DEATHS OF THE POETS

PAUL FARLEY

POETRY

The Boy from the Chemist is Here to See You
The Ice Age
Tramp in Flames
The Atlantic Tunnel: Selected Poems
Field Recordings: BBC Poems 1998–2008
The Dark Film

NON-FICTION

Distant Voices, Still Lives

AS EDITOR

John Clare (Poet to Poet)

MICHAEL SYMMONS ROBERTS

POETRY

Soft Keys
Raising Sparks
Burning Babylon
Corpus
The Half Healed
Drysalter
Selected Poems

FICTION

Patrick's Alphabet
Breath

PAUL FARLEY AND
MICHAEL SYMMONS ROBERTS

Deaths of the Poets

JONATHAN CAPE
LONDON

1 3 5 7 9 10 8 6 4 2

Jonathan Cape, an imprint of Vintage,
20 Vauxhall Bridge Road,
London SW1V 2SA

Jonathan Cape is part of the Penguin Random House group of companies
whose addresses can be found at global.penguinrandomhouse.com

 Penguin
Random House
UK

First published by Jonathan Cape in 2017

penguin.co.uk/vintage

A CIP catalogue record for this book is available from the British Library

ISBN 9780224097543

Typeset in India by Thomson Digital Pvt Ltd, Noida, Delhi
Printed and bound in Great Britain by Clays Ltd, St Ives plc

Penguin Random House is committed to a sustainable future for
our business, our readers and our planet. This book is made
from Forest Stewardship Council® certified paper.

Contents

DEATHS OF THE POETS

Introduction

And as they were afraid, and bowed down their faces to the earth, they said unto them, Why seek ye the living among the dead?

Luke 24:5

We would not want to be in here at night. It's sepulchral enough on a bright spring morning, as the soft-shod denizens of New Bond Street slip out of the boutiques and PR firms to get a rare glimpse of sun after the coldest winter for years. Out there it feels like a corner has been turned. Young men carry coats on their shoulders, women take off scarves and tie them to their bags, surprised by warmth. The ice queen is dead, and life is returning.

Except where we are: in a saleroom at Bonhams, waiting for an auction of *Poetical Manuscripts and Portraits of Poets*. It is a large private collection, full of rare and remarkable poetic relics. We sign in nervously at reception, and pay an eye-watering sum for copies of the exhibition catalogue. We are early. Not being auction-house regulars, we didn't know if there would be a rush for good seats or whether everyone shows up late, having met in the pub beforehand. We are asked if we would like to register as bidders. We shake our heads and the receptionist points upstairs.

The large saleroom is empty, save for a few experts from the Book Department, on hand to answer questions as the buyers arrive. But they're too busy making sure that overseas telephone and online bidders are connected to bother with the likes of us. There's half an hour to go, and we're the first here. The room is quiet, so we look around and take stock. We are surrounded by paintings and photographs of poets, three deep in places, staring out at us. A few are portraits of the living, but overwhelmingly this room is full of dead poets. John Betjeman sits on what looks like a bardic throne, trousers hoisted chest-high by his braces, captured by Christopher Barker moments before or after the famous mid-laughter shot from his book *Portraits of Poets*. This unpublished picture has him pensive, and you can't help but recall his legendary late regret that he hadn't had enough sex in his life. Across the room, W. H. Auden (who probably didn't share Betjeman's regret) is caught by Mark Gerson at a Faber reception in London in 1972. His friend and fellow poet Stephen Spender peers down at a book and Wystan, head thrown back, mouth open, looks at Spender and – in the words of Bonhams' cataloguer – barks at him. What was it? A joke? A piece of gossip? An impromptu review of the unnamed book in Spender's hands? Auden with his mouth open is a feature of almost all those famous Faber party shots. It's as if you could catch the great man (who, according to Alan Bennett, loved to hold court about the difference between 'being boring' and 'being a bore') at any point in any party, and he would be there barking, reliably mid-quip, mid-anecdote. In a glass cabinet on another wall, notebooks and manuscripts lie open. Private notes made public. Siegfried Sassoon's notebook has – handwritten on its cover – the title *Verse, not prose thank God*. There are great treasures in this room. A yellowed foolscap sheet stained at the top with the rust mark of a paper clip turns out to be T. S. Eliot's typescript, with revisions, of 'Journey of the Magi'. And there are autograph manuscripts of poems here by Charlotte Brontë, Keats, Hopkins, Hardy.

But there's something about the photographs in particular that gets to us, the assembly of them, their compound effect. Row upon row of dead poets staring out at us, poets who have written the last line of their last poem, who cannot add to or subtract from their life's work and legacy, poets whose lives and poems are pored over and dissected. Susan Sontag's famous line 'All photographs are *memento mori'* never felt truer than it does now, standing in this poetic necropolis in the middle of London. Her declaration that 'to take a photograph is to participate in another person's (or thing's) mortality . . .' should come with a caveat, 'but with poets, the stink of mortality increases tenfold'.

★

The late Robin Williams, in his role as the inspirational English teacher in *Dead Poets Society,* has his pupils gather round a faded photo of school 'old boys', long dead and fertilizing daffodils, and he gives them voice. In a spooky whisper he delivers their post-humous message to the living: 'Carpe diem, boys.' But the poets on the walls at Bonhams don't seem to say that. We could lean in as close as the auctioneers would let us, but they wouldn't have anything to whisper. In fact, the scale and reputation of their body of work is, it seems, in inverse proportion to the possibility of imagining them as ghosts, as presences. Those less known for their own writing, like Ted Hughes's lover Assia Wevill, seem much more vivid, more haunting in photographs. The likes of Auden and Hughes and Eliot have replaced the weight and presence of their bodies with the weight and presence of their bodies of work. Their work has supplanted them, spent them, spoken everything they have to say. There is nothing deader than a dead major poet.

★

The Bonhams sale is not all about dead poets, though. One of the survivors, poet and retired Professor David Wevill is reported in the Canadian press as being unsettled by the prospect of a batch of his own papers – poems, drawings, cuttings, journals, photographs – being sold here. The story of this archive is itself unsettling. These papers came down to us through the years touched by one of the most disturbing and compelling stories in twentieth-century poetry, that of Ted Hughes, Sylvia Plath and Assia Wevill. David

Wevill was Assia's husband. The two couples became friends in London in the early 1960s when David and Assia rented a flat in London from Ted and Sylvia, who had moved to rural Devon. The rest is terrible and much-debated history. Ted and Assia began a relationship, and within six years of each other both Sylvia and Assia had taken their own lives.

David Wevill's papers were apparently discovered among Assia's belongings when she died, and then stored by Hughes in his own archive, which eventually became part of the Roy Davids Collection, on sale at Bonhams today. When he heard about his own work appearing in the sale catalogue, Wevill was quoted as saying, 'I fear that they might not be owned by me, the way these things go, but they're my stuff.' The issue was quickly and amicably resolved. When Bonhams and Roy Davids heard about Wevill's response, the entire Wevill archive was withdrawn from sale and sent back as a gift to its surviving author. Wevill declared himself touched by the generosity of this gesture, and the sale proceeded without the Wevill papers.

But it did highlight the way in which writers can be curiously led into their own deaths by their papers. With university archives and private collectors keen to invest in the drafts, letters, photographs and even emails of poets as a kind of wager on their future canonicity, it's increasingly common for poets' private papers to be 'collected' long before the poet is actually dead. 'Papers' can include notebooks, shopping lists, receipts, train tickets, postcards, all the disjecta membra of a life worth collecting, a debris field stored in acid-free limbo. We recently heard a story of a senior poet in late career working on a memoir, since published. She had, in the years leading up to this commission, accepted an offer from a major library to archive her papers. In order to refer to her own diaries and letters, she found herself having to travel to another city, sign in as a reader, request her own diaries from the stacks and wait at a table as they were brought up in a buff archive box and placed in front of her. We forgot to ask her if she had to wear archivist's gloves, but it wouldn't surprise us. In fact, it seems oddly fitting that a living poet confronted by the artefacts of her own posthumous reputation should have to handle them with extreme care, for fear that something might rub off.

★

The saleroom fills up with bidders. Some of the lots come with estimates running into tens of thousands. We shuffle to the end of a row and sit motionless, terrified that a cough or a twitch could cost us thousands. Some of these bidders are clearly regulars, waving and chatting. A man in the row behind us talks loudly about an interesting discussion he heard on 'the BBC Home Service'. Either this bidder has not been listening to the on-air trails and idents for the last fifty years, or he is himself a ghost. Come to think of it, his lightweight car coat does look either very cutting edge or a relic of the Sixties. A dead bidder in a room full of dead poets. Along the left-hand side of the saleroom a row of Bonhams staff is poised on phones to manage telephone bids from around the world.

As the sale begins, the clamour builds. We are moving through the lots and poets in alphabetical order, and we are going at a good lick. It turns out that the ghost in a car coat behind us has deep pockets. As bidders wrangle over a portrait bust of Matthew Arnold, we look at the upcoming lots. We are particularly interested in lot Number 17, described in the catalogue as an 'autograph revised manuscript of celebrated poem "Stop all the Clocks"'. The page in question is reproduced in the catalogue, in an uncharacteristically neat hand, with – as the catalogue points out – 'somewhat jagged left-hand edge where presumably removed from a ledger?' And there's an estimated date of 1937.

The catalogue entry is detailed and fascinating. It describes the manuscript as containing 'two *currente calamo* corrections'. *Currente calamo*, Latin for 'on the hoof, pronto, with a stroke of the pen'. The two corrections in question, a crossed-out word – seemingly the beginning of 'guard' before 'dog' in 'prevent the dog from barking with a juicy bone' – and a crossing out of 'ocean' in the final stanza, only to rewrite it more legibly. There's something unsettling about *currente calamo* corrections, the sense of Auden's quickness of mind and hand, his lack of concern that this should be a perfect copy, just clear enough to read, the fact that it is torn rather raggedly from a notebook. It's unsettling because as we pore over these details, the numbers are racking up. What would Auden make of this hastily copied manuscript of his 'blues' about death being sold as a relic, its value secured by his own death, the supply of his manuscripts now fixed, finite and collectable? Of course, this is no ordinary Auden poem. It was famously read by the grieving Matthew (played by John Hannah) at the funeral of his lover Gareth (Simon Callow) in the film *Four Weddings and a Funeral*, and from that moment it became one of the best-loved twentieth-century elegies.

There are several telephone bidders, plus interest in the room. The race to own this piece of paper quickly mounts. Fifteen, sixteen, seventeen thousand, with the auctioneer picking up the subtlest of nods from his colleagues on the phones, and from those sitting in front of him. As the numbers settle at £23,750 including premium, he declares the bid 'all done', but not before giving a last nod to the losing bidders – 'no regrets?' – then the gavel falls.

Auden had a savagely dry wit, and no small ego. Like many of the poets in this sale catalogue, we suspect he would have loved to see his handwritten drafts, letters and notes change hands for thousands of pounds. Sadly, such value increases markedly on condition of death. Not for the poets the stellar painters' gift, to draw on a napkin in lieu of a restaurant bill. To be collectable, a poet really needs to be dead.

★

For many of our generation of British poets, born in the 1960s, it was the previous generation of American poets who caught our attention. There was great work being done in Britain, and particularly in Ireland, but the older American generation – the likes of John Berryman, Elizabeth Bishop, Delmore Schwartz, Anne Sexton, Robert Lowell, Sylvia Plath, Frank O'Hara – seemed to have possessed, or be possessed by, some other force. Many of them wrote directly, nakedly about their own lives, and were dubbed 'confessional poets' as a result.

The term 'confessional' doesn't bear too much scrutiny. It suggests a stronger common purpose, a shared aesthetic behind this movement. In fact, they weren't even a movement. This was a generation of individuals, working in multiple voices, styles and forms. But from our perspective, squinting across the ocean at them, it was not the word 'confessional' that bound them together but another word: 'doomed'. The fact that their work drew on aspects of their lives for subject matter diverted attention towards the character of those lives, and more particularly their deaths. A quick glance across that generation reveals alcoholism, depression, paranoia, relationship breakdown and suicide.

Was there a glamour to that litany of despair? Of course there was. For teenaged or twenty-something would-be poets there was something counter-cultural, some rock star glory to these furiously spent lives that made them far more potent than the Wordsworthian model – to keep writing, gathering in eminence by the decade, until you peg out from old age with your place in the canon secure. But it was more than just bohemian glamour. There was something in those extreme lives that seemed to authenticate the work. Without it ever being spelt out, the implication we drew from this doomed American generation was that in order to access the real poems, the truest, deepest soundings, the poet must put everything at risk – health, family, security, and ultimately life itself. Everything. We say it was never spelt out, but in fact it was. John Berryman, in an interview with the *Paris Review,* about a year before he committed suicide, wished every kind of disaster upon himself in the belief it would further his work. The artist who is struck by the worst possible ordeal which does not actually kill him is 'extremely lucky', says Berryman.

What to make of this? Most poets would agree that there is something of a dark compulsion about the need to write poems. Our British contemporary Don Paterson has looked for the roots of this compulsion in neuroscience and has argued that soon the term 'poet' will become more of a 'diagnosis' than a vocation. And there are many examples of poets suggesting that this compulsion to make poems exacts a price. W. B. Yeats sets out the choice – 'perfection of the life, or of the work', and choosing the latter means turning down a 'heavenly mansion' in favour of 'raging in the dark'. Robert Graves blamed the muse, saying in another *Paris Review* interview that the muse brings 'happening' into a poet's life, because 'tranquility is of no poetic use'. Novelists can be stable, savvy, politically adept and in-control, but poets should be melancholic, doomed and self-destructive.

Where did this leave us? It didn't look good. If you had this compulsion to make poems, you felt like you were joining a slowly shuffling queue, and at the front of the queue were those great twentieth-century American poets, jumping, one by one, off the edge of a cliff. Alternative role models were available, of course, even among that mid-century American generation. Marianne Moore lived to a ripe old age in New York, before passing away some months after looking bewildered as she threw out the season-opening pitch at the Yankee Stadium. More of that story later. And Wallace Stevens served his time happily as a senior insurance executive in provincial Connecticut, dictating poems to his secretary after walking to work. Do they, and the likes of T. S. Eliot, Philip Larkin, Stevie Smith, who made it into (relatively) old age represent another way? Is there another queue a young poet might join, which leads to contentment, a daily word count (or stanza count) like a novelist, and a glowing annual check-up at the doctor's?

★

Lot 480 at the Bonhams Sale. An autograph manuscript of his poem 'This Side of the Truth (for Llewelyn)' by Dylan Thomas. Auctioneer's estimate: £5,000–6,000. It is a beautiful, mid-career lyric addressed to the poet's six-year-old son, declaring that there are 'Good and bad, two ways / Of moving about your death'.

One turn of a catalogue page and there he is, the Welsh wizard, fag on the go, sweaty and pudgy, clutching a pencil as he gives direction to a group of actors at a New York rehearsal of his late, great verse drama *Under Milk Wood*. Within days he collapsed at the Chelsea Hotel and was rushed to St Vincent's Hospital, where he died at the age of thirty-nine. This is Lot 479: a glazed, framed silver print by photographer Rollie McKenna, estimate £600–800.

★

As a culture, we've long paid attention to the last words of the famous and the notable, but language and death converge with particular power in poets, whose foreknowledge of the inevitable can somehow seem especially acute. The death mask and the locket of hair may have fallen out of fashion, but the association between poets and mortality persists, even though few writers today work with a memento mori skull placed strategically next to their laptops.

Laptops? Technology of all sorts is not to be trusted. Most poets can't wire a plug, let alone drive a car. Few of them own PlayStations. The world would tend to swipe left (not that poets would know what that meant). Yet despite all the wretched self-loathing and hypochondria, poets are expected to exhibit a pious devotion to the muse. They never complain, except in sonnet form. The public image of the contemporary poet is, well, odd. And it's certainly not healthy. Poets must live withdrawn and ethereal lives, or if they do socialize must be found minesweeping and stump-shagging outside The Crank & Wanker, while their feral children run barefoot in the beer garden. Poverty is mandatory, as is intemperance or substance abuse of various kinds. So pervasive is this skewed image in society that every now and then, when a poet seems to show one or other of these tendencies, journalists and broadcasters seize upon it, and the poet can find him or herself painted into a corner. Although recreations listed in *Who's Who* such as 'standing in shafts of moonlight' probably haven't helped.

When Samuel Johnson wrote his *Lives of the Poets* in the late eighteenth century, he told the stories birth-first. Now, it seems inevitable, and telling, to start from the death, since the poems are so often seen through the prism of the death. But where and when did this toxic myth begin?

★

We realize it's taken some neck to invoke Johnson in this book's title, and we owe the doctor more than a nod. Johnson's *Lives* began *its* life as a series of biographical and critical prefaces to the work of the English poets, but it outgrew those original intentions to stand independently, by its third edition in 1783, as *The Lives of the Most Eminent English Poets; with Critical Observations on their Works*. Working from biographies, dictionaries, letters, critical introductions and other sources available to him at the time, Johnson's *Lives* takes fifty-two poets, from Edmund Waller (born at the beginning of the seventeenth century) to Thomas Gray (who died just under a decade before the *Lives* was published), and was completed in an astonishing burst of fits and starts over a few years, during which Johnson turned seventy.

His *Lives* is also a book of deaths. In accounting for each of the poets' biographical circumstances, characters and works, Johnson also provides us with a census-taking of their checking out, and what strikes the reader now is often the sadness and melancholy of ambition interrupted or frustrated. Mankind's default setting is misery. Gout, lingering consumption, tumid legs, chills and inflammation of the lungs take their toll. The great leveller shows up in bizarre, random, even tragicomic guises. William Congreve's 'melancholy state was aggravated by the gout, for which he sought relief by a journey to Bath; but being overturned in his chariot, complained from that time of a pain in his side, and died'. The Earl of Dorset 'happened to be among those that were tossed with the king in an open boat sixteen hours, in very rough and cold weather, on the coast of Holland. His health afterwards declined'. Thomas Otway choked on a piece of bread bought with a guinea begged in a coffeehouse. Edmund Smith self-medicated with a powerful purge, despite the warnings of others, 'boastful of his own knowledge, [he] treated the notice with rude contempt, and swallowed his own medicine, which, in July 1710, brought him to the grave.' Of George Stepney's demise, all Johnson has to say is: 'His life was busy, and not long.' And neither, today, is his Wikipedia entry. Next to Milton, Pope, Swift and Dryden, many of these names are unfamiliar to us now, sunk into obscurity, despite their inclusion in Johnson's famous book.

Johnson's poets drink and gamble, suffer blandishments and scorn, are industrious and diligent; they can be vain, foolish, ambitious and sycophantic or learned, scholarly and philosophical. They are usually men of means (and always men), though they also often lapse into penury or decrepitude. Despite their variety, we seldom get the sense that the extreme life – a sense of emotional or physical peril – is a pathway to great work, less still the cultivation of mortal danger for art's sake. Flaring briefly but brilliantly in youth, then suddenly expiring isn't a recognized concept: in the *Lives* nobody dies before the age of thirty (not even George Stepney). William Blake's proverbial 'The road of excess leads to the palace of wisdom' wouldn't be bitten into the etcher's plate for another decade. Johnson is often telling us a sad story or 'mournful narrative', though the alehouse and card table, the vagaries of patronage and favour, the deadening hackwork of Grub Street and ill fortune are all part of the game, occupational hazards.

By the middle of the eighteenth century, the skint and miserable poet was already becoming a cliché: in William Hogarth's print from his painting *The Distrest Poet,* a scribbler waits for inspiration to arrive in his spartan attic. Quill in one hand, scratching an empty head with the other, he has designs on hitting the big time, achieving some measure of fame and making some money, while an angry milkmaid has arrived at his door to present her bill. In Hogarth's image, the poet seems enslaved; there he is, *chained to his desk*. But if at times failure and disappointment seep through the pages of Johnson's book like a stink from the Fleet Ditch, any link between risk, suffering and lyric achievement, or edginess and outsiderdom as a kind of organizing principle, isn't clear, except in one case: the life of Richard Savage.

Savage was a Grub Street legend. We have to admit, we can only think of a single poem he wrote – perhaps because of its title, 'The Bastard' – but his name burns caustically in Johnson's Augustan roster. Savage claimed to be the illegitimate son of an earl and a countess, and in Johnson's *Lives* the poet's mother does not come out of the story well: a poisonous and vindictive character, who harried Savage from cradle to grave (she survived her son and, somehow, Johnson's account escaped a suit for libel). At large in literary London, arrested as a political subversive, involved with two other men in a grubby, small-hours brawl at a Charing Cross knocking shop in which a man was stabbed and killed, Savage seems to blunder from one disaster to another. He comes across as what we'd today call entitled, deprived of his aristocratic birthright, a gentleman poet muddling through a literary landscape that was shifting away from models of patronage towards those of the marketplace, though in Johnson's portrayal what's most striking is Savage's rolling with the punches, living on his wits during long spells of extreme indigence, wandering London's streets at night, as lonely as a murderer:

> He lodged as much by accident as he dined, and passed the night sometimes in mean houses, which are set open at night to any casual wanderers, sometimes in cellars among the riot and filth of the meanest and most profligate of the rabble;

and sometimes, when he had not money to support even the expenses of these receptacles, walked about the streets till he was weary, and lay down in the summer upon a bulk, or in the winter, with his associates in poverty, among the ashes of a glass-house.

And Johnson was, for a time, one of these associates. Arriving in London in 1737, the future giant of eighteenth-century letters was a young schoolmaster down from the Midlands to seek a new career as a writer, and the two struck up a friendship. Savage had achieved fame and notoriety following his trial for murder and subsequent pardon – escaping the hangman's noose was a good career move – but by the time Johnson met him ten years later, his star had waned. Johnson and Savage were partners in penury, walking the city after dark, sustained by their talk, a pair of fleas in the cogs of a giant clock movement.

Savage ended up at Newgate Prison in Bristol over a debt of eight pounds, where he died in 1743. What we're left with from Johnson's version is a glimpse of the poet as outcast and night-crawler, set squarely at odds to the currents of his day. Johnson published his *Life of Savage* the following year, and it made the doctor's name. Could it be that this book contained the germ not only of the *Lives* he was to complete nearly forty years later, but also the idea of a new kind of poet, a new way of being a poet in the world?

*

When Johnson's completed *Lives* appeared, it contained no mention of a seventeen-year-old poet who had died ten years before, in a Holborn attic just a few hundred yards away from Johnson's Gough Square house. Johnson knew about Thomas Chatterton: six years after his death, the doctor and his biographer James Boswell visited Bristol and climbed the steps of the tower at St Mary Redcliffe Church to view the ancient chest where the young poet claimed to have discovered the manuscripts of Thomas Rowley's poetry. 'It is wonderful how the whelp has written such things,' Johnson said, despite the fabrication and forging. But Chatterton's story was about to turn into sharper focus and make deep impressions on the generation of poets who would soon follow.

If you were one of the earliest readers of Johnson's *Lives of the Poets* in 1783 – let's say you've just purchased a copy from a bookseller on the Strand, and have walked back out into the deafening rattle of carriage wheels – how much of an inkling could you have that poetry was about to undergo one of its periodic plate shifts? All the main players of English Romanticism are either children or adolescents – William Wordsworth, Samuel Taylor Coleridge – or will be born over the coming years – Lord Byron, Percy Bysshe Shelley, John Keats – and Chatterton's posthumous moment is about to arrive. You pause to take a pinch of snuff and notice it's later than you thought. There's a taste of thunder in the air and the day has got away from you. Shadows are lengthening. Bells chime. You pick up the pace and hurry homewards.

★

Is it all the fault of these Romantics, with their waxy pallor and unhealthy obsession with mortality? This book is constructed from a series of pilgrimages to the death-places of poets we admire and love, poets whose deaths seem – one way or the other – to shed light on the image of the doomed poet, or to test its mythology. We have many questions, but the biggest and the thorniest question of all is this one: is it true? Is it true that great poems come at a heavy – ultimately fatal – price?

The poets we have chosen to pursue are those whose work and lives pursued us from our first adolescent experiments with writing poems. But more than that, we have chosen poets who – in the manner or time or mythic quality of their deaths – have contributed to the complicated saga of the *Deaths of the Poets*. Some contributed to it by dying young, by jumping or drugging or drinking or fighting themselves into an early grave. Others have contributed by countering it, by living a quiet, scholarly life and writing poems all the way until the light goes out on a solid reputation. Thomas Chatterton, the marvellous boy poet, seemed like a good place to begin.

The act of pilgrimage seemed important. In some cases, we'd be joining a long established trail, though in many others the site of a poet's final days or hours would take us well off the beaten track. In a way, then, this is also a book about places and the charge we feel (or don't) from their associations with a writer. It's also a book about forgetting, and the ways we remember and consecrate some kinds of literary sites, while bypassing others. To Johnson the adopted Londoner, writing his great survey of the English poets, literary pilgrimage and place mightn't have seemed so important. This might simply say something about Johnson's temperament and inclinations to research. The doctor, who famously toured the Hebrides with James Boswell and expressed a wish to visit 'the wall of China', wasn't averse to *travel*, although when William Shenstone – another largely forgotten poet from the *Lives* – once hoped that Johnson might pay him a visit at his home in Shropshire, he was warned by a friend not to depend on it: 'He is no more formed for long journeys than a tortoise.'

*

The last lot has been sold and the auction is over. The event will be recorded, another benchmark in pricing for artworks and collectables. Before we leave Bonhams and re-emerge into the sunlight and noise of the day, we compare the distance travelled between all the post-mortem sifting and valuing we've just witnessed, with any unknown writer's first walk to the postbox in an attempt to find a reader. We wonder how many other poets would recognize this story.

After months or years of sending out hopeful manila envelopes, you have managed to find a publisher for one of your poems. The editor of a little magazine has somehow been persuaded and has devoted some precious space to it. This is a milestone. Somebody not blood related to you, somebody you have never even met, has acknowledged that what you've made is worth publishing. They have taken a chance on you. After what seems an age, your poem finally appears in print, on a page perfumed with fresh ink. And at some point, more likely from the mouths of those most well meaning, somebody who has seen your poem will innocently, encouragingly say: 'Well. Get you. They'll be putting a plaque up here one day, eh?'

A plaque. Because you're waiting to be dead. In your beginning you are already being framed posthumously. No wonder so many poets end up on speaking terms with the dead, writing about death 'as if they had done it', according to the American poet Mary Ruefle, who goes on to explain what an utterly ridiculous state of affairs this is, but also how 'THE MINUTE THEY BECOME DEAD THEY CAN TEACH US EVERYTHING':

> Why, why is that? I think it's because the minute they are dead all of their poems about death become poems about being alive. And we are alive and can be taught something about that.

Now the last straggles of gossipy buyers have broken up, stray bidding paddles are being removed from seats and the gavel has gone back to wherever gavels go. We're sitting in an empty sale-room again, which is where we came in. For some reason, neither of us can resist standing where the auctioneer has just conducted the bidding, though maybe it's force of habit: only now do we make out the similarities between all this and a poetry reading. This lectern, the jug of water with its film of dust, the microphone and the rows of empty chairs facing us: a soundcheck for the afterlife. Time now to leave this inventoried world and go looking for the dead poets, who are out there waiting to teach us everything.

A Portable Shrine

Standing in front of *Chatterton* – commonly known as *The Death of Chatterton* – in Tate Britain is enough to make a poet sick. It's one of the defining images of nineteenth-century painting, a Pre-Raphaelite masterpiece. We are examining it with Tate curator Dr Carol Jacobi, who explains how Henry Wallis painted pure white on to the canvas first, instead of the conventional dull wash. He then worked over it, so the finished canvas looks back-lit, transfigured. She takes us through the details, the painstaking pencil work on the boy's alabaster skin, the torn shreds of his abandoned poems on the floor by his lifeless right hand, the ghost of a London dawn skyline through the open casement window, the empty arsenic phial on the floor beside his bed.

Like many a famous painting, movie star or revisited childhood haunt, *Chatterton* is smaller in the flesh than you expect. But the flesh is what gets you. The artist Henry Wallis was a young man himself – in his mid-twenties – when he hit upon the suicide of a beautiful young poet as the subject of his next painting. It is full of the virtuosic confidence of a young artist trying to make his mark, and it has been read as a critique of society's treatment of artists. But as you stare into the painting, you can't take your eyes off the skin's pallor, the cascade of auburn hair. If this is a polemic about undervalued artists, then it's a strange one. It seems to glory in this sacrificial figure, this secular pieta. There is a death-lust to it, a lustre and a lavish attention. A line from Marlowe's *The Tragical History of Dr Faustus* at the foot of the frame underlines the point:

'Cut is the branch that might have grown full straight, / And burned is Apollo's laurel bough.'

But what makes this painting exceptional is more than its morbid sick-sweetness. After all, anyone who spends time in galleries will have taken in their share of Victorian mortality-porn. Wallis's depiction of Chatterton's death is not just ravishing but culpable. If the myth of the doomed poet starts anywhere, it starts here, with what Ruskin called this 'faultless and wonderful' painting.

★

The poet Thomas Chatterton died not once but twice. Or rather, not once but repeatedly. His first death took place on 24 August 1770 in a garret in Brook Street, Holborn, London. After turning down his landlady's offers of dinner the night before, he was found stretched out on a pallet bed with an empty phial of poison lying alongside him. He was not yet eighteen. His literary reputation amounted to very little, despite his prodigious output – almost 700 pages written under noms de plume – and was overshadowed by his scandalous reputation as a faker of medieval verse. He was interred quietly in the backyard burial plot of a Holborn workhouse.

The son of a Bristol teacher, Chatterton was brought up in a schoolhouse across the road from St Mary Redcliffe Church. The house remains, preserved on what feels like a traffic island on Redcliffe Way, a busy commuter strip in Bristol's central business district not far from Temple Meads Station. It is a modest, four-square Georgian home, lime-rendered and newly re-roofed. It has been Grade 2 listed for its historical importance, but the same cannot be said of the school. A large wall protrudes from the house with elegant windows, a remnant of the grander buildings of the school itself. But the wall is all that's left. Where children once lined up at desks, commuters line up in queues, minds on the day ahead, eyes glazed at a sight of such daily familiarity. Why did the road-builders leave the school wall? We conclude it must have been a structural necessity, because it looks odd, a taster of a more impressive building tagged on to a tiny house, as if they amputated the wrong bit.

There are plans to turn Chatterton's birthplace into a café and visitor centre, but when we arrive it is locked and empty. Morning rush hour, and the schoolhouse is dwarfed and beaten by the city around it. Among the towering hotels and office blocks it looks like a Wendy house. It's hard to imagine the shy kid who lived here, passing tranquil hours in the muniments room high above the north porch of the church across the road, teaching himself to write in a convincing medieval style.

When he claimed to have discovered ancient verses by a fifteenth-century monk called Thomas Rowley, Chatterton's skills as a teenage forger conned many of the great and good, including (for a while) the celebrated antiquarian Horace Walpole. Eager to capitalize on his luck, Chatterton moved to London and began selling squibs and polemics to journals under fantastic pen names like Harry Wildfire, Decimus and Flirtilla.

The phoney monk Rowley was exposed when Walpole's friend the poet Thomas Gray – of *Elegy Written in a Country Church-yard* fame – read the poems and fingered them as fakes. But Chatterton battled on, scratching out a Grub Street living with his pen, until his body was discovered in that garret room at the age of seventeen years and nine months.

It's a sorry tale, seen from any angle. From a literary perspective, what did we lose? Chatterton's mastery (in his mid-teens) of verse forms and his ear for a lyric line suggest a prodigious talent. What would he have written had he lived into his twenties? Even Keats – famously young when he died – had seven more years than Chatterton to leave us a body of work. There are loyal adherents to his literary worth, those who argue that the Romantics would have come to nothing without him, but it's safer to say that here was a genius snuffed out before it could flower. From a human perspective, it's an even bleaker – and more familiar – story. A teenage boy leaves a provincial city in search of experience, money and fame, and without the care of family and friends ends up dying alone in a shabby bedsit.

We wander over to the church, where a café in the crypt is opening up for the day. We sit with a coffee and contemplate the strange posthumous life of this remarkable boy-poet. Lots of people we talk to in Bristol have heard of him. Some of them know where his family house is. But barely anyone can quote a line from his verse. And that's not just the case in Bristol. Gather a group of contemporary poets and literary critics in a room (actually, don't ...) and very few of them could quote from Chatterton's work either. Some may know of him as a famous forger, others as a forerunner of the Romantic poets, but more will know him from him his blue britches and Pre-Raphaelite locks. For most of us, Thomas Chatterton has become the young man in Wallis's painting.

★

In the years following his death, the literary world continued largely to ignore Chatterton, save the odd skirmish about the authenticity of various manuscripts. But the myth was already being seeded. By the late 1700s the poet on his garret deathbed had gained a niche – but growing – following among engravers and printmakers, some of whom pressed rewind to the moments just before his death. In John Flaxman's 1790 *Chatterton receives the Bowl of Poison from the Spirit of Despair*, the beautiful boy (looking rather like a beautiful girl) reaches out to drink from a bowl being offered by the grotesque spectre of Despair, who appears to be a cross between a cage-fighter and the Grim Reaper. In 1783 a romantic mock-ruin was built on an estate in Bath, in honour of the figure Wordsworth called 'The marvellous Boy, / The sleepless Soul that perished in its pride', which bore the inscription 'Unfortunate Boy ... Thy Fame Shall Never Die.' There were even Chatterton handkerchiefs available in red and blue, depicting the tortured poet in his garret. But the merchandise of death was not what gave the myth its next big push. That was down to the poets.

By the start of the nineteenth century he was cropping up in poems by Wordsworth, Shelley and Rossetti, and most notably in Coleridge's 'Monody on the Death of Chatterton', in which the living poet calls upon his dead hero to help him achieve such purity of will: 'Grant me, like thee, the lyre to sound, / Like thee, with fire divine to glow.' The pure and broken boy was an irresistibly perfect icon of devotion to the muse, even in the face of poverty and obscurity, even if it cost him his life.

These replays of Chatterton's death in the poems of celebrated living poets began to make him famous. In the decades after, he became an exemplary romantic figure, an embodiment of what these living poets half-feared and half-believed, that to be a true poet means to push your life to the very brink of ruin and death, and ultimately beyond.

★

Its name may not be up there with the *Mona Lisa*, but everyone knows the image. It's been reproduced on countless postcards, mocked up for films and books (including the one you're holding now), even recently refashioned as a Babyshambles album cover, with Pete Doherty claiming Chatterton as one of his heroes. We walk along the walls packed with Tate Britain's nineteenth-century treasures, but we keep being drawn back to Henry Wallis's painting of *The Death of Chatterton*.

The original, first exhibited at the Royal Academy in 1856, is strikingly more vivid than its many reproductions. The scene is so simple, so elegantly set. In front of the window, on a bare and dirty bed lies the glamorous, young, dead poet. The blue of his britches looks as radiant as the Marian blue in Christian iconography, and his sullied white shirt is open to the navel to reveal his pale chest. His head tilts off the edge of the bed to face us, as his hair cascades towards a wooden trunk, open on the floor, surrounded by the shreds of torn-up verse. His hair is the darkest, richest red, for which we have to thank not just the painter but the young model, the novelist George Meredith. Sadly, George's vivid locks were not enough to stop his wife eloping with Wallis three years later.

An open window of the attic room behind the corpse shows the skyline of the city that turned its back on Chatterton. The painted poet is sexualized, feminized, romanticized. But there is a sacred element here, too. This is the poet as a sacrificial figure, a vicarious victim who gave himself in the cause of his art.

Wallis's painting was copied, exhibited and toured the British Isles. Among its many admirers were the new urban working class, for whom exhibitions of art were staged by philanthropists eager to offer moral and aesthetic improvement, and to show off their cultural and economic power. Exhibitions like the colossal Art Treasures Exhibition in Manchester in the summer of 1857 extended the audience for painting far beyond the London coterie. In five months Manchester's extravaganza attracted 1.3 million visitors. To put the idea of this painting on tour into some kind of context: throughout 2014 the Manchester Arena sold just over a million tickets, for shows featuring the likes of Beyoncé, Kylie Minogue and Katy Perry. And they had dry ice. Wallis's painting tapped into the Victorian public's fascination with death, and for many of the new urban working class this was their first encounter with what a poet might actually be like – sensitive, tormented, counter-cultural, bohemian. Oh, and dead.

It didn't come out of nowhere. It seemed to fit the stories of other poets, notably John Keats, whose line 'A thing of beauty is a joy for ever' was written above the exhibition's entrance. Keats had died in 1821 and, like Chatterton, he died young, poor, sick and broken by his sacrificial dedication to poetry.

★

'I always somehow associate Chatterton with autumn. He is the purest writer in the English Language,' Keats wrote in a letter to

John Hamilton Reynolds in the early autumn of 1819. In Rome, we walk down from where we are staying off the Piazza del Popolo to the old foreigners' quarter, the Piazza di Spagna. Italy has been lashed with an autumn storm this week, and earlier we'd walked along the banks of a swollen and muddy Tiber, watching snarls of trees and branches racing through the bridge arches. To the north of the country, roads are washed out; tourists are wearing swimming costumes in St Mark's Square. Here in Rome, the sewers are backing up.

But the storm has passed, and the tourists are fully-clothed in the Piazza at the foot of the Spanish Steps. And there is the Keats-Shelley House, right beside the Scalinata. Inside, the whole place, with its dark wood paneling and bookshelves, its chairs lining the sides of rooms with old display cases, feels burnished, still, richly textured with age. If it's possible for a museum to feel autumnal, then this one does. As we'll discover, museums to poets don't always behave in this way. The rooms here contain many manuscripts and drawings, including a portrait of the tubercular Keats on his deathbed by his devoted friend Joseph Severn, drawn here in 1821, towards the end of four long months. The pair had sailed south from London on the advice of Keats's doctor. The young poet knew what was happening inside him. Having been apprenticed as a surgeon, he called for a candle to inspect what he had coughed up. 'I know the colour of that blood; – it is arterial blood; – I cannot be deceived in that colour; – that drop of blood is my death-warrant; – I must die.'

In another room there is a life mask of Keats made five years before he died here. We can't help but compare it to Severn's portrait: the drawn features in the latter, the hair sticking to the poet's brow. There is plenty of actual hair here, too, Keats's included. Exchanging locks of hair was common during the early nineteenth century. There is an alabaster urn said to contain a fragment of Shelley's jaw.

And here is the room in which Keats died, small but high ceilinged, shuttered off from the glare of a Roman day. It's the bed that punctures the routine air of looking around at exhibits. Even though we know it's not the original bed that Keats lay dying in – everything was burned to prevent infection – it catches us off guard. It might be something to do with its scale: it feels slightly miniaturized, a walnut boat bed for a boy. His death mask tilts upwards in its case. We look to the ceiling he would have known intimately: plasterwork flowers on a pale blue background, seen from a bed like this. The deathbed turns the whole room into a kind of death mask. Standing next to it, there's an underlying impression of every bedside we've ever visited to wait for a fever to break, to say goodbye to somebody, or to beg somebody to hang on, or to let go. Later, out on the house's terrace, we'll talk about how a sickbed becomes a deathbed, and at what shaded moment as the day and hour drew closer would Keats have realized he wasn't leaving that room. That bed.

Keats was an admirer of Chatterton and saw him as a kindred spirit, dedicating his *Endymion* 'to the memory of Thomas Chatterton'. In particular, Keats loved 'Ælla', perhaps the best of the Rowley poems, and he liked to recite its best-known stanza on love and loss:

> Comme, wythe acorne-coppe and thorne,
> Drayne mie hartys bloode awaie;
> Lyfe and all yttes goode I scorne,
> Daunce bie nete, or feaste by daie.
> Mie love ys dedde,
> Gon to his death-bedde,
> Al under the wyllowe tree.

Once you get beyond the cod-medieval spelling, it's not hard to see – or rather, to hear – why Keats was so captivated by Chatterton. Considering those lines were written by a boy of fifteen or sixteen, the lyric music and elegiac tone are remarkable and memorable. But Keats was also drawn to the purity, as if

Chatterton had tapped into some ancient wellspring, an unpolluted source of poetry. We have to readjust and remind ourselves that many of the objects and furnishings in this museum post-date Keats. Maybe old and pure to him meant the baroque fountains, or rather the water that bubbled in them as it arrived in the Eternal City from the distant hills. It's said he could hear the Fontana della Barcaccia in the Piazza from his sick bed.

*

The painting of *The Death of Chatterton* was a palpable hit, and not just in Manchester. It had a similar impact on the people of Dublin when it was shown there in 1859, and in Birmingham, where a small copy was shown in the city's museum and art gallery. It was a critical success, too, lauded by the likes of John Ruskin.

Henry Wallis produced many more paintings, but nothing surpassed the fame of this early portrait. He is said to have observed in later life (with reference to another of his works, *The Stonebreaker*) that 'dead poets are more saleable than dead labourers'. In 2014 the nineteenth-century collection at Tate Britain, home of *The Death of Chatterton*, mounted a small exhibition which illustrated just how remarkable a phenomenon it was. Alongside the Wallis image, they showed two hand-tinted albumen photographic prints, under the title *The Death of Chatterton*. But these were made three years after Wallis's painting, and by a different artist – a former dentist called James Robinson. At first glance they look identical to the painting. The composition and colours are painstakingly copied. On closer inspection, there are differences. Chatterton's face is not the same. And the colours, though retouched after printing, are no longer as vivid as the oils.

James Robinson was one of the eager visitors who queued to see Wallis's painting when it came to Dublin. By staging carefully reconstructed scenes, he produced a series of stereographic images of Chatterton's death. He would photograph each scene twice and, by changing the angle of the camera between the two exposures, was able subtly to alter the interrelationships between objects in the scene. When mounted side by side – and viewed through a pair of lenses looking like a cross between ancient opera glasses and industrial strength specs – a visitor could experience a 3D effect.

It is an unsettling experience, looking through the viewer at this 3D image of a deathbed scene. Why would you want to apply this 'shock' technique of hyperreality to a scene with no movement save a candle guttering out at the edge of the frame, and no drama, because the tragedy has played out before the viewer got there? It is simply a staged picture of a corpse.

Except it isn't just any corpse. It's a sacrificial icon. The attempt to use technology to make it 'hyperreal' is not to make it lurid, like some morbid peepshow. No, this is an attempt to draw the viewer into the emotional heart of the scene, to feel pity at the sight of this tragic young poet, broken by devotion to the muse. And it's also meant to evoke a sense of gratitude. The Victorians were steeped in Christian theology and iconography, and in that context it's not hard to see Chatterton's death as a surrogate sacrifice. He was our representative, sent to meet the Spirit of Despair on our behalf, and we should gaze upon him and be thankful. At the foot of the explanatory card on the Tate's wall beside Robinson's stereographic images, a note informs the visitor that they are on loan from the private collection of Dr Brian May. It seems fitting that a rock star should have some connection with *The Death of Chatterton*. After all, rock stars have not only muscled in on poets' roles in giving voice to what it means to be alive, but they have also muscled in on our particular reputation for dying.

★

Thomas Chatterton was not the only pre-twentieth-century *poète maudit*. As we've seen, in England, poor consumptive John Keats was a 'cursed poet' when he died in 1821 at the tender age of twenty-five. It was the French writer Alfred de Vigny in his 1832 novel *Stello* who dreamt up the haunting phrase 'poète maudit'. *Stello* conjured in gory detail the vision of the true poet, doomed and desperate, rejected by the world, suffering and dying for his art. In 1835 Vigny took this obsession a stage further with his hit play *Chatterton*, which spread the fame of the 'marvellous boy' across the continent. French poetry produced its own fair share of *poètes maudits* in the nineteenth century, notably Charles Baudelaire, Paul Verlaine and Arthur Rimbaud, but the power of Chatterton's story was such that he became its focus.

There's a strange flush of pride for a British poet to think of our boy Chatterton being such a hit across the Channel. He even pops up in the twentieth century as part of the lyric of a Serge Gainsbourg song. His poetry may have been an influence on few other poets, but the myth of his death was unstoppable.

★

Wallis's painting, incidentally, was also the target for one the most pleasingly amateurish of art thefts, according to Edward Dolnick's *The Rescue Artist*. In 1991 the copy of *The Death of Chatterton* at the Birmingham Museum and Art Gallery was stolen on a clear December day when the thief – who had always loved the painting – strolled through the gallery to the room where it hung, lifted it off the wall and walked out with it under his arm. He then got on a bus and showed off the painting to his fellow passengers, reportedly suggesting that he might sell it if any of them liked it enough to make him a decent offer. Several days later the painting was recovered from the man's house, after police got the nod from an anonymous informant. The thief was let off with a warning, but that wasn't the end of it. In a gesture of great decency, the Birmingham gallery chief invited him back for a guided tour of the Pre-Raphaelite collection, and the chance to gaze in particular at his favourite image, *The Death of Chatterton*.

★

In what he called his 'last Will and Testament', written four months before his death, Chatterton plays with the idea of suicide as a risk that comes with his poetic temperament. It is fair to say that he 'plays', because, despite the bleak subject matter, his acid wit is evident throughout:

> . . . being sound in body, or it is the fault of my last surgeon; the soundness of my mind, the coroner and jury are to be the judges of, desiring them to take notice, that the most perfect masters of human nature in Bristol distinguish me by the title of Mad Genius; therefore, if I do a mad action, it is conformable to every action of my life, which all savoured of insanity.

Running quietly parallel to the legends of these infamous poetic deaths are the plaintive counter-tellings. Within a decade of Thomas Chatterton's death, the myth was being challenged. And the alternative accounts are very persuasive – that the wunderkind was making a decent living, enjoying London society, but killed himself by accident, self-medicating with vitriol and calomel (recorded by the coroner as 'arsenic') for venereal disease, whilst taking laudanum to dull the pain of his medicines. In short, it seems likely he got the balance of his meds wrong.

There are similar counter-narratives of Dylan Thomas's last days in New York, featuring witnesses at the White Horse on his last night who claimed that 'eighteen straight whiskies' was wide of the mark, and that it was medical mismanagement that killed the poet, not his self-destructive drive.

But no matter how much evidence accumulates to complicate these deaths, the pull of the myth is too strong. As the poet and critic Donald Davie suggests, the cultural expectations of poetic genius demand these spectacular denouements: 'A lyric poet is one who is absolved from all civic responsibilities and all moral restraints on the strict understanding that by enacting his own self-destruction under the spotlights he shall vindicate his public in its resentful acquiescence to the restraints he is absolved from.' So when the truth seems to complicate or cut against the myth, we acknowledge these re-tellings, then ignore them.

★

THE FIRST PERSON TO LIVE TO 150 IS ALIVE TODAY an advertising hoarding declares above the turnpike from Newark into Manhattan. We're riding in a stretch limo by mistake, our hotel having thought we were somebody else. Somebody on important business in New York and not two moonlighting poets, flummoxed by the routine Homeland Security questions at the barrier: 'What's the purpose of your visit?' 'Well. We've come to look at the places where some poets died . . .'

The flight was smooth, as flights go. Some of the things we were worried about hadn't happened. We had taken some precautions, of course. Here were two poets steeped in stories of the deaths of poets, on pilgrimage to the death places of our own poetic idols. We didn't want to die on a 737 before the pilgrimage had even started. So we had downed more than our share of aspirin to ward off deep-vein thrombosis, pulled on our calf-hugging compression socks, and one of us took the precaution of walking the length of the plane with exaggerated high-steps roughly every fifteen minutes. The other had mocked this extravagant exercise, then stashed every morsel of the in-flight food down the pocket of the seat in front of him to save for landing – 'Because if you choke on a piece of food up here what can they do to save you?' When this was mocked in turn, it was met with the rejoinder: 'Fuck off. Remember Thomas Otway . . .'

But the accidental limo feels fitting: there is something very funereal about this vehicle, dark and shiny as a beetle's wing-case on the outside, deeply plush and upholstered on the inside, right down to the whisky and water decanters rattling in the doorwells like jars of embalming fluid. At least, we think it's water: parched from hours of recycled cabin air, we pour ourselves huge tumblers and take deep gulps of what for a few panicky seconds could actually be formaldehyde, but turns out to be lukewarm vodka.

Once the coughing has subsided, we take this as a good sign. Whatever these doomed poets of the past did to shorten or preserve their lives, alcohol was rarely far from their lips. We raise a glass to the Spirit of Despair and slump back in our seats. We are here on pilgrimage to retrace the last steps of Chatterton's inheritor, the twentieth century's ultimate doomed poet. And drink is a big part of that story. The familiar skyline looms from Jersey City, Hoboken, before we descend into the Lincoln Tunnel.

★

Our accidental limousine pulls up outside the Library Hotel. We chose to stay here because of its handy midtown location (just a short stagger from the New York Public Library and Archives) but also because of its name. Its website even boasts a top-floor bar with roof terrace called 'The Poets' Garden', where the speciality is a gin cocktail called a 'Shakespeare's Sonnet'. When we booked, we explained that we were British poets on the trail of great American poets, in the hope that we might get a discount. If not a discount, we hoped at least to be shelved in the poetry section. As its name suggests, the Library Hotel is organized by the Dewey Decimal Classification system, so different clusters of rooms and different floors carry particular kinds of books. These books are not just in bookshelves on every corridor, but stuffed into alcoves and shelves in each room too. It seems fitting that we should sleep among the work of dead poets.

At the check-in desk, it is clear that our email attempt to win favour has failed. Not only are we not offered a discount, nor even a complimentary 'Shakespeare's Sonnet', but the receptionist eyes us up and puts one of us in a room in Psychology, surrounded by books on Freud, and one in Zoology, surrounded by books on keeping snakes.

Still, as its name also suggests, the Library is reassuringly sealed off from the midtown din, and way more comfortable than what we're used to. Resisting the urge to nap, we drop our bags and head out to meet the American poet Daisy Fried, who has generously travelled in from Philadelphia to spend the day in New York with us. Our first port of call is Greenwich Village, on the trail of Thomas Chatterton's infamous twentieth-century incarnation, Dylan Thomas. If Chatterton's death became the founding myth of the doomed poet in the nineteenth century, then Dylan's death reheated and re-presented that myth for the twentieth. Here was the Welsh wizard, begotten not made, born with a genius too volatile to handle, a gift he kept in check by anaesthetizing it with alcohol, until his death finally cornered him in New York in November 1953 at the age of thirty-nine.

It is hard not to feel cornered by Dylan as you sit in the White Horse Tavern on Hudson Street. Large, mural-sized photographs of him loom down at you and it feels like a challenge. 'Match me,' he seems to say through a fug of cigarette smoke, with a half-full tumbler of whiskey in his hand. 'Match me drink for drink, poem for poem, or you're only playing at it.' The death of Dylan Thomas, with his reported last words 'I've had eighteen straight whiskies; I think that's the record,' seems integral to his work. Why else would his demise become the most famous and celebrated thing about him? When BBC television commissioned a drama to mark Dylan's centenary it was clear from the outset where its focus would be. Sure, there were marital battles in Laugharne and scenic walks up Fern Hill, but the title of the drama, *A Poet in New York*, says it all: the fascinating bit of Dylan's life is the end. And the unspoken assumption behind the myth of his death is that it was the price he paid for the lasting reputation of the work. Were it not for the straight whiskies and the lovers, would we be as interested in *Under Milk Wood* or 'Do not go Gentle into that Good Night'? Our sensibilities today could not bear a painting of *The Death of Dylan Thomas*, portraying him stretched, pieta–like, along a New York hospital bed. Though we don't mind such images in films, and *A Poet in New York* provided one, complete with his wife Caitlin, insane with grief, trying to thump and kiss him back to life. Our taste in still photographs of Dylan tends towards 'before' shots, complete with cigarette and whisky. But we all know where they are heading.

★

Two British and one American poet are sitting beneath Dylan's mural in the White Horse, eating burgers and chips. There is live coverage of a US PGA Golf Tournament on the TV in every room. We are served by a young English girl who is studying here in New York. Does she know who Dylan Thomas is? 'Oh yes, a famous poet who drank himself to death here.' We feel we are letting the side down by drinking Diet Coke. We have a day's work to do and want to keep our heads clear, but the Welsh wizard looks disgusted with us. *Lightweights*, he seems to whisper, in the voice of Richard Burton. He's the Spirit of Despair, offering us his cup of poison, but we're saying, 'No thanks, we might get a bit dehydrated.' Jack Kerouac, Hunter S. Thompson and Norman Mailer, all one-time patrons of this old Village boozer, might not have been muralized on its walls, but are here in spirit, too. They look down on us, a Mount Rushmore monument to drinkers of true stature. Mount Lushmore. We'll get our coats.

Mind you, there's still plenty of big drinking going on among British poets. You only have to watch them (us) in the bar at any literary festival to confirm that. But are they (we) drinking to oblivion? We ask Daisy about her American contemporaries, living under the shadow of towering drinkers like John Berryman, Robert Lowell, Elizabeth Bishop. Do they still hit the bottle so hard in the service of the muse? 'It's Prozac now', she says, 'not alcohol and drugs. Most poets I know drink slightly too much wine in the evenings.'

Dylan's sneer seems ever more pronounced. Daisy's verdict rings true. Most British poets we know drink slightly too much.

But maybe that caution is a reaction, in part, to that doomed mid-twentieth-century generation. 'Their deaths have come to dominate their lives,' says Daisy, 'and the danger is that it becomes another excuse not to read the poems.' If the story of a poet's death becomes more famous than the poems themselves, then where does that leave us?

The pub suddenly gets noisy: a large group of elderly ladies from Pennsylvania is sitting down for lunch. They are in high spirits. We think at first that they might also be Thomas pilgrims, so Daisy asks them. No, it's a theatre trip to Broadway. Have they heard of Dylan Thomas? 'Oh yes, he was that poet who drank himself to death, wasn't he?' We finish up our Diet Cokes and head off in search of the Chelsea Hotel.

★

As we head up Eighth Avenue, stopping to apply Factor 40 to our noses and earlobes because the sun has come out ('and we *are* on the same latitude as Madrid here . . .'), we reflect on how a more rigorous approach to literary pilgrimage has been brought to bear on the subject, by people equipped with the necessary analytical tools. Twenty years ago, visitors to Laugharne, the town on the South Wales coast that Thomas transformed into Milk Wood, were surveyed about the poet. One of the questions they were asked concerned their sense of him as a person. Over 36 per cent of respondents, perhaps unsurprisingly, went to the dark side, and a list of some of the words and phrases used helps transport us from this sunlit, twenty-first-century city to those final, chaotic November nights sixty years ago, when this was the walk home from the pub:

loud
brash
wild
violent
nihilistic

dissolute

sponger

fraud

drink problems

wasted life

easily led

restless

tormented

unable to cope

own worst enemy

★

In his final week Dylan was tired and unwell. He was in the throes of a punishing reading tour. It was his fourth time on the US circuit and he didn't want to be there. Although he was lauded at every theatre and party and university, it took him away from his work, away from his family, away from himself. And the timing of this trip had an extra bite. He was in the latter stages of a play, a verse drama for radio that was to become his best-known work. He had brought the unfinished script of *Under Milk Wood* with him on the trip, in the hope of working on it in idle moments in his hotel room. Which is where we're heading.

This isn't the first time we've walked down 23rd Street with a mounting sense of excitement, it has to be said; we've both been this way before, in other lives, as different kinds of pilgrims. The Chelsea Hotel used to be Sid and Nancy, Patti Smith, Andy Warhol and the Velvet Underground, Leonard Cohen, Bob Dylan writing *Blonde On Blonde*. Though we knew the other Dylan had been a guest there, too, even back then. Dylan is a gateway poet. We remember trying to keep a lid on things, wising up quickly to how unbecoming any enthusiasm (along with pointing at tall buildings and yellow taxis) might appear in the city that's seen it all before. Though even by New York standards the Chelsea is a node of cool. It's picked up a powerful pop- and counter-cultural charge in the years since Dylan Thomas checked in and checked out, and the Thomas connection must have been part of the draw, though there was a nexus of other writers drawn to the place around the same time he was staying here; we imagine freak alignments, a single day sometime in 1953 when John Berryman, Theodore Roethke, Sylvia Plath and Thomas might all have been found staying, visiting or hanging around its lobby. There's the red awning up ahead.

We arrive at the Chelsea and it's covered in hoarding and scaffolding. We can still see the brass plaques outside the entrance, celebrating luminaries who've stayed here: one plaque reads: 'Dedicated to the memory of Dylan Thomas, who lived and labored last here at the Chelsea Hotel, and from here sailed out to die.' Well, that's one way of putting it. 'As I sailed out to die' is a line from Dylan's 'Poem on his Birthday', so it's a fitting epitaph. But it's also an evocation of the heroic, self-sacrificial poet in all his glory, sailing out like Odysseus, risking all to bring the poems home.

We walk into the lobby and it looks like a building site. There's a guy at reception who explains that the whole place is being refurbished to make it a top-class hotel again. Can we go upstairs to see the room where Dylan Thomas was staying that last night? It's part of someone's private apartment now. Can we leave a message for them and come back? No, they are not allowed to reveal who owns the apartment, and besides, the rooms upstairs have had their walls and ceilings replaced, so even if you could find the room it would be unrecognizable. Things feel stripped back, pared down and under renovation. We seem to remember the walls here being hung with paintings. We sort of miss the fabled air of loucheness, the false ceiling of hash smoke, the big waterbugs with antennae that could pick up the free Wi-Fi.

An elegant, elderly woman walks down the staircase into the lobby, directing a young male assistant, who is struggling with a large blank canvas. He is telling her that the shape and size of the canvas are such that it will never get into a yellow cab. She says she believes it will and he should try. We catch her eye as she stops in the lobby and we get talking. Oh yes, she insists, the Chelsea is still a bohemian place, though it isn't what it used to be. Her late husband was an artist and now they are slowly removing the contents of his studio. She has a sudden attack of coughing, blaming it on pollen, so Daisy offers her a cough sweet. The sweet helps, but not much. She struggles to talk, but manages to say that there's a battle going on here, a battle for the soul of the Chelsea Hotel. Should it be preserved or modernized? The only poet living here now, she says, is the great bohemian poet and painter Rene Ricard. And he is very sick.

*

In a 1977 interview for BBC Television, Dylan Thomas's widow Caitlin (last depicted on British TV screens doing some impromptu expressionist dancing on a windswept beach in *A Poet in New York*) suggested that her husband was all too aware of the romantic image of the dying, sacrificial poet: 'He had the ridiculous, romantic idea, you know, of the poet starving in the garret, and all that helped the image he was trying to build up of the tubercular, consumptive, dying, pale poet. He wanted to be long and sickly and green and all that, but in point of fact, of course, he was square and small, and not like the conventional idea of a poet at all.'

And what was it like to live with the great doomed poet? 'He just liked his warm slippers and his dish of titbits – pickled onions and sardines and anything with a lot of vinegar, and cockles, all put on a plate, which he'd stuff into his mouth when he was listening to the cricket scores,' said Caitlin. 'He was just Mister Everyman until he put on the act of being the poet.'

And it seems that Thomas's destiny as the twentieth-century Chatterton went back a long way. In an early letter, the young Dylan says: 'Give me . . . a Chatterton attic.' He went on to do his best to emulate that garret scene. And there's an early poem, too, called 'O Chatterton and Others in the Attic', which calls on

these doomed poets to 'Drink from the earth's teats, / Life neat's a
better poison than in bottle.' Like Chatterton, the popular myth of
Dylan Thomas circles around self-destruction. His death is commonly regarded as – if not such a direct suicide as Chatterton's
'arsenic' – at least a case of wilful drinking to the point of death,
driven by despair, personal and professional frustration and
anguish, miles from home. Famous and lost. But this account has
been challenged in recent years, with evidence suggesting that –
drunk and sick though he undoubtedly was – Thomas's death was
at least hastened by medical mismanagement in his final days.

His infamous 'eighteen whiskies' boast came in the early
hours of the 4th of November. Later that day he was attended
by a doctor several times, who administered different kinds
of shots to help him rest and recover. He was admitted to
St Vincent's Catholic Hospital early on the 5th and died there
four days later. But it's fair to assume that the whisky didn't
help. In his 1970 *Paris Review* interview, John Berryman, who
was with Thomas in his final days, put it bluntly: 'He wouldn't
have lived, anyway, but they killed him.' Asked by his inter-
viewer if he thought Thomas had a self-destructive impulse,
Berryman was unequivocal: 'Oh, absolutely. He was doomed
already when I first knew him. Everybody warned him for
many years.'

★

As Caitlin Thomas put it, her late husband was in thrall to the idea
of the 'consumptive, dying, pale, poet', and frustrated that he was
too short, portly and insufficiently pallid to match up. Chatterton,
the alabaster, gaunt, dead boy had spawned a myth far more robust
and enduring than he was. By the end of Thomas's life, in America
even more than in Britain, Dylan the man had been subsumed into
Dylan the legend. Writing in the *New York Times* Book Review in
1975, the poet and critic Donald Davie ventured that 'the late
John Berryman and the late Anne Sexton are just two poets who

might, I believe, have had longer and happier lives if they hadn't grown up under the shadow of the Dylan legend.'

But what is the Dylan legend? Davie nails it: 'His readers, acting out a vulgarized parody of the romantic idea of the poet as scapegoat, live out vicariously through him all the risks and excesses which they are too timid or prudent to live out for themselves; and they demand that in the end the poet pays – for their fantasies as well as for his own actions – by suicide.'

But Dylan was no dilettante. His letters and reviews make clear that he was 'sharp and unsparing' in his observations on poetry and culture. As Davie chillingly concludes, 'the horror is that Thomas almost certainly knew what was happening to him, even as he went along with it.'

★

We sit in the penthouse bar of the Library Hotel and muse over our 'Shakespeare's Sonnets'. They seem to be gin and tonics, with a twist. Twelve parts gin and tonic, two parts twist. Clever stuff, we think. So, why is it that, despite the protestations of poet-critics like Donald Davie, and long-lived counter-examples like T. S. Eliot and Marianne Moore, the popular image of poets in our culture still leans towards a Chatterton-Thomas self-destructive bohemian, blazing a trail across the sky in a brief and lurid life? Is it simply an attraction to the drama of the stories, a prurient interest in extreme lives? No, that doesn't quite explain it. Above all, it doesn't account for the link between the life and the work. Daisy Fried is surely right that an infamous death can overwhelm the work of a poet – as with Sylvia Plath – and can be, as Daisy puts it, 'just another excuse not to read the poems'. But the reputation of the poems (cf. Sylvia Plath's *Ariel* or John Berryman's *Dream Songs*) is heightened by the drama of the life and death. To our post-Romantic sensibilities, it is not hard to see a poet's early and tragic death as an authentication of the power of the work.

These 'Shakespeare's Sonnets' are slipping down nicely, and since we're putting them on our room bills we're neatly avoiding knowing how much they cost. We order more. The penthouse bar opens on to a roof garden crammed with young, New York professionals. They look like extras from the TV legal drama *Suits*, just tipped out of the flashy law firms, having a high and loud old time sitting on each others' laps on large sofas. A few more of these sonnets and we'll have to clear them out so we can recline – Chatterton-style – in this least garret-like of attics: 'Excuse us, we're English poets and we've had too many Sonnets.'

★

If it's true that an infamous poetic death can be 'another excuse not to read the poems', then surely Dylan Thomas is the exception? His body of work is not huge, and far from uniform, depressingly asymmetrical in the way he'd only six poems to show for the last eight years of his life. His influences ranged from the complex sound symmetries of his Welsh language forebears to the Modernist experiments of the previous generation. His head was in song and his feet were in concrete. At times, his voice (though never ranging far from the lyric) takes words to the very edge of sound and sense, as in the visionary 'Altarwise by Owl-Light': 'The planet-ducted pelican of circles / Weans on an artery the gender's strip.'

But the handful of his poems known to most readers are – with cruel irony – defiant in the face of death. The villanelle 'Do not go Gentle into that Good Night', with its heartbreaking refrain 'Rage, rage against the dying of the light', is often read as a rallying cry for the poet's father in his final days, but since it was written five years before his father's death (and six years before his own) it is perhaps better read as a gathering of courage, a clenching of fists in the face of what he knew was coming.

Perhaps the saddest epitaph for this master of the memorable line is that 'Rage, rage . . .' is surpassed in fame only by 'And Death shall have no Dominion.' It is sadder still when you hear that line declaimed in the rich, recorded tones of a poet whose death (or the myth of it) has achieved almost complete dominion over his memory in our culture.

★

It is late Summer 2014 and we are standing in Dylan Thomas's writing shed. He has just nipped out for a pie and pint and won't be long, because he's clearly in mid-poem here. His baggy jacket is slung over his chair-back, and the ink is barely dry on the page he's writing. We sniff the air above the stubbed-out Woodbines in the ashtray on his desk, to see if any whiff of smoke still hangs there. There are seashells along a ledge halfway up the wall, and many pinned-up prints of paintings by the likes of Bruegel and Rouault. Not surprisingly for a poet's den, there are pictures of dead poets on the walls, including Lord Byron, Walt Whitman and Edward Thomas. More surprising are the pictures of (at the time) living poets like Marianne Moore and his contemporaries W. H. Auden and Louis MacNeice. We can't think of any other poet who would want the face of a contemporary staring down as they try to write, unless that contemporary is a lover or partner, of course. And even then . . .

We wait for him, but we are not alone. A curator stands at the door alongside a stack of leaflets.

Dylan isn't coming back. At least, not here. This is not his famous writing shed in Laugharne, overlooking the Taf estuary in south Wales. This is the busy seafront at Dún Laoghaire outside Dublin. We are standing in a painstakingly assembled reconstruction of Dylan's shed, built on the back of a trailer now halfway through its grand tour.

In May, at the beginning of this same summer, we'd visited the real thing, set squint in the wall next to a small road that rises up out of Laugharne and looks out over the sea. The real writing shed was not open, so we'd peered through its window into the same small writing room, the same pale jacket left thrown over the back of the same simple straw chair (similar to Van Gogh's famous chair in his bedroom at Arles, occupied by an abandoned pipe as its trace of the artist), the same air of the poet having slipped out to Brown's for half an hour.

Here in Dún Laoghaire, it's hard to know what to make of this. Things are getting too recursive. We feel a kind of déjà vu, but that isn't quite it . . . Every postcard on the wall, every book on the shelves, even the scrawled lists of potential rhyme words on a foolscap sheet at the side of his desk are replicas of the real shed. This was made as a centenary celebration, as an educational resource for schools, as a way into the great poet's work. But standing here on a quiet Saturday morning it feels more like a portable shrine, a medieval reliquary carried by travellers for devotion and protection in dangerous times. This is the spitting image of his shed as he left it in 1953, when he embarked on that final, ill-fated American tour, and its proximity to Dylan's death is what makes it feel hallowed.

Every accoutrement, every detail counts, because somewhere in this studied shabbiness lie clues to the mystery of doomed genius.

The Names of the Bridges

Searching through Robert Lowell's papers at the Houghton Library, Harvard, we come across disturbing references to Dylan Thomas's death, in letters to Lowell from John Berryman. Dated 14 November 1953, a letter from the Chelsea Hotel says: 'My brains are broken by Dylan's illness and death, which is certainly the worst thing that ever happened.' He goes on to tell Lowell that: 'I was with him when he died, and unluckily was the only man who was, because I had to tell everybody.'

The letters are full of Berryman weighing up the impact of Dylan's death on himself and other poets. What did it mean? Where did it leave the rest of them? For a poet, like Berryman, already haunted by death, it made its mark. In pen, handwritten at the foot of the typed letter from the Chelsea Hotel, Berryman writes: 'Dylan murdered himself with liquor, of course, though it took years.'

★

We have been putting off doing this, but now is our chance. We walk up and stand on the Washington Avenue Bridge in Minneapolis at the point where John Berryman jumped, almost a hundred feet above the river's bank. As the New York poet George Green told us : 'John missed the water.' There are students walking to and from their various seminars, lectures, tutorials. The bridge is right at the heart of the University of Minnesota campus. We wonder how much the students know of the poet who made his exit from the world here. We had somehow imagined a more remote spot, perhaps further upriver where the rush of falls fills the air with white noise, where thoughts may be drowned out. But this is mere yards from the place he went to work each morning, the hall where he gave his inspirational lectures.

The *Minneapolis Star* reported on the evening of Friday, 7 January 1972 that at nine o'clock that morning, 'a man sources identified as John Berryman, 56, Pulitzer-Prize-winning poet, jumped to his death.' It then sets out the details: he landed on the frozen bank of the Mississippi River at the west end of the bridge, near the second pier of the municipal coal docks, and rolled fifteen to twenty feet down the embankment. He was found dead at the scene, and identified by 'a pair of glasses with his name on them and a blank check'.

Eyewitness accounts of the jump were unclear. Art Hitman, a university carpenter, was walking inside the bridge's glass-enclosed pedestrian walkway when he 'saw a man climb on to the outer railing'. Newspaper reports quote Hitman saying: 'He jumped up on the railing, sat down and quickly leaned forward. He never looked back at all.' But even on the day he died there were other accounts. Captain John Brooker of the University Police told the *Minneapolis Star* that a witness told him Berryman walked to the rail, 'waved goodbye' and then jumped.

We peer over the edge to try to get the measure of it. This is the sharp end of poetic death. John Berryman, Sylvia Plath, Anne Sexton, Hart Crane, a stellar roll call of American poets who took their own lives. We came to Minneapolis to pay homage to the writer of the *Dream Songs*, to meet his wife and to try to understand what happened to him. As we stand at the point where he jumped, there's a phrase from his widow, Kate, which keeps coming back to us. 'Poetry exacts a price,' she said, 'but it doesn't have to be the ultimate price.'

★

John Berryman's poetry should be illegal. It probably is, in some States. It should qualify as an intoxicant, rendering the reader unable to drive safely or hold down a regular job. For British poets of our generation, the discovery of his *Selected Poems* was an introduction to the seedy seduction of the *Berryman's Sonnets* sequence charting the course of an affair and the wildly ambitious historical fantasy *Homage to Mistress Bradstreet*. But these were in truth just a gateway drug to the *Dream Songs*. Although they appeared in episodic books over more than a decade, you can now buy all 385 of them in a single volume. They are short, almost all eighteen lines long, broken into three six-line stanzas. They are capacious almost beyond categorization. Discovering such a versatile, polyvocal form is both a liberation and a trap for a poet in mid-career. He created a character – Henry – a man described by Berryman as having suffered 'an irreversible loss'. Berryman had suffered such a loss at the age of twelve when his father shot himself but the poet was at pains to stress in interviews that he was not Henry and Henry was not the poet. Other voices in the *Dream Songs* include a narrative voice that jump-cuts between Shakespearean rhetoric and American slang, and a foil for Henry – a fool for his Lear – a vaudeville character in blackface who refers to him as *Mister Bones*.

The poetic liberation of the *Dream Songs* is that Berryman could write about absolutely anything. The flexibility of this form with its range of diction, multiple voices, broken and re-assembled syntax made it almost impossible to think what a Dream Song couldn't contain. And that was the trap too. There are too many *Dream Songs*. Some are, inevitably, weaker or fall flat on the page between finer examples. But at its best (and a lot of it qualifies as 'best') it stands up as one of the most ambitious and astonishing poetic works of the twentieth century. W. B. Yeats believed that 'sex and the dead' were the only subjects that should be compelling to a 'studious mind'. Well, the *Dream Songs* are full of both those compulsions, plus jealousy, joy, fear and wit and a good deal

of wrestling with God. *Dream Song* 4 gives a flavour of most of
these ingredients:

> Filling her compact & delicious body
> with chicken páprika, she glanced at me
> twice.
> Fainting with interest, I hungered back
> and only the fact of her husband & four other people
> kept me from springing on her
>
> or falling at her little feet and crying
> 'You are the hottest one for years of night
> Henry's dazed eyes
> have enjoyed, Brilliance.' I advanced upon
> (despairing) my spumoni. – Sir Bones: is stuffed,
> de world, wif feeding girls.
>
> – Black hair, complexion Latin, jewelled eyes
> downcast . . . The slob beside her feasts . . . What wonders is
> she sitting on, over there?
> The restaurant buzzes. She might as well be on Mars.
> Where did it all go wrong? There ought to be a law against
>   Henry.
> – Mr Bones: there is.

★

Two days ago we flew into Minneapolis–St Paul in a twin-engine
Embraer jet. As we crossed the Great Lakes, the small plane was
cuffed and buffeted. Our seats were on separate sides of the plane,
so we didn't have to own up to each other how sick we felt. As
we walked down the steps on to Minnesotan concrete, the sense
of relief seemed even greater than usual: flying in, the land below
had turned so glassy and insubstantial, vast expanses of sweetwater
creased here and there into the arrowhead of a boat wake.

On our way out of New York, we asked the taxi driver to take us down West 46th Street, past the site of the Columbia Hotel, the flophouse where in 1966 the poet Delmore Schwartz, broken by years of alcohol, barbiturates and amphetamines, collapsed in the lobby and died of a heart attack at the age of fifty-two. In *Dream Song* 151 John Berryman wrote:

> Sick & heartbroken Henry sank to his knees
> Delmore is dead. His good body lay unclaimed
> three days.

Berryman wore Henry as a costume. Michael Hofmann has described the *Dream Songs* as '385 phantasmagoric sketches' with their own scenery and characters. The character of Henry allowed Berryman to perform as himself, but costumed, half-man, half-myth. If the death of Delmore brought Henry to his knees, it had an even more powerful effect on John. The fate of his doomed generation of American poets – Theodore Roethke dead at fifty-five, Sylvia Plath at thirty, Randall Jarrell at fifty-one, Anne Sexton later at forty-five – preoccupied him. And the *Dream Songs*, one of the greatest achievements in twentieth-century poetry, are nothing if not an extended dance with death.

Number 70 West 46th Street flashed past. No sign of the long-gone Columbia Hotel, just a quiet Manhattan crossroads, with banks on each corner shut for the sabbath. Nothing to mark the passing of a poet. And where were we on that night – 11 July 1966? We were toddlers, no doubt put to bed in good time so our parents could gather round the radio or TV to witness England's underwhelming opening to the World Cup. A nil-nil draw against Uruguay at Wembley was an inauspicious start for the home nation. It was hard to believe that three weeks later in the final, Kenneth Wolstenholme would be saying 'They think it's all over . . . It is now,' as jubilant England fans ran on to the pitch. We are now both between Anne Sexton's age and Delmore's age when they died. On a bright, showery Sunday in New York it felt like a blessed, but unsettling age for a poet to be.

Traffic was light as we headed out to Newark on the trail of Delmore's old drinking buddy John. In the back of the taxi one of us was flicking through a well-thumbed copy of the *Dream Songs*, while the other ran through nervous checks – passport, wallet, notebook, camera, pills.

★

Of all the photographs we took in Minneapolis there's one that is particularly hard to look at now. It seems ghoulish, crass. The picture features two British poets standing in the parking lot of a liquor store in East Franklin Avenue, Minneapolis, bodies angled to frame the doorway of this low, blue-painted building. Between and above us is the neon logo 'Zipps Liquors'.

It was taken on our first night in town by the poet Dobby Gibson. He lives in Minneapolis and he has kindly offered to pick us up at our hotel and take us on a tour of the Berryman sites. As we shake hands and climb into his people carrier, it's striking that he is also – and by his own admission – an 'absurdly tall person'. This was a surprise to us. Without comparing notes beforehand, we had both built expectations of Dobby on the only other Dobby we knew – the House Elf from Harry Potter. But instead of a tiny, wizened figure in a sackcloth vest, we were greeted by a slim, elegant man in his forties. Dobby is a busy man. Alongside the familiar poets' round of readings and teaching, he is a successful creative director, working on brand development for a range of Fortune 500 companies. The child seat in the back of his car, and the stack of picture books beside it, suggests he has a busy home life too.

First stop on our tour is The Brass Rail, a favourite dive bar of Berryman's in his later years. Refurbished and rebranded as The Brass Rail Lounge, it's now a well-known and successful gay club, famous for the quality of its dancers. The door is open

to the street, as Dobby slows the car. It's tempting to have our
first drink of the evening there, but we're meeting another poet
for a drink in Dinkytown later, so for now we're on a schedule.
Looking into the Brass Rail's deep gloom, we try to imagine the
late, full-bearded Berryman up at the bar with a bourbon in one
hand, cigarette in the other, holding court with whoever he happened to find there. We imagined ourselves sitting on either side
of him, trying to keep up with the pace of emptied glasses, rapt
with attention to this genius, this poetic hero, this most terrible
of examples.

Next stop on the tour is Zipps Liquors. Dobby tells us this is
where the poet got his regular supply of whiskey, delivered each
day to his home nearby. It's an old family firm, going strong for a
good fifty years. We park up, walk inside and wander round. It's full
of bright banners and special offers on the stacked-high 'Beer of
the Month – Crazy Mountain', and deals on tequila and rye. It's a
friendly place, with young staff keen to help and talk. On the wall
above the counter is a display of merchandise. We each pay $10
for a black T-shirt with the lurid logo from the sign outside. Then
Dobby takes our photo, before we get back in the car. For the first
time on this leg of the trip, we feel we're on the pilgrim trail.

On to the suburbs, to St Frances Cabrini Catholic Church,
where Berryman's funeral took place on 10 January 1972. We
get out of the car for a photograph. It has been raining and the
fallen blossom makes the sidewalk slippery. The air is alive with
all the scents released by rain. We pose again, while Dobby takes a
photograph. A lady turns the corner with her toy dog on a scarlet
lead. She asks what's happened? What's going on with the church
that would bring foreigners here with cameras? Nothing, we say,
nothing. We retreat to the car, where one of us tries to climb into
the driver's side by mistake and feels deeply uncool.

In the post-rain evening light, the Washington Bridge over the
Mississippi looks like part of a train set in its cheerful maroon and
mustard livery. We drive along the riverside below the bridge and

park at the roadside. There are no other cars in sight. We walk down an unkempt grassy bank at the edge of the river and look up at the bridge above us. Dobby tells us this is where Berryman landed. On the morning of Friday, 7 January 1972, he had left his wife Kate to head for the university, where he said he needed to clean things up in his office. At the post-mortem there was no trace of alcohol in his system.

As we stand under the bridge and pose for a picture, clouds begin to gather and the sky darkens. A police car is lurking behind our parked car. Dobby waves us further down the bank into the longer grass. One of us wonders if you can get Lyme disease from tick bites on an urban riverbank. The picture is taken and the policeman walks across to us. Our car is parked illegally, so we are asked to leave. We are not sorry to go. In our haste, one of us goes for the driver's side again.

★

The hotel concierge had told us Dinkytown was the place to eat and drink in Minneapolis. It's fair to say we are a little under-whelmed. Robert Zimmerman moved here from iron-ore country far to the north and west of Lake Superior in the autumn of 1959, and it was in the folk clubs and coffee shops of Dinkytown that he started going by the name of Bob Dylan. The singer initially denied taking his surname from the famously doomed Welsh poet (who, in turn, was given his Christian name after Dylan ail Don, a character in the medieval *Mabinogion* tales), but more recently his autobiography *Chronicles* pointed back towards it. Completely familiar now, 'Dylan' was almost unheard of a century ago, even in Wales. Somebody points out the room above a drugstore where Dylan lived, and it's funny to think of the unknown folk singer up there in the first weeks of the 1960s, the only Dylan in Minnesota, possibly even the country.

We've found an Irish-themed pub with Dobby and another Minneapolis poet, Steve Healey. They are younger than us, and taller.

They seem more sorted, more together, better dressed. They don't seem like the kind of guys who would worry about Lyme disease or the choking risk of eating food on planes. We talk about Berryman and other ill-fated poets. They are both admirers of Berryman's work, and aware of his ghost at the backs of the poets who work in this city today. Dobby cycles under the Washington Bridge every morning on his way to work and never fails to remember the great poet. But Dobby says he thinks the self-destructive poet image is old-hat now. In fact, the whole 'poet as outsider' thing is passé. Steve thinks there's a difference between the dead poets on each side of the pond. American poets kill themselves, he says, whereas British poets tend to cough themselves out, and need to have their clothes burnt after death for fear of infection. We've had a couple of beers, but there is something soul-destroying about this pub, with its framed green rugby shirts and bodhráns on the walls. It feels as far from Minnesota as it does from Dublin.

We suggest to Dobby and Steve that we walk across to the Kitty Kat Klub on 14th Avenue. We had seen it online and, although it didn't look any more authentic than the Irish pub, it did look much more fun – a music and cabaret club done up like a decadent, Belle Epoque dive. The doorman is polite but firm. The American poets can go in, but the Brits cannot, unless they show their passports. But the British poets' passports are back at the hotel. There follows a moment of pleading, masquerading as negotiation. Behind the doorman and down a set of red-lit stairs, we can hear the pulse of nightlife. What would Berryman do? He wouldn't let the evening end here. He would surely charm or blag or joke or fight his way in. The doorman shakes his head. 'Sorry gentlemen, we have a very strict policy on this.'

★

Our first morning in Minneapolis. The vast hotel is almost deserted, and after walking through its wide carpeted corridors to meet in the lobby, we joke about a boy on a tricycle appearing round a corner. A strange conversation occurs over breakfast. It sounds daft in daylight, with refills of fresh coffee being poured, but last night one of us dreamt there was somebody else in the room with them, their doppelgänger, no less. Waking up didn't entirely break the spell; the dream's unsettling atmosphere had seeped into the dark corners of the minibar and trouser press. Flicking on the bedside lamp and sitting up for a bit helped, but the dawn couldn't come soon enough.

In the bar before turning in last night, our talk had turned to stories we'd heard of people arriving in distant hotel rooms only to find they were already occupied; and what had got us on to this subject in the first place were the full-length mirrors placed just inside the doorway of the rooms here. When we'd arrived, both of us had the same jarring sensation of meeting somebody who looked just like us, struggling over the threshold with the same luggage. Earlier, flying in over the Great Lakes and then the watery, loon-haunted landscape of Minnesota, the earth had looked glazed with vast mirrors. And if that wasn't enough, we were travelling to Minneapolis–St Paul: the Twin Cities! See? Easily explained. We relax and turn to our hash browns and scrambled eggs.

And then, as we leave the hotel for the archive, a man who looks the spit of John Berryman, in his later, wild-bearded, back-woodsman phase, cycles past among the Minneapolitans heading out for the day. Perhaps this trip is beginning to mess with our heads. We struggle to remember who said: 'Every dead man is probably still alive somewhere'. We settle on the Portuguese poet Fernando Pessoa, meaning any one of a number of people. Pessoa invented dozens of heteronyms, and after his death in 1935 left a trunk of papers so various and vast it's still being mapped today.

*

On our Berryman ghost tour, Dobby pointed out a huge concrete bunker by the river, just under the Washington Bridge.

'That's where you'll be tomorrow,' he told us. And so we are. The Berryman papers are stored in this temperature-controlled, sun-proof, Mississippi-proof archive store, just a few paces from the spot where he jumped. To get permission to look at his papers you have to approach his widow Kate Donahue. We did this a couple of months ago, and to our surprise a reply came back not only granting us access to the archives, but also offering to meet us. We felt very honoured and rather nervous. Our letter had told her that we were British poets, that we both owed a debt to Berryman's *Dream Songs* as an early influence, and that we both teach in university English departments. We made no secret that our area of research was the deaths of poets, but had she missed that detail? Would we just seem ghoulish? Neither of our two poets from the previous night had met her. The only pictures we had seen of her were of the Berrymans together, more than forty years ago. With a big age gap between the two of them, these pictures show Kate as a strikingly beautiful, dark-haired young woman in her twenties. How would we recognize each other now? She would be in a grey SUV, she said. She would pick us up at 11.45 on the corner by the university law school.

Entry to the Elmer L. Andersen Library of the University of Minnesota was relatively painless: pencils only, one notebook each, no photographs, no food. The extent of the archive runs to fifty-seven cubic feet of manuscripts, notes, typescripts, galleys and proofs, photographs, diaries, awards, financial records and other personal papers. We had written in advance requesting access to all the papers from the last year of the poet's life. We start to work backwards from the letters written to Kate after John's death.

However doomed he was, Berryman shines through these let-ters as a much-loved and inspiring friend and teacher. One of his ex-students – Charles Hirsch – wrote to Kate three months after the suicide, recalling the 'slow, blissful days of the Minnesota spring', and on one such day standing outside amid fallen blossom after one of the poet's lectures:

Your husband came out of the building, robustly breathed and said: 'Sir, just look at the pavement! It's delicious!' I muttered something about performing Stravinsky's *Rite of Spring* on the campus mall, and he believed me. We laughed. Then I mentioned my appreciation for him giving such a fine lecture. He thanked me and said: 'Let's go talk' . . .

Bizarrely, two letters that same month were addressed to Berryman himself. One was from a student asking to switch from writing a paper on Job to one on the Song of Songs. The other was from a student in Brooklyn seeking to complete the requirements of John's humanities proseminar of spring 1971. The Pulitzer prize-winning poet had been dead for three months when these letters were written. These students must have been too busy studying to read the newspapers.

In one of the archive boxes is a small, yellowing notebook, of the flip-over type used by policemen in Ealing comedies. This one was used by the poet on a trip to India. We strum the pages like a flick-book and a visible puff of dust appears in front of us.

Looking through the Berryman papers feels, after a while, overwhelming. They have a stained, creased physicality and an often palpable fug, the faint smell of stale tobacco rising from the archive boxes like a wet overcoat that's spent a long evening in a bar. This is a chaos of papers, in all shapes and sizes: notepapers, napkins, receipts, a London Underground map, covers of pulp crime novels, things torn from newspapers and magazines. There are diaries and notebooks. Dozens of both. You don't have to look hard in the diaries to see lines like 'suicide has been on my mind all three days', or 'I have been considering suicide every day for a month.' The notebooks give the impression of a man struggling to impose order on his daily existence. And one of his techniques of marshalling the emotions, events and expectations of his life seems to have been listing.

There are endless lists in the archive here, lists of famous suicides, lists of current health problems, lists of fears. Lists of

resolve: to smoke less, to drink less, to eat more healthily. Lists
that set goals: to revise 3 songs a week, to work 4 hours a day,
to achieve a good night's sleep. Shower, nails, CLEAR UP. Lists
of money owed. Lists of jobs to do. Lists of things to avoid.
To Do lists. Not To Do lists. LEARN RUSSIAN. Urgent lists.
Lists of census-taking and inventory: of women, of faults and
'life-problems'. The arithmetic and economics of habit, such as
smoking: 'note: 4 packs a day is $60 a month – even x 6 mo's
only is $360!'

In a worksheet from the Alcoholics Anonymous 'Fourth Step
Inventory Guide', the poet had answered the questions with terrifying honesty:

Q: What has bothered me most about myself all my life?
A: Whether I would be a great poet or not . . .

Q: What bothers me most about myself in relation to the
future?
A: Whether I can overcome this.

Q: Any thoughts, ideas, inspirations, feelings as to how best I
can handle my most bothersome bothers?
A: Clean clothes, showers, daily exercise, talk with Kate,
closer relationships with friends, write to brother and
mother, answer letters at once, offer resistance.

One of the most unsettling things we find is a tiny jaundiced
press cutting: 'Moonstruck Man Leaps To His Death', a lurid
tabloid report of a suicide back east involving a man jumping
from a bridge. 'The full moon hung over the Hudson River
as the young man walked slowly from his car early today and
started climbing over the outside rail of the George Washington
Bridge . . .'

★

We leave the archive and stand by the entrance to the Law Building. This is where Kate Donahue has generously offered to pick us up. We feel nervous, slightly ashamed. We haven't even met her and yet we've just been reading the most intimate thoughts and fears of her late husband. She arrives promptly and is welcoming, polite. We get in the car and offer to buy her lunch somewhere. She asks if we would like to see 'the Berryman house' and of course we say yes. As we drive away from the university, we look across at the Washington Avenue Bridge disappearing behind us. She must see it every day.

We arrive at the house and follow Kate inside. This could be a suburb anywhere in the Midwest, with large family homes set back from the street among trees and well-tended lawns. The Berryman home is white-painted with a porch running the width of the house, windows looking down two flights of stone steps to the street. The blossom trees are huge, taller than the houses.

Kate offers us tea in china cups. She points out a desk where John used to write. Across the room is a desk where she now writes. There are shelves of books, but one area of the room in particular is set aside for John's books and books about John. The house is dark but beautiful – a tranquil place to work. There are family pictures framed on shelves, tables, walls. But we can only see one of the poet. He's in his pomp, sitting on a verandah, wearing a white suit, with a pile of manuscripts and notebooks on a table beside him.

We sit down at the dining table. Kate pours the tea and we begin to talk. She has been teaching poetry to a local adult education class that morning. It's a regular part of her work. Does she teach them any of John's poetry, we ask? 'My problem is that it's pretty hard,' she says. 'It's not that easy for me to keep it on the page. I don't teach much John Berryman. If I did, I'd have to spend the rest of the day recovering.' She says she sometimes thinks of the happier poems. She loves the line 'his thought made pockets, & the plane buckt'. We both join in and finish the line

with her; it's probably been cued up in both our prefrontal corti-
ces since the bumpy flight west. 'I don't know why I like that line
so much,' she says, 'but I do.'

How did John work? 'He sat in the living room, just over
there', she points at an old armchair. 'He did lots of brooding. But
frequently I'd be in the kitchen cooking, and he'd say, "Oh come
and listen to this," and he'd be working on something. He liked
company, he liked activity. The students used to follow him home,
and they'd all be sitting on the floor and I would say, "Dinner time
now, time for everybody to go home." '

Kate knows why we are here, but no one is talking about John's
death. It doesn't seem possible to ask. Not yet.

Did he talk about the poems to you? 'He never talked about
Henry, that person, outside of the poems. Henry didn't exist outside the poem. Henry House was not somebody walking around
in here. He was only on the page.' We sip our tea. The wind buf-
fets the blossom trees outside. As soon as she says that Henry is not
'walking around in here' it seems inevitable that he is. Berryman's
double – JB and not JB – sitting in the old armchair with a cigarette or calling from upstairs to see who the visitors are.

Did John feel he had completed his work, at the end? Kate
shrugs: 'I have to realize, realistically, that he was his age, and I was
my age. We were married for ten years, but it was hard for me
to see his whole career. As a young man he was a lot different.
I read about him as a young man and it sounds like somebody I
never knew. He was very ambitious, very classical, wanting to be
part of the major tradition, then developing more of an American
language and style, the slang that he ended up using and liking. As
a young man he can't have imagined that. He ended up finding a
path that only he understood.'

Kate was twenty-two when she married John in 1961. He was
in his late forties. She was a local Minnesotan girl. He was the big-
shot poet and professor. 'He felt like Minneapolis wasn't his chosen
environment', says Kate. 'He considered himself a New Yorker. He

always saw himself as Henry among the Goths, it didn't feel natural to him. I'm Irish and French, and Minnesota is Scandinavian, I was brought up here.' She does a parody Minnesotan accent, a joke voice she used to do to make John laugh. 'The winters here were a bit tough. He wasn't crazy about the weather.'

In the last months of his life, with Kate's love and support, John came off the bottle. Was that dry last year fruitful for writing? 'Yes, but it felt like it wasn't a strong recovery, there was something tentative about it.'

Did he work differently when he was sober? 'John's study was the biggest bedroom upstairs. Before, when he was drinking, he was always down here. But he tried to get back into more of a scholarly mode, I think, working on Shakespeare, with a more disciplined schedule. That was one of the results of not drinking, you could arrange your day however you wanted it. I don't know how much poetry he was writing in those last months. I think he wanted his reputation to last, but was quite nagged with a sense of failure. Wanted to get back into Shakespeare scholarship. He was going through treatment. I don't think any of us – unless we've been through it – knows what it's like to be totally addicted. Who are you? Are you this person who does all these things and needs this stuff, or are you another person?'

The tea is finished. Kate has been generous and open. The stillness here and the darkness under the great trees makes it feel like a trap. We are on edge, in spite of Kate's hospitality. John Berryman in later life had a conversion experience, from a scholastic belief in the divine to faith in a personal 'God of rescue', a God who could intervene in the details of individual lives. Was he hoping for such a rescue? Did he wait for it here? And what about us? Are we here to meet a ghost?

Kate begins to talk about John's late 'conversion'. She calls it 'a real religious coming back'. 'He called me up once, he had gone to give a reading out east, Connecticut, and he called late at night

and said he had had this spiritual experience, and I thought he was
drinking, so our conversation didn't end happily, because he felt
like he wasn't being understood. We never really talked about it
again. I felt I didn't really understand it, and he didn't want to risk
having a big misunderstanding again.'

We mention the pictures – daughters, grandchildren. 'This is
a happy ending,' she says. 'John would have appreciated what the
kids have done.' She knows what we're thinking. Why so few
pictures of John himself? 'You don't see too many pictures of
this guy around here.' The phrase 'this guy' hangs in the air for
a moment. 'What he accomplished I respect and it's still alive in
some sense, but it doesn't do the job of a real person. And in fact
I don't have another person. I never replaced him. But I don't
want to put that in front of my children as something they should
be happy about. I mean they have been deprived of a father. And
that's the fact. They have wonderful husbands and we've managed, but we've paid a price. I was a very foolish young person.
I had my own family history, which helped to make this choice
to marry him.'

When John died Kate was still in her early thirties with two
young daughters. She had counselling after his death, then ended
up working as a bereavement counsellor herself. She is a strong,
impressive woman. She does not seek our sympathy. Her life is
directed outwards and forwards, into her work in the community,
as a teacher and counsellor, a mother and grandmother. But it's
hard not to see John's suicide as the shaping, defining force in her
life, the day around which every other day circles.

Berryman's suicide was more than forty years ago, but Kate
still talks about it as a shock, an essential mystery: 'Suicide is such
a puzzle that you're always looking for the answer. I'm still doing
that. I'm still thinking on that day, what could have gone differently. You never get the answer to that, but you're always looking
for it. It's not talked about, but it's still there. It's difficult to look
at the person's life without that. I mean, John was a very happy,

funny guy. But you say that and it just doesn't fit. He was the steadiest man on the block.'

Before we leave, we ask her if she gets many Berryman admirers like us, beating a path to her door? 'No, because it doesn't really do the job that you need. There's some reason why you guys are doing this, for your own understanding, and it's more than just John Berryman you're trying to understand, it's me, and it's your own lives.'

★

John Berryman is a great poet, but a terrible influence. As students, we discovered not just his electric, macabre poetry, but also his terrifying philosophy of creativity. The heart of this can be found in that infamous interview with the *Paris Review* conducted in 1970. Even now it is a stomach-churning read. As students, that gut-clench felt like a confirmation of authenticity, a sign of truth being told, however uncomfortable. In our early twenties, when death seemed like nothing but a rumour, and when the vision of the *poète maudit* was endlessly intoxicating, we could quote one section of that interview verbatim in pubs to anyone who would listen:

> The artist is extremely lucky who is presented with the worst possible ordeal which will not actually kill him. At that point, he's in business ... I think that what happens in my poetic work in the future will probably largely depend not on my sitting calmly on my ass as I think, 'Hmm, hmm, a long poem again? Hmm,' but on being knocked in the face, and thrown flat, and given cancer, and all kinds of other things short of senile dementia. At that point, I'm out, but short of that, I don't know. I hope to be nearly crucified.

He hopes to be nearly crucified? Of course, there's bravado here, wry overstatement, but underneath all that, yes. We believe he hopes for it. Courts it. Longs for it. Not because he has a death wish, but because of the work. It is all for the sake of the work.

If cancer or crucifixion could allow the poet to access the deepest, darkest wells of the imagination, then bring it on. And if that means losing one's life in the process, then so be it.

★

Where did Berryman's ruinous, fatal aesthetic come from? Donald Davie, writing in the *New York Times* Book Review four years after the poet's death, paints a picture of the young Berryman as a scholarly, intensely serious figure, diligent in his development as a poet and an intellectual. So how did he become what Davie describes as 'the very fierce and shocking and disconcerting poet' of his later years? Davie speculates that Berryman's intense encounter (for a critical study) with the wild energy of Walt Whitman's poetry may be partially responsible. But he suggests that 'the Dylan Thomas bandwagon' may have played a bigger part in Berryman's conversion to 'some vulgarly debased notion of the poet as society's sacrificial scapegoat'. Berryman's love of Thomas, his admiration and horror, his grief as a close witness to those last, self-destructive days in New York make this all too believable.

Davie's essay is not an easy read. His sense of anger and loss at what became of John Berryman is palpable. But the essay ends with a moving eulogy: 'The man behind this book was not only one of the most gifted and intelligent Americans of his time, but also one of the most honourable and responsible. I take no satisfaction in saying this. The time to say it to him was when he was alive. And now it's too late.'

★

As part of our work on Berryman, we track down an early copy of some *Dream Songs* online, in a US edition, with 'assorted press cuttings and notes' folded inside the flyleaf. Fascinated by the idea of these cuttings and notes, we buy it. When the package arrives, we find the cuttings are stranger than they sound. They are yellowing strips cut from local Minneapolis newspapers in the days following John's suicide in 1972. On one cutting, an advert for Little Friskies cat food, every piece of white space between the lip-smacking cats and the bowls of food is filled with scribbled notes in blue pen. It seems to be a record of a phone conversation with a friend who knew Berryman. Written sideways down the middle of the page between columns, it says 'sobbing on phone', and 'complete state of shock'. Down the side is written: 'really in bad shape, heavily sedated, absolutely no idea. Thought everything fine 10 days ago. All my life I've never been able to help anybody. Guilt complex.' Then there are notes from the phone call trying to piece together facts about the poet's life: 'his dad committed suicide? Shot himself? He found him at age 12?' And it's true. He did. But whoever is on the other end of the phone was worried about his state of mind in recent weeks: '1-2-3 weeks ago, John very depressed, almost non-verbal – not drinking'.

In a separate, clear plastic bag, also folded into the book of poems, is a copy of the order of service booklet for John's funeral. It includes recitations from his poems, as well as scripture readings from Luke's gospel and the Book of Lamentations. The music ranges from a setting of Psalm 22 to a Beethoven Quartet and, a little surprisingly, 'Kumbaya, My Lord' as the communion hymn. On the front of the service card are printed four lines from Berryman's *His Toy, His Dream, His Rest*:

> At Henry's bier let some thing fall out well:
> enter there none who somewhat has to sell,
> the music ancient & gradual,
> the voices solemn but the grief subdued.

★

We are in a Chipotle Mexican Grill and we cannot talk. We have to say something to order our burritos, but then our accents are caught by the girl who is serving our food: 'Please don't lean over the glass, sir, it contravenes our hygiene policy.'

'Oh, I'm sorry. Are those refried beans?'

'Are you guys from England?'

She is spooning out black beans, barbacoa and carnitas every spare day she has, because she's saving up to visit a friend who is studying in London.

'I want to see castles, mostly. What are the best castles?'

But the lunchtime queue behind us is long and we are dumb-struck. All we can think of is Kate Donahue driving back to what she still calls 'the Berryman house' in Arthur Avenue, having left us here. She offered us a lift to the airport, but we said to drop us at Chipotle on the corner. We'll get some lunch and take a taxi from here. We didn't want to put her to the trouble of a long drive. But also we need a decompression chamber between those Minneapolis suburbs and the airport.

We eat our burritos in silence, watching the rain on the side-walk outside. We have a brief, tetchy exchange about who is going to call a cab, and who will ask the waitress for the address of this restaurant. And as we tip our trays into the bin, Kate will be park-ing outside 'the Berryman house', on a street heavy with blossom. Then she will climb two flights of stone steps to the white wooden porch, unlock the door and enter the most haunted house either of us has ever set foot in.

The taxi pulls up outside Chipotle. We turn our collars against the rain.

'Good luck!' says the girl behind the counter.

'And you. Good trip. Try Windsor, there's a big castle there.'

★

John Berryman's response to the AA 'Fourth Step Inventory Guide' seems more striking the longer we reflect on it. He lost his father to suicide, struggled for decades with depression, despair and addiction, yet in answer to the question 'What has bothered me most about myself all my life?' he wrote:

A: Whether I would be a great poet or not . . .

What does 'great poet' even mean? The respect of his peers, a measure of fame, awards and accolades? No, he had all those. 'Great poet' is another version of 'major poet', attributed to the death-proof genius of a Milton or a Shakespeare. But your peers don't make you a major poet. Only posterity can do that. What troubled Berryman was whether he had done enough to secure his place in the pantheon. In centuries to come, when the merely good or timely or interesting poets are reserved for ultra-specialist PhD theses, would Berryman's *Dream Songs* still be read, memorized, loved?

Why did he care? If you won't be around to know if you've passed the 'great poet' test, then why let it get to you? Berryman's lifelong engagement with Christian theology (his work is full of religious imagery) culminated in a return to faith in his final years. Does the question of posthumous reputation matter more if you believe in a life beyond death?

It only holds if you assume that the concerns of this world are the same in the next. Berryman's notion of God was too rich and capacious for that. If you believe in an afterlife in which 'the last shall be first, and the first last', then notions of mortal 'greatness' become meaningless. Perhaps that's why he seemed to overcome those fears about canonicity – in a handwritten later addition to his inventory when he qualified his 'great poet' concern with the line 'until recent years'.

★

It's part of the ritual of moving to a big city from somewhere smaller: establishing points of reference, absorbing the colours of the subway lines, poring over a borrowed *A-Z* as the train moves closer to its destination. This is a period where the new city is fluid and up for grabs. 'Those days before I knew the names of all the bridges were happier than the ones that came later,' Joan

Didion wrote of being young in New York. From the north-west of England the train slows on its approach into Euston, and we both remember how we learned to read the landmarks. There must have been a time that we were completely unaware of how, somewhere between the Post Office Tower looming into view and the crossing of the Grand Union Canal, the train passed by the end of a street from a mythic landscape, locked in a legendary winter. Neither of us looked out for it, and neither of us has ever visited it, until now. We're standing outside the flat on Fitzroy Road in Primrose Hill, wondering how exactly we're supposed to write about Sylvia Plath.

We know we want to avoid the tar pits of recrimination and blame. We know we stand before something unparsable, that we can never really understand exactly what led to Plath's suicide in the early morning of 11 February 1963, or what happened in the weeks leading up to it, when Plath wrote poetry in an extraordinary flush of invention and energy.

The critical response to Plath's work has been an avalanche. To Al Alvarez – Plath's friend and most enthusiastic promoter in the period immediately following her suicide – the poems in her posthumous book *Ariel* seemed to fuse poetry and death: 'The one could not exist without the other. And this is right. In a curious way, the poems read as though they were written posthumously'. Beyond her circle of family and friends, a critic more recently described Plath as 'the woman who launched a thousand PhD theses'. So much has already been said.

For the first time on our travels, we're feeling like proper thana-tourists, ghouls out to doorstep the living and chill them with news of their domestic ghosts. Except, in this case, we're sure the present occupants are more than aware of who lived at this address for those eight weeks during the winter of 1962–3. The story of Plath's final stay here at 23 Fitzroy Road has been added to, edited, revised, restored, excavated, extended and redeveloped. It has, in fact, become as layered and labyrinthine as a part of an old city itself – we feel as if we should apply for planning permission, though what kind of little loft conversion can we add to what's already been said?

We wonder, too, about how much of what happened at this flat, in a north London stockbrick terrace, has coloured our reading of the poems. Writing recently on Vincent Van Gogh, Julian Barnes used the word 'deathtime' to look again at the painter's huge posthumous success, following a lifetime of obscurity and failure. Van Gogh's work, like Plath's, carries its own climate and weather system, in his case forever bundled together with the storm clouds and gathering crows of instability and madness. With Plath, it's as difficult to read her poem 'Edge' as it is to look at one of the sunflower paintings without some sense of its maker's essential suffering. The myth modulates and varies the pitch of our relationship with the poems: it's difficult to have anything like an initial encounter. Can we remember innocently reading Plath? How much of her biography, simplified, proverbial and circulating through our wider culture, preceded and conditioned our reading?

★

At the junction of Fitzroy Road and Chalcot Road we meet the poet Jo Shapcott and we walk to the flat where Plath ended her life. Today it's gentrified and smart, and there is the plaque to W. B. Yeats, just as Plath would have seen it. Yeats had spent a few years here as a child, his family having moved from Dublin so that his father, John Butler Yeats, could pursue his career as an artist. 'She must have been thrilled that Yeats had lived here', says Jo. A letter home to her mother in November 1962 indicates as much, heartbreaking now in its italic excitement and optimism, the flukiness of happening to pass by here, where we stand now, and finding it available to let, in a street she liked, with a connection to Yeats, and rushing to the estate agents.

'It's hard to imagine a cold, top-floor flat in the middle of a terrible winter,' says Jo as we crane our necks, 'but she lived here for

eight weeks and wrote thirteen amazing poems.' Here it is, the edge
of the glacier that keeps calving, the point at which Plath slipped
into myth. It's important to remember that she was relatively
unknown as a poet up until this point, despite her first collection,
The Colossus, despite BBC appearances and poems in magazines.
Her first novel – *The Bell Jar* – was just out, but published under
the pseudonym Victoria Lucas. She wasn't 'Sylvia Plath' yet.

'Tomorrow morning some poet may, like Byron, wake up to
find himself famous for having written a novel, for having killed
his wife; it will not be for having written a poem,' wrote the
poet and critic Randall Jarrell. Plath complicates this statement:
by being a woman, by not waking up and experiencing her own
fame, and by having written those poems.

We know the appalling winter had something to do with it.
This was the first proper snow Plath – a New Englander probably familiar with blizzarding nor'easters, ice storms, even a
hurricane – had seen since moving across the Atlantic. It was a
legendary season; we only experienced its antithesis, the gorgeous
summer of 1976, but growing up we both remember older people
talking about it with a kind of hush and awe. January 1963 was
the coldest month of the twentieth century. Some inland waters,
estuaries and rivers froze over, harking back to the frost fairs of
the Little Ice Age.

Plath was glad to be out of rural Devon, where she had lived
with her husband Ted Hughes immediately before moving back
up to London, and Fitzroy Road. Deep polar drifts isolated communities, and many phone lines were down, although you can
sense the closed-off feeling Plath was experiencing in the city
with her two young children, stuck in the dirty pack ice. She
wrote to her mother on 16 January, describing her gloominess
amidst the big freeze-up, the longed-for telephone she was still
waiting to have put in, her sense of being cut off.

In the autumn of 2002, the poet Hugo Williams came across a
street near his Islington home covered in snow. Which was odd,

because it had seemed fairly mild for November. Not only that, but the cars the snow had covered all seemed to be models not seen on the road in decades. For a moment or two, the poet must have wondered whether he'd stepped through a secret portal in the city. It turned out he'd stumbled upon the location shoot for *Sylvia*, a biopic of Plath and Hughes. Special effects had been called in to cover everything in fake snow – made from shredded paper, salt and foam – in order to recreate the awful winter of 1962–3. Imagine a future where scenes from your life are being recreated in such painstaking detail, down to the smell of bacon from the on-set caterers.

We know London had something to do with it. Indeed, a monochrome, peeling, puddly, just-off-rationing country seems bound up with Plath's suicide. Britain was still shabby in its post-war period, trying to clean up its act (and its air). The milk that Plath left out for her sleeping children in their cots upstairs at Fitzroy Road – opening their bedroom windows and sealing the doors to make sure they'd be safe – was delivered to the doorsteps at dawn; the coal gas burned with a pale blue flame. Britain was still on 'town gas' derived from coal, and still a few years away from natural gas piped in from the North Sea oilfields. Town gas, manufactured at local gasworks, contained carbon monoxide and made every cramped kitchen a convenient execution chamber.

And then there was the long wait to get 'on the phone'. In Britain during this period the telephone was still something of a luxury, and the single supplier could take its time in meeting demand. Far from a world where everybody is connected to everybody else via a pocket handset, often the only recourse was the nearest public call box. Today we don't often have to memorize a phone number, but Plath wrote an essay the year before she died called 'Ocean 1212-W', connecting her to her grandmother's house by the Atlantic; and that hurricane we mentioned, the Great New England Hurricane of 1938, making a landfall much anticipated by the five-year-old Plath and her little brother, who wanted a piece of this approaching calamity that might blow their world to bits.

★

Plath's final creative surge resulted in a folder of poems, left out in the Fitzroy Road flat to be discovered following her death. Maybe thinking in terms of 'surges' subtly perpetuates an idea of the extreme life and work. Would we say the same of novelists, working towards a daily word-count goal? Novels can be jigsaw puzzles too, but poets are often writing a book they can't see at all, oblique fragment by oblique fragment. The poems that became *Ariel* were finally collected, compiled and arranged by Hughes and published in 1965, though the book isn't simply a lyric diary of her final weeks. There are the self-elegies, but also the poems to children like 'Balloons' and 'Nick and the Candlestick'. Poems like 'The Moon and the Yew Tree' or 'Berck-Plage' were written well before Fitzroy Road, and the shift up to line speed and peak creativity happened over a longer timeframe, precipitated by birth rather than death according to Hughes, who wrote of how miraculous Plath's development was following the birth of their first child, the more so given the demands of babies and housekeeping; things speeded up following her second birth, her gifts and capacities integrating over a period of months, achieving an astonishing unity of purpose.

We wonder how much of this terminal surge is an expectation of the reader, reading the life as much as the poems, or *into* the poems.

'We should have more Anon,' declares Jo. 'Find some way of allowing poems to float free. I think Plath would live without her life. Her poems would live and glow, and people would be able to see the fun and humour in them. Real sharp control and playfulness with words. For me, she's the poet of momentum, and rapid mood shifts. It does take the reader to the edge sometimes, but at no point is it not under control.'

★

We decide not to hang around, and return to the junction of Chalcot and Fitzroy Roads. We talk along the way. Did Plath mean to be found before she died? And what effect did her medication have on her state of mind during those final months here? There has been plenty of speculation on how Plath's insomnia and depressive illness, and the drugs administered to treat these conditions, may or may not have led to her suicide.

The negotiation with various kinds of anti-depressants is so common now that it seems odd to try to tease out the particularities of their use among poets. But there is something about the mercurial relationship between poets and their poems that means any intervention in emotional chemistry needs to be approached with caution. Some poets feel that there's a price to be paid for a peaceful mind. A medicated narrowing of emotional bandwidth means the poems still get written, but they can fall hollow on the page. Others find that taking the screaming edge off anxiety and depression liberates them to write their best work.

Our growing sense that there is something 'doomed' about the psyche of many poets is not alleviated by a flick through the academic journal *Death Studies*. In a paper from 2003 James C. Kaufman of California State University published the results of his study into the life expectancy of poets, mapped against other writers and non-literary professions. He examined '1,987 deceased writers from four different cultures: American, Chinese, Turkish and Eastern European'. His conclusions were depressingly predictable. Across the board, poets died youngest. The *New York Times* picked up on the research and found some even gloomier academic research to back it up. James W. Pennebaker, Professor of Psychology at the University of Texas at Austin, is quoted as saying that: 'Being a published poet is more dangerous than being a deep-sea diver,' adding the caveat that 'it's possible that if they weren't doing poetry they may have killed themselves off earlier'.

An earlier study quoted in the *New York Times* (by Dean Keith Simonton, Distinguished Professor of Psychology at the University of California) declared that: 'It's hard to find something that poets are not higher on pathology – alcoholism, suicide, drug abuse, depression.'

But is the poetry the problem or an attempted cure? Professor Simonton speculates that poets may be using the making of poems as 'a form of self-therapy' for their problems, and it's their innate pathologies that kill them, not the poems.

James C. Kaufman, however, sees the poetry as part of the problem. Asked about conclusions from his own research, he argues that being in a 'subjective, emotive field is associated with mental instability'. 'If you ruminate more, you're more likely to be depressed,' he says, 'and poets ruminate. Poets peak young. They write alone.'

★

Jo suggests there might be a broader pattern connecting creativity with different mental states. 'Whether healthy or mentally fragile, you could argue that in a creative moment, your mental state is altered. I don't think it's a necessary part of creativity, but it's not surprising.' Jo has recently worked with a neurophysiologist, Mark Lythgoe, and explains his idea of latent inhibition, the very strong filtering function in the brain for addressing the massive amount of sensory stimuli that comes in. If we received everything, we'd be overwhelmed. Latent inhibition keeps things focused.

'He seemed to be arguing that for creativity to occur, the filter has to lift so that new associations can be made – can we say that mental fragility allows for that to happen more easily than otherwise? Though I'd argue mentally sound people can achieve it too – the idea of being "in the zone", drink, drugs. Tragically, one of those is a pre-existing mental fragility.'

Lythgoe published a paper on the extraordinary case of Tommy McHugh, a fifty-one-year-old builder who survived a stroke and found himself overwhelmed by an urge to be creative. The storm that had struck his brain had affected the filtering mechanism in Tommy's frontal lobes. A few weeks after surgery he began to fill notebooks with poems. He started painting pictures, several at a time; when the cost of canvases became a problem, he painted on the ceiling, the wallpaper, the floor. He worked for up to nineteen hours a day. Before his stroke, Tommy hadn't the slightest interest in art. Soon, his house was full of it. The paintings and poems flowed out of him.

★

'The poems read as if they were written posthumously.' Alvarez's line points us in a different direction. Any changes in the brain's weather, its chemistry or structure, can undoubtedly alter our creative capacities. But in emphasizing this, we risk putting something else in the shade. Christopher Hitchens once recalled some advice given to him by Nadine Gordimer: 'A serious person should try to write posthumously.' It's wonderful advice, but perhaps the most challenging for any writer to act upon and accomplish. So good, the novelist Jeffrey Eugenides turned it into an awards speech, passing it on to those new to the game. To turn down the noise of the world, the temptation to follow the latest literary fashions, to bend oneself out of shape in order to find some accommodation among the crowd of voices receiving attention; to resist any urge to self-censor, to be candid and honest with oneself while harbouring no troubled thoughts concerning how one's writing will be received, even among coterie or clique; to achieve all of this while keeping a line open to the world, staying in touch with lived experience.

★

We turn right into Chalcot Road and head northwards towards the Square, going further back in time. Here is the earlier Plath-Hughes residence, Number 3, the big pink house where the couple lived together for eighteen months, from the beginning of 1960, before moving down to Devon. This is where their first child Frieda was born, and where Plath published her first collection of poetry, *The Colossus*. Forty years later, when a blue plaque was unveiled at this address, a reporter asked why this wasn't happening round the corner at 23 Fitzroy Road. 'My mother died there . . . But she had lived here,' answered Frieda.

Blue plaques. We recall our own first few weeks in London. Young and somewhere around peak susceptibility, arrival in the autumnal city left many lasting impressions of newness and difference: mice bristling under the live rail in deep Underground stations; signs that said LOOK RIGHT and MIND THE GAP and TAKE COURAGE; the vivid red of Routemaster buses, bleeding into the steely greys of a rainy day; the smell of hot fat and frying onions and chestnut braziers – and blue plaques were a part of all this.

We've grown accustomed to the commemoration of the artist's living place and the workplace in the form of a plaque. This hallowing of ground is so commonplace in London that the sculptor Gavin Turk could ironize the gesture (and fail his Masters) at the Royal College of Art by presenting a blue plaque in his studio declaring he had worked there, 1989–91. There's a nice historical symmetry to this: the blue plaque as we know it today was designed by a student from the Central School of Arts and Crafts in 1938. Whoever they were, all we know is that they received four guineas for their efforts. In a way, every blue plaque is a Tomb of the Unknown Art Student.

Has there ever been a generation of artists and writers more aware of a commodified afterlife, more self-consciously working sub specie aeternitatis, surrounded not just by the work of the past (though that's never been so plentiful and available), but also the museum of its sources in the world? Writing just before the Second World War, the critic Cyril Connolly invoked Dr Johnson to suggest that not only was an unmarried man only half a man, but a married man only half a writer; domesticity for Connolly was one of the enemies of promise, symbolized famously by 'the pram in the hall'. In a different age of working mums and stay-at-home dads we hope that caution might easily be consigned to the scrapheap, but a new and insidious enemy might have emerged, that of the paralyzing and overbearing presence of the dead (and their visitor centres with free parking) in our midst. Has the pram in the hall been replaced by the plaque on the wall?

★

London in early 1963 wasn't the overlooked, CCTV-haunted and camera phone-infested city we navigate today. And yet there is lyrical footage of the night in question. The streets hushed, the parked cars deformed by snow, and the woman alone with her children, who is not yet connected to the great, frozen intricate thing she finds herself in the middle of, who might have ventured out into the sub-zero Sunday night for the payphone on the corner, to call her husband – who *is* plumbed in to the Post Office exchange – at his flat in Cleveland Street, in the shadow of the half-built Post Office Tower. But there is no reply.

Hughes's poem 'Last Letter' is an excerpt from an outtake. The speaker imagines a phone ringing in an empty room, the caller walking through the streets of dirty snow to reach the call box, over and over. It wasn't included in *Birthday Letters*, a collection of the poems he'd been writing to Sylvia since the early 1970s that was published in 1998, but only came to light recently (it was published in the *New Statesman* in 2010). It runs the same lacerating film, over and over. When people die, we often gain a sense of their whole life coming into view fairly quickly, working against the usual awfulness or circumstances of their decline. Then there are artists and their loved ones who are not easily allowed this, stuck endlessly in the looping tragedies of their deaths.

We've found a café on the main drag at Primrose Hill (terroir coffee, artisanal bread, wheatgrass shakes – where fifty years ago it would have been mugs of tea and fried bread, maybe a Spanish omelette if you were lucky) and ask Jo about the ongoing adjustments and revisions, the difficulty of getting back to the poems. Did *Birthday Letters* change her sense of Plath, or inform her sense of Hughes in relation to Plath?

'The second. It didn't really change my sense of *him* – because I didn't feel they [the *Birthday Letters* poems] were a major part of his work. I'm a huge fan, but other parts are much more significant. I'm intrigued by what the impulse to publish was. I can see the impulse to *write* them – almost a kind of diary working through of emotional difficulty – but the result of gluing them together is quite extreme. I was intrigued how firmly the publication of those poems wove those two poets together even more closely, so that they'd never be read apart'.

★

We had a haunted moment on the walk into Primrose Hill from Chalk Farm station, as we crossed an old iron footbridge. The arched bridge didn't feel long or memorable enough to warrant a name, but could this be the one Ted Hughes calls Chalk Farm Bridge in his poem 'Epiphany'? We start to stare at other bridge-crossers: lumberjack-shirted hipsters blinking in late-morning sun, a man in paint-stained overalls, a woman in gym gear with a Yorkshire Terrier in her tote bag. What are we looking for? An epiphanic encounter with a bloke trying to sell us a fox cub, as Hughes's poem describes? A glimpse of Ted or Sylvia, walking off the film-set of their own lives and making their way towards the Underground, where they would vanish?

The sun is in and out, and feels like it's being rationed, peeping through clouds to ignite brickwork and skips; post boxes flare; tidy north London streets turn illuminated and precise before everything dims again. A van flies past, and from its passenger side window comes the immortal cry: OI! FACK ORF GIN-JAH! We like the idea of a depot somewhere on the outskirts of the city, where a fleet of random abuse-flingers set out each dawn to ply their trade and startle passers by.

Now we stand at the junction of Fitzroy Road and Chalcot Road again, a crossroads that today has come to feel like an axis between life and death, the point where the latitude and longitude of Sylvia Plath meet on the ground. We like Jo's emphasis on the poems, on their imaginative load-bearing capacities, their ability to exist without their author. Strange thing is, even though we've never been here before, we really can't recall reading Plath without being aware of these hinterlands of unhappy myth. Over time, as we learned her poems and grew familiar with her work, an underlying matrix of biography, claims and counter-claims, testimony, anecdote and study developed and deepened. We were learning other lines. Now we're extras too, playing our tiny walk-on, walk-off parts in an old movie, standing where many others have stood, holding their battered, ancestral *A-Z*s like scripts, trying to get their bearings. We like Frieda Hughes's emphasis on a plaque marking lived life. Maybe pinning the map with the end-point of death only sticks us to the script and pins down these poems of mood shift and momentum.

But what about the meeting place? It occurs to us now that some of the most durable poets have come in pairs or gangs, or held allegiances that bolster their stories. Wordsworth and Coleridge, Owen and Sassoon, Auden and MacNeice, Plath and Hughes. Maybe we shouldn't be so surprised that more hasn't been made of this: after all, we are dealing with unpopular culture here. Meanwhile, the meetings of Mick Jagger and Keith Richards on Platform 2 at Dartford Station, the first members of Pink Floyd at the University of Westminster and John Lennon and Paul McCartney at St Peter's Church Hall in Liverpool, are today all marked by plaques.

★

Plath and Hughes first met at the launch of a student journal called *St Botolph's Review* (which ran to just one issue in their lifetimes: a second appeared in 2006, a fifty-year gap you'd have to say is erratic, even for a little magazine). It happened on a Saturday night in late February 1956, and by the middle of that year they were married. Hughes had graduated in 1954, but was back in Cambridge for the party; Plath was at Newnham on a Fulbright Scholarship. The American student had got a little blasted on Whisky Macs before arriving, and was bumping into things. Her college years at Smith College in Massachusetts had been bumpy, to say the least: there had been breakdowns, suicide attempts, months of psychiatric care, and electroconvulsive treatment. Her adolescent turbulence didn't prevent academic success, though it makes it seem all the more remarkable. But then, Plath seemed to live at a certain pitch, what Elizabeth Hardwick, reviewing Plath's work in 1971, described as her 'drifting, rootless rage, the peculiar homelessness, the fascination with sensation and the drug of death, the determination to try everything, knowing it would not really stop the suffering – no one went as far as she did in this.'

At the party, Hughes moved in. Plath wrote an account of what happened in her journal the morning after. The two had pulled away from the main group and into a quieter side room, away from the dancing turtlenecks and piano music and smoky clamour. There was a kiss, and then a memorable description of Plath's bite to Hughes's cheek, so hard it was bleeding when the couple re-emerged from the room.

Plath had certainly been reading the *St Botolph's Review*: she could quote his own poems back at him (they were all to appear in his first book *The Hawk in the Rain* the following year). The party was thrown in the Cambridge Women's Union in Falcon Yard, just off Petty Cury, a warren of medieval yards honeycombed with cafés and old university clubrooms. What is there today? We decide to go and take a look, because, beyond the famous bite, Falcon Yard seemed to have resonated with Plath: she planned a novel based on her life in Cambridge with this title.

★

Of course, it's long gone, cleared away by developers in the Sixties. We visit Cambridge and discover the Lion Yard Shopping Centre standing in its place. This is already the second time on our travels that we've found ourselves wandering through a mall like mystery shoppers from the heritage industry. While in Bristol, looking for signs of Chatterton, we'd visited the site of Newgate Gaol, where the proto-Bohemian poet Richard Savage had ended his life in debt and obscurity; it's now The Galleries, a shopping complex that opened for business in the early Nineties. We found an oval plaque remembering Savage on the wall at one of its entrances. Here, in Cambridge, we begin to wonder how many other retail outlets we'll discover with literary heritage, and whether we've stumbled on a metaphor not just for the deaths of the poets, but the death of poetry?

But Lion Yard in Cambridge isn't a death site. Weekend shoppers are out in force. Joining the footflow and entering the familiar sacred grove of sensory marketing techniques, passing the distracted and desirous faces in the crowd, there's nothing on offer here that comes anywhere close to the excitement Plath and Hughes must have felt on that Saturday night sixty years ago. Then, as if to skewer our haughty, middle-aged grumblings, a group of girls screech and laugh as they walk by, closely pursued by a pack of teenage boys. Places like Lion Yard are great for copping off! People still fall in love, or in lust, anywhere, and we decide to leave Sylvia and Ted like that – an idea or an image before it has been struck, still molten and unknowable, upriver from all of the major building work, renovations and bodged jobs, clapping eyes on each other for the first time somewhere round about here – in the air above us, back when this was called Falcon Yard. And let there be no plaque.

The Dust of England

Ever considered the Russian Matryoshka doll-effect of the Romantic poets' lives and deaths, each nesting one inside the other? It goes like this:

> William Wordsworth 1770–1850
> Samuel Taylor Coleridge 1772–1834
> Lord Byron 1788–1824
> Percy Bysshe Shelley 1792–1822
> John Keats 1795–1821

We really should get out more. But think about the little Keats doll, the innermost heart. Looked at from his point of view, the other four poets are very much at large and all-enveloping. He can know nothing of their literary after-lives. Seen from the perspective of our Wordsworth doll, the younger writers might come and go, flaring briefly, their reputations waxing and waning. In the case of Keats, what Wordsworth can't know is how high the younger poet's stock will continue to rise during the Victorian period, beyond his outer orbit of 1850. We see it all differently from *here*. As young men themselves, when Wordsworth and Coleridge published *Lyrical Ballads* in 1798 the plan almost certainly wasn't to create a paradigm shift in English poetry; it's likely that they were looking to help fund a long stay and walking tour in Continental Europe. They were looking to get paid.

While in Bristol on the trail of Richard Savage and Thomas Chatterton, we try to establish where *Lyrical Ballads* was first published. Or at least, was printed slightly earlier than an almost identical version of the book that also appeared in London. The book's first publisher, Joseph Cottle, was a poet and bookseller in Bristol, well connected with a coterie of writers at large in the final years of the eighteenth century, his support extending in some cases to patronage. Looking even further into the margins, we find Nathaniel Biggs, master printer, with whom Cottle collaborated. Cottle's shop and business was based in Wine Street; Biggs's press was located on St Augustine's Back, a quayside of buildings that ran alongside the River Frome. Today the Frome has gone, or gone underground. A water feature cascades down the Millennium Steps here in the city centre, and we soon work out the course of the buried river along what's now St Augustine's Parade. Biggs never left much of a fingerprint, but we imagine him working somewhere here, his nails grouted with ink, his apron smudged, stooping over the galley proofs, the ships moored outside and the stink of the tanners and dye-works and paper mills. Here, somewhere among Toni & Guy and Boots the Chemist and Pizza Hut, the Ancient Mariner first saw the light of day. 'From Mariner to marinara', one of us offers, then hangs his head in shame.

So much of any writing's larger meanings and resonance lie hidden from its author; its destinies are unpredictable, although oblivion is always a safe bet. It's distorting enough for the reader, where the tendency might be to crowd out their present moment. Anthologies of poetry are often stand-offs between the quick and the dead. The present – let's call it the *long present*, the past few decades – contains work that hasn't really entered the grinder yet. Walking backwards through time, the gangs of poets wobbling on the tightrope of a timeline begin to fall off and thin out, until half centuries, whole lifespans, flicker past represented by single poems. The dead who have walked this earth easily outnumber us, though you wouldn't know it from where we're looking. The sound of the first poem uttered has a long way to travel.

The Romantic poets didn't see themselves, or each other, like we do. From here, we look back towards that group of writers as to a constellation, and though the Zodiac arrives at its alignments and conjunctions over time, its individual stars burn at their own rates and consider their neighbours in a completely different array. But one of these poets woke up one day to find himself gone supernova. He's the aristocratic, mad, bad and dangerous to know doll (maybe more of an Action Man), who, looked at another way, is nested right in the middle of our little arrangement: Lord Byron. Of the famous five, it's his death we know the least about, except that it happened in Greece.

*

We're sitting in a bar off Syntagma Square in the centre of Athens, drinking cold Mythos beer. Like the ginger-haired everywhere, we've long become adept at finding shady places. In the taxi on the way into town, we asked our driver: do you know Byron? She cracked a big smile: 'Of course, of course! He was a great man, a poet and a philosopher. Look!' At that moment, the cab was approaching a statue outside the National Gardens. Greece, personified as a woman, crowning the poet Byron. Scribbling our notes, we worried about how very convenient this would all appear. But there's more.

'Vyron,' she said, as we rattled towards the Plaka. 'Vyron is still a boy's name here. Go into those gardens and call out Vyron! I tell you, somebody will look your way.'

This can't possibly be true, can it? We imagine yelling Keats! or Larkin! on a busy street in London or Hull. That really is fame – though it wasn't what Byron had in mind when *Childe Harold's Pilgrimage* first saw the light of day in 1812. The first instalment of that long poem, which quickly electrified readers and cemented Byron's celebrity overnight, sold out its first edition in three days. The story of its hero's flight into far-off lands was begun in Ionnina in the north-west of this country, where Byron was visiting the court of Ali Pasha during his first journey to Greece in 1809. The Byronic hero was born, reverberating down the nineteenth century and beyond, from the mountain fastnesses of Epirus up near the Albanian border. Here, baby boys are still proudly given the poet's name. 'Byron' means something different here.

★

There's a painting of Byron in the National Portrait Gallery by Thomas Phillips. The moustachioed poet is decked out in the velvety Albanian costume he brought back from that journey to Epirus, a cock pheasant with 'shawl-girt head and ornamented gun'(or scimitar at least), gazing aloofly to his right and off into the distance. But it's a copy, made long after the poet's death. The original is here, in Athens, and it seems like a good place to start. It hangs in the British ambassador's residence and they are happy to let us in to see it. At the end of a Kolonaki street awash with the blue surf of jacarandas, we exchange our passports for passes and are ushered in by the guards.

We're introduced to somebody inside as being 'here for the painting'. They in turn ask us: 'Will you be taking the painting this afternoon?' For a few confused moments we feel like international art thieves, before the super efficient Katerina arrives and takes us through into the ballroom, where the Byron portrait hangs in pride of place. A long-cased clock chimes the hour, while a PA hidden somewhere is *testing, testing* for some future ambassadorial reception or function. And there he is, just as he sat for Phillips exactly two hundred years ago in 1814. He was newly famous then, and must have been pure showbiz to the people who came to view him at the Royal Academy that year. He's supposed to have asked if Phillips could do his nose again before it left his studio. Katerina tells us the portrait is often lent out for exhibitions, and it's strange to think of Byron travelling on ambassadorial business for Great Britain (as well as providing an echo of the nineteenth-century tours of Wallis's painting *The Death of*

Chatterton). But we're not so embarrassed by Byron any more. Even Westminster Abbey finally relented and allowed a memorial. We're standing before an image – however stage-managed – of Byron on his first trip to Greece, as a young man barely into his twenties. After five tumultuous years back in England, Byron left again for Greece, and to understand his death we have to travel to the west of the country, to find out why he returned.

★

Parnassus, seen across the Gulf of Corinth from an air conditioned KTEL bus.

> O thou, Parnassus! whom I now survey,
> Not in the phrenzy of a dreamer's eye,
> Not in the fabled landscape of a lay,
> But soaring snow-clad through thy native sky . . .

It's hot here at sea level in late May, but we can see winter snow has found a few final hiding places on the highest slopes of the mountain. Byron was here on his first Grand Tour, and to the north of us lies the landscape that found its way into *Childe Harold*. 'It was a world of strife, ambush, revenge, burning villages, massacre, impaling and severed heads,' wrote the great traveller Patrick Leigh Fermor, who trudged through the region over half a century ago, though nothing substantial seemed to have changed in the textures and tempo of the remote mountains and villages. He also wrote of how the ramshackle country bus was being replaced by 'commodious charabancs', and we experience the first pang of what we're beginning to recognize as Paddy Fermor Guilt.

Our long and drowsy and very upholstered afternoon intersects with the poet's journey at several points, however. We've passed through Loutraki, where Byron and his companion John Cam Hobhouse sat around the campfire with their soldier escort. The little port of Itea sits almost directly across the water, where

Byron and Hobhouse landed to begin their ascent of Parnassus to Delphi. Aigio flashes by, a small town on the E65, where the two travellers were detained for over a week by bad weather, and then the coach crosses the Rio–Antirrio Bridge connecting the Peloponnese with the mainland, where the Gulf of Corinth and the Gulf of Patras meet. We're heading for Missolonghi, which Byron passed through and saw only briefly on that first Greek adventure, and couldn't have known would be the place where he would return to die fifteen years later.

★

'And thou, the Muses' seat, art now their grave.' We wonder what Byron and Hobhouse would have made of Delphi today. Here is the landscape of Apollo and the Muses, at the very epicentre of European culture, though much of it still lay buried and yet to be excavated when the two young travellers saw it. Byron was a confirmed gouger and scratcher of his name and you can still find a trace of him here: on one of the columns in the gymnasium, among the scratched names of sailors Newton, Hope and Mangles, the graffiti in Hobhouse and Byron's hand still survive.

It has found its way into a poem by Leeds-born Tony Harrison: 'Polygons', a marvellous, many-angled elegy and reflection on mortality among the ruins at Delphi, describes how Harrison used water bottled from the nearby Castalian spring to splash on the stone and ping up the definition of the lettering. Harrison has form as an explorer of mortal traces in the margins: visiting Wordsworth's home of Dove Cottage a thousand miles away in the Lake District, he once found some graffiti written on the back of a window shutter, unseen by the thousands of tourists who file through its gloomy, coal-scented rooms:

'our heads will be happen cold when this is found'
W. Martin, paperhanger,
4th July 1891

This found line of 'five strong verse feet' found its way into Harrison's poem 'Remains', or more likely brought it to life: the poet uses the forgotten artisan's 'one known extant line / as the culture that I need to start off mine'. In the later poem, in Delphi, Harrison catches sight of a newspaper headline in a kiosk:

SEIMOUS XINI

Without having to read any further, he understands that his friend and fellow poet Seamus Heaney has died. They had once dined and drank and swapped poems here in Delphi.

★

On hearing the news of Byron's death, the young Alfred Tennyson walked out by himself and carved *Byron is Dead* into the soft Lincolnshire sandstone near his village of Sommersby.

★

Yesterday in Athens we'd trudged up the dusty pathway to the Acropolis. Standing on its plateau, the place resembles a vast film set – not just in the scaffolding and gantries erected on parts of the Parthenon itself, but in the way the crowds of sightseers aren't sightseeing, but recording everything on their camera phones, holding their mobile devices aloft like amateur film directors measuring the light. We were doing it ourselves.

Seeing the ancient world at first hand is always a complicated business. After knowing it for decades as a place in pictures and books, encountering the thing itself can involve a strange abnegation. The place might be smaller than we imagined, or bigger; it can disappoint or overwhelm us in many different and subtle ways. But there's often a little death involved. Freud suffered what he called 'a disturbance of memory' when visiting the Acropolis. He was standing in front of a place known to him second-hand but centrally all his life. Maybe this was more pronounced a feeling a century or two ago, when educated Europeans would have been steeped in this shared culture from an early age, but we both felt the unreality of visiting somewhere we've never been many times before.

> Where'er we tread 'tis haunted, holy ground;
> No earth of thine is lost in vulgar mould,
> But one vast realm of wonder spreads around,
> And all the Muse's tales seem truly told,
> Till the sense aches with gazing to behold
> The scenes our earliest dreams have dwelt upon ...

At the same time, hadn't Byron come to the very edge of his culture? A place where Europe gives way to somewhere else entirely? This is the poet who, later on this same first journey through the Mediterranean, would famously swim the Hellespont, the great watery rift separating Europe from Asia. Byron went beyond the traditional terminus of the Grand Tour – Rome – and deep into unmapped Greece. Later in the Acropolis Museum, we would view the giant figures and friezes removed from the Parthenon, and find ourselves completing a sad mental jigsaw puzzle: marrying the fragments there with those familiar from visits to the British Museum – the Elgin Marbles – plus the odd hand that's found its way to Munich or an elbow that's ended up in Copenhagen. Byron didn't think much of Elgin's plundering of these artefacts.

> But who, of all the plunderers of yon fane
> On high, where Pallas linger'd, loth to flee
> The latest relic of her ancient reign;
> The last, the worst, dull spoiler, who was he?
> Blush, Caledonia! such thy son could be!

All this bodily scattering and dispersal has other Romantic chimes. Keats took himself south to Rome to die of tuberculosis, and we remember the lock of his hair and death mask in the little museum next to the Spanish Steps, and his room that still retains a gloomy, deathbed air, with its polygonal floor tiles, and beyond its shuttered windows the sunlight and commotion of tourists and students on gap years out on the Piazza di Spagna, where long ago the furniture from the poet's sickroom had been piled up and burnt.

Then there was Shelley, drowned in a storm while sailing from Livorno to Lerici in the Gulf of La Spezia, and cremated on the beach near Viareggio. In the oven heat of Athens we recall rainy visits to the Walker Art Gallery in Liverpool. Inside, beyond the Corinthian-columned entrance that was itself a soot-stained northern echo of what we were sweltering in the middle of, we'd stand before Louis Édouard Fournier's painting *The Funeral of Shelley*. The poet lies serenely on a smouldering pyre of wood, while on the sands a small party of mourners looks on. There's his wife, inconsolable. Edward Trelawny, the ex-naval volunteer who will tell this story many times over his long life, is here. And there's Byron, dark windswept hair and open shirt collar. The day looks overcast, the sea dour as the Mersey at Widnes. We also recall the complicated disappointment of discovering the facts: that the day was actually fine and warm, that the body being cremated had been in the water for ten days, pulled ashore using hooks, then temporarily interred in the sand with quicklime; that local quarantine laws meant the decomposed drowned had to be burned, and a kind of portable iron furnace cage had been rigged up. An appalled Byron is supposed to have gone for a swim, and Shelley's wife didn't show up at all. Still, the story of the poet's heart being snatched like a baked potato from the ashes and ending up in England seems to be true. Byron too was to experience a postmortem scattering, as we were soon to find out.

★

A Byronic detour. After Minneapolis and John Berryman, we fly west to California. We've a couple of days spare, and want to look for Thom Gunn in San Francisco. As a counterpoint to Greece, the West Coast of America is clearly another kind of myth-making centre and source, and we're reminded of this somewhere over the high desert of Nevada, when the drinks trolley malfunctions and a flight attendant asks drily if anybody on board knows how to re-boot the 'flux capacitor'. We're all in on the joke, because we're as steeped in this younger American culture as Grand Tourists from northern Europe once were in the Classical world.

For poets, the Californian epicentre lies further north from the dream factories at Hollywood: Kenneth Rexroth, Jack Spicer, Robert Duncan, and the so-called San Francisco Renaissance; Lawrence Ferlinghetti and the City Lights Bookstore; Allen Ginsberg and the *Howl* obscenity trial; the Beat poets. Somewhere in there is Thom Gunn, wearing a leather jacket like Marlon Brando in *The Wild One*. Far below, the desert is intricate with vast fields of wind turbines and solar farms harvesting sunlight so powerful their arrays of mirrors can cause birds flying overhead to burst into flames on the wing. This is the future, but you can't help thinking of Icarus.

Byron famously shook the dust of England from his feet and headed for the Continent. Thom Gunn struck out west, leaving the England of his birth and upbringing shortly after his first book, *Fighting Terms*, had appeared in 1954. While a student at Cambridge, Gunn met and fell in love with an American student, Mike Kitay, and the move – initially to California to study at Stanford with the poet Yvor Winters – became permanent. In one sense he never stopped being an English poet, his work attuned to the formal shapes of English verse, but different strains of influence moved through his poetry. Most strikingly, his poise in language struck sparks with the subject matter he found in the Bay Area, the new world he found himself moving in so un-English and un-1950s as to seem like time travel: drugs, the burgeoning counter-culture, Hell's Angels, gay pride, the male body and the leather bars and light and heat of the West Coast. When describing the move, Gunn talked in contrasting terms of 'spaciousness' and 'claustrophobia'.

Seamus Heaney told a story to Dennis O'Driscoll in their book *Stepping Stones* about going to dinner at Donald Davie's house in Stanford, some time in the mid-Seventies; Thom Gunn was a guest, and Heaney remembered being particularly struck by the fact that Gunn had hitch-hiked down from San Francisco to be there, not even bothering with the bus. Maybe he liked the community of the open road, America as a site of restless movement, energy, anything-might-happen-ness:

> It is a part solution, after all.
> One is not necessarily discord
> On earth; or damned because, half animal,
> One lacks direct instinct, because one wakes
> Afloat on movement that divides and breaks.
> One joins the movement in a valueless world,
> Choosing it, till, both hurler and the hurled,
> One moves as well, always toward, toward.
>
> A minute holds them, who have come to go:
> The self-defined, astride the created will
> They burst away; the towns they travel through
> Are home for neither bird nor holiness,
> For birds and saints complete their purposes.
> At worst, one is in motion; and at best,
> Reaching no absolute, in which to rest,
> One is always nearer by not keeping still.

The quitting of tired, shabby, small-minded postwar England for prairies of possibilities, though, might be a simplification and myth in itself. A poet whose work managed to hold in balance the analytical and cerebral with the pleasures and travails of the flesh, he also seems a poet of interiors and exteriors – which might seem a minor distinction, but cities have their promiscuous streets and their hidey-holes, and Gunn was a city-dweller. We both remember reading 'Street Song' from *Moly* (1971).

> My methedrine, my double-sun,
> Will give you two lives in your one,
> Five days of power before you crash.
> At which time use these lumps of hash
> They burn so sweet, they smoke so smooth,
> They make you sharper while they soothe.
>
> Now here, the best I've got to show,
> Made by a righteous cat I know.
> Pure acid – it will scrape your brain,
> And make it something else again.
> Call it heaven, call it hell,
> Join me and see the world I sell.
>
> Join me, and I will take you there,
> Your head will cut out from your hair
> Into whichever self you choose.
> With Midday Mick man you can't lose,
> I'll get you anything you need.
> Keys lids acid and speed.

'Street Song' seems to make a dealer hawking his wares in the streets of San Francisco chime with broadside ballads and vendors' songs, the noise and texture of any lively streetscape down the ages. If Wordsworth had his daffodils – and Larkin, in a famous riposte to that, his depression – then Gunn had the streets, the energy of the sidewalk. His work is populated with dealers and down-and-outs and tramps. Though, running counter to that, it has its enfilades of rooms, its crawlspaces. Asked about this once, Gunn recognized the metaphor: 'It's like a house and there are rooms, there are half-hidden rooms in it, there are attics where nobody ever goes . . . I expect Freud speaks about it somewhere. You might almost say it was a cultural metaphor rather than an individual one. I do dream a lot about houses and about rooms, but I've always assumed everybody did.'

A year before Gunn died in 2004, the poet Tom Sleigh had spoken to him about a sex club he had visited (Gunn by now was into his seventies). Sleigh describes how, being straight himself, Gunn entered into an almost anthropological level of detail concerning a club with two floors, one for gays, one for straights, and the supplement paid by gays to descend among the straights (which wasn't reciprocated). Tents were rooms within rooms. Later, checking to see if he could find the details of such a club online, Sleigh came upon a description that might or mightn't have been the same place in San Francisco, but makes clear what was available:

> There are different floors, but there's a bottom floor with a dungeon and bondage room, for a total of three floors, not two. And there was no mention of tents, but rather theme playrooms: among others, an ancient Egyptian room, a boxing ring, and a series of cubicles that would seem to form a maze called Asshole Alley. There is different pricing, but not as straightforwardly gay/straight as I remember. And of course, it's possible he was talking about a different club altogether. What I'm certain of is this: Regardless of the no drugs or alcohol policies, Thom talked about the drugs people were on: Viagra, obviously, but more to the point, speed (methamphetamine), PCP (aka angel dust), and ecstasy, though it was Thom's impression that more straights were into that.

★

We're at the Bancroft Library at Berkeley, California, to look at Thom Gunn's papers, and things are not going well. After visiting the Presidio and the Golden Gate Bridge, after gazing across to

Alcatraz to get our bearings, we'd wandered around the Haight–Ashbury District, ground zero of the hippie movement during the late Sixties. It felt a little tidied up, less the melange of tatty souvenir stores and shooting galleries and bars and dealers than we'd imagined; maybe Midday Mick sells oregano to tourists these days. Gunn had lived on Cole Street from the early Seventies, but a series of mishaps meant we got the address wrong and paced up and down, growing more frustrated and sweaty, eventually taking the BART train out to Berkeley.

Now, recomposed in the cool of the library, we have the archival boxes in front of us and at our disposal. This, we're discovering, is always an exciting moment. Regardless of how detailed the cataloguing of materials has been, nothing quite prepares you for the appearance and touch and smell of the actual 'papers' – that metonym that sometimes seems to cover any number of notebooks, scrapbooks, diaries, letters, postcards, cloakroom tickets, receipts, shopping lists . . .

Thom Gunn was discovered dead at the Cole Street house in the Haight in April 2004. While reading the accounts of various friends in the wake of his death – which was sudden and unexpected, even though he was seventy-four – we're struck by the routine and domesticity Gunn enjoyed at the Cole Street commune (or 'queer household', as he preferred), though in the midst of this settled picture the partying continued. The medical examiner recorded 'acute polysubstance abuse'. According to one friend, the photographer Billy Lux: 'He kept his freak on in a big, big way, doing three-day speed and sex binges when he was in his seventies. PNP, or party and play, it's called. I think one of these party-and-play episodes might have killed him. Although I wasn't part of that whole scene, I did, in a way, admire his aggressive pursuit of sensual pleasure. I just wish he was still around to relay his latest sexcapade in a letter or a poem or over lunch at Zazie's.'

Perhaps ageing was the hardest thing. Gunn's descriptions of his life in California in the Sixties are golden and idyllic. There's an ache in the way he describes its music, the rhythms of its acid-infused occasions, its sense of a possible community spilling out beyond the orgies and bathhouses to irradiate the wider world, which is almost unbearably halcyon. The time of his life. To not only leave that, but to leave behind the corporeal energies required to fully participate in that, must have been agonizing. Towards the end, he didn't. He hung out with a younger crowd, took drugs, and talked of the 'gerontophile' at large who went for the older guy.

In the archive, a strange thing happens when we begin rooting around in the boxes. We thought we'd begun to get the hang of reading other people's mail, but after a short while, we both begin to feel uncomfortable: nosy, grubby. There are things here that make us laugh aloud, breaking the scholarly calm of the room; things that reveal a salty humour, like postcards of pissing pigs (later, we go back to our notes in pencil to check: yes, pissing pigs). Here is Gunn's diary, the pages bifurcated down the centre into two columns of fine, delicate handwriting. There is fan mail, including a card from a well-known English pop star. There are also letters and notes from people we know, people who are still very much at large. We signal to take a break, and in the hall outside we decide we don't want to carry on.

It's all simply too recent; still somehow up in the air. The dust hasn't settled. Our squeamishness interests us: after seeing a few death masks and locks of Romantic hair, after thinking we were starting to get used to handling letters and manuscripts written by dead poets, we've been stopped in our tracks. When does an archive like this settle into something less like a rummage through a drawer in a dead person's apartment or an inspection of the evidence room? Is there a necessary distance, a cooling-off period, where the papers found about a person gradually become less difficult to view? Or is it simply the objects we discovered from the blood-warm and still-living and known to us, a reminder that one day – and soon – we'll all end up in shoe boxes or scrapbooks or – if we're lucky – an archive like this one? All we can say is that, even though we know this is a dereliction of duty, even though we've come all this way for nothing, we're going to leave Thom Gunn in peace.

Fresh air always seems freshest outside an archive. We wander down to one of the cafés on campus, and sit staring over a sun-drenched lawn dotted with students out enjoying the day. And when talk turns to the Bay Area light and the way Berkeley today looks like a painting from the Sixties or Seventies by David Hockney or Richard Diebenkorn, we catch ourselves wondering whether we can ever really leave the archive.

★

Mesologgi.Mesolongi.Missolonghi.Messolonghi.Messolongion. A watery, swampy place, a place of huge lagoons known to migrating birds and spawning fish, that slips its own spelling. A wetland landscape that has been drained and diverted and canalized in our own lifetimes. A place of eel traps and herons, salt pans and mosquitoes. The same, different place that Byron knew when he returned here in 1824.

Byron arrived by water; Paddy Fermor did too, watching the town float towards him 'as though raft-borne on its rank lagoons'. Our bus wails in low gears, winding down a mountainside road into a landscape of orange groves, wayside shrines, then tall reeds and bulrushes. We meet Rosa Florou at the KTEL station, over coffees so bituminous and grainy you could stand a spoon in them. Any poet would be lucky to have somebody like Rosa attending to their afterlife. A small dynamo of a woman, President of the Messolonghi Byron Society, she ushers us into her car and off we go. First stop: the Garden of the Heroes, just around the corner.

Byron found his way back to Greece and Missolonghi following the years of fame and scandal that culminated in him shaking the dust of England from his shoes and quitting the country in the spring of 1816. If you were to tag and track the poet, his

movement south might seem somewhat inexorable – down the
Rhineland to Switzerland, then the famous Villa Diodati meeting
with Shelley, Mary Godwin, Claire Clairmont and John Polidori
in the volcanic-shrouded 'Year Without a Summer'; south again
to Italy and shimmering Venice; Ravenna, Pisa (the period during
which Shelley was drowned), and Genoa, from where he set sail
for Kefalonia in July 1823. 'I love Greece, and take the strongest
interest in her struggle,' he said in 1822. 'I will tell you a plan I
have in embryo. I have formed a strong wish to join the Greeks.'
The tractor beam pulling him south wasn't simply powered by
the memories of that transformative Grand Tour of 1809–11.
Greece was now fighting for independence after more than three
centuries of Ottoman rule. Revolts had broken out in 1821 and
the poet had found a cause. You get the sense, in the letters and
recorded conversations that have survived, of Byron offering his
services to the Greeks and their provisional government. He must
have known the risks involved. 'I should prefer a grey Greek stone
over me in Westminster Abbey,' he wrote a few months before
sailing to the Ionian islands and the war zone beyond, 'but doubt
that I shall have the luck to die so happily.' His epic poem-in-
progress *Don Juan* recorded the general revolutionary alignment.
Poems aren't diaries or manifestoes, but still . . .

And I will war, at least in words (and – should
    My chance so happen – deeds) with all who war
With Thought . . .

★

The Garden of the Heroes is scattered with obelisks and monuments, stonework echoed by the taller cypresses, as deep and
blue-green as Van Gogh painted them. It's a hot day, bristling with
insects, but there's plenty of shade to be found. Here is where
many of the soldiers and philhellenes who sacrificed their lives
for the independence of Greece have been commemorated. For

many, their remains, once scattered throughout this region, were brought here for reburial in the 1830s. Here is Markos Botsaris, who fell in the first siege of Missolonghi just a few months before Byron arrived. Here is Christos Kapsalis, whose house Byron had stayed in, and who would later set alight the gunpowder stored there when the enemy entered, blowing everything to smithereens. There's Georgios Karaiskakis, accused of treason and court-martialled in the troubled days leading up to Byron's final illness, who was killed fighting a few years later. Here is the tomb where the remains of all the fighters were piled in a heap ('Look . . . countless Leonidas are here buried, who courageously fought for freedom'). Maybe most importantly when thinking of Byron's short time here, we find the bust of Alexandros Mavrokordatos, his chief ally, who survived the poet by forty years. All the chaos and rivalries and politics and violence of that time turned into a scented garden with a visitors' guide in four languages.

And here is Byron, at the centre of it all, standing on top of his cenotaph, 'Among the arranged trees and the marble clichés / And the small memorial cannon like staring infants / With lollipops in their mouths', as Louis MacNeice wrote, making this same pilgrimage in June 1950. Rosa explains how Byron's lungs and organs are buried inside its pedestal, in a silver-lined box.

What? Yes. The people of Missolonghi wanted some part of the poet who was more than a poet. Byron died after taking ill with a fever, probably brought on by a soaking he received while out riding in the squally April showers. He had been in and out of poor health for months, and had suffered a seizure in February that appears now like an ominous precursor to what followed. He'd arrived in Missolonghi at the beginning of the year, slipping quietly into its lagoon in a small craft known as a *mystiko*. His arrival wasn't kept quiet for very long: this was a hugely symbolic event in the Greek independence movement. Byron came ashore like a messiah, bearing gifts of hope, credibility and money. Lots of money.

Rosa takes us to the site where the Kapsalis house stood, and where Byron breathed his last. It would be easily missed: a small stone obelisk flanked by a pair of saplings in a quiet residential square. A few parched white roses are gathered at its base (placed here by students attending a conference a few weeks ago, Rosa tells us). She also explains how we're standing right on the former shoreline of the lagoon, which has now receded by several hundred yards; Byron would have taken his punt almost to the doorway of this vanished house. We imagine the threshold, and Byron arriving home soaked through. We imagine Louis MacNeice, also caught out in the rain, arriving home. But we'll cross paths with him again later.

★

We're staying at Nafpaktos a few miles away round the headland, a sleepy resort with an out-of-season feel: stacked plastic chairs on the edge of a grey and gritty beach. The weather has turned stormy and unsettled, and we eat calamari and drink Alfa beer that evening, watching lightning flicker in the clouds out across the Gulf of Patras. It turns out each of our first memories of encountering Byron concerns an entry in the *Guinness Book of Records* under 'heaviest brain' (in Neapolitan ounces). We couldn't have both imagined this. Conversation turns to *The Man With Two Brains* and Steve Martin's Dr Hfuhruhurr, which seems to have both nothing and everything to do with today. We hope the thunder rumbling far out over the Ionian Sea will help tune us back into antiquity. There's a panic over whether we've enough euros to cover our meal – as we're discovering, Greece is essentially a cash economy – but we scrape it together and thank our hosts.

The following morning we wander down into the old port and come across an iron statue of Miguel de Cervantes, as tall and stark from a distance as a Giacometti figure. Nafpaktos was once Lepanto, an important Venetian fortress. In early 1824 this place was full of disgruntled Albanians who had not been paid for their privations, and Byron's first mission – which he did accept – was to take the town. To this end, Byron was training up his own militia, but the plans soon unravelled. There was trouble in the assembled ranks at Missolonghi, Byron suffered his seizure, and there was to be no triumphant march into the garrison. We wonder at the non-memorial, which probably would have stood here above the small harbour, if Byron had made such an entry. Instead, the author of *Don Quixote* has it all to himself. Before helping to invent the modern novel, Cervantes was a soldier in the Spanish navy, and had also fought the Ottoman Empire at the Battle of Lepanto in 1571. Wounded by arquebus fire, he lost the use of his left arm here, 'for the greater glory of my right', as he's supposed to have cracked.

★

Paddy Fermor was on a mission in Missolonghi. Before leaving for the Greek adventure that became *Roumeli*, he'd visited Lady Wentworth, Byron's great-granddaughter, in Sussex, and describes how he spent an hour rummaging through a reliquary of Byroniana, including the same velvet jacket and scimitar that we saw in the portrait at the Ambassador's Residence. Lady Wentworth passed on a letter she'd received from Missolonghi, which contained an offer to return a pair of shoes once owned by Lord Byron to one of his descendants. Fermor volunteered to try and track them down. He began by writing to the current owner, who was wary of sending the precious footwear through the post. But once in Missolonghi, Fermor forgot the owner's name, and had to resort to putting the word on the street: have you seen Byron's shoes? Eventually the niece of the shoes' owner presented herself and took Fermor to meet him. They were not shoes after all, but a pair of 'light, slender, faded slippers, with their morocco leather soles and the uppers embroidered with a delicate criss-cross of yellow silk and their toes turning up at the tip in the Eastern mode.' You can sense Fermor's huge excitement as he turns them over to discover the difference in each slipper's imprint: it was as though the club-footed Byron 'had limped into the twilit room . . .' Yesterday in the small museum at Missolonghi, we'd looked into the eyes of Byron's personal boatman John Kazis, who had lived well into the age of still photography and poses in his *priari* on the lagoon in 1884. Kazis remembered seeing Byron wearing these slippers at the house of Kapsalis, after he rowed him to the vanished threshold where we'd recently stood, and it was he who had handed the slippers down to their present owner. Story lies within story. Words and pictures spark across huge gaps. Byron's slippers were never returned: their owner had a change of heart and couldn't bear to part with them.

★

Byron and relics. Such was his celebrity that friends, lovers, chancers and archivists would squirrel away anything connected with the poet.

Take these: peach stones in a Petri dish, held in the archive of Ravenna's Classense Library, from fruit picked by Byron's lover Teresa Guiccioli on a pilgrimage after his death to the English family seat at Newstead Abbey.

Or these: next to the peach stones, another Petri dish, this one with a dozen flakes of cream-coloured blossom. 'Is it cherry?' we ask the curators, 'from Newstead, perhaps?' But no. It's his skin. There's a tale told here that these flakes of sunburnt flesh were from the grieving poet's swim at the beach cremation of his friend Shelley. When the peelings fell, Teresa kept them. As pale redheads, we've done our share of post-beach peeling, but nobody has yet put our blossom in a Petri dish.

★

Byron's last illness was recorded by his doctors and companions, though the poet was a difficult patient, and reading their accounts today produces its own miasma of leeches and claret and opium and mustard blisters and senna enemas. Nobody seemed to agree on what was causing his fever. The doctors were young, inexperienced, and acutely aware of being at the bedside of one of the great celebrities of their day. Byron didn't want to be bled – 'many more die of the lancet than the lance' – and some doctors today would agree that a dirty lancet probably caused a fatal sepsis, but eventually blood was taken. Pietro Gamba, one of the poet's closest followers – who also died of fever three years later – produced an eyewitness narrative of those final days in April 1824. It can be collapsed into a horrible prose poem:

The next day he felt himself perpetually shuddering.

The next day he kept his bed with an attack of rheumatic fever.

He rose from his bed the next day, but did not go out of the house. The fever appeared to be diminished; but the pains in his bones and head still continued: he was melancholy and very irritable.

The following day he got out of bed at twelve; he was calmer; the fever was less, apparently, but he was very weak and suffered from the pains in his head.

The fever was still upon him: but the pains in his head and his bones were gone.

It happened unfortunately that I was myself confined to my bed this day by a sprained ankle and could not see my lord; but they told me that he was better . . .

The next day I contrived to get to his room. His countenance at once awakened the most dreadful suspicions . . .

During the night of the seventeenth he had some attacks of delirium, in which he talked of fighting; but neither that night nor the next morning was he aware of his peril. This morning his physicians were alarmed by appearances of inflammation of the brain and proposed another bleeding, to which Lord Byron consented, but soon ordered the vein to be closed.

He awoke in half an hour. I wished to go to him – but I had not the heart.

It was about six o'clock in the evening when he said, 'I want to go to sleep now'; and immediately turning around, he fell into that slumber, from which, alas! he never awoke.

A great many leeches were applied to his temples and the blood flowed copiously all night.

He continued in this state for four-and-twenty hours; and it was just a quarter past six o'clock on the next day, the 19th, that he was seen to open his eyes, and immediately shut them again. The physicians felt his pulse – he was gone!

★

Standing before the Byron Memorial in the Garden of Heroes we wonder whether a cenotaph can really be a cenotaph if it contains at least some corporeal part of the commemorated. The poet's body was embalmed for its long voyage back to England; various organs seem to have travelled home separately in Canopic jars. Some doubt there are any bodily traces of Byron here at all. It's said that the lungs might not have survived their residence in Missolonghi much beyond 1826, long before this memorial was erected, the year this place was besieged and devastated by the Turks. Others believe the story of a monk rescuing the remains from under the church where they were buried during this volatile time. It seems Missolonghi got Byron's lungs *and* larynx, which were preserved in an urn, whatever their eventual fate, and we want to believe they're here. The source of the poet's voice and breath.

★

We're leaving Missolonghi for Athens, and then back to England, in a fraction of the time it took Byron's spirit-preserved body to make the journey by sea, or even for the news of his death to reach home shores. Famous in his lifetime, the dead Byron provided an even more virulent culture, multiplying memoirs, reminiscences, accounts, pirated editions, gossip, legend. The fever is still running. Blossoms in a Petri dish.

We head east on the roads running north of the Gulf of Corinth, the land greener and fresher than when we'd travelled west a few days earlier. Greek bus drivers seem very house proud, or bus proud: this one has pennants hung like bunting around its huge windscreen, rosary beads that click softly as we slow into bends, and photographs of what must be the driver's family and friends run along the upper sill as if it were a mantelpiece or a mobile shrine. Place names from the ancient world appear as road signs, coming towards us, rising up, then falling back into the past. The country seems quiet and settled from our air-conditioned seats, miles of sun-stunned olive groves and deserted way stations, and it takes an effort to remind ourselves that Greece is back in the news again. The rumbling debt crisis means the country could be in danger of slipping off the edge of the Eurozone. At some point on the long journey, the driver switches on his radio and Barrett Strong's 'Money (That's What I Want)' is playing. Sealed in a Tamla bubble, we imagine a new philhellenic movement. We try to picture how much money a poet arriving by boat would need in order to make any real difference today. A shipping container filled to the brim with euros, lifted by crane on to the dockside at Piraeus? Stirred from our stupor and the hypnosis of the road, we make our notes, before tiredness gets the better of us. Later, we wake to graffiti and streetlamps in the dusk on the outskirts of the ancient city, having slept through Mount Helicon.

Going to the Inevitable

Larkinland. It sounds like something to rival Dismaland, the artist Banksy's bemusement park, which flourished briefly in Weston-super-Mare. Upon purchasing your all-day, all-rides pass at the gates of Larkinland, you are issued with a confusing mixture of pre- and post-decimal money with which to pay for various rides and amenities. Mr Bleaney's Room is a favourite: there is always a queue to look in on this cramped and boxy space with barely enough room for its single bed (only two visitors at a time, please); a sound installation creates the effect of a television jabbering away downstairs, and you are invited (one at a time, please) to lie on the candlewick and contemplate a stain on the ceiling. The Large Cool Store is a trove of Fifties and Sixties vintage clothing, restored and presented as a retail experience (if you can tell your half-crowns from your threepenny bits). The Arundel Tomb is impressive indeed: a stone effigy surrounded by a 360° screen showing time-lapse footage. Similarly, the High Windows Camera Obscura looks down on a Sixties street scene; look, there are a couple of kids; viewers exit via The Long Slide, where they are encouraged to yell or scream 'like free bloody birds'. Kids love this, although one criticism of Larkinland is that there could be more for children. Still, if rides are your thing, there are two must-dos: The Swerving East From Rich Industrial Shadows takes you rattling along in British Rail rolling stock towards Hull, through post-war edgelands and brilliantly staged panoramas of big skies, industrial froth, cooling towers; wave as you pass The Whitsun Weddings, bombing along in the opposite direction towards the south. Later, after dining on an awful pie, there is comfortable, themed accommodation at The Royal Station Hotel. Guests are encouraged to explore its shoeless corridors before spending a homesick night in their room.

★

We're travelling through north Lincolnshire on a summer afternoon. In the distance, power stations loom and 'the tall heat that slept / For miles inland' still seems to inhabit the landscape rolling by. But today the wide, flat fields are corrugated with rows and rows of solar panels, working against our idea of finding Larkinland from a train window (Larkin wrote a lovely lyric called 'Solar' in the early 1960s – 'Coined there among / Lonely horizontals / You exist openly' – which can be read as a poem in praise of renewable energy, though we don't think this is exactly what the poet had in mind). The air streaming through our carriage sometimes smells grassy and sometimes of brassicas: not the pungent, institutional, remand-centre smell of cabbage, but fresh leaves, a vegetable, green, caterpillar scent. The post-war past wavers in and out of focus as a radiant bar of sunlight makes its slow photocopy at each bend . . .

Enough. Stop. It's autumn in England. The clocks went back last night and the trains are in utter chaos. We're not sure if the two events are related, but the upshot is we've found ourselves at Doncaster, our third change, running more than an hour late. Ahead of us, in Hull's Royal Station Hotel, the poet Sean O'Brien is waiting. Sean isn't the kind of man we'd want to keep dangling, and we speculate nervously on his furious, over-caffeinated demeanour. Sean grew up in Hull and is himself a great evoker and elegist of the out-of-the-way and round-the-back, the country of railways and rivers. He knows Larkin's adopted city well and has offered to show us around. We hope the offer still stands when we eventually limp into Paragon Interchange.

When will that be? Boarding our fourth train of the morning, we consider the shortfall between taking a train through England today, thirty years after the poet's death, and those rich poems of approach and departure: 'The Whitsun Weddings', 'I Remember, I Remember', 'Dockery and Son' and 'Here'. In poetry there are never any announcements from the buffet of there being no hot water available. As we fret over our Virgil, growing angrier by the minute, we also fret over what we might – or might not – find. Larkin died in a Hull hospital in 1985 and there might lie ahead only an impossible institutional labyrinth if we attempt to simply visit the actual site of expiry (today, the Nuffield Hospital is the Westbourne NHS Centre, just round the corner from Pearson Park, and the top-floor, university-owned flat where Larkin lived from 1956 to 1974: the years of peak output for this famously fastidious and meticulous poet).

As the train picks up the course of the Humber and we pass through Goole, we finally begin to tune into something like Larkinland, entering into a slower landscape. The river broadens; the suspension bridge looms into view. An end-of-the-line feeling is evocative in another way, too: Larkin overlaps us, dying just as we were becoming aware of his work. He was once within living range, at the other end of the M62 connecting Hull with Liverpool, via Manchester. The thought that, in our teens, we could have taken a coach or a train and visited him, easily, with a day-return ticket in our pockets, is immediately undercut by the idea of turning up unannounced on his doorstep. We're guessing the Hermit of Hull would have sent us packing.

★

A friend once beat a path to Philip Larkin's door in the Brynmor Jones Library at Hull. It was at the beginning of 1978, a few days into the new year, and our friend was a young English Lit student who'd heard about a new Larkin poem published in the *Times Literary Supplement* right on top of Christmas. His tutor Andrew Motion (future Poet Laureate, Knight of the Realm and Larkin biographer) had told him about it, but he'd missed the edition. Arriving back in Hull for the new term, he visited the library, looking to find a copy, only to be told all copies of the *TLS* for 1977 had been sent away to be bound. The Assistant Librarian said he knew there was a copy on the Librarian's desk upstairs, and that if he went and asked politely for a photocopy he might be in luck. Nervously, he knocked on the door. And there was Larkin, large, pasty-faced, thick glasses, though perhaps not yet the self-styled 'egg sculpted in lard, with goggles on' of the final years. Our friend explained his request and Larkin sat back in his chair and smiled: 'Wait there, I'll go and make a copy for you.' He took his copy of the *TLS* to the photocopier along the corridor and lay his poem face down against the light.

Needless to say, our friend still has the Xerox Larkin made for him that day. It's a nice story, and we're always intrigued by a kind of imaginative marginalia: did Larkin leave the copier lid up and press the poem to the glass, and, if so, is there a black edging to the copy he made containing an image of the poet's hand or shirtsleeve or wristwatch, preserved in fading toner? We're too scared to ask. The poem was 'Aubade'. Our friend stood outside in the cold, reading this new Larkin poem: 'There was one line in particular that just overwhelmed me: "The sure extinction that we travel to / And shall be lost in always". It was the "sure" and the "always", as much as the extinction and the lostness, that really got to me. That line has stayed with me. It has never lost its power.'

★

The whiteness of Larkin. Whitsun, White Sunday, the seventh after Easter, and its white vestments. 'A wild white face' beneath red stretcher blankets in the back of an ambulance. 'The white hours / Of young-leafed June.' The white steamer on a horizon. The white rows of 'unseen congregations'. A glass of gin and tonic raised, 'Though white is not my favourite colour.' Albums – a young lady's, a wedding – and the whiteness they contain. The whiteness of lambs that learn to walk in snow, of collars, of blossom, of a sky 'white as clay, with no sun'. White out.

★

'Aubade' was Larkin's last big artistic statement, a poem that stares into the pre-dawn abyss and tells us how it's always darkest just before it goes completely black; that's made all the more powerful by the way it figures the very ordinary, close-to-hand world: a morning song where the edges of the bedroom curtains grow light and turn into a sombre, domestic Rothko; where a wardrobe reveals its distinct, definable shape and edges, and the plain hollowness of an upended coffin. 'Death is what gets poets up in the morning,' the American poet Billy Collins once said. Larkin doesn't even need to get his slippers on.

Death might have got Larkin going as a poet, too. 'An April Sunday brings the snow' from 1948 was written for the poet's father, who died on Good Friday 1947. Stephen Regan – the student who knocked on Larkin's door and asked to see a copy of 'Aubade' thirty years later – is now a Professor of English and he tells us how he thinks this poem was the beginning: 'Larkin never included it in any of his individual books of poems. My guess is that it was just too personal. But it's far better than a lot of the other early material that appears in *The North Ship*. I think he found his voice in that poem. He was only twenty-five at the time.' The poem is full of Eastertide imagery, but ultimately rejects any sense of resurrection:

> An April Sunday brings the snow
> Making the blossom on the plum trees green,
> Not white. An hour or two, and it will go.
> Strange that I spend that hour moving between
>
> Cupboard and cupboard, shifting the store
> Of jam you made of fruit from these same trees:
> Five loads – a hundred pounds or more –
> More than enough for all next summer's teas,
>
> Which now you will not sit and eat.
> Behind the glass, under the cellophane,

Remains your final summer – sweet
And meaningless, and not to come again.

★

Arriving at Hull, we're practically met on the concourse by a bronze of Larkin (it looks like the one of John Betjeman at St Pancras) seemingly caught in a wind tunnel between the bar at the Royal Station Hotel and the ticket barriers, rushing with manuscripts under his arm, 'late getting away'. It's a sign of things to come.

We find Sean in the lobby of the Royal Station Hotel. He waves away our apologies. He understands the shortfall between the railways of the mind and those of the urinous vestibule. There are still a few hours of daylight left. We decide this day should be called Gloomsday and set out to find the car-hire offices.

It turns out Larkinland has already been built, and while it mightn't be so immersive as our daft *jeu d'esprit* (or *jeu de tristesse*) The Larkin Trail already carefully overlays this part of the world with three zones of interest: Larkin's Here in two parts (Hull's city centre, and also its penumbra containing the Pearson Park flat together with the university), and Elsewhere, which casts a wider net through Holderness, from remote Spurn Head inland along the banks of the Humber and north to Beverley, all a bike-clipped ride away from the city. 'To follow in Larkin's tracks is to take not only a literary journey, but also journeys through diverse land-scapes and rich architecture and, seeing the city through a poet's eyes, to gain a philosophical view of the place where Larkin lived and worked for three decades.' It's possible to alight at Paragon Interchange and follow The Larkin Trail for hours, from geocode to geocode, each location 'easily identified by its unique, bespoke sign'. We've never seen such a fastidious contextualizing of place. The hermitage welcomes visitors.

The detail is overwhelming. The Trail comes with an excellent archive and an accompanying set of podcasts. The walker with a handheld device can listen to Larkin reading his poetry or Pee

Wee Russell playing clarinet or an interview with the current owner of Larkin's Newland Park house, the one he moved to after the university requisitioned his high windows overlooking Pearson Park. Of all the poets whose places we've journeyed to, Larkin's – perhaps befitting a chartered librarian – are easily the most catalogued and curated.

★

We enter Pearson Park through an ornamental arch, into a leafscape of quiet Victoriana. Tall houses guarded by trees and hedges stand on the fringe of the old free park itself, its glasshouse and benches and 'blurred playground noises', which manages to feel both private and welcoming, human in scale. Sean leads us to Number 32. The postman has just visited on his round. Beyond the brown wheelie bin, iron gates and dense overgrowth, we can see the famous high windows, the central pane being arched and vaguely ecclesiastical: Larkin's temporary attic flat of eighteen years. The BBC *Monitor* interview with John Betjeman. Jazz and whisky. The poet pulling open the curtains after a nocturnal piss. But there's no plaque and no getting any further. Just inside the gate, sacks of builder's sand lie piled up on the path amongst the dead leaves, and the place has a wary, provisional, work-in-progress feel.

Sean then leads us next door and, pointing to this building's upper storey, throws us a curve ball: 'I don't know why they've let the hedge get that tall. My parents rented the ground-floor flat here from the old lady who owned it, then my mother and her sisters bought the whole house ... And I ended up in that room there with the ecclesiastical window. Three or four years after Larkin had left.' And we thought *we* had a tantalizing connection! 'Yes. Pretty strange.' Sean had the same high-windowed view over the park as Larkin.

Betjeman called this 'the classy part of Hull'. We look towards the park and imagine Larkin's view, his fastness looking out over the post-war world. There's an interpretation board for wet woodland biodiversity, its thrushes and moorhens overwritten with graffiti. We didn't plan it, but the autumnal mood has intensified our visit here to such a degree all the doors between place and poem have blown open: it's difficult not to read the park through the poems, and to imagine its huge presence in Larkin's work. 'It's impossible to say for certain,' says Sean. 'But the place is so loaded with asso- ciations for me that I'm almost about to burst into tears!' His own first book of poems was called *The Indoor Park*:

> I am in love with detail.
> Chestnut trees
> Are fire-damaged candelabra.
> Waterbirds are porcelain.
> The plant house is the room within the room
> And all this is England,
> Just left here, and what's to be done?

It's always an odd experience, visiting a place where poems you know and love emerged. Poems have many sources, of course, but we feel the mediating alchemy that was once at work here. The trees are coming into leaf and the leaves are falling in ones and twos. Larkin is simultaneously both more alive and more dead to us than ever.

★

At Larkin's Newland Park house a toad the size of a small hippo (in suit and tie and glasses) squats above the entrance. We always had the impression this was an unpleasant kind of gaff – 'the ugliest one-roomed house in Hull' – and one Larkin had been somewhat forced to seek after the university had asked for Pearson Park back. But it looks fairly agreeable. This was Larkin's last home in Hull, and behind the toad a plaque declares the dates.

As we stand at the gates, the toad asks: 'Can I help you?'

We look at each other. Whoever just threw their voice, it isn't funny.

There is a woman at the upstairs window. 'Can I help you? Would you like to see the garden?'

Yes!

'Wait there, I'll come down and let you in'.

The gates are buzzed open and we meet the present owner, Miriam Porter. Miriam grew up nearby in a Hull orphanage and became a successful businesswoman in London before buying the house when it came up for sale in 2001. She's funny and fast-talking and delighted to show us round the place, ushering us straight through the living room and its big glass doors on to the garden. 'I bought a garden, not a house. It was just wonderful'. We spy another toad on the grass.

The toads are refugees from an arts event in the city in 2010, Larkin 25, when the fibreglass amphibians were stationed across the region as far away as Beverley. Like Wallace Stevens's blackbirds and W. H. Auden's forest trail (as we'll discover on other pilgrimages), this is one of the ways we're encouraged to remember now, a cultural boundary walk around the writer's neighbourhood. More than a hundred thousand people came to Hull to see the toads, and this summer a 'where are they now?' series of events mirrored Larkin's own answer poem, 'Toads Revisited'. The list of participating toads is working against our notion of Gloomsday: there was a Punk-phibian Toad, a Fish & Chips Toad, a Global Pop Toad, a Typographical Toad. There was no toad called Work. At auction, Miriam managed to buy the Larkin Toad – surely the alpha toad? – for her front balcony, along with Tigger the Toad, who gawps at us now across the lawn.

Miriam encourages us to have a look around. She has recently thrown a party and the foliage is festooned with streamers and bunting. It's a lovely garden. We remember the story of Larkin accidentally killing a hedgehog with a lawnmower here, and being sufficiently rocked by this little death to produce a (rare) late poem, 'The Mower'. The grass is sown with windfall apples, but no hedgehogs make an appearance.

Back inside, we go through to a room that was once Larkin's garage. We're standing in the space formerly occupied by the poet's Audi. Didn't we read somewhere that Larkin liked the car's name because it reminded him of Auden? This in turn brings to mind a story of Larkin watching Wimbledon during one of his early stays in hospital in 1985. Larkin liked the seventeen-year-old Boris Becker because he thought he resembled a young Auden.

The Audi melts away. The garage too.

Miriam has renovated the house beyond recognition. 'This was all full of Monica Jones's furniture.' The women in Larkin's life could easily be the subject of a separate book. Jones was an English lecturer Larkin had met while he was beginning his career as a librarian in 1946. The two shared a holiday cottage at Haydon Bridge in Northumberland, and when Monica fell ill in 1983 she moved here to Newland Park. Outliving Larkin by sixteen years, she stayed on, a recluse, until her death in 2001. By the time Miriam arrived, there were still plenty of traces. Books, letters and papers went to the Brynmor Jones Library and the Bodleian in Oxford, but the Philip Larkin Society managed to save other objects for the Hull History Centre.

Do many people come? Miriam smiles. 'Yes. We get a lot of visitors.' Even a minibus full, on one occasion. And does she like Larkin's poetry? 'I like "Aubade".' It feels like an apposite choice: that poem would have been finished here in this house, his last major work. It isn't very Gloomsday, but as we leave, crunching across the gravel and saying our goodbyes, we can't help feeling a little rejuvenated. Miriam is a kind of custodian, too, and her enthusiasm and generosity has put smiles on our faces. As the gate swings shut, Sean turns to us: 'And that, gentlemen, is a Hull accent.'

★

The Westbourne NHS Centre, just a few avenues and tenfoots from Pearson Park, is on The Larkin Trail. Each point of interest has its own information plaque, and here, instead of a line of his poetry, we find what were reputedly Larkin's last words, according to the nurse at his bedside: 'I am going to the inevitable.'

At this small hospital's reception we get a warm greeting, despite just showing up unannounced, but we're told there's nobody around who'll remember the place thirty years back. Do you get many visitors on Larkin's trail? The two receptionists look at each other, but can't think of any others: we're the first. Or at least, the first to have the cheek to cross the threshold and ask daft questions.

Larkin had been ill with an oesophageal cancer for several months. He'd been in and out of hospital by the time he was finally admitted here in late November. The poet's last few years seem relentlessly grim, stoked it has to be said by his own sense of the darkness closing in. His letters to friends are full of sad details (bottles of port left downstairs overnight, so at least he would have to get up in the morning) or candid autobiography: 'So now we face 1982,' he wrote to his old friend Kingsley Amis, 'sixteen stone six, gargantuanly paunched, helplessly addicted to alcohol, tired of livin' and scared of dyin', world-famous unable-to-write poet.' Letters survive, but his diaries don't: in the ambulance on the way here from Newland Park that final time, he told Monica Jones to destroy them all.

'I am going to the inevitable.' Outside again, we find ourselves admiring Larkin's last words. For a book full of the deaths of poets, there have been remarkably few. Larkin clearly had a sense of occasion. It sounds like a good name for a pub – as in 'I'm just going to The Inevitable.' We press on with our journey. Keep Calm and Go to the Inevitable.

★

The last words of writers. Talking about Larkin's parting shot put us in mind of the pre-eminent British television dramatist Dennis Potter. When Potter was dying of cancer in 1994 he gave a final interview to Melvyn Bragg for Channel 4. It was utterly compelling to watch. Potter's reflections on the state of British culture, on his own work and history, were lent the overwhelming authority of a dying man. Now, with his work almost done and his life petering out, you felt he could say anything. But more than any single phrase or opinion, what we remember most from that interview is a detail, the fact that it was not tidied or bookended in the way we expect on TV. The beginning and end of the interview, the shuffling on to the set, taking seats while microphones were adjusted, introductory small talk, were all left in the final broadcast. And it ended with the standing up, the off-mic reflections on how the interview had gone, the slow walk off the set. Every minute was broadcast, because there were so few minutes left. Every aside made by the dying writer was worthy of our attention, because these were his last weeks, his last months. He was passing into death and had already been lent some of its commanding authority.

Potter's reputation was not damaged by the broadcast of his interview's rough edges. Quite the reverse. But then, interviews were not his work. How would we feel about the broadcast of unedited rushes, rejected retakes of scenes from his TV dramas? That, effectively, is the posthumous fate of many poets. Any legible scrap from a notebook is faithfully recorded and republished. With some poets, this process may not be injurious. In William Carlos Williams's case, for example, his composition process was a building up of fragments, a constant shifting and reshaping of multiple materials. To see more of those fragments, those materials in motion, would do no harm to one's understanding of an unfinished epic like *Paterson*. But for poets like Larkin, should we apply a different standard?

Paul Muldoon's *New York Times* review of Larkin's *Complete Poems* argues that the book is too complete. 'Like Elizabeth Bishop,' he argues, 'Larkin is not particularly well served by having every napkin-or-matchbook-jotting published.'

★

We discover another Larkinland. In September 1976 Michael Kustow, an Associate Director at the National Theatre, got in touch with Larkin: 'I'm writing to ask for your permission and encouragement for a reading of a selection of your poetry here at the National Theatre ... I have tentatively thought of titling the programme "LARKINLAND".' Larkin replied: 'LARKINLAND sounds a delightful title: rather like a fun-fair, but as long as the reality is not too much like one I am happy with it.' And so Larkin was encouraging, if not willing to perform in any way himself. The show was a reading of Larkin's poetry – the evening book-ended by the two 'Toad' poems – together with a few prose excerpts, and featured four actors, jazz and a slideshow. A version of Larkinland was eventually broadcast on BBC radio in the summer of 1977 ('It is all rather like a mixture of <u>Ghosts</u>, <u>Tristan and Isolde</u> and Max Miller live at the Palladium, but I expect it will be alright,' he wrote to his editor Charles Monteith at Faber); and it rode again in a much revised and retitled incarnation – Philip Larkin's Blues and Other Colours – staged at the Ilkley Literature Festival one Saturday evening in July 1982. But during that first run at the National Theatre, the director was keen to see if Larkin would consider attending – and eventually, one night, he did.

*

All that remains of Larkin's diaries are their covers, and we look at some of these in the Hull History Centre. After he died, Monica passed the diaries – over thirty years' worth – to his secretary Betty Mackereth. As he'd wished, Betty took them to his office at the library, where she tore their pages out, shredded them, and sent the tatters to the university incinerator.

We hold them: non-books, purplish, oxblood, gutted old binders, all the signatures torn from their spines. A few fragments remain on the inside covers or endpapers. We can sometimes piece together a sense of where he was: 1950–52 has a Guinness label stuck over a picture of Queen's University, Belfast (and a small mugshot of Larkin collaged in, looking down). This particular book has MY LIFE AND HARD TIMES on the spine. Also: 'Faint heart never fucked the pig' (motto: Ox & Bucks Light Infantry).

A tourist leaflet for Ireland Pleasure Island – again, we look at the collage work: Larkin, cutting and pasting himself into things.

Some of what's survived is oddly mundane – a note for a pair of Veldtschoen from Saxone Ltd, Leicester, seems to track the progress of a pair of shoes he's bought from 1949 to 1952, adding their original price to subsequent heel, toe and re-soling work, coming to £6.14.9. Then there are lists of quotes – from Proust, Aristotle, Rossetti, Joyce, Wilde – which makes us imagine them as commonplace books. But beyond these peripheral scraps there's nothing to see here: the Archive with a Hole in It.

Even so, we feel a bit squeamish, given Larkin's explicit desire to remove all traces of these books. But this is far from the sharp end of archive research. We felt that jab with Thom Gunn's journals, with John Berryman's desperate lists, and it will reach its sharpest point later, on the trail of Rosemary Tonks. With these Larkin covers the charge is in the relic voltage of the handwriting and the handcrafted collages, but the content is nothing more than trivia, though it is *his* trivia.

★

At his office, the University Librarian takes a box from a drawer and opens it. Inside, wrapped in paper, are a pair of Larkin's glasses. They are the familiar, Harry Potter by-way-of Eric Morecambe frames, glazed with lenses as thick as the bottoms of gin bottles. We have seen the ceramic desk toad. We have seen the photographs of Guy the Gorilla. The drawer seems filled with objects that Larkin kept close at hand here, his place of work. But the glasses present us with a new problem. We look at each other. We've stood before various thresholds and had our pictures taken. We've even sat at the huge desk here in Larkin's office (at 8' x 4', bigger than the one in the Oval Office). The glasses are largely what made the shy and retiring librarian one of the most easily recognizable poets of his day, or any day, and the temptation is to pick them up and put them on. Glasses seem to want to be worn. But there's something stopping us, and we're interested in where the line is; the line we'd feel we were crossing should we start acting as if we're trying on sunglasses in Boots. We remind ourselves that many of the reliquaries and *Wunderkammern* we've encountered contain objects of morbid fascination, but decorum insists we maintain some respectful distance from the dead. And anyway, Larkin was good at making us see the world afresh through his eyes, as poets do.

Gloomsday would not be complete without a visit to the Brynmor Jones Library, where Larkin spent most of his working life. We were not expecting to see a great deal beyond its facade – in the months before our visit, the whole building has undergone a huge redevelopment – but after announcing ourselves at the barriers and a phone call upstairs, incredibly the University Librarian would be glad to show us Larkin's original office, which he still uses. Richard Heseltine is only the fourth such post holder at the Brynmor Jones (Larkin was the second) and there's an air of lived connection as we're ushered into a large and tidy room, with a tiled electric fireplace, bookcase, photographs, and, over in the corner, a typewriter that catches our eyes. 'Yes, that was Larkin's,' Richard explains. But a laptop is charging on the desk: if this is a museum, it's very much a working museum.

We realize how much of Larkin we must have absorbed, not only through his poems but as images: photographs and footage. On the door of the office is a small sign – Librarian – recognizable from the *Monitor* documentary, where Larkin enters in raincoat and, through a trick edit, re-emerges de-cloaked and ready for the working day.

Larkin's toads famously squat as symbols of the daily grind, but standing in the University Librarian's office it's hard not to admire what he oversaw here, what got built. We stand looking out through his view of a quarter of a century: the trees on the lawn, the University buildings glowing in the late October sun. Before we leave, Richard hands us two postcards as keepsakes; two photographs separated by a similar timeframe. In the first, taken in June 1958, Larkin is standing in front of the foundations and geometric skeleton of the new building, hands in pockets. A sheet of groundwater elongates him in reflection and he gazes down into the bottomless sky beneath his feet. It's a selfie: Larkin was a keen amateur photographer and must have fixed his new Rolleiflex on its tripod, set the self-timer and walked into his composition. In the second photograph – trick edit – it's 1979: the library has not only been built, but extended. Larkin sits on a bench in front of the library building (with fellow poets Douglas Dunn and Andrew Motion), laughing. Larkin was curmudgeonly about his job, especially in the later years once computers had begun to move in, but we can't help feeling his 'Shetland pony' that turned into a 'frightful Grand National winner' must have given him some measure of pride and satisfaction. And of course, it stands as his monument.

★

It's Valentine's Day, 1977. Larkin has shown up to see Larkinland. He'd told Charles Monteith that he planned to meet Kingsley Amis in the foyer of the National Theatre. Later this year he would finish his last great poem, 'Aubade', published just in time to ruin a few Christmas dinners. The handful of poems that were to trickle out afterwards would suggest the poet had run out of energy. But here he is, on the brink of that silence, not wanting to be spotted, furtive at the cloakroom, wary at the bar ordering interval drinks. The house lights go down. The readers file gravely on to the stage. 'Why should I let the toad work squat on my life? . . .'. Larkin wrote afterwards:

I came away rather subdued. It was like having your entire life thrown at you in forty-five minutes. But stranger than that, it no longer seemed like my life, or not exclusively my life, but something I could look at along with the rest of the audience without being personally responsible for it. In fact, a paradoxical effect of LARKINLAND for me was to make me wonder whether I had ever lived there at all.

We end our trip to Hull in a pub round the corner from Pearson Park. There is (inevitably) a Larkin's Bar, but Sean takes us to an old-school boozer he once frequented, with roughcast thick as porridge on the outhouse walls. We're not sure if Larkin ever drank in here (he didn't seem to be much of a pub man), but Sean is experiencing that slightly dislocating intoxication of sitting in a once familiar room with a pint in front of him. People have been and gone, parties gathered and broken up, and there is something wrong with the mean sea level of the tabletops: didn't they used to be higher? All day in Hull, there have been moments when we've also felt like we've been here before.

'Deprivation is for me what daffodils were to Wordsworth' goes one version of Larkin's line (he later changed it to 'depression'). But both poets are doing well in one branch of the afterlife business, because both have established a reinforcing physical place in the world that people can visit. Perhaps it doesn't matter that one lies surrounded by the National Park he largely helped to conceive of and create, and the other is a former whaling and trawling town at the end of the M62. In the end, maybe what matters is a venue, a postcode you can enter into your satnav, something you can point at, solid enough to sink rawlplugs in and fix a plaque to. Pilgrims need their sacred places, sources, relics, destinations – and a minicab to get us to our lodgings after the alehouse. Before we say goodnight and Gloomsday draws to an inappropriately satisfying close, we're faced with a huge wall map of Kingston-upon-Hull, divided into the concentric circles of fare zones. We retrace our steps through the streets and parks, the broad blankness of the Humber to the south, the knot of rails terminating at the station, and marvel at the way Larkin has been so wired up to it all. Soon Hull will be UK City of Culture, but work began on Larkinland long ago, while the poet was still alive, when this famously sceptical writer was given a disconcerting sneak preview of his theme-park afterlife.

★

Some poets resist the toxic bind between the poetic life and work. It's a resistance movement cheered on by many younger poets, offering hope of assuaging the need to write poems without having to die prematurely as a result. Chief among the leaders of this movement are Philip Larkin and his American near-contemporary Elizabeth Bishop. Writing in the *New York Times* Paul Muldoon links them for their 'characteristic modesty, meticulousness and, even, anti-Modernism'. Both were well aware of the popular power of the so-called 'Confessional' movement, in which the life becomes the direct subject of the work, but both were wary of it.

Temperamentally, Larkin and Bishop were reticent, careful to protect their privacy. And both were suspicious of any whiff of bohemianism. Larkin wrote, perhaps more in hope than conviction, that the 'big sane boys' would rise to the top of the poetic canon, seeing off the Confessionals, and Bishop (always discreet when she wrote about friends, lovers or family) chided her friend Robert Lowell for quoting from private letters in his poems, asking him if he isn't 'violating a trust' and declaring that 'art just isn't worth that much'. Both fought extended battles with depression and drink, but tried to keep these battles private.

And both moved to edges, to eastern seaboards, settled, wrote and died there. Perhaps, in those places, we can find the roots of their resistance.

★

On 6 October 1979, at the age of sixty-eight, Elizabeth Bishop died in her apartment at Lewis Wharf, Boston, of a ruptured cerebral aneurysm. A year before her death, an interview for *Paris Review* by Elizabeth Spires begins with Bishop taking her visitor on to the balcony to look at the spectacular harbour views and point out famous landmarks.

It is a May Sunday morning and, having tracked down Lewis Wharf, among the old dock buildings of Boston Harbor, we are looking up at her balcony on the fourth floor, the home where she spent her last years. It sits in a grey stone building above what is now an insurance office, in a part of the harbour now given over to leisure. Families from the city have come out here to look at the luxury yachts and cruisers, and to patronize the smart sea-food restaurants at the waterside. The apartment in question is the only one with a fine double balcony, with a table and chairs set up facing the bay. There is a small ornamental tree in a pot, waving in the sea breeze. What a view it must have.

This building, like those around it, reminds us of the almost identical mercantile monoliths at Salford and Liverpool docks, where bills of lading were issued and stamped. At the time she lived here, Elizabeth Bishop was teaching at the Massachusetts Institute of Technology in Cambridge, a couple of miles inland. But she chose to live here, right on the brink, among the cries of gulls, the chinking of ropes on masts of boats as they bob in the gentle swell, the salt stink of the ocean.

The mood is buoyant. Ferries packed with sightseers pass on the horizon. The weather is unseasonably sweltering, well up in the 90s. The whole season seems oddly out of kilter with the Bishop we know from her poems. We walk to the edge and look over. The water looks stagnant and fetid, not cold, salt and clear like knowledge.

★

We walk into the main lobby of the apartment block at Lewis Wharf to see if there's any trace of the poet, to try to find out who lives there now. The lobby walls are lined with blown-up vintage photographs of fishermen plying their trade. We ask the concierge if he has heard of Elizabeth Bishop. 'Who?' We explain who she was, who we are and why we are here. 'Yeah, I've heard of a poet living here, but not much detail. Michael will know the detail. You need to talk to Michael.' It seems that Michael is the Building Manager. He is in the building, but currently upstairs. We can hear a vacuum cleaner and wonder if he's a hands-on Building Manager. We are told he will be down in a minute, then we can talk to him.

In the meantime, the concierge tells us about himself. He does weekends here, because it's easy. He just sits here and says hello and goodbye to the residents as they pass. In the week, he's a truck driver. That's harder work. He has had three wives and six kids. 'Do you guys write poems every day?' he asks. We mutter something about writing when the poems come, but they don't always come. 'You should write every day', he says. 'How can you get really good if you don't? My son, I tell him to play hockey every day if he wants to be a hockey player.' We nod and look towards the lift, willing Michael to emerge. But the concierge has a point. Whatever you do, if you want to get better you have to work harder. And we are on the trail of a poet who worked very hard. She worked on fine-tuning her poems over many years and multiple drafts, and struggled to perfect them. Her *Complete Poems* is a relatively slim and very hard-won volume.

★

We know how hard Bishop worked because all the drafts of one of her most famous poems – 'One Art' – are in the public domain, and available in a book of her notes and drafts. And that's not the only poem of hers to 'show its workings'. When a book of her 'uncollected poems, drafts and fragments' was published in 2006, the eminent poetry critic Helen Vendler (based down the road at Harvard University) wrote in the *New Republic* that 'it should have been called "Repudiated Poems" ', adding that 'the real poems will outlast these, their maimed and stunted siblings'. Vendler argued in her review that if Bishop wanted to publish her unpublished notes and drafts, she would have done so. She concluded that 'The eighty-odd poems that this famous perfectionist allowed to be printed over the years are "Elizabeth Bishop" as a poet. This book is not.' The rights and wrongs of this case rest on whether the poet herself would be happy to see these notes and drafts published after her sudden death, or whether, had she had the time to prepare for her death, she might have asked for these unpublished papers to be destroyed.

In her *New Republic* review, Helen Vendler acknowledges that there will be many devotees eager to buy 'the new book by Elizabeth Bishop', before citing the example of Gerard Manley Hopkins as an exemplary case: he asked his sisters to burn his spiritual journals, and his wishes were followed to the letter.

It is a tough dilemma and it gets tougher the more you love a poet's work. When they were published in Britain, we were delighted to read Bishop's notes, drafts and fragments. It did not lessen our admiration for her poetry. Quite the reverse. It served to underline how hard she worked, and it confirmed just how tough and rare is the making of such immaculate and precise poetry. But whether it is honourable to publish without the consent of a dead poet is another question entirely. Many poets now manage their own paper trail even as they are creating it. Deals with notable archives are often struck in late middle-age, and papers are sent and catalogued long before the demise of the poet. After the death, everything seems hallowed. It is the instinct to venerate relics, which never quite left us after the medieval iconoclasts smashed up the reliquaries and burnt the bones. There are e-reliquaries all over the Internet, where collectors of signed books, private letters or the personal effects of 'celebrities' can be bought and sold, often for absurd sums.

★

Michael the Building Manager has finally emerged. He is carrying a vacuum cleaner, so we conclude that he is a hands-on manager. The concierge introduces us and Michael turns out to be a good talker, with what sounds to us Brits like a broad Bostonian accent. It's past lunchtime, but he's worried about our stomachs. Where are we planning to eat? Are we OK to wait this long for lunch?

He knows about Elizabeth Bishop too. He tells us that she lived here in her final years with her partner Alice Methfessel. He recalls that when she moved in 'she brought all these crazy white plank-boards up from the Amazon, she had figureheads from those old ships they have down there, she had them hanging all over the walls in her place.' He says she was a 'real character' – 'very avant-garde, you might say'. She was one of the first people to move into condos here, when the warehouse was renovated. We have read it wrong, says Michael, it wasn't a dock office, but a spice and grain warehouse. The wharf itself, he explains, was owned by John Hancock, 'the guy with the big signature on the declaration of independence'.

He tells us that Bishop was one of the first to buy into the new dock conversions. She had vision, he says. She could see the potential here. When she bought it, her apartment would have cost around $55,000, now it's worth upwards of a million and a half. She was one of his favourite residents, a friendly presence around the place. She used to wear jeans and roll them up like Capri pants, always with a button-down white shirt and sneakers. She was, he says, smooth and relaxed. He knew Alice, too, and it was clear that Alice was the love of her life. When Elizabeth passed away he was very sad and surprised, because she seemed like such a healthy, vibrant lady. He looks sad as he remembers her. Then he starts to talk about the other notable residents of the building, including a Nobel Prize-winning economist and an academic working on Irish history. But we're more interested in the new residents of Bishop's apartment. Are they aware of their illustrious predecessor?

★

At Harvard we are photographed for our ID cards that will gain us access to the archives. One of the items we've requested isn't, strictly speaking, a document of death at all, but it proves irresistible. We take our seats in a hushed reading room and the trolley squeaks over to our table, bearing a small notebook with a beautiful cover, intricate and slightly faded, the colours of a fruit label or a cigar-box lid.

This is one of Elizabeth Bishop's notebooks. As with Larkin's salvaged covers, there's an electricity to it. What does it mean to hold and touch such a thing? Why do we feel – we both feel – a connection and a charge? A poem, once printed and published, has a life of its own to lead, with any luck far and away beyond the time and place its author occupies. This is as it should be, but the excitement must derive from finding a record of the first moments a poem entered the world, and the hand that brought it here, into light and language. Does it restore the poet? From the careful hand-writing, crossings out, reworkings, are we imagining the lamplight or sunlight it was written in, the table or desk where the notebook lay, birdsong, traffic fumes, the smell of food being prepared – and the writer absorbed in this? Is any inspection of an original draft an act of imaginative restoration, working against the idea of the death of the author? The ink has long dried, but somebody called Elizabeth Bishop came this way, following the lines of blue feint, trying to make something called 'The Burglar of Babylon'.

Looked at the other way, for Bishop, maps and gazetteers and almanacs and encyclopedias, the printed reference materials of the last century, carried a charge of their own, fertile and almost erotic when a newspaper compositor slips and misspells 'mammoth' as 'man moth'. She sensed the illustrator's excitement when a cartographic colour bled beyond its boundaries. If we treat the notebook as relic, Bishop could turn our attention to the anonymous authors and makers of the kind of books never meant to be infused with lyric powers.

★

Oh yes, says Michael the Building Manager. The new residents were aware of the history of their apartment, even before he told them. And they have been good custodians. They have done wonderful work on the travertine stone floor. It was a mess when Elizabeth first brought it in, but when it was laid and polished it looked amazing. The afternoon heat is rising, despite the fresh breeze off the water. We keep thinking about that cool floor and the ghost of a great poet padding barefoot across it. We try to talk our way in, but Michael is having none of it. The owners are away and he is the custodian of these buildings. None shall pass.

Michael returns to the subject of lunch. He's a genial host, who wants us to experience the best of harbour life, and that means seafood. He writes down the name of a place and tells us to be patient. 'There are sometimes long queues there, but the fish is fantastic. It's worth the wait.' And all we can think of is the deathless eyes of the 'tremendous' catch in Bishop's famous poem 'The Fish':

> which were far larger than mine
> but shallower, and yellowed,
> the irises backed and packed
> with tarnished tinfoil
> seen through the lenses
> of old scratched isinglass.

That fish was a survivor, its lip threaded with 'five big hooks' from previous battles. It becomes a symbol of survival, of a toughness that can stare down death and swim away. The poem could only end the way it does: 'And I let the fish go.'

★

Elizabeth Bishop chose her own epitaph, a suitably down-to-earth quotation from her poem 'The Bight', carved on to her monument at Hope Cemetery, Worcester, Massachusetts:

> All the untidy activity continues,
> awful but cheerful.

Poet Interrupted

'Not Waving but Drowning' is the poem that defines Stevie Smith for most of us. Like Auden's 'Stop all the Clocks' it achieved a popular fame that outstripped all of her other poems, so now it seems to sum her up. And that summary goes something like this: eccentric, lonely poet in London suburbs writes poetry of quiet desperation:

> Oh, no no no, it was too cold always
> (Still the dead one lay moaning)
> I was much too far out all my life
> And not waving but drowning.

And parts of that summary are true. From the age of three until her death at sixty-eight she lived in the same semi-detached house in Palmers Green, north London, commuting daily to her job as a secretary at the Newnes Publishing Company in the city, before returning to the suburbs to write poetry. And those poems are hard to describe without reaching for words like eccentric or idiosyncratic or odd. They conjure a world of dogs, cats, birds, figures from fairy tales and nursery rhymes, often accompanied by her own child-like, stick-figure drawings.

To misread these clues and consign her to the bin marked 'light verse' would be a big mistake. Sylvia Plath, in a letter to Smith in November 1962 (just months before her suicide) declared: 'I am an addict of your poetry, a desperate Smith-addict.' And it's not hard to get hooked. Smith's poems are like a crash course in truth-telling – stripped back, deceptively simple, eyes-wide-open examinations of human conscience, motivation, behaviour.

But among the cast of characters shuffling on and offstage in the music hall of Stevie Smith, one character recurs in poem after poem. By the time she died of a brain tumour, while visiting her sister in Devon in 1971, Stevie had been courting Death – as a familiar, a saviour, a lover, a friend – all her life. It is not far-fetched to say he was the love of her life.

★

In Devon, on Stevie Smith's trail, we find ourselves waylaid by Benedictine monks and strong tonic wine. Our car is parked in the grounds of Buckfast Abbey, where they make Buckie, fortified vino and scourge of temperance activists north of the border in Scotland (where it has been regarded as a menace to society by health ministers and MSPs). We buy a couple of bottles from the Abbey's gift shop for old time's sake. The green glass and that jaunty yellow label (grapes and an abbey that turns out to be completely real: we hold the image on the bottle up to its actual tower and compare them) are enough to have us swapping lurid stories of youthful excess and catastrophic hangovers. Walking back to the car, with the sun on our backs and the background hum of bees working the flowerbeds, we feel a long way from blasted bus stops and caged off-licences and the drink's unofficial slogan: 'Buckfast: gets you fucked fast.'

★

The South Hams in Devon are England on toast. Lush, rolling, verdant – a long way from suburban Palmers Green. We've driven west, then north through this creamscape towards Dartmoor and the villages of Buckfast and Buckfastleigh. This is where Stevie Smith's story ended. Shortly after retiring from teaching in Aylesbury, her elder sister Molly had moved to the South West and a bungalow in Buckfast, not far from the Abbey (she had converted to Roman Catholicism in 1928); but had suffered a coronary in 1963, followed by a debilitating stroke in 1969 that for a time affected her speech and left her partially paralysed. Stevie moved down to Buckfast to look after her, and began dividing her time between Palmers Green and Devon (with plenty of reading engagements all around the country besides: this was a busy time for the poet-in-demand). The bungalow is still there, on a quiet road, and the present owner doesn't mind at all if we want to take a couple of photographs of its spick-and-span facade; no, nobody comes here asking about the poet Stevie Smith. A bell had once been rigged up between this bungalow and its neighbour, should Molly need to alert the people next door in an emergency.

Stevie died nearby, at a cottage hospital in Ashburton (now a Community Hospital). In the late autumn of 1970 she had begun to feel ill, suffering faints and blackouts and a ringing sensation. She was forgetting words. Tests revealed a brain tumour. She wrote a letter to the poet Anthony Thwaite on 17 January 1971, giving her address ('At the moment, but I don't know for how long ha ha') as Ward 2 of Freedom Fields Hospital in Plymouth, where she describes her condition:

I had a very peculiar toss down. I wasn't very well for about a month & even then I did often find myself using all but quite extraordinarily odd wrong words. It is like the telephones scrambling their eggs – but I never manage for about 10 minutes at least to spike any proper eggs. Then I'm afraid on Jan 5th (I was of course & had since Nov 10th been living with Molly, my sister, in Buckfast) then on Jan 5th I fell almost dead, I mean ridiculous, etc.

We held this letter a few weeks earlier, in an archive in Hull (where Smith was born and spent some of her childhood): one side is heavily annotated, crossed out, rewritten, the scrawly handwriting running sideways up one edge, difficult to read; a small, eggshell-blue envelope (franked: REMEMBER to use the POST CODE!) and matching writing paper – Queen's Velvet stationery – with two stamps for 1d and 4d. Not that it mattered. Smith's letter was delayed: for the first time ever, British postal workers had walked out on strike after their demands for a pay rise weren't met, and it lay in limbo somewhere between Devon and London, finally arriving the day after Thwaite had heard the news of her death.

While in hospital, she also wrote to her editor at Longmans, who was helping her arrange poems for her next collection, *Scorpion and Other Poems*, mentioning two new pieces, 'The Stroke' and 'Come, Death' (she struggles with the latter title: 'Dauth', 'Daugth'). Before she drifted out too far, there were moments of sharpness, not least when reading 'Come, Death' to visitors at her bedside.

> I feel ill. What can the matter be?
> I'd ask God to have pity on me,
> But I turn to the one I know, and say:
> Come, Death, and carry me away.
>
> Ah me, sweet Death, you are the only god
> Who comes as a servant when he is called, you know,
> Listen then to this sound I make, it is sharp,
> Come Death. Do not be slow.

She'd published a poem called 'Come, Death' more than thirty years before, but here the consolations of religion are lost and the address has turned more urgent, head-on, familiar. Through late winter towards the first ignitions and edges of spring, as the letters piled up in the post boxes and sorting offices, as the country decimalized and severed its ties with a thousand years of palm-stained history, Stevie Smith lay in the tiny cottage hospital under Dartmoor, where her condition, 'this awful medical case that to me is rather like Hampton Ct. Maze', worsened, and she was finally picked up and carried away at Ashburton on 7 March.

★

In the village we can imagine a slight figure at Boots or the Spar or the Post Office. Things have changed here, but we get the sense that places like this – built up during a medieval wool boom – take a longer view and hang on to their skein of history for more years than most, despite the incursions of the global high street. Deep, absorbent England. Frances Spalding's biography of Stevie Smith paints an intriguing picture of the two sisters here in Buckfast during the Sixties as the poet began to visit from London more often, getting to know the neighbours, attending Mass at the Abbey (Molly regularly, Stevie reluctantly), cadging lifts from car owners or requesting essentials – library books, Bounty bars – from far flung places like Newton Abbot:

> Her [Molly's] capacity for boredom was another reason why Stevie began to visit, her appearance in Buckfast serving to confirm Molly's eccentric reputation. Few were aware of Stevie's fame and saw only the oddly dressed woman who queue-barged in the Ashburton Co-op and walked the lanes at night when unable to sleep. When the two sisters have a Sunday morning drinks party all knew that the sherry in the cut-glass decanter was, as usual, bought from a keg in the chemist's.

Eventually, Molly wanted Stevie to be buried in the grounds of Buckfast Abbey, and the monks had agreed to this. But her will had not been changed in time, and so Stevie Smith's remains were taken to the crematorium in Torquay. Nevertheless, her funeral took place here, in the Church of the Holy Trinity at Buckfastleigh, though when we ask for directions, things are not looking good. 'Which church? D'you mean the old, burnt-out one?' That's the only Holy Trinity around here; and so with stones in our hearts we find the bridge over the River Mardle, as directed, and begin the climb up a wooded path.

Which is long and steep, and we pause a couple of times to catch our breath (we discover later that there's a much easier route by road). Near the top, as we pass a railed-off mobile mast, we see the grey spire – it's here! But as we get closer, we realize we're looking at a shell. The parish church that stood here for more than 800 years was destroyed by fire in an arson attack in July 1992.

> YOU ARE WELCOME
> IN THE CHURCH,
> BUT AT YOUR OWN
> RISK.

The roof has completely gone. It's like standing inside a Caspar David Friedrich painting on the edge of Dartmoor, a ruin scorched back to its skeletal masonry. On the ledges running where the roof would have met the wall our old friend buddleia is in bloom, loosening the stonework with its roots.

'Come, Death' was read here as part of the service that day in 1971. It feels like an oddly Gothic end of the line; a feeling only compounded when we decide to crack open a bottle of the screw-top tonic wine from the Abbey that we can see in the distance, and find ourselves standing next to a railed-off tomb which a sign says was an inspiration for Arthur Conan Doyle. The place is more the Hound of the Baskervilles than 'O Happy Dogs of England'. Maybe this is a bad idea.

Or maybe it's far enough from the dotty spinster of Palmers Green to help us look at her again. The place of worship transfigured by fire into art. Smith's abiding familiarity and fascination with (big caps on) Death is matched only by her lifelong dispute with Religion. We make our way back down the wooded hillside path, before it goes dark.

★

A trip to Palmers Green feels necessary, to understand the world of Stevie Smith. Like John Betjeman, she is forever associated with the ends of London's tube lines, quiet commuter streets where curtains twitch and anything is possible behind them. Stevie's lifelong home was in Avondale Road, where the current residents have agreed to meet us. We are intrigued, having read her hymn to the street:

> How sweet the birds of Avondale
> Of Avondale, of Avondale,
> How sweet the birds of Avondale
> Do swoop and swing and call.

And we are fascinated to see her home, too, to tune in to its house-ghosts, to test whether it still feels, as she described it, like 'A House of Mercy':

> It is a house of female habitation
> A house expecting strength as it is strong
> A house of aristocratic mould that looks apart
> When tears fall; counts despair
> Derisory. Yet it has kept us well. For all its faults,
> If they are faults, of sternness and reserve,
> It is a Being of warmth I think; at heart
> A house of mercy.

It seems only fitting to travel to the house on the commuter line, to Palmers Green Station and then left, up the main street with its identikit set of suburban shops and cafés, out towards the quiet streets of redbrick houses, past the Anglican church of St John the Evangelist where she – a self-described 'Anglican Agnostic'– went to wrestle with God, up to the corner of Avondale Road. We have come here in the company of the poet Jo Shapcott – on the same day as our Plath pilgrimage – and on the walk up we explain what we know about the current owners, Lisa and Kevin. It's Kevin we're meeting today, and he's been very welcoming on the phone, whilst stressing that he's 'no expert' on poetry.

★

Kevin may feel he's no expert on poetry, but he's hugely knowledgeable about Stevie Smith, and is also very good company. He's a Londoner, a big Spurs fan and an evangelist for Palmers Green. Stevie would approve. Although it was (still is) fashionable for the literati to look down their noses at the suburbs, she was a devotee. She liked the twin faces of Palmers Green – one gazing back towards the city and one out into the countryside.

The house is now broken into two flats and Kevin and Lisa's is the top half. Their kitchen is what used to be Stevie's bedroom, overlooking the back garden. In Stevie's early years, this view represented imaginative potential, wilderness. She describes a route over the back garden wall, down the alley to the railway line, under the culvert and into Winchmore Woods stretching out towards her beloved Grovelands Park. She was warned that the railway was dangerous, and the woods even more so, which made them irresistible. The wild woods now remain only in the names of the streets on the other side of the railway: Woodland Way, Woodcraft, Beechdale, Oaklands. We gaze out of the kitchen (once bedroom) windows and try to imagine it as the outer edge of London, gateway to the back of beyond. It is hard to recapture that sense, as the city now spreads north as far as the eye can see.

Kevin points out that the window frames are 'hammered'. They considered fitting double-glazing, but Kevin said they couldn't go through with it: 'No, it wouldn't be right. We've just got to bodge these windows up and put up with the draughts, because otherwise we'd be leaving less of Stevie here.' He goes on to explain that when the roof needed repair, they had to go for original slate 'because of Stevie'. 'If we won the lottery, apart from buying a Lamborghini, we've spoken of turning it back into the original house.' Do they get many visitors? Yes, he says. In recent years there's been a resurgence. It's not unusual for them to get a knock on the door and find sheepish students from China or the United States wanting to ask about Stevie. The blue plaque outside (unveiled by Andrew Motion in 2005) seems to have encouraged this.

He takes us from room to room, bathroom, parlour, second bedroom, once occupied by Stevie's 'Aunt Lion', whom she nursed devotedly until her death in 1968. Jo points out that while Aunt Lion got the bay window, the most light, the bigger room, Stevie's room had the hinterland, the head space. We are all thinking the same thing. If this was our house, we would want the back room too.

★

As her fame grew in later life and Stevie Smith became the subject of profiles in newspapers and magazines, she would coax the photographers up the road from her house to Grovelands Park. This is a classic suburban park, but for Stevie, as she posed under the damp trees in front of the lake, it was a place of transformation: 'When the wind blows east and ruffles the water of the lake, driving the rain before it, the Egyptian geese rise with a squawk, and the rhododendron trees, shaken by the gusts, drip the raindrops from the blades of their green-black leaves. The empty park, in the winter rain, has a staunch and inviolate melancholy that is refreshing.'

Ten minutes walk north, through the streets that once were Winchmore Woods, we arrive at the gates of Grovelands Park.

Kevin leads us through the grand gates into what looks to us like a slightly shabby green space. It's impressive in its scale, rolling lawns extending to the horizon. There are plenty of mature trees, open spaces. But the real jewel is the lake in the middle. We step over a low fence on to its slimy bank. 'It's absolutely teeming with life in there', Kevin tells us. It's very slippery on the edge. 'I would really laugh if you went in . . .', he says. In Stevie's day, there were boats on the lake. She used to row out to the island for picnics. Now the island looks impenetrable, one great mass of brush and bramble. Kevin is a fisherman. He tells us there are huge, clever carp in here, wily old fish, tough to catch. He thinks they have been here for most of a century, since the lake was built. He is alarmed by the growing number of fish-eating birds.

Stevie praised the park for its 'inviolate melancholy' and we are getting that. We are struggling to find it 'refreshing', though. Suddenly we see a flash of colour in a tree – a bright emerald bird. These are the London ring-necked parakeets, wild progeny of caged birds. They come with their own creation myth, that their ancestors were released by Jimi Hendrix from his Carnaby Street apartment in the late Sixties as a gesture of love and liberation, a psychedelic avian Adam and Eve. That story in itself sounds like a Stevie Smith fairy tale. Despite her penchant for melancholia, we think she would have loved these exotic escapees.

★

Like many suburban parks, Stevie Smith's Grovelands Park was originally the landscaped garden of a big house. In this case, that big house is still there, about three hundred yards from the lake, surrounded by trees. Built as an expression of financial and social triumph, it now stands for something different. Now part of The Priory Clinic, this place is familiar from tabloid newspaper stories about celebrity breakdown, addiction, depression.

It's a strange presence in the middle of the park, among the ordinariness of pram-pushers and pensioners taking the air. Of

course, the point of The Priory is treatment, healing, but nonetheless it's come to stand for a place of last resort in the public
imagination, a place to go or be sent when you have lost control
of your life.

Stevie mainly kept her battles with depression to herself and close
friends. But in 1953, at the age of fifty-one, she had a breakdown
at work and attempted suicide. It's a strange episode, apparently
triggered by an incident in the office, but the facts are still unclear.
What is clear is that Stevie harmed herself, cutting her wrists,
and that she gave up her secretarial job in a publishing house from
that point, to concentrate on her writing and reviewing, whilst
caring for her elderly aunt.

There are clues in later poems that suggest she felt suicidal again
in her final years, but she came back from the brink. Her relationship with Death was so close, the courtship so long, the assurance of
his presence so comforting, that she was prepared to wait for him.

★

Does Stevie line up with the survivors or the bohemians? We
sit on a bench in Grovelands Park to weigh it up. The park is
getting busier now it's school pick-up time, with parents and
pushchairs and kids running on ahead of them. Jo suggests that
Stevie doesn't quite fit in either line: 'She does survive, yes, and
there's a sense of exuberance, but also a sense of darkness in her
work. We know from her biography that she had periods where
she had vulnerabilities. But then she made it all work. She turned
a life that a lot of people would have seen as dreary, into something extraordinary.'

A small suburban drama is unfolding in front of us. It's a dog-
versus-bird stand-off by the lake in front of our bench. A small
terrier shrinks back from the water's edge, barking weakly, and a
swan is hissing, arching, protecting six cygnets. We don't fancy the
dog's chances.

★

W. H. Auden was one of many poets who tried to warn us off their lives. He believed that the poems should stand for themselves and that the notion of a poet's biography (or even worse, autobiography) was a misguided one. Larkin, leaving instructions for the destruction of his diaries, shared that view.

Are we better off without the lives (and especially the deaths) of poets intruding on their work? In Stevie Smith's case, the separation between life and work seems stronger than with Larkin or Auden. As Jo puts it: 'I think with these poems it wouldn't matter a hoot if you didn't know anything about her. You could completely inhabit the poems and engage with her characters, her places, and in that sense she has made something archetypal, about human life.'

But what if, in that breakdown of 1953, her suicide attempt had succeeded? If all Smith's poems remained exactly as they are, not a line added or taken away, would we see those poems differently through the lens of a suicide? Of course we would. It would change the critical context of her work and would lend it a different emotional temperature. But she didn't. She lived on in the suburbs for almost two decades, nursing her ailing aunt.

★

Within seven years of Stevie Smith's death a feature film of her life was released, starring Glenda Jackson as the poet, based on the play *Stevie* by Hugh Whitemore. It was filmed on location in Palmers Green, including her favourite haunts like Grovelands Park, and in Avondale Road. They did not, however, film in Stevie's actual house. Instead, they picked a property a few doors down, because, as Kevin explained to us, it had more original features.

★

The voice says: 'T-2-9-4-6-0 . . . Reel Two.' Then for a few seconds, there's a level test tone, before the drama continues. We've ordered up a radio play from the BBC's Sound Archive:

Persons from Porlock, written and produced by Louis MacNeice. We're familiar with its themes and characters, but even though we've read excerpts from the script in print, this is the first time either of us have heard it as it went out on the Third Programme on a Friday evening in August 1963. It came to us as two zipped files, and we're listening on an MP3 player with a headphone splitter, but it isn't difficult to imagine a wireless set in walnut or bakelite, the dim green glow of the bandwidths and the geography of the airwaves: Paris, Luxembourg, Stockholm, Hilversum, Stuttgart . . . Places where the signal would have travelled, miraculously, over dark hills and deep valleys, through troughs and ridges of atmospheric pressure, finding its way into the creases and folds where we live, except neither of us has been born yet, and the signal has travelled even greater distances to arrive here, in the future. Before we rejoin the cast and characters, we hear this unexpected voice: an unknown and anonymous sound archivist, filer of quarter-inch tape, gatekeeper, guardian at the threshold. The voice disturbs us, expressionless and flat, but speaking out of an air pocket, trapped in the indeterminate past, the dark of a vault, jamming the signal for a moment, stalling us at the mouth of the cave. A discontinuity announcement.

(Fade up cave)

Broadcasting House – or rather Old Broadcasting House, now there's a new one. We've walked in under Eric Gill's statue of Ariel and Prospero to listen to some radio drama from the BBC vaults.

   The death of Louis MacNeice has a proverbial power amongst poets. He didn't flare then burn out like his BBC friend Dylan Thomas, but there's a strain of doom and Romanticism detectable in his death nonetheless. He hadn't exhausted his early promise: with MacNeice there was a sense of dip or lull after the first flush of books, but this was followed by a return to full force, cut off unexpectedly. He didn't die young, but he was too young to die, and – strangest of all – dying when he did gave a symmetry to his writing life, the younger and older poet meeting each other inside a spiral chamber. And he caught his death while building a sound world from a subterranean place, making a play about an artist meeting Death.

His radio play *Persons from Porlock* needed the soundtrack of an underworld, and so MacNeice travelled up to Yorkshire with recording engineers to capture the atmosphere inside the limestone of the Dales. It was a wet summer, cold and damp above and below ground, and he got a drenching. Over the following days and weeks a cough and 'mystery temperature' became suspected bronchitis, and eventually viral pneumonia. He died in hospital on 3 September 1963, just over a week shy of his fifty-sixth birthday.

★

Persons from Porlock takes the listener through twenty-odd years in the life of Hank, a frustrated artist (the play is subtitled: *The Story of a Painter*), who finds some kind of solace as a speleologist, an explorer of caves, despite suffering from claustrophobia. His guide to the underworld is called Mervyn.

MERVYN: Sit down. Don't impale yourself on a stalagmite.

HANK: I don't see any stalagmites.

MERVYN: There aren't any. Don't mind me. I'm just a mad hatter. But if you want stalactites and stalagmites, just wait till you see Scrimshank's.

HANK: Scrimshank's?

MERVYN: Hush, it's a secret. My Unknown Quantity. I've only so far explored the first chamber but, man, it's a symphony in dripstone. The chamber ends in a chimney, that's what we go down next.

There's always been a slight uncertainty about where MacNeice actually went underground on 7 August for his final field record-ing. We know (from a letter to his daughter Corinna) that the day had ended in Leeds, at the Palace of Varieties, an old music hall 'now much invaded by strip: there was one lurid act where the girl was chased by a gorilla'. The Varieties was also the venue for the BBC's long-running light entertainment show *The Good Old Days*, where the weekly TV audience got dolled up to the nines in period Victorian-Edwardian garb. MacNeice might have baulked at that, though *any* costume change might at least have got him out of his wet clothes.

Depending on who you listen to, he had spent the day visit-ing the Settle Caves, or caves at Ingleton. Sometimes it isn't caves but potholes. Often, it's simply Yorkshire or the Yorkshire Moors. Somewhere up north. Does it matter? Well, yes, we think it does. MacNeice was fastidious himself – the fact that he accompanied BBC sound engineers on this expedition to capture the noises used to furnish his fictional underworld suggests as much; a less scrupulous producer might have taken their Uher a few hundred yards north up the road from Broadcasting House and dangled a microphone into a fountain in Regents Park. We decide to get as close as we reasonably can.

But before we decide on which cave might have been the fictional Scrimshank's, MacNeice's meticulousness also inspires a trawl through the historical weather reports. August 1963 was cool and dull and unsettled, with rainfall more than twice the average for parts of Yorkshire. Frontal rain reached western Scotland late on the 6th, spreading to all districts the following day. We also notice the dates to either side of MacNeice's field trip seem relatively clear, prompting the thought that if he'd hastened or held off by a day he mightn't have caught his death. And then the further thought that the passage of a depression to the north of the country interrupted the course of English literature, cutting the lifeline and closing the circle of MacNeice's writing.

HANK: I find it . . . excitingly timeless.

MERVYN: That's right. You leave time outside. With the weather.

PETER: The weather outside can affect us inside though.

★

We can both recall going underground in our own childhoods, usually on school trips, and the gritty-slithery-ness of squeezing through gaps in rock, our luminous cowls or cagoules, the chill of the underworld, the plasma glow of a hand held over a torch. For us it was the Blue John Cavern at Castleton in the Peaks or the caves and potholes of the Alyn Gorge in the Clwydian Hills – but never Yorkshire.

HANK: What I like about caves is their names.

MERVYN: Oh yes, their names, man, they're marvellous. Alum Pot and Gaping Ghyll, Lost John's Cave and Wookey Hole.

Looking at the OS map, we soon realize this is a landscape of fissure and rain gauge and limestone pavement, intricately raddled with shake holes, potholes and plenty of caves. Quaking Pot. Black Shiver Ridge. Lead Mine Moss. Dead Man's Cave. Our eyes squint and water. We scour the tiny type and symbols, from grid to grid, in the hope of finding a clue to the fictional Scrimshank's on the surface. This isn't going to be easy. But we have one steer.

In his letter to his daughter, MacNeice mentions the many stalactites and stalagmites he saw that day in Yorkshire, as well as an underground stream and a waterfall. This sounds to us like a large and accessible cave. Settle and Ingleton are within a few miles of each other, and both plausibly within striking distance of Leeds. We find ourselves dithering between White Scar Cave, which forms its system under the Ingleborough limestone, and Ingleborough Cave itself. Both are show caves (White Scar is the longest in the country) and would have seemed fairly accessible on a day trip. Both have all of those features MacNeice's letter details in abundance. Both have been open to visitors for a long time, but in the end Ingleborough shades it. It lies just above the village of Clapham, about halfway between Settle and Ingleton, not far off the A65, which runs north-west, shadowing a giant fault line. It also connects via an underground stream to Gaping Ghyll, the cathedral space under the hills. We'll meet at Ingleborough Cave.

★

Persons from Porlock takes its cue from the famous interruption Samuel Taylor Coleridge suffered while he was working on the poem 'Kubla Khan'. Coleridge regarded that poem as a fragment, 'composed, in a sort of Reverie brought on by two grains of Opium taken to check a dysentery', and many years later described what happened, referring to himself in the third person:

> On awakening he appeared to himself to have a distinct recollection of the whole, and taking his pen, ink and paper, instantly and eagerly wrote down the lines that are here preserved. At this moment he was unfortunately called out by a person on business from Porlock, and detained by him above an hour, and on his return to his room, found, to his no small surprise and mortification, that though he still retained some vague and dim recollection of the general purport of the vision, yet, with the exception of some eight or ten scattered lines and images, all the rest had passed away like the images on the surface of a stream into which a stone has been cast, but, alas! without the after restoration of the latter!

While on business for the BBC ourselves, we've both, on separate occasions, sought out the Somerset farmhouse where this is supposed to have taken place, 'between Porlock & Linton, a quarter of a mile from Culbone Church', set in the creased, deep coombes leading down to the sea. The identity of the caller has kept scholars busy for years: was it Coleridge's dealer? His friend and rival William Wordsworth? Bloody kids? Did he imagine it? Or make it all up? Was he simply, as Stevie Smith once put it, looking for a fall guy, a get-out clause to release him from his own poem?

> Coleridge received the Person from Porlock
> And ever after called him a curse,
> Then why did he hurry to let him in?
> He could have hid in the house.

The Person from Porlock has come to mean the interrupter, the disrupter, any breaker of the creative spell or distraction from the one true path. In MacNeice's play, the plural Persons come thick and fast. Hank the young idealist painter, who we first meet at the Guernica Exhibition in London, is interrupted, sidetracked and distracted by the Second World War, by the temptations of working as a commercial artist, by the need to keep afloat financially, by booze, by bailiffs, by women. Running beneath the increasing turmoil and disappointment of his life is caving, the deep place outside of time, although by the end of the play the cave has become a trap, and all of Hank's Porlocks have speaking parts. The final Person from Porlock is Death.

★

Can a cave harbour spores or moulds that grow on damp walls, hold themselves in waiting, decade after decade? Do they wait for that once-in-a-blue-moon intrusion of hot breath, close enough for them to cross? Did Louis simply die of cold or was there something down in the dark that took to him? We meet on an overcast August morning and take the short walk along a nature trail above the village of Clapham. The cave mouth looms into view and, as is so often the case, we begin to have second thoughts. Maybe we should go and have a scone and just imagine what it was like?

MacNeice didn't die here – St Leonard's Hospital still stands off Kingsland Road in Shoreditch, though now it's a primary care centre, and most of its original infirmary buildings seem to have been demolished in the Nineties – and we can't even be absolutely sure he caught his terminal chill in this cave. Still, there's no question of us making any recordings here. And it now seems odd even trying to play back some of *Persons from Porlock* underground. The idea of returning the sound to its source had seemed interesting, even redemptive, the closing of a circle we were sure MacNeice might have approved of. However, in the cold light of day, facing the dark hole in the rock, it seems like an empty gesture. 'What's the point in painting black on black?' as a voice at Hank's exhibition whispers in MacNeice's play. But we've come this far.

★

Persons from Porlock wasn't the first of MacNeice's BBC plays to go below ground. A decade before, *Prisoner's Progress* imagined a camp of war prisoners, and an Escape Team trying to dig their way to freedom beyond the wire, into the woods; so far, so familiar, except the course of their tunnel meets another tunnel, a neolithic monument that is being excavated by female camp inmates who want to protect it.

Undergrounds and underworlds are detectable throughout MacNeice's poetry, a bedrock beneath the pavement, though we have to remind ourselves that the 'thumbnail nightmares' of his final poems, or a meeting with the great interrupter Death in a cave, were written with no foreknowledge of their being last things. Tombs and graves, 'below worlds', tunnels, the moving stairs down into Blitz stations, the womb, 'a brangle of talk from the floor below', a bus conductor as the ferryman

Charon ... It isn't the half of his work, but it does trickle like an underground stream, perhaps all the way back to a childhood source: a visit to the salt mines beneath Carrickfergus, 'a black labyrinth of galleries under the carefree fields'.

★

Louis MacNeice had never really fitted in easily anywhere. He was born in Belfast in 1907, to a family that came from the West Coast of Ireland, and grew up in Carrickfergus on the shores of Belfast Lough. It's all there in a poem called 'Carrickfergus': 'Where the bottle-neck harbour collects the mud which jams / The little boats beneath the Norman castle, / The pier shining with lumps of crystal salt', the whole landscape of his childhood overshadowed by the Great War:

> I went to school in Dorset, the world of parents
>   Contracted into a puppet world of sons
> Far from the mill girls, the smell of porter, the salt-mines
>   And the soldiers with their guns.

MacNeice joined the BBC in 1941, and would remain there for the rest of his life, although being a card-carrying member of the Corporation didn't mean he ever settled down exactly; he travelled and spent time in the United States, India, Africa and Greece. In his essay 'The Man from No Part' Tom Paulin describes how there was 'a sense in which he was a visitor everywhere, the man from no part. For the English reader he appears to be Irish, while for certain Irish readers he doesn't really belong to Ireland.' The boy from Carrick never quite seemed to get his head around that first dislocating journey down through England after crossing the water:

> Transported across the Irish Sea and seated in an English
> train ... I kept saying to myself 'This is England' but I did

not really believe it and, as it was night, could not see those differences which stamp a thing as real. But, though full of disbelief, I was vastly excited, and when daylight came I perceived that England was not just an imitation of Ireland; the fields and hedges and houses were different, and as for London when we got there . . . it was not Belfast, it was foreign. And foreign it has remained to me.

★

The cave is beautiful, certainly a 'symphony in dripstone'. We make our way in hard hats deeper into its chambers. The echo of our footfall grows richer and more reverberant as we leave daylight behind. The rolling green of the Dales is forgotten, and while we might have left one kind of time outside – the kind printed on our parking permit – another kind comes to the fore. We're in geological time, the inch-to-the-century of a stalactite's calcium salts, and the constant chill of the underworld beyond the surface's seasons and harvests. Best of all is when we close our eyes. Suddenly the cave becomes a sound picture, and maybe this is what Mervyn really meant by 'symphony': tricklings and drips and the distant roar of rushing water falling into a cavern. It feels like the weather inside our skulls. This is what MacNeice came to gather.

As a star in the firmament of the BBC's Features Department, MacNeice would have spent a lot of time in the studio. He worked alongside such writers as Dylan Thomas: another poet who, as he is supposed to have said, in times gone by might have run away to sea, 'but now ran away to the BBC'. (*Prisoner's Progress* was runner-up to *Under Milk Wood* for the 1954 Prix Italia Prize.) The radio studio is a kind of subterranean space – we've both spent enough time in one to recognize the sensation of entering a chamber, a vault – where the clock marks the seconds relentlessly, and each one becomes significant and precious where Time underwrites the entire enterprise, pointing to another very MacNeician theme.

Radio – on the studio side of the microphone – has its own argot. We remember thinking we were *real* broadcasters when first asking to wear the 'cans' (headphones), or referring to the 'top' of the 'show'. Tragic. It only occurs to us now that having a top, as in the starting point, the place from which a programme sets out and takes its bearings, implies some kind of descent.

There's also that strange ritual which takes place at the end of any recording, which is the taping of 'room tone' or 'atmos'. The producer will ask for about thirty seconds of silence, with any actors or readers remaining quietly in their places. No two atmospheres are exactly alike to the radio microphone and this period of enforced silence resembles a kind of prayer: for the drama you have just made, for luck, for good ratings or kind reviews. It also reminds us of that moment in childhood caves when the guide would always ask everyone to switch off their torches and sit still for a few scary moments. The dark that resulted was absolute, one that the eye could never adjust to. A single stray photon would glow in it like a firefly in a coal shed.

★

MacNeice was busy at the BBC. As the Fifties wore on, he seems to have become disillusioned with the Corporation and its aims. TV was in the ascendant, as was the Drama Department, and the grind began to get to him. The boozing also began to increase and MacNeice became a regular fixture in some of the pubs near Broadcasting House and New Cavendish Street: The Stag, The George. We wonder how much of a sap on his energies the BBC was during these years. MacNeice made all kinds of dramas, but those he set in underworlds become impossible to listen to without some sense of his own predicament, as if he was trying to tunnel his way out from under all that Portland Stone, the artist dramatizing the day job in the studio. *Persons from Porlock* also invites an obvious question: was the

Corporation his interrupter, the monolithic thing preventing him from getting on with his poems? Lord Reith himself as one of the Persons from Porlock?

★

The earth and the ephemeral. The BBC has form with caves and underground spaces. In September 1930 engineers recorded a broadcast featuring The Wookey Hole Male Voice Choir singing a musical arrangement of Metcalf's poem 'The Song of Wookey Hole' from 600 feet beneath the Mendip Hills in Somerset. 'Recorded' isn't quite right. What's extraordinary about this event is it went out live. Recording technology at the time would have meant taking disc-cutting gear underground, to carve the noise into shellac for playing back later. The programme was a success and was repeated a few times, including a famous outside broadcast in 1935:

> THRILLING BROADCAST FROM WOOKEY HOLE CAVES.
> ATTEMPT TO FIND LEGENDARY SIXTH CHAMBER.

> Once again the BBC has chosen Wookey Hole Cave for a novelty broadcast, and this time their relay will be one of the most thrilling and daring ever attempted. On the night of August 17th a man in diving suit and helmet, will walk along the hidden bed of the underground great subterranean cave believed to exist many feet below the level of the river . . . The search is due to commence at 10.30 p.m. and will be broadcast over the National wavelengths . . .

Did MacNeice ever catch any of these broadcasts on the wireless (emanating from a West Country Coleridgean source)? Perhaps on a simple crystal set? We wonder. Before this, while still a schoolboy at Marlborough, he seemed to have felt the draw and allure of the underworld that he'd perhaps first recognized in the mazy Carrick salt mines. In the spring of 1922 he wrote a letter to his sister explaining how he fancied exploring nearby Silbury Hill; a year later, he made the expedition:

> Silbury Hill is about 7 miles away and is a common resort in the summer term ... On Tuesday we had not time to go to the top, though we examined the door at the beginning of a tunnel once used for excavation purposes. Sad to relate, the door was locked. I don't think the excavators found anything of worth inside although they penetrated to the centre ... Silbury Hill is a prehistoric artificial mound, far larger than the Mound behind A house.

The Mound is the prehistoric structure that Marlborough School is almost built upon. In the years immediately following MacNeice's death, the upstart medium TV, and a new channel – BBC2 – took its cameras underground to broadcast live from inside the chalky tunnels and chambers of Silbury Hill. The pictures went out, but nothing much was found, and the programmes appear to have flopped. By then, the television audience's attention was tuning in to pictures beamed down from the skies above.

★

As we make our way deeper into Ingleborough Cave, old instincts arise. Caves suggest a huge pre-human past, but also the prospect of signs and objects as clues to that past. Even though this is a well-explored old show cave, our eyes dart about in the tangle of flashlights that glitter and ripple across the walls and ceiling and passages up ahead, as if we might be the first to uncover the bones of a mammoth or something much older, a fossil from the warm shallow sea this once was. To the south of us lie the great coalfields of Lancashire and Yorkshire, the old horizons of a vast swamp, and we scan the limestone for mineral clues.

(Pause: sudden increase of stream noise – and build behind)

DONALD: Hank! Do you hear what I hear?

HANK: My God! It must be raining outside.

DONALD: Is the stream higher?

HANK: I'm just trying to check. I noticed a funny bit of crystal in there in the wall of the tunnel – No, my God, it's
submerged!

In *Persons from Porlock* Hank catches this glimpse of a strange
crystal (this echoes a childhood dream MacNeice had about the
Carrick salt mines, featuring hostile gnomes who had kidnapped
him in order to search for a jewel in the dark). But the water
level rises and Hank is caught in the Stygian trap, plunged into a
valve through which he can never return. The play ends with the
uncomprehending Hank being addressed by a roll call of voices,
the 'persons' of the play's title, and the final voice we hear – in a
broad Somerset accent – is Death himself, come to lead Hank
across a suddenly Classical underground river.*

---

* Here, we enter the submerged cavern of a footnote. Water in limestone might lead
to one of the sources of modern European poetry. In the limestone landscape
of Provence around Avignon, the great poet-scholar Petrarch fell in love with the
unattainable Laura. We know very little about who she was, and nobody is even sure
as to whether the two actually met and exchanged words, but Laura proved a deep
source for Petrarch, who wrote hundreds of lyric poems – ballads, sestinas and, most
famously, sonnets – that speak to us out of the fourteenth century, collected as the
Canzoniere. In the village of Fontaine de Vaucluse, Petrarch is remembered in a little
museum on the banks of the River Sorgue, and the story of the poet and Laura has
been attracting visitors for centuries. Napoleon had a neoclassical column erected
there in 1804 to mark Petrarch's five-hundredth birthday (and claim the Florentine
poet for the Republic), but His Imperial Majesty was following in the footsteps of
tourists dating back to the 1540s, when it was not unusual for a traveller on business
in Avignon to take a trip to Vaucluse to visit Petrarch's landscape of love. These early
literary pilgrims would have explored the nooks and recesses of the same enclosed
valley where Petrarch had sought solitude and consoled himself following Laura's
death, heard the birdsong that echoed her voice, fallen into following the same
pathways where he burned and wept for love, and wondered at the deep turquoise
pool beneath a limestone cliff where the Sorgue that flows through his poetry rises.

Persons from Porlock, featuring the sounds gathered in this, well, this Yorkshire limestone (because that's all we can say with any certainty), aired at the end of August 1963. By then, MacNeice was lying in a hospital bed, and four days later he died. A week after this, his collection of poems, *The Burning Perch*, was published.

He sees Laura everywhere. Everything is brimful of her. And it's tempting to think of this limestone pool as a source of the sonnet.

For a few weeks every spring the quiet pool swells, surges and turns torrential. This phenomenon, like its depth, was for a long time something of a mystery. It was reputed to be bottomless. Six hundred years after Petrarch loved and lost Laura, Jacques Cousteau arrived in Vaucluse; the same Jacques Cousteau in his red Phrygian cap who turned our television screens into the thick glass window of a submersible and bathed our Sunday night living rooms in a rippling, undersea light. Cousteau and his team had studied the history of dives at Vaucluse, including a recent descent to ninety metres (whose diver claimed to have discovered the zinc boat of an earlier nineteenth-century expedition), and would be using the new aqualung gear they'd developed. In 1946 these were the most sophisticated techniques and equipment available. But things didn't go according to plan. Being a poet might be more dangerous than being a deep-sea diver, but diving into the source of poems is another matter.

'Our worst experience in 5,000 dives did not come in the sea, but in an inland water cave, the famous *Fountain of Vaucluse* near Avignon,' Cousteau wrote later. Loaded down 'like donkeys' with air cylinders, torches, rope and pig iron for ballast, he and another diver, Didi Dumas, dropped beyond thirty metres down into the darkness and silence, but before they could discover the secret of the spring they ran into trouble; both men grew stupefied; thoughts slowed down. Sea dives can intoxicate a diver, but usually at much greater depths, and this felt different from nitrogen narcosis. Dumas seemed to black out completely, and the pair's rope signals to the surface became febrile and confused. Somehow, Cousteau managed to haul Dumas back towards a faint green haze above them. They emerged in a bad state and were revived with brandy and the heat of a petrol fire. Later, they discovered the diesel compressor they'd used to charge their cylinders was sucking in its own exhaust: they'd been breathing carbon monoxide. The dive into Petrarch's source had almost killed them.

Cousteau knew all about how Petrarch had been addicted to the mysteries of the Vaucluse fountain and cave, but also its attraction to other writers, such as the Provençal poet Frédéric Mistral. He explained how the fairy of the fountain had changed into a beautiful maiden and accosted a passing minstrel – this neck of the woods being prime minstrel territory – who she led into the water, deep down to a submerged prairie where seven diamonds plugged seven holes, and told him how, when she removed the seventh precious stone, the waters would rise. We catch a

And then? The cave we're crouching in now could double for the dark of forgetting and obscurity, the silence of a writing life cut short. Here is the wildtrack of an underworld that MacNeice wanted to capture instead of mocking-up in the studio. We imagine how a foley artist would recreate this, working with a palette of drips and tingles of tapwater in a studio so full of pails and tins it might resemble a leaky submarine; and a huge amount of reverbed presence, building an atmosphere of emptiness and radio silence, which is never really total silence.

MacNeice's death was unexpected and sudden in middle age, and such a death has its ramifications for the durability of any artist's work. The man from no part wasn't straightforwardly associated with any source in particular, and, unusual as his death was, it didn't easily fit the Romantic paradigm. Like Stevie Smith, MacNeice was a modest poet who fought his demons in private, but by most people's standards also 'made it all work'. Both lives were unspectacular compared with those bohemians – including some of their friends and contemporaries – who blazed across the sky. Luckily, MacNeice had admirers who were able to boost the signal in time. Auden – a poet whose mid-century pre-eminence might have overshadowed and reduced MacNeice to a less audible hiss – wrote an elegy addressed to

---

glimpse of another strange crystal. The fountain bubbles up in Mistral's long poem *Mirèio*, written in Provençal:

> Once, when by Vaucluse grotto I was going,
> I saw a fig tree in the bare rock growing;
> So very spare it was, the lizards grey
> Had found more shade beneath a jasmine spray.
>
> But, round about the roots, once every year
> The neighbouring stream comes gushing, as I hear,
> And the shrub drinks the water as it rises,
> And that one drink for the whole year suffices.
> Even as the gem is cut to fit the ring,
> This parable to us is answering.

his old friend, 'The Cave of Making' – the 'cave' in this case being the writing room of Auden's newly established home at Kirchstetten in Austria. MacNeice also eventually found his way into the work of Americans such as John Berryman and Robert Lowell, taking walk-on elegiac parts.

> A month from his death, we talked by Epstein's bust
> of Eliot; MacNeice said, 'It is better
> To die at fifty than lose pleasure in fear'

Perhaps even more importantly, younger poets were tuning in, not just to commemorate (though they did that too: Derek Mahon's 'At Carrowdore Churchyard' feels like imaginative geo-caching; early bearings taken from the site where MacNeice's ashes rest and 'will not stir'), but also to enlarge and build on and be excited by. Michael Longley has noticed how poets from Northern Ireland 'picked up frequencies which were inaudible in Dublin or London'. MacNeice is now one of the last century's touchstone poets, but seen from today it's hard to remember how there was a moment when the torches were turned off and for a while all was steady archival cold.

★

We leave Broadcasting House by its new entrance, blinking in the sunlight, and cross the wide piazza towards the familiar wedding cake of All Souls Church. The ground beneath our feet is carved with the names of hundreds of places near and far, the old litany of place names found on a wireless dial set like a memorial into the paving stones. Voices whisper from the ground. We are walking on art. WORLD is the work of Canadian Mark Pimlott, and he's included place names from the realms of fantasy and mythology, too. Wouldn't it be great to find Scrimshank's here? we say, loitering about like we've dropped something, but after searching a while we give up. MacNeice would surely have liked this.

He recalled an early love of place names in his 'unwritten book', *Landscapes of Childhood and Youth*.

Scrimshank's still bugs us. Later on, it occurs to us that we might have been looking in the wrong place in a different sense. As a place name in Yorkshire, we drew a resounding blank, but 'scrimshanker' turns out to mean something along the lines of 'skiver' or 'shirker'. And we end up wishing MacNeice had gone AWOL on that August day, had walked up Portland Place from the BBC with his sound engineer and recorded some of the water features in Regent's Park. The fountains there must have stood in for many places: the Alhambra Gardens in Granada, the rainforest of Guatemala, a carp-haunted pool in Kyoto, the sewers of Vienna. A shadow World Service.

Free to do as he liked, MacNeice could have spent the rest of the day round the corner in The George, drinking, talking, on the fringes of the crowd, but content in a blue haze of cigarette smoke, the busy decade getting underway in earnest beyond the taproom dark, happy knowing he was meant to be somewhere else.

Coda

Maybe we knew each other better
When the night was young and unrepeated
And the moon stood still over Jericho.

So much for the past; in the present
There are moments caught between heart-beats
When maybe we know each other better.

But what is that clinking in the darkness?
Maybe we shall know each other better
When the tunnels meet beneath the mountain.

Two Ferries

Arromanches is one of the key stopping points on any Operation Overlord pilgrimage. It is a small former seaside town in the middle of the Normandy landing zone, halfway down Gold Beach, between the American beaches codenamed Omaha and Utah to the west, and the British and Canadian beaches of Juno and Sword, to the east. *Former* seaside town is perhaps a bit unfair, since it still has all the accoutrements – seafront bars, crêperies, ice-cream stalls and vast beaches – but history has rather overwritten it. Most of the souvenir shops sell replica regimental badges, books and World War Two merchandise. Some even sell Overlord relics – jerrycans, spent and rusted bits of ordnance, military helmets. The larger shops have a back room or a spare shelf selling non-Overlord souvenirs, including local calvados and cider. On the doors and windows of many of the bistros and cafés there are pictures of aged veterans with rows of medals, and the slogan: 'Welcome, our liberators'.

The beach looks idyllic. Some of the strands along our home patch – the Lancashire resorts of Southport, Blackpool, Formby – are expansive, but these beaches are a different scale entirely. You could set land-speed records here. Further west, on the Brittany beaches at this time of year, you would be pushed to find enough space to spread out your towel. But here, there are acres of space. Perhaps it's the Mulberry Harbour that puts people off. In a remarkable feat of engineering, a temporary port was established here at Arromanches in the immediate aftermath of D-Day, to ship in thousands of tons of supplies, men and vehicles. Vast concrete caissons were towed across the channel and a working harbour was assembled in situ. It did its job for six months, until deeper, bigger ports were liberated, but it hasn't disappeared. The caissons, cut loose and displaced after seventy years, are being reclaimed by seaweed and limpets and gulls. But their presence is an unmistakeable reminder of what happened here.

It is early morning, but the town is filling up. School parties gather with their workbooks outside the Overlord Museum. In the souvenir shops we hear mainly American voices. One middle-aged man wears a brown leather jacket with a technicolour frieze of beach combat printed on the back, topped by the words 'All Gave Some, Some Gave All'. In a café down the street a British veteran is walking slowly to a table, flanked by his daughters. Younger men, perhaps grandsons, follow behind. As he sits down, we see that he is in full regalia, medals and beret. We decide to escape before the coach trips arrive.

On the headland east of Arromanches there is a 360-degree circular cinema. Billed as 'a trip at the heart of D-Day', it offers an immersive experience in surround sound, projected on to nine high-definition screens, of the Battle of Normandy. The pay desk offers a long list of exemptions from the entry fee, including teachers, children under the age of ten, journalists, war veterans, deportees, members of the Resistance, Maquis, draft evaders and war widows. We buy our full-price tickets and go in.

The film begins. Hitler makes a speech on the wall to our right. Churchill makes a speech on the wall behind us. Men file on to boats at either side. Ahead of us, close-ups of nervous-looking soldiers, smoking and laughing as they wait to board. Every now and again, we see a map of the Channel and the Normandy Coast, showing us the beaches and charting the progress of the invading forces. Apart from the maps, everything we see is archive footage. We keep turning on our heels, so as not to miss anything. The sound is intense. A shell cries as it crosses from one side of the room to the other. At one point, in a clever bit of digital trickery, the layers of detail in a piece of film are separated – man from beach from sky – and the perspective dips and deepens. For a moment, we are at the shoulder of a soldier moving up the beach. Why? Because that is why we are here. Like those Victorian stereoscopic images of the *Death of Chatterton*, or medieval paintings of the wounds of Christ, this film is intended to draw us so fully into the scene that we are changed by it, moved to feel gratitude or pity.

On the screen ahead of us, a young girl holds up a flower, perhaps to hand it to a liberating soldier. Battalions of men in uniform emerge from the sea all around us and troop from sand, to fields, to streets. The grainiest and least distinct clips are of the heat of battle itself, men running off the transporter craft into a wave of machine-gun fire. To the left of us, one screen shows a wide shot of a section of beach on which one man is clearly hit, and falls. Was he dead? Wounded? Did he survive? Whatever became of him, his seminal moment is the one we take away with us, his daily duty to take a hit each day at twenty minute intervals to challenge our imaginative failure to connect. As we file out through the gift shop, a recording of a Forties swing band accompanies us. No one speaks.

★

In a cluster of apple trees just outside the Normandy village of Fontenay-le-Pesnel, a young member of the 12th SS Hitlerjugend takes aim to launch a shell. He is lining up a target two kilometres north, to the brow of a hill called Point 103, where a cluster of British Sherman tanks is sheltering, overlooking a village called St Pierre. It is a drizzly, grey morning in June 1944.

The 12th SS Hitlerjugend is a Panzer division noted for its focus on young recruits. Most of its soldiers – as its name suggests – are drawn from members of the Hitler Youth. Many of them are new to the battlefield, but they are led by older, more experienced officers. The young recruits have a reputation for zeal and a hunger for action. Three days ago, British, American and

Canadian troops landed in vast numbers at beaches across the Normandy coast. The 12th SS have been travelling west to stop them, as part of a counter-assault to defend or take back strategic centres like Caen and Bayeux. On the morning of 9 June their task is to prevent British tank squadrons moving south into Tilly-sur-Seulles. They know the advance is coming. They have seen a cluster of eight tanks sheltering under trees.

Now their job is to pre-empt the attack, to shell those tanks, perhaps make a kill or two to unsettle them, to flush them out. There are reports of recces being made by soldiers of the Sherwood Rangers from Point 103, sizing up the roads and bridges around St Pierre. The young recruit has got them in his sights. The shell is launched and traces an arc ahead of its own tearing sound.

★

One of Keith Douglas's most famous lines of poetry is his plea to 'Simplify me when I'm Dead'. But like most poets' deaths, the more you look at him through the lens of his own, the less simple he seems. The detail that sticks in your mind when you read about the death of Douglas is that he died without a mark on his body. It is not unknown for soldiers to protect a comrade's next of kin by reporting an unbroken, unblemished corpse at the death scene. A recent re-evaluation of the death of the poet Edward Thomas on the Western Front in the First World War has challenged his own version of the 'woundless corpse' myth. The literary scholar Jean Moorcroft Wilson discovered a letter from Thomas's commanding officer Franklin Lushington, revealing that the poet was 'shot clean through the chest'. The story of a shell blast killing him without a mark on his body was, perhaps, a benign fiction to protect Thomas's widow Helen.

Twenty-seven years later, and less than three hours' drive away, the same myth of the unblemished body attached to the death of Keith Douglas. But perhaps it wasn't a myth in Douglas's case. The army padre, Skinner, who lay Douglas's corpse in a temporary grave under a hedge, attested to the body being unmarked. It is certainly possible that a shell blast in a tree directly above him could have killed the poet instantly without any shrapnel wounds. And there is something strangely prescient about his description of the moment of death itself at the end of his poem 'How to Kill', depicting death as a mosquito, weightless, that 'touches / her tiny shadow on the stone, / and with how like, how infinite / a lightness, man and shadow meet'.

In 'How to Kill' Douglas makes us feel, more vividly than any poet of the First World War had done, what it is like to pull the trigger, to end a life. His description of the moments before the death are unforgettable, a final few seconds in which he holds 'the soldier who is going to die' in his gunsight, and watches him as he 'moves about in ways / his mother knows, habits of his'. And as a reader you are made complicit. Your eye too is pressed against the 'dial of glass'. Is the soldier being held there simply to perfect the aim? In part, yes. But there is an element of power play. The poet has already named the victim as 'the soldier who is going to die' and with that absolute mastery he holds the frame, like an angler playing out a fish before reeling it in.

*

Douglas was a Sherwood Ranger, part of the 8th Army. Their Normandy landing came on the back of a long and shattering Desert Campaign in North Africa. Their war was done, and many of them felt that France was someone else's battle to fight. They were spent in mind and body.

The death he got was not the one he prepared for. His most celebrated poems are full of the imagery of a parched, fly-blown, bleach-boned desert death. In *'Vergissmeinnicht'*, written in Tunisia the summer before he arrived in Normandy, Douglas revisits the scene of a recent desert battle and finds, 'sprawling in the sun', the body of an enemy soldier. Douglas had a cold eye. Ted Hughes compared him to Elizabeth Bishop for their 'inner detachment', and his work stands as one of the strongest poetic underlinings of

Chekhov's advice to 'write more coldly' if you want to move your reader. The eye of the poem lingers over the corpse of the enemy soldier, killed three weeks before by the narrator. As a reader you are forced to look at the 'swart flies' on his skin, 'the dust upon the paper eye / and the burst stomach like a cave'.

'If at times my eyes are lenses,' Douglas wrote – and his poems from the deserts of Libya and Tunisia vividly evoke its 'wide land-scape' and 'hard land', a plain scattered with the wreckage of warfare, the legions of strange, unburied dead, and the space and distances of the desert. It's an optical space, a space of demon projectiles and a hot dry wind like a knife. Danger is reckoned in thousands of metres; shells shred through the air with a noise like paper being torn.

Douglas was alive to the ghastly oddness of warfare in the Western Desert. 'It is tremendously illogical – to read about it cannot convey the impression of having walked through the looking glass which touches a man entering battle,' wrote the officer who carried cop-ies of *Alice in Wonderland* and *A Short Survey of Surrealism* in his kit. Beyond the surreal dead left waiting where they fell above ground – 'a man with no head / has a packet of chocolate and a souvenir of Tripoli' – there is the reality of life in the tank to consider. Douglas and the Sherwoods crossed the open vistas of desert inside cramped metal boxes, where the tank crew's horizon had been screwed down to a turret, and the stink of petrol blended with that of stale piss col-lected in empty shell cases. And the reality of death in the tank, too. Protected by armour plating, the tank soldier's situation might seem preferable to the infantryman's exposure, but tanks made targets, and direct hits caused awful carnage; the Shermans in particular were given the nickname 'Ronsons' (after the lighter), because of their tendency to 'brew up' and burn like furnaces.

★

Within hours of landing at Gold Beach, the veterans and old sweats of the Desert Campaign must have found themselves in another world, backed up in traffic jams made of their own invasion forces, stuck in tiny lanes as deep-cut as ravines, and never a vista of more than a stone's throw. This was a lush land of orchards and hamlets and hedges. The Sherwoods had entered a forest. The death that stalked Keith Douglas through the deserts of North Africa was a paper-eyed, reedy wraith of a death. What kind of death would stalk him here, among the apple trees and dairy farms?

As clear as the evidence is that Douglas did fear and anticipate his death in France, even perhaps willed it, it is hard to underestimate the shock of the Normandy bocage. What was the bocage like? Like the holloways of Dorset, but far deeper. Some hedges were so steep and enveloping that you couldn't see the sun as you walked down a sunken lane. Enemy soldiers would lean over hedges to drop grenades into passing tanks below, or fire an armour-penetrating round from a handheld Panzerfaust at close quarters. This was ambush country. Many tank commanders were killed in the first days of the battle, accustomed as they were to desert vistas, where trouble could be seen coming from a long way off. Here, they would put their heads out of their turrets and be picked off like targets at a fairground range.

In those first few days in France, the desert fighters barely knew how to navigate through Normandy, let alone conduct a battle here. Douglas died before he could write a single poem about the place, yet he is now inseparably linked with this landscape. He is a victim of the Battle of Normandy and he is buried in a cemetery here. This is his ground. Yet it wasn't his at all. Keith Douglas landed at Gold Beach on 6 June. He was killed three days later.

★

A ferry from Portsmouth on an evening in early June. We are retracing the journey – as closely as we can – of the Sherwood Rangers at this exact time of year. The sky is overcast and griddled silver, and we remember how important the weather was in the Channel seventy-odd years ago. There is barely any other resemblance between then and now: we are making the overnight crossing to Caen on a ferry the size of a small housing estate, complete with bars and shops and restaurants, and we are not sailing towards MG42s or navy guns or Panzers. Perhaps out of guilt or a desire to rough it at least a little and get a Longest Day vibe going, we've neglected to book a cabin. We wander the decks. It seems fairly deserted, until we follow a hubbub that leads us to the fluorescent blue light of a cavernous bar, which is packed. There's a small dance floor, scattered expectantly with the spangles of a mirrorball. We decide not to stick around to see who or what will be appearing, but slink off to find an empty canteen, where we eat miniature Port Salut and Roquefort and drink miniature bottles of vins de pays.

After putting it off for as long as we can, it's time to face our airline-style seats in one of the fore galleries. We soon realize we're complete amateurs at this lark: our fellow travellers have come prepared with eye masks, pillows, sleeping bags, earplugs, thermos flasks. A chapter of bikers appears to be making the crossing, and by the time we find our seats most have bedded down on any available surface. Stepping carefully in the dimmed light for fear of treading on somebody's motorcycle dreams, we prod what appears to be luggage in the space we've been allotted, only to realize it's a pupating biker. So, we settle in, all of us facing the rolled-down blinds blocking our view of the sea at night. The temperature drops steadily, until by about three o'clock it's as cold as a meat safe. At half-past four we go on deck to look at the sunrise over a steely Channel. Back in our cryogenic chamber, we recall a friend who'd asked about our larger project: 'Oh yes,' he'd said to us, 'I remember. Holidays on the backs of dead poets.' The occupant of the sleeping bag next to us turns in his sleep and expresses a long, pitch-shifting fart. Finally, just as fatigue gets the better of us and we begin to loll and nod, the lights flicker on, the blinds rattle open and there is the coast of France. We disembark and wander ashore, looking for the car-hire offices with a kind of bloodshot desperation. It's 0730 hours: this is going to be a long day.

★

Gold Beach today is a quieter stretch after the hustle of Arromanches a few miles to the west. We drive down a sandy track from Ver-sur-Mer on to a lovely littoral zone. After landing on the vast beach itself – and the tidal range is huge, much greater than we'd expected – Douglas and the Sherwoods would have crossed *le marais*, this marshy, indeterminate region that lies just inland. Walking westwards, we discover a place of makeshift, weathered, clapboard houses and photogenic sheds, rushy and overgrown and very birdy: there are yellowhammers and several kinds of warbler singing away in the tangled overgrowth. It's a truism that nature will find a way to heal and restore itself, but we both agree it takes a fairly big imaginative adjustment to square this ground with the decades' worth of collected sediment from war movies, photographs and eyewitness accounts. Only a few days ago we'd looked at wartime maps of this beach – TOP SECRET charts that declared they would NOT be carried in operational aircraft – that warned of UNDERWATER OBSTACLES 'HEDGEHOGS', urgent and criss-crossed with symbols like the most frantic diary entry. A huge invading army passed this way. On the beach, where KING sector once gave way to JIG sector, a lone turnstone runs along the high-water line, stopping at intervals to fuss and probe the sand. We imagine it minesweeping, but other than this the day is empty and sun-struck and stitched with birdsong.

★

We are outside the Musée de la Bataille de Tilly-sur-Seulles 1944 to meet the curator and local historian Stéphane Jacquet. He has agreed to be our guide, to take us to the place where Keith Douglas died. But first he offers to show us inside the museum, which is in the twelfth-century former chapel of Notre Dame du Val.

Our guide looks younger than us, almost as young as some of the soldiers pictured on the walls. He picks up a long cane to use as a pointer, and starts to talk us through what happened here in 1944. He is giving us background, context. He explains that the

Sherwood Rangers (Douglas's regiment) had a relatively painless start to their Normandy campaign. At Gold Beach, where they landed, Douglas's A Company found little resistance and moved inland towards Bayeux. They faced nothing on their beach to match the horrors experienced by American troops at Omaha Beach, west along the coast. Their progress inland was not as rapid as they hoped, but this was due to traffic jams, not fighting. The narrow, winding lanes and tight stone bridges of Normandy were not designed for a colossal invasion force.

Having taken Bayeux, the next target for Douglas and his men was Tilly-sur-Seulles. More specifically, a cluster of trees above the village of St Pierre, codenamed Point 103. By 9 June they were there, and had still encountered little more than occasional shell-fire. They managed to take Point 103, to defend and secure it. But all that was about to change. The Panzer Divisions, slow to move in response to the landings, were closing in.

The interview pauses as Stéphane looks towards the door of the chapel. The museum is full of relics, rusted pieces of Tiger Tanks, the large cracked engine of a Typhoon 'tank-buster' fighter plane. It is hard to get a clear view. Is there someone moving behind the map screens across the chapel? Stéphane calls out in French. He tells us he heard someone say something. 'I thought there was someone? Was there someone? I thought I heard someone? No one? The wind. A ghost.' He continues . . . So they counter-attack, in their mission to take back Bayeux . . . but he keeps glancing across to the other end of the chapel. He is sure there is somebody there.

★

We leave the museum and get into Stéphane's car. He is taking us to the end of Keith Douglas's life. We drive through Tilly-sur-Seulles and he points out the one house that escaped the flattening of 1944. We head east out of Tilly up a rising street into the adjoining village of St Pierre. On the way through St Pierre he points out a beautiful detached house in fine gardens overlooking the village: 'This is my house. I live here,' he says. It is a lovely house. We have a moment of house envy. We drive uphill out of St Pierre to Point 103. Stéphane parks the car on the brow of a hill on a track between two fields. Our coats billow like kites as we try to put them on. In the hours since we arrived at Caen ferry port there has been a storm brewing. In the next field is a wind farm. The sails are a blur. This will be a good day for the grid.

Stéphane gives us our bearings – that way towards Bayeux, that way towards Caen – then shows us how the Sherwoods, when they arrived here, parked a tank in the middle, just behind the hedges, then infantry around the outside to create a defensive square. The plan was to use Point 103 as a base to make an assault on St Pierre. The village was not heavily defended, but there were some German troops. Time was tight, because the Panzers were coming. Not just Panzers, but the more feared Tiger tanks, with their 88 mm guns. 'This is called Tiger Hill now,' says Stéphane.

We have to keep reminding ourselves that the vista we see, the agrarian plain swept by these gales, is a feature of the last few decades. When Douglas stepped out of his tank to look at this view, he saw no more than a few hundred yards in each direction. He saw orchards and hedges and walls and farm buildings.

★

Stéphane has spent years meeting veterans on pilgrimage to Tilly, among them Sherwood Rangers who fought with Douglas in the desert and here in Normandy. We ask him what they said about this poet in their ranks. 'They said he didn't really want to be here. Some of his friends said he wanted to die. He walked everywhere. He was out of his tank all the time. They told him not to do it. So some say they were not surprised he was killed quickly after his arrival in Normandy. In the desert, you could move on foot, because you could see enemy tanks miles away. In France, the enemy could be anywhere.'

Was he just putting himself at risk, or them too? 'Many of them loved him,' he says. 'But others didn't like him at all, because he was always going his own way. The commanders especially didn't like him, because he was difficult to manage.'

Another short ride in the car and we are there. This is where Douglas died. In a feature for BBC Radio in 2004, the poet Sean Street tracked down an archive interview with Douglas's friend John Bethell-Fox, a fellow tank commander in the same regiment, and Padre Leslie Skinner. In a clip from an interview with Bethell-Fox there is a striking account of that final recce he made with the poet:

> We went off and did whatever we had to do, which was to try and identify some enemy movement. The other side of a small stream we were fired at. We had to get back as quickly as we could and in the process he was slightly nicked by a bullet. That was the first time I saw him scared. Paralysed with fear. I'd never seen him like this before. It impressed itself upon my mind, naturally. But he knew with absolute certainty that the day had come.

As Douglas snapped out of his moment of stasis, he grabbed Bethell-Fox and they dived into the river, swimming downstream to fox the snipers. They climbed back on the bank 100 yards further down and scrambled up the hill to get back to their tanks. They then drove back up the hill to the rest of their squadron, to report back on the recce. What happened next was put clearly and simply by Bethell-Fox in his interview: 'We rejoined the other tanks on the hill, and he was killed as soon as he got out of his tank.'

★

On the morning of 9 June, Rev. Leslie Skinner was informed that a man had been killed. He knew Douglas well, but the report came without a name. He responded to the call and rushed up the track from Tiger Hill. Rev. Skinner was attached to the Sherwood

Rangers as a padre. He had spoken to Douglas the previous day in Normandy, and at length in England before D-Day, when Douglas had approached him after a communion service, wanting to talk. In an archive interview broadcast as part of Sean Street's documentary, Skinner recalled that he and Douglas had wandered in the New Forest for most of the night. They talked, he said 'about everything, but he kept coming back to his conviction that he wasn't going to see the war out'.

Stéphane leads us up the track. There is a hedge under some tall trees at the edge of the field. Under the hedge is a hollow, and this is where Douglas's body was temporarily buried by Rev. Skinner. The padre recorded that he faced occasional rifle fire as he dug the grave and stood over it to read the brief funeral rite.

Douglas was probably shelled from Fontenay-le-Pesnel, a village two kilometres south of here held by the 12th SS Hitlerjugend with the experienced troops of the Panzer-Lehr. In the short time they were here, before advancing on Tilly, the Sherwood Rangers were hit hard by this shelling. We ask Stéphane if Douglas's reportedly reckless 'walking about' could be seen from the German positions. Was his wandering the reason for the shelling? 'No,' he says, 'they were shelling the tanks, not the men.' But then he qualifies it. 'Perhaps they saw a man approaching the tanks?'

Stuart Hills, a survivor of the Sherwood Rangers' Normandy campaign, described Douglas as fatalistic. But why such fatalism in a man so young? According to Hills: 'He probably felt, "Well, I've done what I was born into this world to do, there's not much more I can do except to be a hero."'

Douglas's delighted batman, when Douglas disobeyed orders in North Africa to get himself back to fight on the Front, declared, 'You're shit or bust, you are,' and so he was. Hell-bent on putting himself in the way of risk, even of harm. If Douglas had played it safer, lasted just a few weeks longer, he might have survived the whole campaign.

★

The final stop on our Douglas tour. We park at the side of a busy road west of Tilly-sur-Seulles, opposite a Commonwealth War Cemetery. There are five such cemeteries around this small town, a testament to the heavy cost of the battle for Tilly. This one has a crop of German graves in the far corner. As Stéphane leads us down the rows of identical white stones it all seems guiltily familiar. It could be one of countless identical cemeteries across the north of France and Belgium, containing the dead of two world wars. The guilt comes from the familiarity, from the lack of shock we feel, even as we walk along the rows and read out the ages on the headstones : '19, 22, 24, 18 . . .'

It's been a long day following the last days of this soldier-poet. We have held his poems in the highest regard since first encountering them in our teens, and his age when he died became a benchmark in our own lives. In our early twenties, not confident enough to own the title 'poet', but writing and reading voraciously, two deaths of poets loomed particularly large – Keith Douglas at twenty four, and Keats at twenty-five. In particular, Douglas, as the younger of the two, seemed to stand as an unmatchable example. Here was a poet consciously completing his body of work in his early twenties, tying things up. Did he share John Berryman's anxiety about having 'done enough' for his work to survive him? Berryman had the advantage of another four decades. W. H. Auden stressed that as a poet you should act your age. 'One might ask,' he said in a *Paris Review* interview, '"What should I write at the age of sixty-four?", but never "What should I write in 1940?"'

How does that work for Keith Douglas? In 1940 he writes like a young man, full of longing, to his Oxford lover Yingcheng: 'Today, Cheng, I touched your face / with two fingers, as a gesture of love, / for I can never prove enough / by sight or sense your strange grace'. But that same poem contains the lines 'today I touched a mask stretched on the stone- // hard face of death.' And underneath that verse in his published *Collected Poems* is the ascription 'Royal Military College, Sandhurst, 1940'. In the four years that followed, Douglas was to witness the horrors of war, to kill and to know that he would be killed. How could he not be both a man of his age and also a man of his time? What should I write in 1942 or 1943 was an essential question for him, and the answer was to write as dispassionately as his powers would allow him to, to make the reader see and do what he had seen and done.

We cannot help but wonder about the missing Keith Douglas poems. We reach his grave and stand in front of it in silence. We wonder if this poet – who had honed his craft on battlefields – had some lines in his head about the wild stretch of Gold Beach or the sudden shock of landscape folding into pocket squares of orchards, pastures, tree-lined tunnels.

On the stone it reads: 'Captain K. C. Douglas, 2nd Derbyshire Yeomanry'. The second line is indistinct. We lean in to try to read it. The gales that have been cutting across these fields all day have worn the stone. But we can still make it out: it describes him as 'Poet, Artist' and then there is a quotation from Philippians 4:8, plus the line 'these things he loved, he died in their defence'. What are these things? The bible passage lists: 'whatsoever things are true, whatsoever things are honest, whatsoever things are just, whatsoever things are pure, whatsoever things are lovely, whatsoever things are of good report . . .'

As we are about to leave the graveside, we notice that the dates along this whole row of stones match up – 9 June, 10 June, 11 June. We turn to walk away and there's a sudden awkward moment as we realize this is the end of our tour with Stéphane and we haven't paid him. We agreed a fee of fifty euros for this personal tour and had forgotten all about it. We make apologies and fumble for our wallets, then the camera pulls back and it's as if we are watching a wide-shot of ourselves standing in a war cemetery, handing folded banknotes across the grave of Keith Douglas. Stéphane's skin creeps as much as ours. He says, 'Later, in the car park is fine', as we stuff the notes back in our pockets.

★

One last question for our guide: where can a visitor see some true bocage these days, to understand what it was like? No chance. There are efforts to preserve a small part of it miles to the west, but the terrain encountered by the Sherwood Rangers is no more. The former 'Peasants' Forest' and its network of woodstock and apple orchards is in decline, and it's a disappointment to discover that agribusiness and a policy of land *remembrement* has meant the hard-pressed open field has gained ground in the decades since the war, while miles and miles of hedge banks have been flattened. This part of Normandy is a vista now. Those North African Campaign veterans fighting their way south from Gold Beach seventy years ago would have felt at home here. This was their kind of battlefield. What was the bocage has become a kind of desert.

This means we have time to go and see the Bayeux Tapestry. It feels initially like an aside, a 'may as well while we're here' sidetrack, before the hire car has to be returned and the Portsmouth ferry caught. The big historical rhyme between the two battles – 1066 and 1944 – is widely known; the images of the contraption-like comet or the arrow lodged in the King's eye are stock footage in our collective memory. But when we form up in a long line to file through the dark in an orderly shuffle along the Tapestry's illuminated seventy metres, the bright fields and lanes of Normandy come rebounding back on us; it's like looking through a camera obscura that translates landscape into wool and embroidery. The cavalry of William and Harold, the camped soldiers in their fish-scale mail, the ships that cross and re-cross the threadbare sea of nine centuries ago . . . We see it all again for the first time, at a slow walking pace, in detail. Woodsmen hack down trees to build the invasion fleet. The dismembered dead lie about the battlefield. Looters strip their unburied bodies.

Back at Caen ferry port we find a café. As we order coffee the storm that's been gathering all day bursts with astonishing force. The sound alone rules out conversation, so we watch until the deluge swells the awning above us and we have to take refuge indoors. This tempest feels necessary, cleansing. Retracing Douglas's last steps was fascinating, but utterly nauseating too. Where does bravery become bravado, recklessness shade into a death wish? We think of the cold eye behind his poems, on our backs as we walked the same paths and tracks, twice his age and worlds apart. Our time has run out. We pick up our bags and sprint for the boat. We are drenched in seconds, but it feels like an expiation.

★

Frank O'Hara seems to have suffered one of the more banal deaths of the poets. Retailing the details to people who don't know what happened is likely to lead to surprised looks, open mouths, and yes, even an edge of mirth. You're kidding? He was run over by a beach buggy? The bare facts are that Frank O'Hara left his Manhattan office at the Museum of Modern Art one Friday afternoon in July 1966 to spend the hot weekend on Fire Island, staying with friends. Sometime in the early hours of Sunday he was hit by a beach buggy, having been stranded on the beach along with the other passengers of a taxi that had thrown a tyre. O'Hara wasn't killed outright. He was transferred to a hospital on Long Island, but by Monday evening he succumbed to his injuries. He was forty years old.

Does the vehicle involved in a fatal accident colour the death? We remember how Roland Barthes was struck by a laundry truck in a Parisian street. Beach buggy invites a kind of category error. Buggies are seen at golf courses. Babies ride in them, as did the Banana Splits over on the opposite coast in California. Buggy sounds harmless and we associate it with harmless fun. That is, until we consider how all along the sandy beaches and inlets and spits of the East Coast a culture of water taxiing and sand ferrying had sprung up. The vehicles involved – beach buggies – were in fact anything from old Model Ts to army-surplus jeeps to Land Rovers. The buggy that hit O'Hara that night on Fire Island was

a metal jeep, travelling at speed. The speed itself was disputed by
both driver and witnesses, but the mass and momentum involved
were enough to leave O'Hara's body swollen and broken, his skin
dark and his liver ruptured.

★

In *Dime-Store Alchemy* the poet Charles Simic looks for the artist
Joseph Cornell, haunter of mid-century Manhattan's junk shops
and used book stores, and in doing so he navigates a secret city
untouched by the map makers:

> On the street again, the man in the white suit turning the
> corner could be the ghost of the dead poet Frank O'Hara.

Plenty of other writers ran into O'Hara this way, only in life.
Like this: 'I liked the way he walked. Once I saw him going up
Second Avenue. An angel with sneakers.' Or this: 'I remember the
first time I met Frank O'Hara. He was walking down Second
Avenue. It was a cool early spring evening but he was wearing
only a white shirt with the sleeves rolled up to his elbows. And
blue jeans. And moccasins. I remember that he seemed very sissy
to me. Very theatrical. Decadent. I remember that I liked him
instantly.'

Up and down the avenues, running into Frank O'Hara in the
street seemed to leave an impression, and also seems the most
appropriate means of encountering this poet. Crosstown traffic.
A buffeting intersection wind. The surprises a city like New York
can throw up, the sudden shifts in scale and tempo as you walk its
sidewalks and rub shoulders with its crowds. A headline glimpsed
while passing a news stand. A pause for a papaya juice. 'I can't even
enjoy a blade of grass unless I know there's a subway handy, or a
record store or some other sign that people do not totally regret
life,' he once wrote.

★

We decide to start out from MoMA and the galleries on the fourth floor. Standing in front of Jackson Pollock's *Full Fathom Five* feels like a good fixed point of departure, a place to weigh anchor that links O'Hara to the Manhattan art world. We also take a look at Frank O'Hara's Papers in MoMA's archives. O'Hara worked here for a long time, from the early 1950s, mainly organizing exhibitions. He was good at it. We look at the exhibition catalogue for the sculptor Reuben Nakian (whose work was on display when O'Hara died), and it's clear that enormous knowledge, curatorial skill and energy were being brought to bear. For all the martinis and gossip and parties, there he is, in the memos and minutes: Mr O'Hara, present, hardly missing a meeting.

Outside, we enter the boom and buzz and fall to walking vaguely in O'Hara's footsteps, the trails left behind in his poems. The larger structure of his city endures – Second Avenue, Times Square – and the cabs are still 'hum colored', but much of the detail is unrecognizable, or obliterated. Where did the soon-to-be-torn-down Manhattan Storage Warehouse actually stand? Downtown is more pungent; it smells like cities used to smell, even how we imagine they smelled: manholes, hot dogs, rain on warm sidewalks. We can point to the spot where the 5 Spot Club must have opened its doors for business on the Bowery, where Billie Holiday sang without a cabaret card for no money; a cavalcade of jazz greats passed through this patch of urban park and O'Hara held his breath. This must be the site of the original Ziegfeld Theater, on the corner of 54th Street. 515 Madison Avenue – O'Hara's 'door to heaven' – is still the DuMont Building, famous for its early broadcasting antennae, long outgrown and interfered with by the surrounding skyscrapers. But where is the Olivetti typewriter store that O'Hara, taking his lunchbreak walks from MoMA, is supposed to have stopped off in to bash out the lyrics that became *Lunch Poems*, at least according to that book's spoofy anti-blurb? Down among the countless chain pharmacies and vitamin stores, in the noonday gloom of street level, we realize how much of his mid-century, midtown New York has gone, and how neon in daylight isn't always a great pleasure.

★

We buy day-return tickets for the Long Island Railroad at Penn Station, bound for Fire Island. After the streets and avenues of Manhattan, New York's outlying regions feel convoluted and fractal. We're going off grid. Getting to the edge of the ocean proper is a complicated affair. Albert Camus once heard a tugboat in his insomnia and realized 'this desert of iron and cement is an island', but leaving the insular city leads to many other islands whose names have slipped their geography, names we all know: Ellis, Coney, Riker's, Staten. We cross the East River, passing through Brooklyn and Queens, heading eastwards through Long Island, separated from the mainland by Long Island Sound. To the south, the coast feels like land's end, but the Atlantic Ocean is still a step away from us, because what we're really looking over is the Great South Bay.

Out there is one final ribbon of North America, a long spit of land, the thirty-two-mile barrier of Fire Island. We change at Babylon. The day feels overcast and deserted, and we begin to wonder whether we'll reach our destination and find ourselves alone, like overenthusiastic day-trippers everywhere. We're so anxious at this stage that we hear ourselves airing our anxieties, introducing them into any conversation or exchange. 'Hello, we're trying to get to Fire Island. Is there a train from here? We've come all the way from England. Are we too early?' The guy in the ticket booth at Babylon waves away our misgivings: he thinks it will be rocking down there. This is the beginning of the Memorial Day weekend, traditionally the start of summer here. We should take a cab from outside the station. By the time we reach Sayville, where we hope a ferry will take us across the Bay, it has started to rain.

The hostelry at the Sayville Ferry dockside is indeed rocking. The bar is two or three deep with day-trippers getting drinks in before the next sailing, and in its cosy, low-ceilinged, wood-panelled way it feels maritime. Sayville is oysters and clams and wireless telegraphy, almost the very edge of the continent. This could be The Spouter Inn in *Moby-Dick*, and even though we're only crossing to Fire Island, rather than going away to sea, we're all about to take to the waves and there's an excited, boozy camaraderie in the air. Would O'Hara have waited here forty-odd summers ago with a martini, reading a slim volume of Pierre Reverdy? No. We find out later that O'Hara drove out from New York that Friday afternoon with three friends and crossed to the island in a private boat. But we're glad we don't know that yet. Fire Island, in particular Cherry Grove and The Pines (where we're heading), is famous as an LGBT resort, a relaxed escape from the city, though things have probably changed a great deal since O'Hara visited. Among the posters pinned to one wall, we notice an advert for something called Boy Butter ('It'll open you up for the summer'). The rain is beginning to pelt down hard against the windows and awnings. Thoughts turn to our inadequate waterproofing.

★

'I remember one very cold and black night on the beach alone with Frank O'Hara. He ran into the ocean naked and it scared me to death,' poet and artist Joe Brainard once wrote. O'Hara knew the sea. Before New York and MoMA and the Cedar Tavern and his friendships with the painters and sculptors and composers, before 'I do this, I do that' and Personism and the poets John Ashbery and Kenneth Koch and James Schuyler and the loose, constellating label 'New York Poets', before coldwater flats and lofts on Broadway and parties, Francis Russell O'Hara from Irish-Catholic small-town Massachusetts, conservatoire-trained classical pianist, had enlisted in the US Navy during the final year of the Second World War. He saw active service on a destroyer in the Pacific, which took him all the way to the Bay of Tokyo, but before that, in Key West, he'd been inducted into the world of echo location at Navy Sonar School. He recalled his sonar instructor years later: 'When you see the button you press it. You must determine the target by sighting along this line and squeezing like on an orange. There are several million Germans in the world and more Japanese who are utter horrors: we shall plant them, not like dragon's teeth but like Parma violets. You get right about center by listening for the mean tone, that's right, sweep back and forth across the target and determine its center by your hearing, you've had musical training, haven't you? I just love the Symphonie Espagnole. Milstein, of course. That's right, fire.'

★

Boarding the ferry to Fire Island, we notice many of our travelling companions are couples and that quite a few are holding hands. As the boat's engine kicks in and we pull away from the land, the plural pronoun buckles and groans as we both catch each other's glance and have exactly the same thought, at the same time: we are undercover straights, voyaging to a gay haven. Should we pretend to be a couple? We must seem convincing enough.

Our ferry slaps through the whitecaps of Great South Bay in squally conditions. The crossing takes just long enough for the colour to drain from our faces and for us both to regret our second beers, but there is no chundering over the gunwale. Somebody says the Bay is a lot cleaner since Hurricane Sandy made landfall just a few months ago. The septic tanks of Long Island have created a vast algal lagoon over time, which the storm surge seems to have broken up. Thinking of clams, we return to our hard plastic seats, packed in with the bright Gore-Tex and oilskins of our fellow passengers, sharing the available space with the boxes and crates of motley supplies you see on island ferries everywhere. The city of only a few hours ago has now completely dissolved.

There's a good story that begins with O'Hara making a ferry crossing. He is supposed to have written 'Poem' on one bound for

Staten Island in 1962 (O'Hara wrote dozens of 'Poem's, so you usually go on the first line: this is the one that begins with the memorable 'Lana Turner has collapsed!'). We know this because he was on his way to give a poetry reading (slightly inexplicably) with Robert Lowell at Wagner College. The two must have cut very different figures on the podium that night, and it can't have helped the occasion that O'Hara decided to announce his ferry poem, freshly riffed from a headline in the *New York Post*, and very hot off the press itself, to the audience. As veterans of many poetry readings ourselves (and as Seamus Heaney's widow Marie has famously remarked, there is no such thing as a short one), we speculate on the decorum of such events. 'And now I would like to read something longer . . . ' is probably the most chilling phrase encountered, though 'And now I would like to read a new poem . . . ' might run it a close second, depending on who's reading. Declaring your new poem was written on the way to the gig takes real chutzpah, indeed, takes a Frank O'Hara. Lowell wasn't impressed. Introducing his half of the evening (which was starting late because O'Hara had overrun), he offered a backhanded apology to the audience: he was very sorry for not having any poems composed in haste. It's an interesting fault line in American letters to mull over (and a helpful distraction from seasickness), though Elizabeth Bishop was more of a fan, writing to Lowell years later after hearing the news of O'Hara's death, 'I was sorry to see about Frank O'Hara in TIME – I liked him a lot the 2 times I saw him, even if he was drunk and a bit disorderly . . .'

★

Fire Island is barely smouldering. The chilly rain has long set in, and grey, state-sized sheets of cloud snuff out our hopes of a lift in the weather anytime soon. The sombre day has put a dampener on the little clutch of shops, cafés and bars near the ferry landing and marina; the drag-queen parade and disco inferno feel a long way off.

Perhaps the weather helps take us back in time, though. We know this place was a little quieter back when O'Hara visited. It also makes things feel more elemental, as we head towards the Atlantic oceanfront of the island, following the slippery board-walks over the sand, pine straw and scrub, and soon find ourselves in a warren of pathways, which all seem to lead to secluded wooden cabins. Though 'cabin' doesn't feel adequate.

The poet W. H. Auden had shared ownership of a tarpaper shack near here in the 1940s (in which he kept, pinned to the wall, an OS map of Alston Moor in the English Pennines, his limestone landscape). 'Shack' doesn't cut it, either.

This feels like serious real estate, the wooden retreat in the dunes meets architectural Modernism, though many of the properties are showing signs of Hurricane Sandy's visit. Notices on fences and gateposts everywhere declare: 'This Structure Is Unsafe and Its Occupancy Has Been Prohibited by the Code Enforcement Official', next to recent, defiant flyers picturing well-structured, naked men: 'Broadway Bares: Fire Island Calendar Girl'. The bar-rier strip lost more than half of its beaches and dunes as Sandy reminded everybody that this whole island is a map-defying work in progress, evolving, breaching, forming new inlets or sealing up older ones.

Through the rain, between the shacks, along the boardwalks, we snake our way towards the point where Frank O'Hara took his final steps. There are plenty of young couples passing us, some carrying bags of food or bottles of wine. The whole commu-nity feels like it's on holiday, and we suppose it must be. Most of these men seem well-off, well-dressed, slim and good-looking. But not all. As we traipse along the dockside, we pass a couple in their forties. They are holding hands, but walking slowly and in silence. They seem out-of-sync with the vitality and ebullience so evident here. As we pass them, they give us what we take to be sympathetic glances, as we are also past our prime. This doesn't feel like a place for the old, nor even the recently young.

That couple looked dispirited because, we guessed, Fire Island
Pines no longer belonged to them. How would the night pan out
for them? Would they end up at the bar-disco, as O'Hara did on
his last night? Would they feel – as do many middle-aged men
on forays to clubland – like spectators at someone else's party?
Was that a turning point for the poet, in the first summer of his
mid-life?

Many of his friends said they expected him to pre-decease
them. At Frank's funeral, his former lover Larry Rivers described
the death he had expected for the poet: 'a romantic death brought
about by too much sex, by unhappy love affairs, by writing too
many emotional poems, too many music and dance concerts, just
too much living.' But no one predicted the death he met here.

★

And then here it is, Crown Walk, Fire Island Pines, leading down
to the ocean and its huge rollers. It happened somewhere here,
although it's impossible to say exactly where. X can't mark the
spot in the sand, and we realize now how this has all been about
the approach, the getting here, the distance travelled from the city
to this edge. The beach is long and straight and forlorn, flensed
with dark tyre tracks.

Somewhere here, it happened. We compare this scene to our
earliest impressions of O'Hara's death from what scant details were
available (beach buggy, run over): a bright red beach ball with a
Kodachrome blue sea, a yacht from a boy's birthday card, polka-
dot bikinis and camp Sixties swimming trunks. Brad Gooch's
biography adjusted all of that. In *City Poet* Gooch describes how
it happened at night, in a moonless, island dark. O'Hara had been
drinking with friends and was sharing a water taxi heading east
to where he was staying. The taxi broke down. The passengers
milled about, waiting while another was called. For some reason
O'Hara seemed to break off from the group and stray away from
the landward side of the taxi towards the ocean – and into the

path of a buggy being driven by a twenty-three-year old seasonal odd-job man. This was how the poet received his mortal wound.

There's nothing else to see – what did we expect? – and after splicing together our old conjectures with what hard facts there are and today's desolate scene for a little while longer, we realize we're both soaked through and cold, and maybe it's time to find somewhere out of the rain.

★

The bar by the marina, with its deserted dancefloor and mirrorball (its orbiting glitter making the place seem even emptier), turns out to be one of the friendliest we'll drink in during this visit to America. One of the young men tending to the drinks tells us there's a special offer on white wine and pours us two huge glasses. We soon forget we're shivering. We ask him about Frank O'Hara. No, he doesn't think he comes in here. It will get busier later.

On the night he was drinking hereabouts, O'Hara didn't know he was going to die, that he would never walk along a Manhattan sidewalk again, admire somebody's new painting or smoke a cigarette. He didn't know his last poem was already written and would be found along with many others, unpublished, in his Broadway apartment, or that the prints and drawings in his office would soon be placed in storage, the letters chasing him for permissions finally answered by distraught colleagues. He'd thought about ageing, death and posterity – in an autobiographical fragment from several years before, he'd written: 'Nevertheless I am aware that I am now six years older than Keats when he died and four years younger than Byron in the same situation' – but these anxious comparisons with the Big Anthology in the Sky are pretty common among poets. It was a summer night, and maybe he'd had too much to drink and it was time to call a halt. Being here, though, has us wondering about why he wandered into harm's way down on that beach. Once, on film, he'd said:

'Don't be bored, don't be lazy, don't be trivial and don't be proud. The slightest loss of attention leads to death.' Was it a slip, a loss of focus, fatal in the writer who went on his nerve and had always engaged nimbly with happenstance and the accidental? Or was it the opposite of this? Looking out into the dark ocean, was his imagination sonar-sweeping beyond the curve of the earth, picking up an echo towards dawn two thousand miles away, and the O'Haras of Ireland? Later, we'll ruin what lyricism there might be here with a map and a ruler. Looking straight out to sea from this shoreline, the first place a viewer's gaze would be likely to make landfall is, in fact, the coast of Brazil.

The topographies of Frank O'Hara's and Keith Douglas's final journeys are a chiasmus. One moves from the deep-cut, high-walled streets of Manhattan, where he knows how to live, to the endless vista of the Atlantic, where he dies. The other moves from the endless vista of the desert, where he knows how to fight, to the deep-cut, high-walled lanes of the bocage, where he dies. Both died too young. Both left behind a smaller body of work than their many admirers would wish for. Although it's impossible to read their thoughts in those final days, both seemed, to some extent, to anticipate their trajectory, to be gathering to a point. And in both cases questions have been raised about whether and to what extent they courted death.

The bar is beginning to fill up a little. At some significant moment the dance music we had hardly noticed pulsing in the background is cranked to a rib-registering volume; seeming to take this as their cue, the barmen reach around as one and pull their T-shirts over their heads, revealing the torsos of Apollo. Suddenly everything is telling us: you must join a gym. Happy hour has begun, but we can see the Sayville Ferry shuddering into the dock outside, and it's time to head back, from island to island, to the distant island city.

The Dugout

It is hard to avoid the conclusion that David Jones, like Keith Douglas, died the wrong death, or at least that he died in the wrong place. Instead of a heap of bleached bones in the desert, Douglas ended up in a rain-soaked uniform under a hedge in Normandy. For Jones, another poet forged in combat, his place of death was a bed in the Calvary Nursing Home of the Little Company of Mary in Harrow on the outskirts of London. He was seventy-eight years old, and had been struggling for several years with illnesses of old age. But his death had been a long time coming.

The place of his long dying was what he called his dugout, a single-room in a shared house, where he lived and worked for more than two decades. At various points the location of his dugout changed, but its layout and accoutrements remained constant. He rarely ventured out, but he welcomed visitors, and they were struck by the claustrophobic intensity of his room, dedicated to the service of his work. The bed and desk were a patchwork of poem drafts, letters, paintings, books and drawings. He was by all accounts fine company, chain-smoking his way through conversations on his passions: history, politics, war, painting, myth.

To say that his death had been a long time coming is not to say he wished it upon himself, nor that he lacked a passion for the here and now. He was painting and writing even in his final months. His preparedness for death was akin to that of the nuns who nursed him. Calling on Jones in Harrow was not unlike visiting a monk. A Catholic convert from his mid-twenties, Jones regarded his work as a vocation and a sacrament. When he died, he left a collection of drawings, watercolour paintings and inscriptions – many of which he kept in his dugout, and did not try to sell – plus four books of poetry.

His final illness came in the autumn of 1974, a turbulent year of two British general elections and a heightening of the IRA's terrorist campaign in England. To Jones, steeped as he was in the history and myth of the Matter of Britain, it must have felt like the end of days. Except that Jones had already lived through the end of days. He died on 28 October, but all the coordinates of his death were set sixty years before in the place he didn't die: Mametz Wood on the Somme.

★

A remembered visit to Mametz Wood, at the end of a long day of travels, interviews and encounters in northern France for a radio programme on the poets of the First World War. Jones has had barely a mention all day, despite the fact that *In Parenthesis*, his account of serving as a private soldier on the Somme, is one of the most admired of all war poems, at least by other poets. Jones is difficult, or rather, his work is difficult. He was a high Modernist. He believed that the job of a poet was 'to make a shape out of the very things of which one is oneself made'. In Jones's case, as an Anglo-Welsh art school graduate and self-educated literary and history scholar, this meant everything from the Arthurian myth cycle through Greek and Roman military history and the ancient Welsh tales of *The Mabinogion* to more personal 'things', such as his grandfather's trade as a shipbuilder on the Thames, and his own service as a private soldier in the Royal Welsh Fusiliers on the Somme. Everything was poured into huge, intricately structured, capacious epic poems with momentous titles like *In Parenthesis* and *The Anathemata*.

On our way back to the hotel at the end of the recording day, we chance upon a sign for the village of Mametz. The car is full of people who want to get back to their rooms, to call home, to get changed or get a drink. But when will we next be this close to Mametz Wood? We decide to make a detour. This will not take long. Ten minutes max. We follow the signs out of the village. We are heading further and further from our route. At the end of a tight lane we find it, nestling between ploughed fields, ringed by low wooden fences with signs saying this is private land.

We get out and climb the gate. There is no point in coming here without entering the wood. It is lit like a film set. Late afternoon sun breaks on the trees and picks out particular clumps of brush and thorn for spotlit attention. A bird scutters in the dry leaves. The details are chillingly close to Jones's description: 'you find yourself alone in a denseness of hazel-brush and body-high bramble'. And it is only a small step to picture what follows: 'You tug at rusted pin – it gives unexpectedly and your fingers pressed to released flange. You loose the thing into the underbrush.' No one says a word. We have been on battlefields all day, but this is different, out of bounds, barely marked and fenced off.

A hundred yards into the wood we catch a flash of scarlet among the dead leaves. It is a wreath of poppies, and the card with it tells us that an old man – a survivor of the battle – was buried here according to his wishes just a year before. We stand for a few minutes in silence, among the rowan and the hazel, trying to picture what David Jones saw, what so shocked Robert Graves that he described it as 'a certain cure for lust of blood'. What would make a man want to be buried here, all these decades later? Did he believe that this was his designated death-place, that he somehow dodged his bullet, when so many of his friends took theirs? This was the site of one of the Somme's bloodiest, costliest battles. The autumn sky is darkening. In more than one way, we have a sudden conviction that we shouldn't be here.

★

When T. S. Eliot first saw the manuscript of *In Parenthesis* he declared himself 'deeply moved'. More than that, he wrote that he regarded it as 'a work of genius'. Like many a work of genius, it was a long time coming. It was over twenty years between Jones's survival of the Battle of Mametz Wood and the publication of this richly poetic account of it.

It is one long poem, broken into chapters, written in a form of prose poetry. It describes, simultaneously, the everyday experience of a private soldier on the Western Front, plus a parallel track of mythic and historic soldiery. It follows an Everyman squaddie, a private like Jones himself, not the officer classes from which most of our war poets emerged. It begins with training and drilling in England and culminates in the horror of battle itself. At each moment, even when battle is at full pitch, the narrative is not just horizontal – the progress of battle, the journey of our soldier anti-hero – but vertical, thick with mythic resonance and a sense of the weight of history at the soldier's back:

> LoweryouloweryouprizeMariaHunt, an' gammy fingered upland Gamalin – down cantcher – low – hands away me ducky – down on hands on hands down and flattened belly and face pressed and curroodle mother earth
> she's kind:
> Pray her hide you in her deeps
> she's only refuge against
> this ferocious pursuer
> terribly questing.
> Maiden of the digged places
>   let our cry come unto thee.
> *Mam*, moder, mother of me
> Mother of Christ under the tree
> reduce our dimensional vulnerability to the minimum –
> cover the spines of us
> let us creep back dark-bellied where he can't see

don't let it.
There, there, it can't, won't hurt – nothing
shall harm my beautiful.

In Parenthesis is not just multi-layered, it's poly-vocal too. Among the David Jones riches in the BBC archive is a Fifties dramatization of the poem, produced by the brilliant Douglas Cleverdon. As well as producing Dylan Thomas's *Under Milk Wood*, Cleverdon's BBC career included work with Ted Hughes, Stevie Smith and Sylvia Plath. For *In Parenthesis* he assembled a top-drawer cast, including Richard Burton and Dylan Thomas. Once you have heard Richard Burton reading the passage beginning '*Mam*, moder . . .' it is very hard to hear any other voice in your head as you read it.

That power of a voice to colour words as permanently as registrar's ink is there in Jones's own voice. The BBC archive contains several recordings of the poet, in that fruitful period in the Forties and Fifties working with Cleverdon. Like many dead poets, he is revivified by recordings of his voice in a way that photographs can never achieve. Jones, the working-class son of Anglo-Welsh parents in London, speaks his poems with a low, rhythmic growl, a smoker's gravel. But the big surprise is his accent, a soft cockney now as obsolete as the cut-glass, post-war, pukka tones of Robert Graves. Press *play* and you hear passages from *The Anathemata* rhythmically intoned in an accent straight out of an Ealing comedy.

★

The poet Kathleen Raine visited Jones's 'dugout' in Harrow, and described him as a kind of ascetic, increasingly withdrawn from the world into a small room filled only with his own sacramental objects, charged with meaning: 'his mother's silver teaspoon, a glass chalice in which he arranged the flowers he painted, a small knife, a slender pair of scissors, a photograph of the little dog Laika, sent up by the Russians into space'.

Another friend, Nest Cleverdon (wife of radio producer Douglas), described just how other-worldly Jones became in later years, and how his friends supported him in that withdrawal: 'Somehow we all took for granted that we would trail to Bond Street to buy special string vests, drive him to have his hair cut, chase up the art galleries who had cheated him.' She recalls offering to buy him a radio, which Jones declined with the words, 'I don't want a bloody machine.'

★

In Parenthesis is not the catchiest title for a war poem, nor indeed for any poem. But as soon as Jones gives the reason, no other title will do. In the introduction, he explains that he chose it because 'for us amateur soldiers (and especially for the writer, who was not only amateur, but grotesquely incompetent, a knocker-over of piles, a parade's despair) the war itself was a parenthesis – how glad we thought we were to step outside its brackets at the end of '18 – and also because our curious type of existence here is altogether in parenthesis.'

Perfect though it is as a title for the book, it belies most survivors' experiences of fighting on the Western Front, including that of Jones himself. He hints at this in the phrase 'how glad we *thought we were* . . .' For Jones, as for many, stepping out of those parentheses was far from the end of turmoil and suffering. In 1943 he produced a beautiful work in pencil, ink and watercolour under the title *Map of Themes in the Artist's Mind*. Like his famous painted inscriptions of sacred texts, this 'map' uses every square inch of the paper, with words snaking up the margins and straying on to the mount paper behind. Seen from a distance, it is a crazed pattern of headlines, subtitles, faint marginalia and multiple arrows establishing connections between all these elements. Step closer and you see, bang in the middle, FRENCH & GERMAN ROMANCE, with the thickest arrow heading down to the left where we meet MALORY, the fifteenth-century writer who brought the Arthurian cycle into English. GREECE & ROME sit above MADONNA WORSHIP and PROVENCAL COURTS OF LOVE in the top right, and PREHISTORIC BRITAIN to the top left, feeding down into CORNWALL and WALES.

At first glance this map makes sense, as these are the founding myths and places for Jones's epic *The Anathemata,* his major project at the time. But on reflection, the map is perhaps better seen as a mask to conceal the artist, or an inventory of what the artist *wanted* his mind to contain. There is no mention of Mametz Wood or the First World War. Late in life, he admitted that those experiences were still very much part of the map of his mind: 'The memory of it is like a disease,' he said, before admitting that he still thought about it more than anything else.

★

For years after side-stepping death in Mametz Wood, Jones seemed to slip back into his former life. He returned to Camberwell Art School, then to Westminster School of Art. In the early Twenties he worked with the sculptor Eric Gill in Ditchling, Surrey, and later at Capel-y-ffin on the Welsh borders. He was even, briefly, engaged to one of Gill's daughters. But by the late 1920s there were signs that his past was catching up with him and he returned to live with his parents at Brockley, still working on his paintings and engravings. In 1947 Jones suffered a catastrophic nervous breakdown. He had survived a previous collapse in 1933, but this time he needed intensive psychiatric care and was moved to Harrow to work with Dr Bill Stevenson, based at the Bowden House Clinic there.

It is a cold October morning and we are walking through Harrow with Jonathan Barker – formerly of the British Council's Literature Department and a longtime Jones fan – and Vivian Wright, a local who has mapped the details of Jones's years in this north-west London suburb. We knew about Jones's history in Harrow. Much of his work as a writer and artist was done here. But until we visited we didn't realize there are two Harrows. When we met Jonathan and Vivian outside the tube station, we were standing in the Harrow we associated with Jones – commuter-belt London, a typical outlying suburb with its Betjemanesque bedsits and leafy avenues.

But now we are at the site of Northwick Lodge, his first London 'dugout'. And it's not what we imagined at all. This was a lodging house for masters at Harrow School, and it was very much a part of Harrow-on-the-Hill, with expansive views over the Home Counties below. This is the 'other' Harrow. It has the feel of a village, and a very particular kind of village at that. This is one of England's most famous public schools, alma mater of prime ministers, industrialists, judges and eminent writers like Lord Byron. But Jones was no Byron. He was a working-class Londoner whose war poetry is marked out from the ranks of Owen, Sassoon and Graves by the fact that its author was a private soldier. For this shy autodidact, Northwick Lodge was a foothold in another world. He lived here for two decades in the convivial company of the schoolmasters who were his fellow-lodgers.

On the walk up, we passed shop windows with displays of straw boaters and school gowns. We also ran into a few boys wearing them. It all feels like a dugout in a larger sense than Jones had in mind, a place in which a version of Englishness has retreated to fortified positions and can still be sampled in highly concentrated doses. This feels like an escape in itself, a flight from modern London. Jones's withdrawal into his dugout, forswearing even a radio, was a retreat within a retreat.

One of the many school entrances we passed leads to the Fourth Form Classroom, a rich and gloomy wood-panelled room textured with the carved names of old boys. It's so archaic that it was used as the location for Professor Flitwick's Magical Charms Class in the screen version of Hogwarts. One of the names is Byron's, and Harrow might be where he first learned to love scratching and gouging his name. As we've discovered, Byron was to become a bit of a fiend for tagging. Such was Byron's fame that the classroom walls bear several fake signatures, carved by later boys in adulation. If you want to run your finger round the curves of Byron's true 'B' it takes an expert guide to point it out, high on a wall between PAXTON and BROWNE.

★

The psychiatric treatment David Jones received in Harrow was subtle and effective. He later praised the work of Dr Stevenson and his team, recognizing that their job was not simply to make him well, but to equip him to continue with his work. Vivian pulls a sheet of paper from her bag and reads from a letter Jones wrote in 1947: 'I have to try and paint now. I paint trees from my window. It's part of the curative game, as, in their judgement, I've now reached a period when I must paint, because they maintain that my major conflict displays itself in relation to painting and it must be fought out in that terrain – that's not the whole story – but a very important part of it, whatever the inclinations, results, difficulties, feelings.'

When you look at Jones's paintings from his decades in Harrow, many seem to begin with the simplest compositional impulse – looking out of the window. *Trees in a garden* would be a fair title for much of Jones's painting in the early years here, even when those trees are transfigured into mythic forests. Those limber, interwoven branches in paintings like *Vexilla Regis* are rich in mythology. Much of it comes from Jones's familiar deep wells of Christian and classical symbolism – the tree as the Cross, with the crucified thieves on either side. But again, the painting was central to the healing. On the making of *Vexilla Regis*, Jones wrote:

Of the trees which started me off on this picture, one was a pine and the other a fir (the other, I believe, a chestnut). They were outside my bedroom window in the nursing home when I was jolly ill for seven months – and I did a number of drawings of those trees and then, in the end, did this complicated picture, very much influenced by the previous drawings, though quite different. The picture went through many vicissitudes, and suffered much alteration and was nearly torn up more than once. The psychiatrist, under whose care I was, *made* me go on, so that it was produced under rather special circumstances. In a sense the doctor could be said to have been a 'part-producer', I feel.

To understand the importance of these painted trees, you need to look beyond the Christian symbolism into Jones's personal history and mythology. Mametz Wood before the First World War was a dense tangle of oak, beech, lime, hazel and hornbeam. After five days of unimaginably brutal combat, much of it hand-to-hand, almost 4,000 of Jones's comrades lay dead, with similar losses on the German side. The poet Robert Graves, who witnessed the immediate aftermath of the battle, declared that 'not a single tree in the wood remained unbroken.' Perhaps Jones could only begin to recover from the splintered wreckage of Mametz Wood by putting the trees back together, re-seeding them, filling them with birds, forcing them back into leaf.

★

After a stroke and a fall in 1970, the poet moved into Calvary Nursing Home, Sudbury Hill, just down the hill from Harrow School. There he was nursed by the Blue Sisters. The Nursing Home is now Chasewood Park, an opulent-looking development of private apartments. We walk up the driveway, past signs warning of CCTV and guard dogs on patrol. This place is gated and tended, set in ample grounds with floodlit tennis courts, secure parking for residents, automatic sprinkler systems built into the manicured flower beds. On the other side of the driveway a young child plays in the fallen leaves as his mother attends to her mobile phone.

A recent advert shows a three-bedroom flat in the new development for sale at £700,000. As well as a heated swimming pool and steam room, the former chapel has been turned into a full gym, complete with badminton and table-tennis facilities. The sales pitch concludes the description of the gym with 'beautiful stained-glass, leaded windows'.

The chapel has been incorporated into the apartment complex, but the developers left one incongruous feature from the convent intact. Above the entrance to the underground car park, a colossal crucifix is underwritten by the phrase 'Ecce Homo'. A local newspaper cutting, marking the last days of the convent, features a picture of a patient's bedroom. It looks cold and bare, with a metal-framed hospital bed, a small table and chair, a bedside cabinet and a TV on a trolley pushed against the wall. Four years is a long time to spend dying, as Jones did in this monastic waiting room. But the death he missed in Mametz Wood nearly sixty years before caught up with him here on 28 October 1974.

★

David Jones didn't choose Harrow. He came here to find the right psychiatrist, but once here, he stayed for the rest of his life and produced some of his finest work as a poet and artist. Why did it suit him so well? His Harrow was very much Harrow-on-the-Hill, school Harrow, that anachronistic village where a young Byron or Trollope might walk the streets, alongside today's frock-coated, straw-hatted pupils, and be indistinguishable from them. For Jones's blasted nerves, it offered tradition, routine at its most secure, a place of safety and recovery.

Like many poets, Jones was nothing if not complicated. Would he have suffered a breakdown anyway, even without the horrors of Mametz Wood? He was not the type of war poet we expect. For a start, he believed that soldiery was a noble and ancient calling. And his battlefield poetry was written in the broken, fragmented structures of a Modernist epic. But also his war took so much longer to be processed. The report of *In Parenthesis* came a long time after the flash, being finally completed and published more than two decades on from the events it describes. Whereas Wilfred Owen received psychiatric treatment at Craiglockhart Hospital while the war was still raging, Jones's treatment under Dr Stevenson – famous for his work with shell-shock sufferers – didn't begin until three decades later. Jones saw the role of artist as a sacramental 'maker' and eschewed 'mere self-expression'. Do we believe him? There is a beauty and a purity to Jones's aesthetic, something of the vocational, even the monastic. If his insistent separation of the life and the work sounds like an act of will, of self-protection, then it's no less admirable or true for that.

★

What would we have made of the Normandy bocage or Mametz Wood or the Sambre-Oise canal? Would we, like Edward Thomas, Keith Douglas, Wilfred Owen, have gone to war as poets half-ter-rified but half-aware that it might be 'the great subject'? Not for the first time – thinking of sons, nephews, the next generation – we are reminded that our generation is an exception, that we have lived to middle age without conscription, without a world war. There are contemporary war poets, notably Americans like Brian Turner and Kevin Powers, who fought in Iraq. But for most poets of our generation, war has been distant, mediated through TV news reports. A poem like *In Parenthesis* can still hot-wire an over-familiar piece of our history, just as the First World War, like so many wars before it, vanishes into commodification and cliché. At the end of the poem, Jones has a wry line for his hero John Ball as he drops his rifle: 'Leave it for a Cook's tourist to the Devastated Areas and crawl / as far as you can and wait for the bearers.'

★

We're standing on the towpath running alongside the Sambre-Oise Canal, just outside the village of Ors in northern France. This is a warm October many years ago and the day is peaceful.

There are no boats and not a whisper of wind disturbs the water, a long corridor of silver kinking away from us up ahead. Before dawn on the Monday morning of 4 November 1918, 2nd Lt Wilfred Owen and his Company of the 2nd Manchesters attacked the opposite bank here. The fighting was fierce. Royal Engineers were trying to construct a floating bridge under heavy fire, so the troops could make the crossing. Owen never made it to the other side, and was killed along with many other men that day. It's difficult to square all that with the scene before us. A dabchick forages along the reedy water margin. Earlier, we'd walked up the towpath from the lock house that was captured from Germans that day; the place was sun-struck and deserted, only a few pockmarks in the building's masonry to hint at what had taken place there ninety autumns ago.

Owen had arrived in France in the first weeks of 1917, where he found himself occupying a former German dugout in no-man's-land at Serre with his men. 'I have not been at the front. I have been in front of it.' The dugout was half-flooded and the enemy knew they were there. 'Those fifty hours were the agony of my happy life,' he wrote to his mother afterwards. Between this 'seventh hell' and the canal at Ors the following autumn, Owen wrote the poems that today are taught in schools and read the world over. But following his trail, we soon realized how little we knew about where these poems came from.

★

Owen's death – just days before the Armistice was signed – happened during a phase of the war very different from our stereotypical view of trenches and stalemate: things had begun to move quickly and the enemy was in retreat. We'd imagined – naively as it turned out – an officer, appalled by what he was seeing, scribbling instinctive verse in dugouts and shell holes in between barrages and raids. But it wasn't like that.

His poem 'Miners' begins, like a good story, by the fire:

There was a whispering in my hearth,
   A sigh of the coal,
Grown wistful of a former earth
   It might recall.

It listened for a tale of leaves
   And smothered ferns;
Frond-forests; and the low, sly lives
   Before the fawns.

Soon, though, the coals whispering and shifting in the grate lead the poet elsewhere:

But the coals were murmuring of their mine,
   And moans down there
Of boys that slept wry sleep, and men
   Writhing for air.

And I saw white bones in the cinder-shard,
   Bones without number.
For many hearts with coal are charred
   And few remember.
   . . .
The centuries will burn rich loads
   With which we groaned,
Whose warmth shall lull their dreaming lids,
   While songs are crooned.
But they will not dream of us poor lads,
   Lost in the ground.

This poem was written in Scarborough in January 1918, only weeks after Owen had been discharged from Craiglockhart Hospital with orders to rejoin his unit. Days before, a pit explosion at Halmer End in Staffordshire had killed more than a

hundred and fifty men and boys, and Owen quickly responded
by writing a poem on the colliery disaster, describing later how
'I get mixed up with the War at the end'. It was one of only five
poems he published in his lifetime; he also described how he'd
sent it off to *The Nation* the same evening as writing it, deciding,
in a letter to his mother, that 'for half an hour's work I think Two
Guineas is good pay.' Just over a year before, Owen had been
writing poems like his sonnet 'Purple': 'Purest, it is the diamond
dawn of Spring, / And yet the veil of Venus and youth's skin,
/ Mauve-marbled; purpling young Love's mouth for sacred sin.'

What had changed? Most obviously, Owen had been to the
front line in the early days of 1917 and seen first-hand what modern industrial warfare did to the natural landscape, the human
body and the mind. He'd seen the ground 'cobbled with skulls'.
He'd been underground himself. He'd also met with a few people
who had utterly recalibrated him. Sent to the Front – or beyond
the Front – Owen was quickly able to draw on the sum total of
his experience to date in ways that were fresh and exciting to
him, and so, continually, to us. His writing after that first terrible
exposure in the dugout can't help being 'mixed up with the War'.

★

Looking for Wilfred Owen took us, of all places, to Birkenhead,
across the river from where one of us grew up. The Owens
moved there from Shrewsbury in 1900, his father Tom Owen
having been appointed stationmaster at the Woodside terminus.
All sulky red bricks and wheelie bins today, back at the turn
of the last century Birkenhead was bustling and industrial. New
York's Central Park was modelled on Birkenhead's; the first cinema outside London was established here. Walking around its
backstreets, we find the three houses the family had lived in,
the site of Birkenhead Institute, where Owen was a star pupil,
and Christ Church, an all-important focal point in those early
years. The young Wilfred grew up in an evangelical atmosphere:

frequent services took place at home, as well as in church, and
we discover how Wilfred liked dressing up, donning the priestly
robes. His mother had hopes of him making a career of it.

Despite this, a major epiphany seems to have occurred out
in the countryside to the south-east of Birkenhead, above the
Cheshire hamlet of Broxton in about 1904, and it had nothing
to do with the church. Climbing the wooded sandstone ridge up
from Broxton today, it's not hard to see why. From the crest you
gain a panorama, stretching from the Wrekin and Shrewsbury,
round past the line of Clwydian Hills (including Moel Famau,
which every Merseyside schoolchild, including Wilfred, seems
to have climbed) to Chester, the Wirral peninsula, Birkenhead
and the towers of Liverpool. Here was the landscape of Owen's
childhood, laid out before him. His brother Harold claimed it
was Broxton that made Wilfred a poet, and even though you
soon learn to take much of Harold's hagiography with a pinch
of salt, a fragment of a poem written later seems to say as much:

> For I so repassed into my life's arrears.
> Even the weeks at Broxton, by the Hill
> Where first I felt my boyhood fill
> With uncontainable fancies . . .

It seems, from this moment, as if poetry and religion might
be something the young Owen would have to choose between.
For a while, he managed to work at both. Otherwise, it seems a
calm, Edwardian time of plant identification, of collecting rocks
and fossils. He led classes: we began to realize how much of a
teacher and a leader Owen was used to being, even from an early
age. In 1911 he took a job as a Parish Assistant in Dunsden, a
Thames Valley textbook village complete with a well and a
green, surrounded by little lanes. One of us had met with the late
Dominic Hibberd there, scholar and author of a fine biography
of Owen, and after visiting the vicarage and wandering down

to the village green (its well has been plugged up and moved a few yards), we'd sat on comically tiny plastic chairs in the school hall for an interview. It seemed that by the time he arrived at Dunsden, Owen was already sold on Romantic verse, especially Shelley and Keats. Good examples of the young Owen's early infatuation with both can be found in poems like 'Written in a Wood, September 1910', which begins like this:

> Full ninety autumns hath this ancient beech
> Helped with its myriad leafy tongues to swell
> The dirges of the deep-toned western gale,
> And ninety times hath all its power of speech
> Been stricken dumb . . .

★

Throughout the offices of his post at Dunsden – parish duties followed by soul-destroying suppers with the reverend – Owen was writing poems, sonnets full of Love and Beauty and Death, rich in Romantic tropes and allusions, but he was always learning how to make a poem, feeling how the parts fit together. He quoted Keats to his mother, encouraging her to read the poems, and made literary pilgrimages – echoing ours – to Keats's house, even tracking down a granddaughter of Coleridge in Torquay. A bicycle ride into nearby Reading brought him into contact with something a bit newer: Harold Monro's *Before Dawn*, and the Georgians. Owen eventually rejected the one true path, leaving Dunsden, and eventually England, to teach English in Bordeaux for a while. During the hot summer of 1914, as the European superpowers were locking into a chain reaction that would lead to declarations of war, Owen was tutoring at a villa and hanging out in Bagnères-de-Bigorre with the French poet Laurent Tailhade, himself a disciple of Mallarmé and a friend of Verlaine. There was a Decadent Owen, an aesthete who wore purple. He finally entered the Artists Rifles towards the close of 1915, beginning a long year of training and army routine that led to his awful baptism of fire at Serre and Beaumont-Hamel.

★

Discovering Owen's hinterland of writing adjusts our sense of the young officer: these weren't poems simply springing up from nowhere, shocked into existence by howitzers and machine-gun fire. But we also began to understand, in a very practical sense, how difficult writing actually was on the ground. Letters home were one thing – and the Western Front's postal system, which could get mail from England to the front lines in a day, was an organizational wonder – but composing verse?

We soon realized that Owen drafted almost all of his poems either in casualty clearing stations or, mostly, while back in Blighty, at places like Scarborough or Ripon. Standing in his tiny attic room, under the same skylight where 'The Send-Off', 'Mental Cases' and 'Futility' were written, was one of the most unexpectedly moving points on this particular journey. He needed time to reflect and re-gather himself.

And to recover. Surviving the chaos, pressure and extreme conditions of war might involve a deep drawing on imaginative resources. It might involve a reinvention. On a simpler level, another by-product of large-scale conflict is that people get thrown together. As those artists and poets who'd fled to neutral Switzerland coalesced into something called Dada, the shell-shocked Owen quietly took the overnight train north from King's Cross to Craiglockhart War Hospital for Neurasthenic Officers, just outside Edinburgh, in June 1917. The hospital buildings became part of the campus of Napier University: the sound of young people shooting the breeze over lattes made it difficult to imagine the building's former life, and the nightmarish period between dusk and dawn when corridors echoed with shrieks and groans. We asked some students if they knew about Wilfred Owen. 'No,' one group of girls said, 'but we're doing Business Studies.'

What if Owen had never met Siegfried Sassoon? Sassoon, a second lieutenant in the Royal Welch Fusiliers, is supposed to have thrown his Military Cross into the Mersey at Formby, while home on convalescent leave. He was sent to Craiglockhart in an attempt to get him to shut up and quit his anti-war protesting. Sassoon might never have had anything to do with somebody so 'perceptibly provincial' as Owen, but there was nowhere for him to hide when the younger poet came nervously knocking at his door, armed with copies of his latest book to sign. Owen was besotted: of this there is no doubt. Whatever Sassoon might have felt privately, a connection was made: he told Owen to 'sweat your guts out for poetry!' and provided him with an urgent reason to be writing the stuff. Sassoon's work satirized the war: he wanted a complacent Blighty – used to newsreel propaganda and exhibition trenches in Kensington – to wise up. The effect on Owen's poetry is palpable still, a jolt of angry energy, undermining the Horatian 'Dulce et Decorum Est' (it's sweet and decorous to die for your country):

> If you could hear, at every jolt, the blood
> Come gargling from the froth-corrupted lungs,
> Obscene as cancer, bitter as the cud
> Of vile, incurable sores on innocent tongues, –
> My friend, you would not tell with such high zest
> To children ardent for some desperate glory,
> The old Lie: Dulce et decorum est
> Pro patria mori.

And still very evident in 'Smile, Smile, Smile,' one of the last poems he wrote, this time subverting the Tommy's popular song 'So pack up your troubles in your old kit-bag / And smile, smile, smile':

> Head to limp head, the sunk-eyed wounded scanned
> Yesterday's *Mail*; the casualties (typed small)
> And (large) Vast Booty from our Latest Haul.

Also, they read of Cheap Homes, not yet planned ...

Sassoon also put Owen on to Robbie Ross, former companion of Oscar Wilde, slipping him an envelope containing a tenner, plus an address in Mayfair. Owen loved being among the artists and poets. But equally important to the recovering officer was the counsel of Dr Arthur Brock. Brock was an ergotherapist, unique at the time in his field. Shell-shocked patients were suffering a detachment from their landscapes, histories, surroundings – Owen had been blown into the air by a shell at Savy Wood, and had lain in a hole for days – and Brock attempted to reconnect the mind, body and total environment: to make the patient whole again. He set Owen what we'd now call a creative-writing exercise: to write a poem on the theme of Antaeus, who had been lifted off the ground by Hercules and killed because of his break with mother Earth. At the same time as he was falling head over heels for Sassoon, Owen was learning how to reintegrate all the bits of himself. With Brock's help, Owen *pulled himself together.*

★

For the rest of his short life from Craiglockhart onwards – throughout stationings at Scarborough and then the vast northern army depot at Ripon – all of Wilfred Owen's experience to date became creatively available to him. New work poured out. Old poems got redrafted. 'The Send-Off' (originally titled 'The Draft') is a good example of the kind of thing Owen was suddenly, surprisingly, able to do. The poem begins:

Down the close, darkening lanes they sang their way
To the siding-shed,
And lined the train with faces grimly gay.

Their breasts were stuck all white with wreath and spray
As men's are, dead.

Dull porters watched them, and a casual tramp
Stood staring hard,
Sorry to miss them from the upland camp.
Then, unmoved, signals nodded, and a lamp
Winked to the guard . . .

Owen was writing in his attic at Ripon, near the army depot where he would have seen trains leaving daily full of troops bound for the Front. As an image of a cold, mechanistic route to death, conducted by railway timetables, it echoes down the century in ways its maker could never have imagined. By the poem's end:

Shall they return to beating of great bells
In wild train-loads?
A few, a few, too few for drums and yells,
May creep back, silent, to still village wells,
Up half-known roads.

This brings to mind the well on the village green at Dunsden – it's as if the soldiers leave from north Yorkshire then arrive back in the Thames Valley five years earlier – although the actual sources mightn't matter so much as Owen's newfound ability to draw deeply on them for the poem's sake. His early death in France meant there would be no return to pre-war themes, no dalliance with Modernism, nor any long decline or change of direction. His poems fused to their theme for ever. But then, many of those who survived this war – like David Jones – found it stuck to them, the mud of the Ancre Valley and the Somme.

We've each found ourselves in this haunted landscape before on several occasions. The centenary of the War has meant journeys along the Somme, to Mametz Wood, Albert, Baupaume, recording our impressions in a region that has long since returned to rolling downs and belts of woodland, crossed by alien pylons. And in a way, when visiting the former battlefields of Flanders and

Picardy, on the trail of Owen and Jones, Sassoon, Ivor Gurney, Edward Thomas, Robert Graves, Isaac Rosenberg, we're returned to a state before poetry, a darkened, deeply embedded place where the intermingled dread and thrill of the place-names re-asserts itself, and the primal shapes of family stories and myths come back. Our fathers tell us how their fathers pissed on to handkerchiefs during gas attacks. A grandmother remembers as a girl seeing men shaking suddenly, uncontrollably, throwing their arms in the air.

We find Owen in the village of Ors, not far from where he was killed (the telegram announcing his death was delivered to his home in Shrewsbury just as the Armistice bells were ringing). Sassoon died, aged eighty, in 1967. A few years ago his Military Cross was discovered in a cobwebbed trunk, together with a revolver in a Jiffy bag. Owen's poetry eventually found its huge readership during the same decade. For a long time, the work of Rupert Brooke was far more popular. Owen lies at the back of the graveyard at Ors, between two of the other soldiers who died that day.

We visit on a balmy evening, with the sounds of kids playing somewhere close by and scooters buzzing along the road. We take a few photographs kneeling at the graveside, tidying up the cards and flowers.

House Calls

It is one thing to define yourself as a poet on the margins of society, dancing with Death on a nightly basis, while sending back missives from bohemia to the wage slaves at home. It is quite another to be a poet who is also a professional, a pillar of the community. And by 'professional' we mean here one of 'the professions', the kind of vocation that would read well under your signature as you sign some neighbour's passport application or write them a job reference.

If poetry is a vocation in itself, and an all-consuming, life-threatening one at that, then what can life be like for poets who have vocational day jobs? For the sake of clarity, let's exclude the teaching of poetry from this category. Since universities became the primary patrons of poetry in Britain and the United States, many poets have found themselves teaching poetry alongside writing it. For at least some of those poets, teaching is vocational, an extension of the writing itself, forcing you to read and reread great poems of the past, come to terms with them anew, and debate their merits with students who care as passionately about good poems as you do.

But for some poets, their secondary vocation has no explicit connection with poetry at all. Take, for example, the hard-working paediatrician William Carlos Williams, making house calls every day from his home town in Rutherford, New Jersey, out along the densely populated, post-industrial sprawl of the Passaic banks through the city of Paterson towards New York. Or the

Welsh poet-priest R. S. Thomas, tending to the pastoral needs of his flock on the Llŷn Peninsula in rural north-west Wales. Do the two vocations play against each other, creatively or destructively? Does the worldly vocation afford some sort of protection – a sense of purpose – to get you through the despairing times as a poet?

★

The doctor's grave lies in a cluster of Williams graves at the Hillside Cemetery on the eastern outskirts of Rutherford. His stone is simple, bare, with just his name and dates on it: WILLIAM CARLOS 1883–1963. The plain headstone is barely distinguishable from his wife Flossie's headstone next to it. The only thing that sets the great poet's grave apart from the rest is a stick with some fake pearls twisted round it, like a misplaced Christmas decoration. The cemetery rises in the middle, where the Williams graves lie. And from that rise you can see, on the horizon, the glistening towers of Manhattan. These were the twin poles of the life of Dr William Carlos Williams. A twenty-minute walk through leafy Rutherford will take you past his birthplace, the church where he married, the house where he practised as a paediatrician and the piece of earth in which he's buried. Without the opposite pole of literary, glamorous New York, this would look like an exemplary life of local service. But that was only half the story.

Rutherford today feels like commuter belt. Its old name – Boiling Springs – is preserved only in the name of a local savings bank. We guess it has good, nostalgic associations for its customers, but it sounds pretty off-putting to us, visiting as we are from a Britain in the grip of austerity. Placid Pools Savings Bank sounds to us like a much safer place for a nest egg, but our local guides don't seem to share that concern. Rod Leith and Della Rowland are Williams enthusiasts. Both knew a little about him before they pitched up in Rutherford, but got really hooked when they moved to the town and realized what a mark he made here. Della remembers moving here with young children and asking other mothers to recommend a paediatrician. They pointed to a tall, blue-painted clapboard house on the corner of Ridge Road, and recommended Dr Williams, who practised there. It was a paediatric dynasty. The Dr Williams recommended to Della was not the poet, but the poet's son, also called William, who took over not just his dad's practice, but also his house and his role as physician of choice for the parents of Rutherford. Now, Rod and Della run an academic symposium on Williams and his writing, and they work to develop Rutherford's recognition of its most famous son.

We stand outside the house and Rod and Della fill us in on its history – how so many great poets came to visit, how the likes of Allen Ginsberg and Ezra Pound used to get off the train from New York at the foot of Union Street and walk up to see their friend the doctor; how Williams himself contained both vocations within the same house: a study in the attic for the night work of poetry and a consulting room in the annex for the day work of medicine. We don't quite know what to say, because this is not what we expected. The house is, frankly, shabby. They would like it to become a birthplace museum, like Emily Dickinson's house in Amherst, but it doesn't look open for business at all. We walk around the side and are shown the stone steps up to a side door where Williams (and later his son) would welcome their patients during open surgery. But the steps and the path are overgrown and the annex looks unused. We pose for photographs in front of the place, then walk off to the liquor store across the road. We have a special invitation for tonight and we need to take a nice bottle with us. But before we leave the house, one of us says what we've been thinking all along:

'So, was this the house with the fridge?'

'The fridge?'

'Yes, the fridge with the plums in it. The plums he ate, and his wife didn't want him to.'

'Yes, this is the house. The fridge was here.'

★

Unless and until literary fame strikes in later life, most poets have a rather unclear sense of community. A playwright or composer creates a sense of community every time a work is performed. Even a novelist (especially with the advent of social media) has a wider sense of a community of readers. Poetry readings tend not to sell-out theatres. They are usually more intimate (putting it kindly) happenings, and the famously small world of poetry and poets is sufficiently fractious to make social media well worth avoiding. So poets, for the most part, get their daily sense of community elsewhere. Often this comes from a day job, fellow-journalists, fellow-civil servants, fellow-professional gamblers. This enables those poets who still believe in poetry as a vocation to keep that vocation separate from their occupation. And it can be very useful to be able to play one side off against the other in times of trouble.

The Latin roots of the word 'vocation' are in *vocare*, 'to call', and the rather old-fashioned term 'a calling' is still used in the context of the priesthood. But the idea of vocation has become so firmly attached to poetry (much more so than for novelists or screenwriters) that the *Oxford English Dictionary* uses 'her vocation as a poet' as its example of the usage of the word. Why should poetry in particular be more vocational than any other form of writing? The answer probably lies in poverty and pain. Poets tend not to make a lot of money, or at least, not from their writing. This is perhaps why most poets we know love Martin Amis's short story 'Career Move' so much. It's not seen as a key part of Amis's oeuvre, but in its imagining of a world in which the rewards of poets and screenwriters are reversed, it's the stuff of heady fantasy for contemporary poets. With sales of poetry collections rarely tipping over 5,000 in Britain, even for established figures, no one writes poems for money. But if relative poverty is part of what singles out poetry as a 'vocational' form of writing, then pain is an even bigger factor. Great poems don't land in your lap, or so the legend says. Great poems are hewn from great suffering and risk and pain. It must be a vocation.

So how do you manage, as William Carlos Williams did, twin lifelong vocations as poet and physician? And if the word vocation is often applied to the medical profession, how much more to the church? Worlds apart in many ways, but strikingly similar in others, Williams shared that double-vocation bind with the Welsh poet and priest R. S. Thomas. If poverty and pain are the twin pillars of the poetic vocation, then Thomas developed a reputation for both. He lived very simply in rural Wales, surrounded by the skulls of animals, bare white walls, the bleached fruits of beachcombing, paintings and books. As for the pain, well, although his dry wit was celebrated by those who knew him well, he had a reputation for misery. This was underlined for many in a discovery by the critic Jeremy Noel-Tod. In December 2013 during a stop at a motorway services, Jeremy bought a packet of Tyrrell's potato crisps emblazoned with the offer: 'Win a fleeting look of contempt or £25,000.' Next to the headline, to illustrate the look of contempt, was a photograph of R. S., wild-haired and scowling. Noel-Tod tweeted a photo of the pack to Tyrrell's, asking if they knew that the contemptuous man in the dog collar was a major (dead) twentieth-century poet. Tyrrell's tweeted an apology, but not before Twitter had its say on the irony of this highly principled anti-consumerist Welsh-language activist being used to drive sales of 'Hand-Cooked English Crisps'.

Thomas's uncompromising, pared-back poems show the clear influence of early American Modernists, and Thomas admired the later, more ambitious Williams poems in particular. Both were embattled poets, struggling against the dominance of the English poetic tradition. Thomas was born into an English-speaking family and was educated in English. He learned Welsh as an adult and thereafter conducted as much of his life as he could in that language. But because English was his first language, he felt he had no choice but to use it as the medium for his poetry. Like Williams, who struggled to forge a new kind of poetry in American English, Thomas sought to break and reshape an English fitted to the landscape and spirit of Wales. But it's not just their poetry and their struggles against (and with) English that connect them. Just as Williams's poetry became more and more inflected by the people whose lives he entered, making house calls in urban and suburban New Jersey, so Thomas's poetry wrestled with the hopes and tragedies of his rural Welsh parishioners, as he made his visits to the sick, the bereaved, the lonely.

★

This Is Just to Say

I have eaten
the plums
that were in
the icebox

and which
you were probably
saving
for breakfast.

Forgive me
they were delicious
so sweet
and so cold.

It's either the fridge, or the red wheelbarrow. Those are the two William Carlos Williams poems everyone knows. Two of the most perfect short poems ever written. They are like netsuke: intricately carved and small enough to hold in the palm of your hand. One describes the simplest of scenes, a wheelbarrow in a garden in the rain. But it places the redness of the wheelbarrow alongside the whiteness of the garden's chickens, and prefaces this vignette with one of the most famous opening lines in twentieth-century poetry: 'So much depends upon . . .'

The equally famous fridge poem is just as perfect, but some-how more intimate, seems to tell us more about him. It reads like a short note, left on the kitchen table by a man for his spouse to read when she gets home. It's an apology, for eating plums from the icebox. They were not just any plums. They were glorious, chilled and ripe, as perfect as the poem itself. He knew his wife was sav-ing them for herself, but he couldn't resist them. 'Forgive me,' he says. And, we assume, she did. Bill and Flossie married young and stayed married until he died in 1963 aged seventy-nine.

In his late play *A Dream of Love* Williams tells of a physician (Dr Thurber) who travels to New York and dies suddenly during extra-marital sex in a hotel room. He then comes back as a ghost to apologize to his devastated widow. It is the perfect nightmare for a male poet, combining as it does hypochondria, a death-wish, sex and guilt. Some biographers have suggested that Williams him-self had affairs, and the New York connection seems to fit too. In Rutherford everyone knew him. He was a pillar of respect-ability. His parents lived around the corner. He could walk down the street and tip his hat to countless patients, former patients, children whose births he conducted, friends of his wife, friends of his kids. But in Manhattan he was the great Modernist poet, a doc-tor among the bohemians. Was it in the pull, the polarity of these two lives, these two selves, that he found the energy to write?

According to WCW's biographer, Paul Mariani, he wrote *A Dream of Love* 'to come to terms with his own feelings, to apologize for his momentary crazinesses in having slept with other women'.

This push and pull between two vocations – the respectable doctor in Rutherford and the famous poet in New York – was powerful fuel for his work. In a late interview, Williams says that what keeps him interested in life, what gives him his zest and energy after so many years and so many achievements, is the look in a woman's eyes.

★

By all accounts Williams was good company. He and his wife were generous hosts to the many visitors – writers, journalists, scholars – to their house on Ridge Road at the height of his literary fame. The genes for hospitality seem to have been passed on intact, because his granddaughter Daphne Williams Fox knows how to make English visitors feel welcome. We had got in touch with her – as literary executor of her grandfather's estate – to see if we could meet and interview her, but she also offered us dinner and rooms for the night. Her email, received on a typical drowned rat of a day in north-west England, tempted us with the idea that their pool would be warm by the time we made our trip, and that the New Jersey tomatoes would be ripe.

Like many of our fellow Lancastrians, we are of the opinion that swimming pools are to sit by, with a drink, not to get into, with all the flesh-baring implications of that. So it was that we found ourselves sipping beer by a large pool in the backyard of a beautiful house in Rutherford, a couple of blocks away from Ridge Road.

We talk about the town, about how hard Daphne is fighting to try to keep her grandfather's work out there; how hard it is to maintain a literary reputation, even for a figure as famous as WCW. She always refers to him as 'WCW' and it's a habit we start to pick up too. She takes us through to the dining room, where several large archive boxes are lined up on the table. 'These,' she tells us, 'are WCW's letters to his wife Flossie.' Throughout his life, whenever he was travelling, on medical or literary duty, he would write back to Flossie. The letters are, she says, tender and witty and full of love. She is trying to get them published, but nobody will take on such a huge project. She shows us the family albums, and there he is, the well-to-do, small-town doctor, always smartly dressed, rakish-looking in the earlier photographs, distinguished and scholarly in the late ones. Here he stands in his garden at Ridge Road, here in the park on a family picnic, here at a birthday party. It looks a picture of orderly calm, the life of this poet. Daphne tells us how WCW used to go out on his house calls, come back at the end of the day and empty his pockets of all the cash, cheques, prescription slips and reminders which Flossie would file away. He would eat his dinner, then head up to the top of the house and start hammering away on his typewriter. Daphne says her father remembers that clattering of keys going on deep into the night, long after he and his brothers had been sent to bed.

The guest rooms in Daphne's house are as comfortable as the rest of the place. Ceiling fans hold off the dead weight of a summer night, but to those unused to them, their breeze wards off sleep too. A dog barks. It's so quiet here that the dog could be three blocks away, or three states. A freight train sounds its horn for no apparent reason, because there are no other trains, no signals, nothing except a lone dog between this house and the Atlantic Ocean. We've forgotten to lock the hire car outside on the street, but we don't bother. This is quintessential suburbia and seems like the very safest place on Earth. John Berryman went to teach in Minneapolis and began a love/hate relationship with that strange city. His years there produced many of his finest *Dream Songs*, but also claimed his life. The weird extremes of frozen Minneapolis, marooned on the Great Plains, seem strangely fitting for Berryman. Bleak, elemental and bloody freezing most of the time, Minneapolis could bring out the mad genius in anyone. But WCW's Rutherford feels like a town to cure your madness, a rest cure of a town. Writing poems here would be like writing poems in Seahaven on *The Truman Show*. Perfect. Perhaps those two famous Imagist poems – plums and wheelbarrow – are what happens when poems are written in Rutherford. But WCW's work wasn't all about miniatures. He also wrote *Paterson*.

★

Paterson is a place and a poem. As a poem it is WCW's late, great masterpiece; a sprawling modernist collage of reportage, archived news reports, poetic personifications, letters and journal entries.

It is full of violence, sex and death. As a city it is Rutherford's off-the-rails older brother, the one nobody in the family refers to, except in hushed and regretful tones. Paterson is less than ten miles away from Rutherford, but could be on another planet. WCW famously insisted on 'no ideas but in things'. To understand *Paterson* the poem, you need to connect with the thing-ness of Paterson the city. You need to walk its streets, drink in its bars, eavesdrop and hang out. That's how WCW described his own process as he began to research and write the poem in the Forties. Except nowadays it's not quite so easy.

WCW chose Paterson as the setting for his magnum opus because it wasn't Rutherford. His home town was not 'distinguished or varied enough'. New York City was not far away, but that contained and evoked too much. It was simply too big to be the focus of even the most epic of poems. Paterson struck him as the perfect solution. It had a rich history, as one of the cornerstones of American industry, and it was a place he knew well. In his short, vivid memoir *House Calls with William Carlos Williams, MD* the physician Robert Coles gives an account of his time as a trainee doctor in the Fifties, learning on the job doing house calls in Paterson with WCW. He paints a picture of a devoted and popular paediatrician, driving too fast from house to house, visiting sick children and expectant mothers. Paterson fascinated Williams. Coles recalls that WCW's process of diagnosis would begin as soon as he stepped out of the car, taking in the social conditions, the buildings' state of repair, the food on offer in the local stores. He was, in Coles's words, 'almost like a sociologist, making connections between homes and streets and opportunities, checking out schools and libraries and the states of the homes'. He didn't just treat the kids, he would talk to them, get them to explain what their lives were like, to describe the neighbourhood. He would teach the kids how to test reflexes and how to use a stethoscope . . . on him. But at the same time as he was showing Coles how to behave as an empathetic doctor, he was working on his other job too. Often, as he got back in the car after a house call, he would make a page of notes for poems. Even before he conceived of the idea of 'Paterson – the epic' he was captivated by the place.

★

Our guide to Paterson is Professor Steve Hahn from William Paterson University, a notable Williams scholar and, happily for us, a former Boston taxi driver. After a few years driving a taxi, he tells us, you get a nose for trouble. You know which streets to avoid and when to turn around and get the hell out. And those skills are pretty useful in Paterson these days. Like Manchester, Paterson was a nineteenth-century boom town, built on the early industrialization of weaving. Specializing in silk, Paterson became a magnet for skilled workers from the north of England and Poland, and it grew and flourished. Like Manchester also, it collapsed when the bottom fell out of the weaving business. But unlike Manchester, Paterson has not yet reinvented itself as a thriving modern city. There are plans afoot, and in a decade or so this city could be one of America's newest success stories. There's even talk of a tourist boom following the designation of Paterson's historic Falls district as a National Park. But at the time of our visit, such a transformation is hard to imagine.

Steve drives us round the key sites in WCW's poem – the park on Garrett Mountain where a street preacher plies his trade; the city library with its classical columns and the names of great writers carved into its walls; and the spectacular Passaic Falls themselves, the dead drop that gave water the force to drive the mill wheels. The sound of the Falls became WCW's great preoccupation in Paterson. How could his poem capture the distinctive sound of that particular waterfall? An American waterfall would not sound like a Chinese or an English waterfall. And an American poem must not sound like a Chinese or an English poem. The American language was a distinctively different music, WCW believed, and that distinctive music should be there in its poetry.

The public library is particularly incongruous in its setting, in what is now one of Paterson's most notorious neighbourhoods. Steve drives us to it, and back out of it, via a circuitous route that avoids the district around Summer Street and Rosa Parks Boulevard. The city's new plague is drive-by shootings. Just days before we arrived here, a twelve-year-old girl was shot dead as she rode on a scooter to her aunt's house. The age of the girl, and perhaps her name – Genesis – made this case a rallying cry for the people of Paterson. Church and civic leaders led marches, vigils against violence and the drug culture. But Paterson has a reputation for violence that will be hard to shake off.

Before we head out of the city, Steve has one more place to show us. Paterson had its share of violence and madness when WCW was doing house calls here, and that was part of its appeal to him. But River Street always had a special reputation. Even by Paterson standards, River Street was edgy, and it still is. There are disused factories and boarded-up houses, dark cellar bars with plastic chairs outside and people sitting drinking in the middle of the street. And we do mean the middle. We have to slow right down and mount the kerb to get round them. One of the letters WCW includes in his poem-collage about this city is from another of its famous sons – Allen Ginsberg. On the face of it, the letter is a useful offering of local knowledge. 'Do you know this part of Paterson?' asks Ginsberg, recommending that the older poet spends time on River Street as part of his research. 'I have seen so many things,' says Ginsberg of his own time spent in the dives there, finishing with the claim that River Street 'is really the heart of what is to be seen' in Paterson.

But it's hard not to read the letter also as a bit of a jab, a jibe. Poets are fiercely territorial about their subject matter. And when that subject matter overlaps with geographical territory, even more so. Ginsberg, who also wrote about this place, is trying to out–Paterson the old poet. Who *really* knows the city? The guy who was born and raised in it? Or the guy who was born and raised in the suburbs, but has been in countless Paterson homes and delivered countless Paterson babies?

Either way, WCW, the suburban doctor, found his portion of madness in Paterson. He wrote to his publisher and friend James Laughlin in 1943: 'That God damned and I mean God damned poem *Paterson* has me down. I am burned up to do it but don't quite know how. I write and destroy, write and destroy.'

★

Less than a month after Sylvia Plath took her own life in 1963 in a gas oven in Primrose Hill, William Carlos Williams's life petered out after a debilitating series of strokes. WCW's biographer Paul Mariani describes his wife Flossie going to wake him up on the morning of 4 March, and finding him lying still, facing the wall. Their puppy – Stormy, usually full of life and a joy to the old poet – lay outside the door and whimpered. His son Bill was called upstairs, examined his father and pronounced him dead, exactly as WCW had done for his own father.

Not many poets – or certainly few major poets – can claim to have lived a life of service, unless you count devotion to the muse as service. And we don't. Many poets are driven by a compulsion to write, a dedication to poetry, an obsession with it, but that rarely constitutes the self-giving associated with true service. To the people of Rutherford, New Jersey, WCW's people, he was first and foremost a doctor. And not just any doctor, he was the man who delivered many of them safely into the world. According to Mariani, the policeman who led the funeral procession from Rutherford to Hillside Cemetery was himself delivered into the world by Dr Williams. Had WCW never written a single poem, he could have looked back on his life and known that he had made a difference, a big difference, to his community. But he had two communities. The people of Rutherford and Paterson were his first, the one he served in his daily life and work. But his wider community was the fellowship of poets, and of American poets in particular. His lifelong struggle to define a new kind of authentic American poetic measure, an authentic American poetic, is still being weighed and calibrated in seminar rooms and lecture theatres. His notion of the 'variable foot', which marks out the music of a truly American poetic line, is – depending on your point of view – a canon-defining perception of genius or an impenetrable piece of sophistry.

★

There is something noble about WCW's profound struggle with his late, unfinished masterpiece, falling over itself with sheer ambition. Is *Paterson* a failure? On one level, the answer must be yes. Matched against its aims – to forge a new kind of Modernist epic, to define an authentic American poetic voice, to explore the nature of violence, the mystery of relationships between men and women – it was doomed to fall short.

But even in its unfinished, fragmentary form it holds more beauty and power and surprise than countless far more famous poems. Is some measure of failure essential to the making of what John Berryman called 'a great poet'? Few would argue that the *Dream Songs* are a flawless body of work, and like *Paterson* their scale and ambition almost guarantees a falling short. Is there a pattern here? Do average artists play it safe, map out career moves, never frighten the horses? 'Mediocrities develop,' as Oscar Wilde has it. Does real achievement in poetry demand genuine risk? Do you have to risk losing career, reputation, stability, to make the big leaps? It's not straightforward. Some of the most groundbreaking poets in this book passed lives of outward calm and lived to see their dotage. But for some, it's clear, the risks they took to access the great work became their undoing. As Berryman puts it in *Dream Song* 36: 'The high ones die, die. They die.'

★

The legacy of WCW the poet lies where it should lie, in the poems themselves. He's still not read in Britain as widely as he should be. *Paterson*, his masterpiece, is currently – and regrettably in our view – out of print in Britain. However, his role as a Modernist father of American twentieth-century poetry is secure. Ginsberg wasn't the only young poet to call him master. But WCW paid a heavy price for poetry, and for sticking to his guns. His last eleven years were characterized by torment and frustration. His first major stroke in 1951 forced him out of medical work. The fragile but fruitful balance that had held his life together – medicine by day, poetry by night – was broken. The stroke left him with impaired movement, speech and vision. He could only type with one hand on his treasured electric typewriter. Through the Fifties he suffered a further debilitating series of strokes and a major operation to remove a malignant tumour from his colon. As if he didn't have enough to contend with, this last decade also saw him caught up in the McCarthy-era witch-hunts, for his avowedly left-wing sympathies and his friendship with Ezra Pound. Yet through this bleak final decade he remained stoical, committed to his work, supportive and encouraging to younger poets.

One of the most beautiful elements of the *Paterson* poem is a repeated refrain – 'so be it'.

> . . . Rain
> falls and surfeits the river's upper reaches,
> gathering slowly. So be it. Draws together,
> runnel by runnel. So be it. A broken oar
> is found by the searching waters. Loosened
> it begins to move. So be it.

The refrain, he told Pound, was 'copied verbatim from a translation of a Plains Indian prayer'. He went on to say that 'It meant what it says: if it so is then so let it be. In other words, to hell with it.' WCW bore the particular pain of a doctor witnessing the slow dissipation of his own health, knowing precisely what each step means and how it is likely to progress. By the end, after years of opposition and relative obscurity, he was a literary lion. He had achieved the fame he had hoped his work would win, and his death was marked and mourned by the great and good. But on his home patch, the people for whom and about whom he wrote, he was still little known and little read. The city of Paterson when we visited bore few traces of being the subject of one of the greatest American poems. There was a run-down arts centre bearing WCW's name, but that's all we saw. Rutherford, through the efforts of his granddaughter Daphne and the work of passionate advocates like Steve Hahn, Della Rowland and Rod Leith, is trying to make more of its famous son. But when we visit there's no WCW trail, no WCW museum, not even a plaque on his house. When Rutherford lost WCW, they lost a much-loved physician, but gained another in his son. So be it.

★

'So be it' was only part of the story. For much of his life as a doctor, WCW was socially and politically engaged and committed. Robert Coles reveals how WCW saw social conditions as an integral part of the health (or lack of it) of his patients, and he was strident and committed in his attempts to change those conditions. *Paterson* is full of this. At one point in the poem, the inventory of a dead local man (one Cornelius Doremus, who died in 1803) is listed, his meagre possessions laid out verbatim and without comment:

24 shirts at .82½ cents, $19.88: 5 sheets, $7.00: 4 pillow cases, $2.12: 4 pair trousers, $2.00: 1 sheet, $1.37½: a handkerchief, $1.75: 8 caps, .75 cents: 2 pairs shoebuckles and knife, .25 cents: 14 pairs stockings, $5.25: 2 pairs 'Mittins' .63 cents: 1 linen jacket, .50 cents: 4 pairs breeches, $2.63: 4 waist coats, $3.50:

5 coats, $4.75: 1 yellow coat, $5.00: 2 hats, .25 cents: 1 pair shoes, .12½ cents: 1 chest, .75 cents: 1 large chair, $1.50: 1 chest, .12½ cents: 1 pair andirons, $2.00: 1 bed and bedding, $18.00: 2 pocketbooks, .37½ cents: 1 small trunk, .19½ cents: castor hat, .87½ cents: 3 reeds, $1.66: 1 'Quill wheal', .50 cents.

Such is the measure of a man's life.

★

WCW's publisher, the poet James Laughlin, encouraged him to keep writing to the last. As progressive strokes took their toll on his brain and body, WCW would spend hours in his study at Ridge Road trying to type letters. His final letter to Laughlin said:

Dear Jim,

   I finally got your letter enclosing your letter enclocussing your letter which was so ompportant foe me, thannkuok youn very much. In time this fainful bsiness will will soonfeul will soon be onert. Tnany anany goodness. If Slossie eii wyyonor wy sinfsigna-ture.

   I hope I hope I make it
   Bill

★

A memory: it is a grey, gale and rain-striped day. We park down a lane on west Wales's remote Llŷn Peninsula, not far from Aberdaron, where R. S. Thomas served as vicar of St Hywyn's Church. The address we have been given is that of a seventeenth-century Welsh longhouse, and it feels like visiting a museum as we knock on the door. We are fully expecting a curator with an information pack, and a room full of glass display cases full of Iron Age tools. Instead, the door is answered by a gentle, elderly poet who ushers us through the large, narrow living room to his study at the side of the house. As we pass through the living room,

we nudge each other and nod towards a hunched figure sitting
in a chair facing the wall with her back to us, completely still.
We later learn that this was the poet's wife, Elsi, a painter whose
work could be seen on the walls. She was very ill, so we weren't
introduced to her. We heard that she had died a few months later.

★

We are making a radio programme with the poet and critic
Jeremy Hooker. We got here an hour early, having allowed too
much time for the long drive west. We passed that hour sitting
in a local pub, flicking through our notes and books of Thomas's
poems. Perhaps it was the long drive, then the long wait, but
there's something momentous about this visit. It feels like we are
here to meet William Wordsworth or George Herbert. It's not
just R. S. Thomas's fame – and our admiration for his work – that
makes us feel we are visiting an august and long-dead poet. It's
his utter seriousness, too, his uncompromising life and work. We
feel rather, well, trivial. We couldn't imagine RST drifting from a
book of poems to talk about the weekend's football, or wandering
across the pub's snug to put 'Hit Me With Your Rhythm Stick' on
the jukebox.

   To our relief the poet greets us warmly and leaves us sitting in
the study while he goes to make tea. We feel awkward being able
to speak just one or two words of Welsh. We suspect we only
landed this rare interview because Jeremy Hooker is a friend and
noted scholar of Thomas's work. The study is small, book-lined,
orderly. As the producer sets up spools on the immensely heavy
portable Uher, the reel-to-reel, quarter-inch tape recorder used
by radio producers in the olden days (they can now use their
iPhones), we are running fingers along the bookshelves, full of
poetry (Welsh and English) and theology, as well as books on the
Welsh landscape and birds.

   The house is quiet beyond quiet. We are struck by how difficult it must be to write anything here. Unless your work is – as

Thomas's is – so deeply rooted in silence that it has to come from something akin to a monastic cell. As we wait for our host to return with the tea, we gaze out of the window above the poet's desk, a vista over open water. And in the window, peering out above the Irish Sea, is a large telescope. This is not just a hobby, it is part of his vocation. The more you read of his work, the more strongly that telescope stands out as a symbol of the man and his twin vocations.

★

In one of R. S. Thomas's most celebrated poems 'The Empty Church' he describes the church – his own at Aberdaron, per- haps – as a kind of ancient 'stone trap', designed to catch a glimpse of God, or maybe, once in a lifetime, to catch the whole being, 'like some huge moth' trapped in a box. Empty churches, bare stones, the qualities of silence, these are the fabric of R. S. Thomas's poetry. In an interview for the Contemporary Authors Autobiography Series he said he was sometimes asked if he felt a clash or tension between his twin vocations. He replied that: 'Christ was a poet, the New Testament is poetry.'

That telescope in his study at Y Rhiw on the Llŷn Peninsula was not for birdwatching. It was for absence-of-bird-watching. He explained it to us when we asked about the telescope, but the instruction manual is laid out in his poem 'Sea-Watching'. This is birdwatching only in the sense that his poems are God- watching. The telescope is trained out above the surface of the waves, preferably – if the telescope is powerful enough, as his was – miles out from land. Then the watcher simply waits, in the hope that a rare bird too fugitive to fly inland might flash across the lens. If ever there was a more powerful unity between a poet, his work and his hobby, we are yet to come across it. 'You must wear your eyes out / as others their knees,' he writes.

He comes back with a tray of tea, already lukewarm, as if he's walked through several centuries to bring it to us. The house itself seems to hold so much cold that nothing could stay hot for long here. The tapes are fixed to their spool and the interview begins.

★

The more we think about it, the less sure we are about the tele-scope on the desk. Perhaps, in the decades since that Llŷn visit, RST's seawatching poem has telescoped itself into our memory of his study. We flick through our Thomas books to find a reference, but nothing nails it one way or the other. Maybe this is the flip-side of Daisy Fried's fear that, in thrall to poet's lives and deaths, we forget to read the poems. Can reading the poems make us mis-recall the life?

★

Everything R. S. Thomas says on our tape sounds like a lament or an elegy. He is in his late seventies and sounds weary (though he was to live almost another decade), but there is a sharp edge to his words. Asked about the state of contemporary poetry as we approach the end of the twentieth century, he is bleak in his eval-uation: 'What troubles me is the superficiality, the shallowness. As you know, you've only got to sit in the Underground in London and see this panorama of humanity passing and to glimpse behind the masks of the faces before you the joy and the glory and suf-fering and disappointment and frustration. Here you've got major themes for poetry, and they're not being . . . not all the stops are being drawn out. Contemporary poets are guilty, I think, of play-ing around the fringes of the human psyche.'

★

R. S. Thomas is a considered, thoughtful interviewee. We have a number of questions about his priestly vocation, and a number about his poetic vocation. But all his answers seem to address both. How does his love of the natural world impact on his work?

'According to Aquinas, God mediates himself according to the ability of the receiver. And I think possibly that God – using that word – mediates himself best to me through nature, in all its different aspects ...'

But he adds that: 'Of course, I am troubled, on behalf of the Church, by the fact that Jesus' ministry was largely in the country, amongst country people, and his imagery was drawn primarily from nature.'

In a world increasingly dominated by urban and technological life, how is the Church to survive and connect with people? How, for that matter, is poetry ...?

★

The interview, like the sea-sky outside, is darkening.

'The crisis, it seems to me, as we're approaching the end of the twentieth century is: is poetry in the twenty-first century going to maintain its position as one of the great arts, or is it going to drift further and further into what it's already in danger of being, a minority art?'

We are running out of time and tape. The presenter asks a final question, in an attempt to end the interview on a different note. Does R. S. Thomas regard himself as working in the ancient Welsh tradition of praise poetry, in which a key element of the poet's vocation is the celebration of God and the created world?

'What would a Welsh late-medieval poet know about the suffering all over the world? About the ways of the bacteria and the viruses, the reproductive cycle of the mosquito? What would they know of these things, that we know? So, I think it's much more difficult now to be a praise poet.'

RST goes on to discuss his sense of despair that God says in the Bible 'I create good and I create evil.' 'I mean, this knocks you flat,' he says. And it does. We drive back east along the Llŷn Peninsula in near silence.

★

R. S. Thomas died, after suffering from a heart condition, at the age of eighty-seven. For this most committed of poets, political engagement became a key part of his vocation, and his growing reputation as a poet gave him a public platform to express his views. He became a leading voice in Welsh nationalism, in the campaign to save and regenerate the Welsh language. He was a trenchant critic of the role of consumer technology in what he saw as a growing materialism. Like WCW and his patients, R. S. Thomas's life of service to his poor and hard-working parishioners convinced him of the threats he felt were gathering – in the mid-twentieth century – to our essential humanity.

For poets like John Berryman or Sylvia Plath, the turmoil that drove the poems arose out of their lives, their relationships, the struggle with their own inner demons. For R. S. Thomas and William Carlos Williams, the turmoil came in part from the particular encounter with humanity afforded by their secondary vocations, and in part from the language itself, which sent WCW back and back to the page in search of an authentic American poetry, and condemned Thomas to produce work of great beauty and acclaim in the language of his political enemies.

For both WCW and RST, their secondary vocations of service to the lives of others gave them a different slant on their vocation as poets. Dr Robert Coles described how he had attended a home birth in Paterson, whilst doing his training rounds with WCW. The labour was premature and there was no time to get the mother to hospital. As WCW took off his jacket and rolled up his sleeves, the woman was apologizing, and he said, 'Look, we're in this together, and we'll both learn from each other. Let's you and I help this future citizen of the world join us.' According to Coles, WCW sang the national anthem as the child was emerging, so that the child 'knew she was an American' from the word go. 'Young lady,' he said, after the healthy girl was delivered, 'I'm so glad to welcome you to your new American home.'

As with RST's concern for the ordinary, rural working people of Wales, WCW was always trying to cut through differences of class and race and education and authority to fully communicate and learn from people. The first thing he said to Robert Coles when he joined him on house calls was: 'Let's go and meet some ordinary American people, and maybe they'll teach you and me a thing or two.' And this impulse drove the poems too. He wanted his readers to meet the people he met as a doctor, and challenged himself to see if he could do justice to them. 'My words are inspired by my fellow human beings,' he told his young trainee.

★

At the time we interviewed R. S. Thomas in that cold stone trap of a house, the church he had served all his adult life was undergoing slow but significant change – theologically and liturgically. Although Thomas welcomed some of the new, more liberal theology, which meshed better with his own doubts, there was one liturgical change that he disliked. In the old rite of the Mass, the priest would stand at the head of his congregation with his back to them, leading his people in the incantations and prayers, representing them. Once the rules changed and the priest turned around to face the congregation, Thomas felt that something crucial had been lost. As did David Jones. Fortunately, his poetic vocation still permitted RST to take on that role, to turn and face the emptiness on behalf of his people, to cast words into the void of God for them.

Both Dr Williams and Rev. Thomas died in old age after lives of duty to the people they had committed to serve. Neither man was a saint, and neither is an entirely comfortable influence for a contemporary English poet. Both, for different reasons, railed against the historic dominance of the English over English poetry, and in Thomas's case over Wales itself.

Both poets struggled to hold their lives in balance – their outward-facing lives as pastor and doctor, and their inward-facing lives as poets. Both could be described as wounded healers. But at least both demonstrated that you don't have to fling your life off a ledge to access the great poems. They managed to hold down demanding second vocations and to write some of the twentieth century's most important poems. Perhaps, in both cases, their sense of duty to the people they served helped them to avoid the meltdown of poetic self-destruction. Or maybe they found in their twin vocations the necessary tension to generate poems. Does the call of a parishioner or patient trump the call of the muse? Do you put your pen down halfway through a draft poem when the phone rings to call you to a death or a birth?

There are other poetic counterweights to the doomed and prematurely dead. Along with Thomas and Williams, the likes of Wallace Stevens and Marianne Moore would seem to earn a place on Larkin's 'big, sane' list. But more of them later. First, we must consider *the disappeared*.

The Burning of Some Idols

Some poets are so dead that it's hard to believe they ever lived. This seems to be in inverse proportion to the amount of life they managed to cram in when they were with us. Lord Byron's blaze of hedonistic glory made him the most famous man alive, and has given him a status as the ultimate icon of self-destructive poetic bohemianism. But when you read his letters now, or look at those portraits of the curly haired dandy, it's hard to imagine that he ever lived and breathed at all.

Emily Dickinson is perhaps as far as you can head in the opposite direction. This remarkable, singular nineteenth century visionary was born, raised and died in the sleepy Massachusetts town of Amherst, in a house owned by her father. She went to school there, went to church down the road, until she gave up going to church in her twenties. She talked to her family, corresponded with a select group of editors and friends, but spent most of her last three decades in one room, dying in her mid-fifties of suspected kidney disease, and was buried in the family plot in Amherst's West Cemetery. And now we are standing in her room. It is early on a Sunday morning and it is hard to feel that she is entirely absent. Even though this is well-trodden tourist ground, the Emily Dickinson Museum a very professionally run and popular site of literary pilgrimage, and even though we are in a tour group standing in her study–bedroom, it still feels full of her.

★

Emily Dickinson famously withdrew, in her thirties, leaving us more than 1,700 short, intense, idiosyncratic poems. This was a death before death, a death-to-the-world that had a famous echo in the twentieth century.

In April 2014 the British poetry publisher Neil Astley wrote an obituary and accompanying article in the *Guardian* newspaper marking the death of the poet Rosemary Tonks. It was greeted with excitement by the many readers – in the poetry world and beyond – who had been captivated by her story. Tonks had lit up the rather dry poetry world of early Sixties London with two collections of poetry (and several novels) full of the sensuous surrealism of the French nineteenth-century Symbolists. Her books were also alive with scents of the city and sex, assignations in hotel rooms and pick-ups in smoke-filled bars. She attended literary parties, book launches, appeared on BBC radio and was photographed and interviewed in newspapers.

Then in the late Seventies Tonks vanished. She changed her name, left no forwarding address and would not permit reprints of her poems. Occasionally, poet-admirers like Brian Patten and Andrew Motion would write a piece in a newspaper or issue a plea on radio (like the 2009 Radio 4 documentary *Lost Voices*), telling the story of this 'death before death' and lauding her poetry.

Her poems (notably 'Story of a Hotel Room') circulated in anthologies and later online, kept the flame of her work alive, and the myth seemed to add to the power of the work. The story was that after twenty years of travels, affairs, marriage, divorce and literary fame, Tonks in her mid-forties had a powerful religious conversion. She was, the rumour told us, caught up in a very strict and fundamentalist form of Christianity. As a result, she turned her back on the literary world and on her own work, eschewed all reading matter save the Bible, and lived out her years as a kind of anchorite.

Dickinson and Tonks both managed to outwit death by vanishing in advance. As far as the world was concerned, both were long gone by the time their deaths caught up with them.

★

Philip Larkin, in an essay called 'Big Victims', saw Emily Dickinson's withdrawal as a form of arrested development, a willed perpetual childhood. Insisting that her best poems are 'when she is at her least odd, her most controlled', Larkin asserts that 'This is worth remembering in an age when almost any poet who can produce evidence of medical mental care is automatically ranked higher than one who stayed sane.'

The spectre of madness looms over both Dickinson's and Tonks's vanishings, but the accusation often reveals more about the teller than the tale. In both cases, an idiosyncratic mysticism rooted in (but sometimes at odds with) Christianity seems to confirm the diagnosis. Tonks *must* be mad, the rumours seemed to say, to give up London literary life and join a 'religious sect'. It's an assumption that goes back to the medieval female mystics, who were and are often 'diagnosed' as hysterics, anorexics, agoraphobics, epileptics. Some of these diagnoses may have some purchase, but all can serve to take the edge off their achievements and insights.

In the case of these two vanishing poets, their stories lend them and their work a compelling sense of mystery, and a series of questions. But the crucial difference is that Dickinson's disappearance liberated the poems. Most of the *Collected Works* of Emily Dickinson were written in the concentrated years of her anchorite life. In Tonks's case, the disappearance was the end of the poetry.

★

This, in a letter Emily Dickinson wrote to a friend in 1866, at the height of her seclusion: 'Friday I tasted life. It was a vast morsel. A Circus passed the house—still I feel the red in my mind though the drums are out. The Lawn is full of south and the odors tangle, and I hear to-day for the first time the river in the tree.'

The intensity of experience is so intoxicating. It's the intensity John Berryman sought by pushing his life to the very edge and beyond it. But Dickinson went the other way; closing in the confines of her life in the world meant that her inner life burnt ever brighter.

In her poem 'Wild Nights', written in the same period, this recluse, this near-hermit, produces a poem of erotic longing every bit as vivid (if not more) as a Byron or a Donne:

> Wild nights—Wild nights!
> Were I with thee
> Wild nights should be
> Our luxury!
>
> Futile—the winds—
> To a Heart in port—
> Done with the Compass—
> Done with the Chart!
>
> Rowing in Eden—
> Ah—the Sea!
> Might I but moor—tonight—
> In thee!

★

The drive from Boston was long and hot. Massachusetts is experiencing something of a heatwave, with temperatures reaching the nineties. The sat nav is useless. We made an early start, and stopped at a roadside service station for a breakfast burger. As we entered the town, we passed Amherst College, with white marquees set out across its manicured lawns, and banners saying 'Congratulations'. It is graduation day at one of America's most celebrated liberal arts colleges. Awkwardly besuited students and their proud parents stand on lawns with wine glasses or walk the grounds. Robert Frost taught here, and now has a library named after him. And Emily Dickinson knew the place too. Mabel Loomis Todd was a faculty wife, to the astronomer David Peck Todd, who became Professor of Astronomy in 1881. Mabel's affair with Emily's married brother Austin was the talk of the town, and a source of great scandal and distress to the Dickinson family. Ironically, Mabel's role in the dissemination and publication of Emily's work after her death was so crucial that without her we may never have known the poems.

Standing in Emily's room, we look out across the lawns towards the Evergreens. Emily lived with her parents in 'The Homestead', but her brother Austin and his family lived within shouting distance of the window in an impressive Italianate house. Emily's world may have been small, but it was far from calm. Today the lawns are radiant, transfigured, as the landscape looks in her poems. At the top of the stairs on the way to her room we had a shock as – caught in a shaft of sunlight – we were confronted by a replica of Emily's famous white dress. She didn't wear it to look like a ghost. She wore it because it was a practical house-dress, easy to bleach. But here, outside her room, it is hard not to feel haunted by it, by her. Mabel Loomis Todd never met Emily, so complete was the poet's withdrawal from public life. It's not hard to see why Mabel – and others – referred to her as 'the myth'.

With white seeds floating up and down outside the windows and the house full of light, it's hard to negotiate the presence and absence here. The house feels full of her, but there are pockets of absence too. Her beloved kitchen strikes us straightforwardly like a museum exhibit, despite the guide's explanation of Emily's passion for baking; and the large living room with its faded furniture and small-town grandeur feels like a film set. But the upstairs rooms seem to float. They are as full and empty as Emily's poems, with their unpindownable subjects and their peppering of dashes, as if each dash covers a space, a notion, an intuition for which no word yet exists.

★

There is another Emily Dickinson house in Amherst, no longer standing but almost possible to conjure in the early afternoon glare. Between 1840 and 1855 the family moved out of The Homestead to live a few blocks away in a clapboard property on Pleasant Street. This house stood right next to the town graveyard, and at a tender age Emily would have seen many funerals passing by. So far as we can tell, a gas and service station stands there now.

★

One room in the Dickinson Homestead is set aside for the poems themselves. This is right, and rare. For a dead poet's house to give such attention to the poems, a room with interpretation boards and a guide schooled in Emily's use of poetic metre, can only be a good thing. The lesson is clear, and delivered with energy and enthusiasm. There are roughly twelve of us and it feels like school. The group is asked questions, but neither of us puts our hand up. We are told that Emily's use of dashes in her poems was an accepted alternative at the time to other forms of punctuation in handwriting. We are told that the dashes were originally edited out of her published work. We are told that the rhythm of her poems is 'hymn rhythm', a four-stress line usually followed by a three stress line. They don't tell us one of the disquieting side effects of 'hymn rhythm', which is that much of Dickinson's visionary poetry can be sung to the tune of 'The Yellow Rose of Texas'. Try it. O . . .

. . . Because I could not stop for Death—
He kindly stopped for me—
The Carriage held but just Ourselves—
And Immortality.

It is all good. But we are reverting to old schoolroom patterns, gazing out of the window. A beautiful early spring afternoon is taking shape. Across the road from the Dickinson homestead, large houses now obscure the view across what Emily knew as fields. In those fields, she would walk her huge Newfoundland dog and collect flowers to press. As she got older, and withdrew more and more to the confines of her room, the view out across those fields would be a landscape every bit as rich and infused as the landscapes of Renaissance religious paintings, in which Umbrian fields or Tuscan hills became places of annunciation, resurrection and transformation. For Dickinson, who gave up attending church in her youth, the landscape was not so explicitly charged with Christian significance, but it was far from just a piece of ground:

> We paused before a House that seemed
> A Swelling of the Ground—
> The Roof was scarcely visible—
> The Cornice – in the Ground—
>
> Since then—'tis Centuries—and yet
> Feels shorter than the Day
> I first surmised the Horses' Heads
> Were toward Eternity—

★

Some poets really disappear. One morning in San Francisco on the trail of Thom Gunn, we walked along the edge of the pine-wooded Presidio and looked out over the Golden Gate Bridge. Some miscalculation meant we seemed to be at the wrong level for the road approach to the bridge, though the view from sea level was pretty spectacular, with the added thrill of realizing this was where James Stewart jumped into the cold water of San Francisco Bay to save Kim Novak in Hitchcock's *Vertigo*. A couple of years before principal photography began on that film, an abandoned 1954 Plymouth Savoy was found over on the Marin County side of the bridge, its keys still in the ignition; it had belonged to the poet Weldon Kees. Between 18 July 1955, when he was last heard from, and the following day, when his car was discovered, nobody has any idea what happened to Kees.

Originally from Nebraska, Kees was many other things beside a poet: he played jazz piano, wrote short stories and criticism, made experimental films and had some limited success as an artist, who had shown his work back east with some major, up-and-coming figures of the Abstract Expressionist school, and who had been a member of the so-called Irascibles, one of the undersigned in a letter to MoMA protesting at a perceived conservative bias among that gallery's jury in an upcoming competition. After moving to San Francisco, he was friends with Pauline Kael, then a young film critic broadcasting her reviews on KPFA in Berkeley. But all was not well.

A few days ago, while in New York, we visited the archive at Columbia University to look at the Weldon Kees papers they hold. We found this letter: 'Ann & I were divorced about three months ago. She has been in bad shape for a long time, but the last year has been fierce. Withdrawn, sloppy, drinking a hell of a lot more than she ever did. I tried to help, but I guess I didn't know how to handle it –' he wrote to Bob and Lorraine Wilbur in November 1954. His wife had begun to imagine a McCarthyite nightmare of tapped phones and secret agents lurking. A month later: 'Dear Herbert, my book is finally out, and so am I, almost; but wanted to wish you a joyous Yom Kippur + all that,' written on a tiny square of card with torn edges, in red ink.

And then, the vanishing into a Pacific fog. There have been reports of sightings in the years since. In 1987 the journalist Pete Hamill reported meeting Kees in a cantina in Mexico in 1957 – and Kees had spoken of leaving the United States to head south of the border. But Kees has enjoyed a different kind of afterlife as a poet, and as the critic Dana Gioia has noticed, it is one engendered through the agency of other poets:

> Poems about Kees began appearing in small magazines. Whereas most literary reputations today are made by prose criticism or biography, Kees's public legend grew largely through verse. This appears to be a unique accomplishment among modern American poets. While certain writers have become popular subjects for poems, especially elegies— Sylvia Plath, John Berryman, W. H. Auden and Anne Sexton, for example—their reputations were all made and sustained through prose criticism and biography. This singular fact may also partially explain both Kees's general fame among young poets, who assiduously follow new verse, and his obscurity among academic critics, who generally read only verse already canonized by other critics and anthologies.

We first discovered him via Simon Armitage's poem 'Looking For Weldon Kees', which in turn makes its debt of poetic insider tip-off explicit:

> I'd heard it said by Michael Hofmann
> that *Collected Poems* would blow my head off,
> but,
>   being out of print
>   and a hot potato
>   it might be a hard one
>   to get hold of;
> more than a case of shopping and finding
> nothing on the shelves between Keats and Kipling.

Armitage's short book, *Around Robinson*, and the TV film he subsequently made on the trail of the poet, clearly has something to do with Kees's lyrical alter ego Robinson, a persona somewhat like John Berryman's Henry. Appearing in just four poems by Kees, perhaps Robinson gave Berryman a key to the *Dream Songs*? Robinson was Kees's mid-century Everyman, spotted in Grand Central, the Park and in East Side bars. A kind of foreshortening or convergence seems to have happened over time, and the mythological Weldon Kees has proved irresistible to many poets, a tantalizing rumour passed on and passed down. There are now enough homages to fill an anthology.

The strangest item we found in the archive at Columbia was an old envelope, printed by Paramount News ('The eyes and ears of the world') containing a few snipped frames of 35 mm film. The envelope told us absolutely nothing else, except 'Kees?' We held the filmstrips up to the strip lights to get a better look: they showed the face of a man, ghostly in negative. We thought we heard thunder – either that or the subway passed directly under the archive.

After we'd signed out of Columbia, it felt like a good idea to get some fresh air and walk the forty-odd blocks back downtown. The sky rumbled away, scene-shifting from spring into summer, and about ten minutes into our walk the rain was unloosed. We needed to get in out of it, and spied a bar on the other side of Amsterdam Avenue called – no! – The Dead Poet. Drying off in the hardwood and mirrored gloom, we sat with our drinks, watching the bright cabs hissing past outside, half-expecting a man in a Glen plaid jacket and Scotchgrain shoes to come in seeking shelter.

★

Dingles has been rebranded. It's still the top button in a Bournemouth department store lift, but there's no sign of the name anywhere. Too old-fashioned, we assume, since it calls to mind the ringing of a service bell, waitresses with doilies on their heads and the taste of seed cake. None of these is evident this morning. We queue up with our trays to order pots of tea and wonder where Rosemary Tonks used to sit. Did she have a particular table?

We settle in a corner with panoramic views over the town. It is a sullen January morning and in the park below us a hot-air balloon lolls drunkenly, refusing to take off. Judging by the logo and the lurid colours, we reckon it's some kind of health promotion. Bedraggled seagulls tilt on rooftops. We know we are near the sea. We can smell it. But there's no glimpse of it from Dingles. This feels like the very edge of England. A good place to come if you want to vanish.

It has been an odd morning so far. On our separate crack-of-dawn journeys south to Bournemouth we heard the news of David Bowie's death, and within hours his last album *Blackstar* is being read as code, a subtext of last words for his fans and clues about his preparedness for the next world. It's hard not to read Rosemary Tonks's slim oeuvre in the same way. Surely, if we look closely enough, some pattern will emerge to explain the great fracture in her life. We are awaiting the arrival of Rosemary's editor Neil Astley, who will be our guide to her post-vanishing existence. The phrase 'Rosemary's editor' – like most aspects of the Tonks story – is not straightforward. Neil never met her. Nor did they speak or correspond. He sent her postcards, books and letters, tried to visit once and peered through the letterbox when she didn't answer the door. He knew she was at home, but her silence confirmed the received opinion – this poet didn't want to be found.

★

When Rosemary vanished, Tonks vanished too. It was her maiden name, her byline as a writer for the *New York Review of Books*, her introduction at literary parties, the name on the covers of her novels and poetry collections. Although divorced by the time she left London, she decided to use her ex-husband's name to begin her new life.

'I didn't even know her as Rosemary Tonks, she was always Rosemary Lightband,' says Lisa Stillman. We have walked round the corner from Dingles to a smart estate agent's shop marked with the legend 'Stephen Noble: covering the coast-line'. Lisa Stillman is PA to the Managing Director Nigel Still. We are wondering why Neil has brought us to an estate agent. We must confess that the pictures on the wall are enticing – pools and all – but a bit beyond our price range. There is clearly money on the south coast, no doubt bolstered by the advent of Premiership Football here. We wonder if any of Bournemouth's new millionaire strikers or playmakers will be languishing by these pools this summer. Lisa and Nigel pull up office chairs and sit with us.

They met Mrs Lightband when infirmity forced her to sell her home – Old Forest Lodge – a short walk up the road from here. She stayed in touch, warmed to Lisa and Nigel, became a regular caller at the shop. They describe a hunched, frail elderly lady in a navy-blue, full-length coat and a baseball cap. She often wore dark glasses, not for anonymity but to protect her damaged eyes after operations for detached retinas. Whenever they saw her, she carried a notebook bound with elastic bands, and would refer to it in conversation, checking details. Both Lisa and Nigel remembered her skin in particular, describing it as lovely, beautiful, translucent.

Lisa goes to her desk and pulls out a leather-bound copy of the New Testament, inscribed as a gift from Rosemary. We ask if Rosemary ever mentioned her own books. Once, says Lisa. 'She said that she used to write and then stopped.'

We talk about the sale of Old Forest Lodge, and Nigel explains that Mrs Lightband quickly approved or disapproved of any potential buyer he showed round. 'We could almost certainly have sold it for more money,' he says, 'but she wasn't interested. She liked the Rosses, so she decided they were going to have the house. She was very articulate and knew her own mind.' But as we get up to leave, they seem concerned that we might form the wrong impression. 'She was really sweet, a lovely lady,' Nigel assures us, 'and she had a wry smile, a glint in her eye.'

One detail remains with us. Nigel had shown us the vendor's photos of Old Forest Lodge, taken when the property went on the market. Usually, he explains, there'll be the odd dud, unusable because the current owner has strayed into shot. As out-takes go, this is real ephemera, down there with passport-photo booth rejects of ill-timed blinks. But the margins of these photographs – kitchen, bathroom, master bedroom, hallway – aren't haunted by the householder: there is no trace of Mrs Lightband in any of them.

★

Lightband. It sounds like a missing part of the armour of God, as laid out in the New Testament. To withstand what Ephesians 6:11 calls 'the wiles of the devil', you must put on 'the breastplate of righteousness', the 'shield of faith', 'the helmet of salvation' and the 'sword of the Spirit' . . . but how about the band of light? We imagine it replacing the fauld in a traditional suit of armour, just below the breastplate.

If ever there was a poet in need of the armour of God, it was Rosemary. Her journals demonstrate a starkly Manichaean view of the world. Every day was a battle between good and evil, spiritual warfare played out in Asda, Dingles and Beales, the streets and parks of Bournemouth. This sense of a parallel narrative of everyday life – a narrative unheard by most people, but disturbing and inspiring for the believer – has deep theological roots. In most religious traditions that narrative is mediated by a community. In Rosemary's case, no single church or fellowship group or denomination or affiliation seemed to stick. Once she decided that the Christian God was the true God, she was utterly single-minded. She travelled to be baptized near the River Jordan, and saw her day of baptism – aged fifty-two – not just as a second birth, but as her true beginning. From that moment on, only the New Testament could be trusted, so she eschewed all other books and took her bearings from a very vivid and personal reading of it. Her notebooks are full of references to God's love and forgiveness, but on every page there are accounts of 'the enemy' trying to tempt, tease or taunt her, often at night, when she's alone and sleepless.

Her search for a spiritual home had begun in earnest when her mother died in 1968, and it led her into a series of encounters with mediums, gurus and spiritualists. As a result (she believed) of some punishing Taoist eye exercises, she suffered two detached retinas, and by the late Seventies she was fighting to save her vision. She fled to Bournemouth to stay with an aunt. She knew the town from childhood, having boarded at a school here. In the long tradition of heading to the coast for a cure, it offered the chance for a period of respite, recovery. But she never left.

★

Duncan Ross of Old Forest Lodge comes out to greet us in his socks. As soon as we step into the house we can understand why. It is immaculate, bright and elegant. It looks like a show home with its cream carpets and beach-themed ornaments of driftwood, pebbles, shells. Neil is thrilled to cross the threshold of this house for the first time, having got no further than the letterbox before. We put our bags down in the kitchen and wonder if we should take our shoes off, but Duncan's not insisting. He offers us coffee. We have just had lunch in Beales, one of Rosemary's haunts, so we decline. Beales was very much like Dingles, another old-fashioned English department store with a penthouse café. Mrs Lightband knew what she liked.

As we do the tour of Old Forest Lodge, Duncan tries to explain the scale of what he and his wife took on when they bought this place from Mrs Lightband three years ago. He describes a house in deep neglect, inhabited by a tiny, birdlike woman with a tweed skirt pulled up high. He confirmed what the estate agent told us, that her voice was surprisingly clear and strong, that she was witty and likeable. He also mentions the baseball cap. We are fascinated

by the baseball cap. What would be written on a baseball cap worn
by the poet formerly known as Rosemary Tonks? I HEART NY?
BOURNEMOUTH FC? Duncan says he can't recall. No one
can recall what was written on it. Nigel half-remembered something about a cruise line, but wasn't sure. The tour is done. We are
back in the living room. Music plays softly through inconspicuous
speakers. Easy listening. We had an early start to get here from the
north-west, and those plush sofas look inviting. How embarrass-
ing would it be for us to doze off in Rosemary's old house? We
decide not to sit down. It's so peaceful here, although it's just off
the busy St Peter's roundabout. We can't imagine Rosemary had
much time for the sainthood of Peter, nor any of the saints for that
matter. Roman Catholicism was well beyond the pale for her. But
then, the pale stopped as soon as you left the New Testament. She
was nothing if not a purist.

Duncan explains that it took a team of builders and decora-
tors three months to rescue the house. He talks about reclaiming
garden from jungle, discovering walls and flowerbeds when it was
hacked back. The detached garage was stacked to the gunnels
with paintings and books and papers. He flicks through some
albums of pictures taken before renovation. He clearly thinks we
haven't grasped it yet. And he's right. There were bathroom suites
in spearmint green and bubblegum pink, frilly floral lampshades,
but the big shock is the dust. The house was not just dusty, it
lay like indoor snow on the carpets, so the photographs show
desire paths through it, routes habitually used to get from room
to room. It hangs in swags from the ceilings like Spanish moss. It
is hard not to conjure Miss Havisham, living among the wreckage of her past.

But that's not the impression Duncan wants to leave us with.
He remembers how she would break off in conversation, excus-
ing herself to dash out into the courtyard off the kitchen. They
would hear her greeting visitors – 'Darling, it's so lovely to see
you again' – only to realize she was talking to the birds.

She rejected her poems, her literary life, let the house go to seed, but all of this — she believed — was in the greater service of her God. That constant narrative of spiritual threat from 'the enemy' was woven into her everyday encounters. To say a wrong word or to give too much away to the wrong shop assistant or waiter would be to open the door to evil. When the stakes were that high, everything else must have seemed trivial. But the Rosses were on the side of the angels. Before we leave, Duncan shows us one very moving letter from Rosemary, apologizing for blanking him in the street, saying how 'ashamed' she is of her behaviour.

One of her last journal entries, at the end of 2013, gives a sense of her life on two levels. On the surface, little happens. She is ill, in pain, listens to the radio, goes for a walk, speaks to a porter at her apartment building. But the emotional range is — as ever in these journals — dramatic, swinging from elation to desolation within hours. At the heart of it all is her birdscape. For Rosemary, birds were harbingers and messengers. Particular birds (Nanny G seems to have been a seagull) and particular calls could bring comfort or admonishment or warning. Not just the skies, but the trees, parks, the windowsills outside her house were a text to be read, messages from God.

29 December 2013:
Sunday. Was listening to Radio 3 I think, & <u>Borodin</u> came on!!! Oh! Then later in the morning, listening to Classic FM and <u>again Borodin</u>!!! <u>Again the 2nd String Quartet</u>. Was <u>so</u> happy.
But felt <u>so ill</u> & in pain.
Lay down after lunch: but Nanny G. came after 15 mins & then again about 15 mins later.
So got up, after ½ hour lie down, & dressed to go out.
Finally got up to Car Park. Lovely, lovely coo-coos from the left!!!! And then ahead on the path a darling baby magpie!!

<u>But</u> came back & most foolishly said something wrong and obnoxious about the other porters – can't remember what it was. Felt <u>terrible</u>. Went back to his office & asked him to forgive me for speaking <u>foolish</u> & <u>untruthful</u> words.

Walked about miserably & was comforted by some kind little sounds from Nanny G.

★

Her life in London continued, but it was a different city, not the London of literary soirées and book launches. Her regular visits (often weekly) took in cafés around Waterloo Station, libraries where she sought out different translations of the Bible, and Hyde Park.

We like to think that on one of her trips to hand out Bibles and listen to the preachers at Hyde Park Corner, Rosemary may have brushed past Brian Patten, Andrew Motion or one of the other British poets who took to the airwaves to lament her disappearance, as they walked through the city on their way to the BBC.

Neil Astley, writing in the *Guardian* after her death, summed up neatly the general consensus on her vanishing: 'Commentators over the years have made her into a nun; consigned her to a sect; had her communing with the ghost of Charles Baudelaire, or put her in a shed at the bottom of someone's garden. For some reason, these mythmakers always required her to be living in poverty.'

In fact she was comfortably off from her ex-husband's investments on her behalf. She lived relatively simply, but ate most of her meals in cafés and hotels near her home. She tithed 10 per cent of her income each year to various charities. She had a limited social life, but she was far from a hermit. Nigel Still, her estate-agent friend, gave us the parting shot that she was witty, very dry. 'She was delightful, absolutely delightful', he said. We were surprised, all day in Bournemouth, by the warmth towards this reputedly hermitic poet from those who had known her.

★

Is there such a fracture between Rosemaries Tonks and Lightband? Neil sums up the pre-vanishing poet as: 'headstrong, willful, obsessive, rebellious, judgemental, fiercely intelligent and given to extreme ways of thinking'. It's hard to think of any part of that which doesn't fit the vanished poet too.

But more than that, her fierce rage for truth, her rejection of the superficial and the inauthentic, is as evident in her poems as in her later journals. There's a radical impulse to overthrow anything that might damage or compromise the truth.

In his introduction to her *Collected Poems*, Neil quotes a list:

> Three Tang horses with riders, four Sung priest figures, a Japanese warrior, a Korean dancing figure, Chinese jade and small bronzes, Chinese silk robes embroidered with dragons, carved Chinese letter seals (rose apricot stone), Chinese dogs on stands, chess-set and lion mask, along with other artefacts of marble, terracotta, porcelain, plaster, mother-of-pearl, ivory, wood and stone, from China, Korea, Japan, Africa, Greece, Bali and Persia.

This is a sample of over forty ancient oriental treasures in a collection left to Rosemary by an aunt. The list was made in Rosemary's hand, under the heading 'The burning of some idols'. Convinced that these objects were 'graven images' that broke the Second Commandment, she burnt them all – five suitcases of them – in garden incinerators, then pummelled the ashes until all the objects were reduced to 'dog-biscuit size'.

But they weren't the only idols in need of destruction. The garden incinerator saw off the only copy of a huge unpublished novel, written in the six years before her vanishing, and regarded by its author in her past life as 'the best thing I had ever written'. The last traces of her despised 'profession' were gone.

★

People do bow out. Our books and films are full of them. They feel trapped, go to work one day on their usual commuter train, then surface ten years later running a bar on a Thai beach. Depression can fuel it, and we know that Rosemary suffered from what she called 'the flood', and tried to get wise to its triggers. Although she didn't expressly forbid republication of her poems after her death, Rosemary Lightband asked for her journals to be destroyed, and did all she could to prevent the circulation of her poems and novels. Before we part company in Bournemouth, we ask Neil how he squares all this with his new role as her posthumous publisher. 'You're publishing the work of someone else,' he says. 'She was no longer the person who wrote the poems. But you feel an obligation to understand why she chose to turn her back on that person, and on the poetry which is of great literary value. She's an important writer of the twentieth century.' Neil has gone out of his way to try to understand what happened to Rosemary Tonks. He consulted three psychotherapists, but there was no clear diagnosis. If you change the language from psychological to theological, her volte-face seems less singular. In the evangelical and Pentecostal traditions she was (at least initially) drawn into, notions of a 'second birth', of the centrality of scripture, the reality of idols and demons and messages from the Lord are far from unusual. Rosemary took it to extremes. Her Manichaean view of the world, her equally Manichaean readings of the people she met, her sense of birds as spiritual messengers, all push her to the extreme edges of religious faith and experience.

But then, wasn't she always on the edge? The evidence is there in many of her poems. Take this, from the opening of 'Addiction to an Old Mattress', from her second (and last) collection *Iliad of Broken Sentences*, first published in 1967:

No, this is not my life, thank God . . .
. . . worn out like this, and crippled by brain-fag;
Obsessed first by one person, and then

(Almost at once) most horribly besotted by another;
These Februaries, full of draughts and cracks,
They belong to the people in the streets, the others
Out there – haberdashers, writers of menus.

Salt breezes! Bolsters from Istanbul!
Barometers, full of contempt, controlling moody isobars.
Sumptuous tittle-tattle from a summer crowd
That's fed on lemonades and matinées. And seas
That float themselves about from place to place, and then
Spend *hours* – just moving some clear sleets across glass
    stones.
Yalta: deck-chairs in Asia's gold cake; thrones.

Why is the literary world so shocked by Rosemary Tonks's disappearance? With Emily Dickinson's withdrawal, the myth only serves to enhance the authenticity of the poems. Such intensity, such sensitivity, could only be forged in isolation. The fascination and distress surrounding Rosemary's vanishing is different. Perhaps, in part, it's because she gave up a literary career so many people now (as then) long for. Why doesn't she want to come to our parties any more? Her *Collected Poems* quotes an interview with Peter Orr in 1963 on why she didn't feel connected with other poets: 'They are a rather lost set, you know, in London. They form movements.' No change there then.

But the real scandal of the Tonks story is that, unlike Dickinson, she took the poems with her when she left. She gave up on her work. That's what the many poets and readers who admire her poems find so troubling. However, we're not sure we fully accept Neil's and Rosemary's sense that she became a different person when she turned from London's Tonks to Bournemouth's Lightband. From the evidence of those late journals, and from conversations with those who knew her in her final years, her work never stopped. It may have moved from poems and novels to Bible study, constant prayer and soul-searching, but the rage for truth, the sheer voltage and intensity was constant. 'Addiction to an Old Mattress' ends with this:

> Meanwhile . . . I live on . . . powerful, disobedient,
> Inside their draughty haberdasher's climate,
> With these people . . . who are going to obsess me,
> Potatoes, dentists, people I hardly know, it's unforgivable
> For this is not my life
> But theirs, that I am living.
> And I wolf, bolt, gulp it down, day after day.

Confessional

No point feeling nervous about looking for Robert Lowell's death place, we decide in the taxi over to West 67th Street, just off Central Park. If he could have, he'd have written about it. And there's the rub. What would Robert Lowell, the poet who seemed to single-handedly invent Confessionalism, have made of his own death? In September 1977, the sixty-year-old Lowell returned to the United States from a trip to Ireland, where he had visited his third wife, the writer Caroline Blackwood. Their marriage was disintegrating. Hailing a taxi at JFK, he headed over to the Upper West Side and the duplex apartment he once shared with his second wife Elizabeth Hardwick, who still lived in the building. But the cab pulled up outside the apartment block with an unresponsive passenger: Lowell had suffered a heart attack at some indeterminable point between the airport apron and here, where we're pulling up. The taxi driver, unable to rouse his fare, rang the apartment bell, and that was how Elizabeth found him. In his arms, wrapped in brown paper, he was clutching a painting of the woman whom he had just broken up with. He'd once said he wanted 'a natural death, no teeth on the ground, no blood about the place'.

★

Limestone gothic arches. The West 67th Street apartments are impressive, old money, an example of medieval Manhattan. We hesitate on the threshold: the lobby is decorated with murals painted by members of the Artists' Colony that was based here around a century ago, and it turns out the entire street is one of those dense cultural ganglions you find in a city like New York. Isadora Duncan, Rudolph Valentino and Marcel Duchamp, among many other luminaries, have all lived hereabouts. The building super comes out to see what we want, and is more than happy to let us take a closer look at the lobby, but there's no question of disturbing the residents, and anyway, we don't try very hard to talk our way in. Lowell never got this far. But this isn't Frank O'Hara's New York, a few blocks south in Midtown, and it certainly isn't W. H. Auden's New York and the cold-water apartments of the East Village. The building is telling us this much.

Lowell takes much of the Confessional heat, because the term was first used in a review of *Life Studies*, his fourth book of poems. Confession time: when did you first get hold of a copy of *Life Studies*? It turns out we both bought the book sometime in the late Eighties. One of the powers of poetry, or any literature, is the way it can strike a chord a long way from its source. Indeed, most poets would probably confess that the idea of a reader completely unknown and culturally distant from them reading one of their poems is hugely gratifying. And so, the poems of a well-to-do, well-connected Bostonian poet of the mid-century found readers like us, buying the book largely on its word-of-mouth reputation after sampling a few poems in bookshops long since given over to mobile-phone franchises or pop-up supermarkets.

Life Studies isn't a simple book. We remember the fussiness of its four sections, only the last of which, called 'Life Studies', contains the poems that take us into the world of his parents and grandparents, his incarceration for conscientiously objecting, his marriage, medication. The second part, '91 Revere Street', is in prose, and, we discovered many years later, a glimpse into an autobiography he'd begun writing under contract in 1955, but never completed. It's hard to see the book straight now, because the new available space these poems created has been occupied and explored so many times in the decades since it was published in 1959, but this book altered the landscape of poetry. It also introduced a stance, a mode, a lyric tilt to the world that was easily absorbed, easily misunderstood.

★

Something happened to Lowell on a busy reading tour of California in 1957. Ginsberg's *Howl* had been published two years earlier and audiences were getting used to something very different. The North Beach coffee-house crowd, by Lowell's own admission, turned him off his older work; its style 'seemed distant, symbol-ridden and wilfully difficult . . . ' Lowell had just turned forty. He was staring extinction by Beat poetry in the face: 'My own poems seemed like prehistoric monsters dragged down into the bog and death by their ponderous armour,' Lowell said of the experience. It's tempting to imagine the road to *Life Studies* in parallel to the paradigm shift that the painter Philip Guston underwent the following decade, lurching seemingly overnight from abstract textures and colourfields to slapdash canvases of Ku Klux Klansmen, painted like Krazy Kat cartoons, cruising the streets and smoking; or the gear change that occurred in popular music during the same febrile period, when Bob Dylan – himself of course alive to Ginsberg – abandoned his folksy, acoustic sound, plugged in the backline and went electric. It's tempting to imagine a new poetry, forged in the hash smoke and heckled air. But Lowell went on to say how biography might also lie at the root of what happened: 'What influenced me more than San Francisco and reading aloud was that for some time I had been writing prose. I felt that the best style for poetry was none of the many poetic styles in English, but something like the prose of Chekhov or Flaubert.' Either way, the result was a huge freedom won, the freedom, as Seamus Heaney put it, 'from the anxiety to sound canonical'.

★

Cal. We realize we have no idea where Lowell got this nickname, or how. Can we even think of another poet so recognizable by their nickname? Not the sheltering nom de plume or unsure pseudonym – from Decimus to Incertus, poets have always had recourse to those – but a name known to insiders and familiars, given such a wide circulation. It turns out he became Cal while at school, and it stuck. There are two sources: Caliban and Caligula. Prospero's slave and ambiguous monster, and the Roman emperor remembered as a cruel tyrant. So we're guessing he wasn't milk monitor. 'My namesake, Little Boots, Caligula . . .,' as Lowell put it. Dearest Cal . . .

★

Lowell and Elizabeth Bishop had been writing to each other for ten years by the time she saw the poems that became *Life Studies*. 'They all also have that sure feeling,' she wrote to him, 'as if you'd been in a stretch . . . when everything and anything suddenly seemed material for poetry – or not material, seemed to *be* poetry, and all the past was illuminated in long shafts here and there, like a long-waited-for sunrise. If only one could see everything that way all the time!'

In Brazil, Bishop received no reply and learned from Lowell's wife Elizabeth that Cal had been hospitalized in the final push towards the completion of these poems. She spared Bishop the details – 'the details are always like a Russian novel because of the immense *activity* of these stages' – except to say Lowell was far from well. By the time he wrote back, in March 1958, he was in the McLean Hospital at Belmont. Lowell had long suffered from oscillating bouts of mania and depression. 'I am tired. Everyone's tired of my turmoil' goes the last line of 'Eye and Tooth', and there are plenty of Robert Lowell stories in circulation, forming an amalgam of a statue-climbing, raving, declaiming handful who you wouldn't want in the back of your cab. His reply to Bishop from McLean's is funny and sad, but mostly impressively detailed in the way it notices the rhythms of the institution and the characters of his fellow patients. Hospitalization became art, and a poem called 'Waking in the Blue'. He did a similar thing in another poem that ended up in *Life Studies*, remembering his time locked up in a New York jailhouse in 1943, arraigned for refusing the draft:

> I was so out of things, I'd never heard
> of the Jehovah's Witnesses.
> 'Are you a C.O.?' I asked a fellow jailbird.
> 'No,' he answered, 'I'm a J.W.'
> He taught me the 'hospital tuck',
> and pointed out the T-shirted back
> of *Murder Incorporated's* Czar Lepke,
> there piling towels on a rack,
> or dawdling off to his little segregated cell full
> of things forbidden the common man:
> a portable radio, a dresser, two toy American
> flags tied together with a ribbon of Easter palm.
> Flabby, bald, lobotomized,
> he drifted in a sheepish calm,
> where no agonizing reappraisal
> jarred his concentration on the electric chair—
> hanging like an oasis in his air
> of lost connections . . .

The following day we find some of the manuscript versions of this poem, 'Memories of West Street and Lepke', at the Berg Collection in the New York Public Library. There are many changes and revisions between the first typed draft and the final carbon copy: 'Fire-eating' becomes 'fire-breathing'. Two 'Porto Rican draft-dodgers' vanish completely. The journey up the Hudson, where 'Both sheriffs sat in the front seat / So as to have room to swing, if we made trouble', has bitten the dust with them. Whatever Lowell's Confessionalism was, it was no spontaneous outpouring.

Its candour and sincerity must have been something of an illusion, a modulated, carefully poised 'I'. As he told the *Paris Review*:

> There's a good deal of tinkering with fact. You leave out a lot, and emphasize this and not that. Your actual experience is a complete flux. I've invented facts and changed things, and the whole balance of the poem was something invented. So there's a lot of artistry, I hope, in the poems. Yet there's this thing: if a poem is autobiographical – and this is true of any kind of autobiographical writing and of historical writing – you want the reader to say, this is true. In something like Macaulay's *History of England* you think you're really getting William III. That's as good as a good plot in a novel. And so there was always that standard of truth which you wouldn't ordinarily have in poetry – the reader was to believe he was getting the *real* Robert Lowell.

★

We have no qualms about a taking a few photographs on West 67th Street. We could easily be architectural students – *mature* students – studying the Artists' Colony Historic District, the arches, pinnacles, gables and lobby murals. Lowell had arrived where he'd asked the taxi driver to take him that day, and there's no air of gloom or dread. As we frame the building, its doorway, its mailbox (imagining long-ago letters franked with Brazilian postmarks), its ornate address cut into the stone, we remember how Lowell's late poems are full of photographs.

It's hardly surprising Lowell's eye was drawn to the stilled image. He'd said he'd hoped the poems of *Life Studies* 'might seem as open and single-surfaced as a photograph'. Life's 'complete flux' captured, the image and reader travelling along their own timelines. His final collection, *Day by Day*, is full of photographs. It's a quiet, more melancholy, autumnal book than much of what came before, but lit by flash, ghosted by negatives, and populated by dead poets. The book's final poem, 'Epilogue', seems to point somewhere else, to the 'fact' of photography, and things which have passed before a shutter, transmuted into the thicker, impasto, richer imaginary realm of art:

> Those blessèd structures, plot and rhyme –
> why are they no help to me now
> I want to make
> something imagined, not recalled?
> I hear the noise of my own voice:
> *The painter's vision is not a lens,*
> *it trembles to caress the light.*
> But sometimes everything I write
> with the threadbare art of my eye
> seems a snapshot,
> lurid, rapid, garish, grouped,
> heightened from life,
> yet paralyzed by fact.
> All's misalliance.
> Yet why not say what happened?
> Pray for the grace of accuracy
> Vermeer gave to the sun's illumination
> stealing like the tide across a map
> to his girl solid with yearning.
> We are poor passing facts,
> warned by that to give
> each figure in the photograph
> his living name.

What will these photographs tell us when we look back? What is there to learn or understand from a sidewalk, a lobby? The painted angels look down from their mural, their wings folded high behind them.

★

'The *real* Robert Lowell.' To some degree, all poets gather details from their lives, but what kind of risks are involved when poetry tries to move head-on into the territory of documentary, the candid revelation of some private or painful subject matter? One danger might be your work being received and framed as mere biography. What's more, the conflation of life and work attracts unwanted attention. 'The tendency is to overdo the morbidity. You just wish they'd keep some of those things to themselves', Bishop told *Time* magazine in 1967 (though she wasn't told the interview was for a piece about Lowell). 'They had collected about 1000 pages', Lowell wrote to her, 'questioning people I hardly knew, and asking impertinent personal questions'. Bishop was hardly a model for settled domesticity and stability, but her work plots a course wide of the shallows of anguish and confession, moving into deeper waters.

★

We remember a poet telling the story of his father's death, and being asked if he wished to view the body. After steeling himself, he entered the chapel of rest and slowly approached the open coffin. Many confusing and contradictory thoughts pinballed about as he looked down at his father's made-up face; most disturbing of all was a voice that seemed to rise above the jumble of others in his head, which said: 'Fucking hell. If I don't get a poem out of this ...'

Is this simply evidence for that cold particle, that chip of ice, the necessary distancing lens, an opportunistic instinct all artists are said to need in order to make art in the face of trouble and turmoil? The idea is a long and deep-rooted one, durable enough to have generated its own handy, off-the-peg axiom: 'Happiness writes white.'

★

What about the painting Lowell was found clutching in the back of the cab that parked up here?

In *Life Studies*, '91 Revere Street' opens with a portrait painting – of 'Major Myers in his sanguine War of 1812 uniform with epaulets, white breeches and a scarlet frogged waistcoat' – that in turn opens a corridor into Lowell's past, on his grandmother's side. The portrait has been 'mislaid past finding', but Lowell can find it in memory, fixed in his childhood home, in its place.

At the end of his life, Lowell was holding on to a portrait of his third wife Caroline Blackwood, painted by her first husband Lucian Freud in 1952. *Girl in Bed* hangs on the wall of the National Portrait Gallery in London. It comes after Freud's Paddington interior with the big yucca plant and red carpet, but precedes the later, looser, impasto brushwork that he developed into, hogshair replacing sable, as William Feaver once put it. Blackwood had run away to Paris with the painter around the time *Girl in Bed* was painted, and married him the following year.

The girl resting her head in her hand, in silvery white bed linen, is striking, luminous, the big dark eyes in the heart-shaped face working like magnets. It seems Lowell carried it across the Atlantic to be valued, but trying to find out where the painting has been in the decades since draws a blank. We want to join it to 'Epilogue' and the gesture towards art, book-ending Lowell with portraiture. But the girl in the portrait was reportedly a bored sitter, tired of posing for hours on end. The story goes that before his second wife Elizabeth unwrapped the brown paper parcel and came face to face with the image of her marital successor, the dead poet's arms had to be broken in hospital in order to wrest the painting from his grasp.

★

Robert Lowell may be the Daddy of the Confessionals, but he's not the one that seized the public imagination. Two of his students at Boston, classmates of almost the same age and competitive to the last, outstripped him on that score. We are on the trail of one of them now, but we haven't been able to make contact with the current owners of the house. In fact, we can't be completely sure that it's still there. We know it's in a place called Weston, off the Massachusetts Turnpike outside Boston, and we know the name of her road. How could you forget it, once you know what happened there? Black Oak Road.

Our attempts to research this trip online were confounded at every turn. There's no rail connection to Weston, so driving is the only option. An online search before our visit comes up with no sales records for the address in question, but a few property sites estimate the value of the house at around $2 million. Google Maps allows a virtual 'walk' as far as Highland Street, but when you get to what should be the junction to Black Oak Road, it's just a void. It's like reaching the end of the world in a video game, so remote from the centre that the game designers didn't bother to render it.

So we set out on Highway 90 with a paper map and no real idea what we'll find there. This route west of Boston works like an accidental tourist trail of famous American poets. With small diversions from this artery a pilgrim could take in the birthplaces, death-places or sometime homes of Amy Lowell, Anne Sexton, Robert Lowell, Elizabeth Bishop, Emily Dickinson and Robert Frost.

We have spent most of the day at the Dickinson house in Amherst, on the trail of the white-frocked 'Myth' of nineteenth-century American poetry. But now we are heading east towards the Boston suburbs, on the trail of another kind of myth, the suicidal poet who makes poetry out of her own madness and is burned up in the process. It is a myth often attached to Sylvia Plath, but which reaches its apotheosis in her friend Anne Sexton.

★

We are heading west towards Weston and it is beginning to snow. This is so unseasonal it seems crazy. But the plunge into cold fits our conversation. We have spent a shimmering afternoon in Amherst, standing in a room so flooded with light from tall windows that the ghost of Emily Dickinson might be conjured by it. Now we are trying to perform a mental gear shift, towards a dusk encounter with the ghost of Anne Sexton in Black Oak Road.

Perhaps the dubbing of many mid-twentieth-century American poets – Berryman, Plath, Sexton, Lowell – as 'doomed' or 'confessional' is an attempt to understand why they seemed to push themselves to such a brink – and over it. If their own lives were the essential subject of their work, then the plain life, the life of routine and comfort, must be death to the poetry. Is there something in this? Is there anything in the idea that Philip Larkin's 'sane' team, the solid, well-balanced poets like Eliot, Stevens and Marianne Moore were able to live more conventional lives because their work was less dependent on the vicissitudes of love, loss, despair, paranoia, excess? It sounds plausible.

Except it doesn't quite stack up. Berryman was adamant, when asked, that he was not Henry and that Henry was not he. There was clearly some overlap, in that Henry knew and visited some of the same places and people that Berryman knew and visited. But that's the negotiation between any writer and their fictional narrator. On the occasions he was asked what he felt about the 'confessional poet' label, Berryman rejected the term with utter defiance and disdain. How about the other so-called Confessionals? Robert Lowell's work is far too complex and allusive in its 'making' to qualify as reworked pages from his diary. Though he did (in the portraits from *The Dolphin* in particular) draw very heavily on real members of his family and – to his friend Elizabeth Bishop's distaste – incorporated extracts from private letters.

Perhaps Anne Sexton qualifies as the most clear-cut candidate for the Confessional crown. Her letters and notebooks are – like her poems – full of turmoil and passion and lurid imagery. Sexton and Sylvia Plath were competitive friends from their first encounter in Robert Lowell's poetry seminars. When news of

Sylvia Plath's suicide reached her, Sexton poured out her feelings in a poem – 'Sylvia's Death' – which is two parts elegy, one part jealousy:

> Thief –
> how did you crawl into,
> crawl down alone
> into the death I wanted so badly and for so long,
> the death we said we both outgrew,
> the one we wore on our skinny breasts,
> the one we talked of so often each time
> we downed three extra dry martinis in Boston,
> the death that talked of analysts and cures,
> the death that talked like brides with plots,
> the death we drank to,
> the motives and the quiet deed?

★

We are struggling to find Black Oak Road. Weston seems like a ghost town anyway, with no one on the streets, no cars on the roads. There is a lot of money here, and a lot of class. It strikes us Brits, whose sense of American towns is filtered through years of film and TV, as something like Stepford. The unseasonal snow is beginning to ease off as we drive through the town a third time on Highland Street and see the understated sign for Black Oak Road. It seems to point up, as its name suggests, into thick, tall woods.

Probably the last interview given by Anne Sexton was granted to a student at nearby Wellesley College. Beth Hinchliffe's account of her visit to the house in Black Oak Road offers a stark contrast to the way it looks today. They met in Sexton's study, 'just off her sunny kitchen with incongruously cheerful gingerbread men on the curtains. She ionized the room,' Hinchliffe recalls. 'In my memory everything else was black and white (ironically, except her dalmatians), whereas she exploded through in drenched technicolor.'

Nothing on Black Oak Road looks technicolor to us, as it snakes up the hill through the trees. The houses are large, opulent, but closed in on themselves, few and far between, tucked into clearings at the end of long driveways. We see no one. At one house, just on the edge of visibility through the trees, a dog stands at a gate and barks at our car. We are counting down the house numbers on the mailboxes.

★

Anne Sexton's house. We pause outside, engine still running, nowhere to park. We stare at the number on the mailbox, then at the long, low residence beyond it. All is quiet. Although dusk is falling, and the weight of trees accelerates that fall, there are no lights visible, no car outside, no dog on patrol. The scant details we found online misrepresented the place. One real-estate site told us it was a five-bed house built in 1964 in Colonial style, with a forced air-heating system and 3.5 bathrooms. It sits in a plot of 1.39 acres under a wood and shingle roof.

But none of this describes it properly. Now we are here, it reveals itself to be an unstable place where the membrane that separates life from death is disturbingly thin. Of all our pilgrimages to poets' death-places, this is the most unsettling. We are discussing whether to go up the drive, to get out and ring the doorbell. Which of us will do it? What will we say if we get an answer? We stare at the house to try to work up the courage. But one detail from the realtor's list of features keeps coming back to us. Under the heading 'Garage' there is just a dash. No details, no denial, just a lacuna.

What we know about the garage is that on 4 October 1974, after lunch with her friend the poet Maxine Kumin to discuss the manuscript of her forthcoming collection *The Awful Rowing Toward God*, Anne Sexton went home, locked herself inside, and started up her sporty red Mercury Cougar. She was found dead with a vodka glass, wearing her mother's fur coat, having taken all the rings off her fingers.

★

With most of our visits to the death places of the poets, or to their homes, we've tried to set up a meeting with the current owners, and if that has failed, we've just turned up and knocked on the door. But with Anne Sexton's house, setting up a meeting or knocking on the door becomes a very different proposition. Because what if they don't know about her suicide?

We could perhaps just say we're researching a famous American poet who used to live at that address, but what if they go and look her up after we've gone? What if they are living there happily, maybe a family with kids, and then – through us – they find out what really happened there? Sitting in the car on Black Oak Road, we can't imagine living in that house, parking in that garage. And we can't imagine knocking on the door to drop the name of this dead poet into their lives. We drive away.

Anne Sexton suffered episodes of severe mania and depression throughout her adult life. Accounts of her therapies paint an all-too-familiar picture of mental health treatment in the Fifties and Sixties, much of which seemed to deepen her problems. She lived here in Black Oak Road with her husband and two children, but her private life was damaged too, and she divorced a year before her suicide at the age of forty-five.

How much blame for Sexton's fate can be laid at the door of poetry itself? Or, more precisely, the tight bind of life and work encouraged by 'Confessional' poetics?

Her fellow-poets tried to challenge that bind. Denise Levertov made a plea in response to Sexton's death that: 'We who are alive must make clear, as she could not, the distinction between creativity and self-destruction.' Adrienne Rich put it even more starkly in a eulogy at Sexton's funeral: 'We have had enough suicidal women poets, enough suicidal women, enough self-destructiveness as the sole form of violence permitted to women.'

★

About a year after the trip to Black Oak Road we arrange to meet American poet Anne Stevenson for tea in London, on her way to a memorial service for her fellow-poet and friend Lee Harwood. Raised in New England and a graduate of the University of Michigan, Anne has lived for many years in Britain. She wrote about her near contemporary Sylvia Plath (they were born two months apart) in the book *Bitter Fame*.

Now in her eighties, Anne was one of that doomed generation of American poets, but her path was different. We meet her for tea at the Horseguards Hotel overlooking the Thames, not far from the Houses of Parliament. She is at pains to stress that she's not a regular here, but that she and her husband found a special deal and decided to see a few friends in London on the way to the memorial service.

We are surrounded by businessmen and tourists. Anne's husband decides to take a walk and leaves us to it. We begin by asking her about her contemporaries Sexton and Plath:

'It's these screwy girls, these screwy girls . . . You have to understand how very seriously Americans took themselves then. I'm not without my own vanities in this way, but it is very serious. You take yourself as an individual so seriously, you are the centre of the universe. You are brought up that way, competitively, to get to the top of the ladder, and then you discover it's a bit dizzying up there! Then you run into personal troubles – somebody lets you down or betrays you – something you feel you can only remedy by this particular kind of vengeance against yourself.'

She goes on to say how much she admires Plath's poetry, much more than Sexton's. We discuss the near impossibility of seeing either poet's work clearly, past the ever-present facts of their suicides. Did she ever get drawn into this view herself, the inescapable bind between the life and the work?

'Part of my life I believed the notion that the worst things that could happen in your life would be the best things for your poetry. I wanted to be famous. I would take anything that would make me write better, but Elizabeth Bishop was a great help to me in this.'

She roots in her bag to find a stanza from a poem she has copied for us. It is by the English poet James Fenton, a satire on the Confessional aesthetic:

> He tells you, in the sombrest notes,
> If poets want to get their oats
> The first step is to slit their throats.
>   The way to divide
> The sheep of poetry from the goats
>   Is suicide.

As a survivor of that generation, Anne Stevenson's views on poetry are an antidote to that Confessional aesthetic. But when we ask her if she thinks poets are just the same as novelists or playwrights, if the myth of the doomed poet is indeed mere myth, she shakes her head.

'No, it is not a myth. I would rather have been a novelist. I would have much preferred to write like Jane Austen, I envy Dick Francis . . . I can't write poetry unless I have something that really needs to come out.'

*

Three years before her death, and two years before her divorce, Anne Sexton wrote a poem with its date as its title – 'May 30th' – full of bleak wit and foreboding, but full of vitality, too, a taste of life in Black Oak Road:

> Don't look now, God, we're all right.
> All the suicides are eating Black Bean soup;
> the Dalmatian, our turnip, our spotted parasite

snoozles in her chair. The trees, that group
of green girls wiggle at every window;
a sea bird, all nude and intimate, comes in low.

The house sinks in its fill, heavy with books;
in the kitchen the big fat sugar sits in a chamber pot;
in the freezer the Blue Fish vomit up their hooks;
the marriage twists, holds firm, a sailor's knot.
Last night he blamed the economy on Roosevelt and Truman.
I countered with Ike and Nixon. Both wrong. Both human.

Please God, we're all right here. Please leave us alone.
Don't send death in his fat red suit and his ho-ho baritone.

Are our dead poets forming two lines? Is it the Self-destructive
Gang on one side, and the Big Sane Group on the other? It's
tempting to see it that way, but then again Larkin's description of
these admirably well-adjusted poets could be seen as a feint. After
all, he was hardly as big and sane as he wanted us to think. Perhaps
the difference is not so much between victims and survivors, as
between those who believed their life and work were separable,
and those who allowed them to become too entwined?

Again, the lines aren't clear. T. S. Eliot's stable public life as a
respected banker and then editor was complicated by his guilt
and horror at the illness and long-term hospitalization of his first
wife. In a letter reflecting on his life with Vivienne, he says: 'To
her the marriage brought no happiness . . . To me, it brought the
state of mind out of which came *The Waste Land*.' Even in a man
who championed 'impersonality' in poetry, it's not hard to see the
working out of the life in the poems.

The Intelligent Whale

We are in a hire car in Hartford, Connecticut. It is a bright, clear afternoon and the mood in Hartford seems pretty buoyant too, at first. As we peel off the freeway into the city centre we see people carrying flags and balloons. But two streets further on the flags run out. If there's a festival, it's either very local or very unpopular.

Gaze too long into a satnav, and the satnav will gaze into you. Ours was good on the broad-brush stuff that got us from Amherst to Hartford, but now that we're down to particular streets it has no idea. We're looking for an address off Albany Road, near Elizabeth Park. But Elizabeth Park is huge and Albany Road is long. In fact, Elizabeth Park is billed on the signs as 'one of the great parks of the country'. It does look beautiful, full of mature trees and open spaces, but for now it's just an inconvenience. We switch off the satnav and drive slowly round the park's perimeter until, finally, we enter the road in question. And what a road it is. These are huge, sprawling detached properties in their own substantial grounds. In England they would be seen as 'executive homes', and the smart cars parked outside them underline that view.

We count the houses down to the right number, park the car and steel ourselves before walking across a manicured lawn, notebooks in hand. By now, we know how rubbish we are at cold-calling, and don't like doing this one bit. We'd imagined a kind of gumshoe glamour, but it feels like we're peddling encyclopedias or *aloominum* siding. By the time we get to the door, we can't decide whether we look more like Jehovah's Witnesses or Republican canvassers. At least this poet died of natural causes. After several attempts at the bell, a barefooted, middle-aged woman in loose summer clothes answers.

'Hello. Hi. So sorry to bother you, but we're over here from England on a research trip . . . We're both professors and we're trying to research a book, a book about poets, dead poets, we're English professors, and we've just driven over here from Boston today, and, er . . . '

She puts us out of our misery. 'Wallace Stevens freaks, huh?'

★

For young poets seeking to dodge the shuffling queue to the cliff edge, counter-examples are important. For all the self-destructive glamour of the bohemians, shouldn't we cling to the survivors? How about this: one of America's pioneering Modernist poets, who died in hospital a month after John Berryman's suicide in 1972, peacefully at the age of eighty-four? Or this: another Modernist hero – a lyrical mystic, a philosopher-poet – who dies quietly in hospital in Connecticut in 1955 at the age of seventy-five, two years after Dylan Thomas's bacchanalian last trip to New York?

Marianne Moore and Wallace Stevens have the highest of literary reputations, yet they managed to live relatively tranquil lives, active and working well into old age, before succumbing to common geriatric illnesses – strokes and cancer. But even these strong counter-examples are touched by the mythic status of poetic death. In both cases, their deaths were turned and shaped and retold in the years that followed, complicated by rumours. Did the atheist Wallace Stevens secretly convert to Roman Catholicism on his deathbed, requesting that his family should never be told? Was Marianne Moore's love of baseball the death of her, when she appeared in public for a final fatal flourish at the Yankee Stadium?

★

'Yes, I guess we kind of are . . . Stevens freaks, that is . . . ' She finishes a phone call we've interrupted, just as her son arrives home
and parks his car on the drive. They are friendly, open, not unac-
customed to talking about Wallace Stevens with strangers from
overseas. The front door is ajar, but we are not invited in. None
of us knows quite what the terms of engagement are here. Is this
a passing chat in the street or are we guests? She tells us she is the
wife of the Dean of Christ Church Episcopal Cathedral here in
Hartford. They would show us around, but the house is all packed
up because they are about to move to New Hampshire, where her
husband has a new job.

We ask if they get a lot of visitors because of the old poet.
Not a lot, says the son, but those that come are mainly from
the Far East. Stevens is big in China. We ask where his study
was. They are not sure, but they think it was a top-floor room
in the extension on the right-hand side of the main house. It
has windows to the front and back, so the light can pass right
through it. This seems fitting, we say. His poems are like that.
If you look at them long enough, you see that the light passes
right through them.

'I'm an English major,' she says. 'And I don't fully get his poems.'
Her son nods. 'They're really difficult.'

★

As we stand on the lawn in Hartford, being half-hosted by the
wife of the Dean of Christ Church Cathedral, we can't help but
wonder how this house – of all houses – ended up in the keeping
of the Church. Stevens was not an orthodox believer, though he
declared in a letter four years before his death that: 'I am not an
atheist although I do not believe today in the same God in whom
I believed when I was a boy.'

Despite Stevens's disavowal of the term 'atheist', the death of
God was often held to be a cornerstone of his work. The philosophical ambition of his poems aspired – we were told – to a kind

of secular mysticism, a search for a poetry that would function as some sort of stand-in for religion. At times, Stevens seemed to give his assent to this idea.

But since his death there has been great speculation about – and fascination with – a story concerning his alleged deathbed conversion. When the great poet was dying of stomach cancer at the age of seventy-five in St Francis Hospital, Hartford, the story goes that he summoned the Catholic chaplain, Father Arthur Hanley, to his bedside, and was baptized by him. The rumour was quickly denied by some of Stevens's friends and family, but it continued to circulate.

★

The Dean's wife is still not inviting us in. We are dropping hints about the study upstairs, but she repeats that the house is full of boxes. There is a local password, she tells us, to establish whether people you meet in the street are from this neighbourhood. 'The river is moving,' says the local. If the passer-by is a local too, they will reply 'The blackbird must be flying.'

This password comes from Wallace Stevens's most famous poem, 'Thirteen Ways of Looking at a Blackbird'. And there is now a walkway from roughly opposite the house through Elizabeth Park, marked by thirteen stones with the blackbird poem inscribed on them. If you follow the stones, the walk you take pretty much retraces Stevens's own daily walk to his office. This poet's day job has disappointed some poets of a more bohemian inclination. Like T. S. Eliot and his bank career, Stevens was not just a time-server at the Hartford Accident and Indemnity Company, he was a very accomplished insurance executive. Indeed, by the time he retired, he had risen to the rank of vice-president. No wonder he lived in such a fine house. After the Pulitzer Prize made his reputation as a poet secure, Harvard University offered Stevens a faculty position, but he turned it down so that he could maintain his duties in insurance.

Reputedly, he would dream up the extraordinary fantasies of his poems on his morning walk to work, then dictate them to his secretary when he arrived in his office. If this isn't true, it should be.

★

'The Emperor of Ice-Cream' is not only one of Wallace Stevens's best-known poems, but surely one of the best unused (to our knowledge) epitaphs. Who would not want 'Here lies the Emperor of Ice-Cream' on their headstone? Like many of Stevens's poems, it is slippery and elusive in its meaning, but utterly intoxicating in its music and its network of connected images:

> Call the roller of big cigars,
> The muscular one, and bid him whip
> In kitchen cups concupiscent curds.

So starts the first of two stanzas, while the second seems to come from a different world:

> Take from the dresser of deal,
> Lacking the three glass knobs, that sheet
> On which she embroidered fantails once
> And spread it so as to cover her face.

The critic Helen Vendler was among those who ventured a clear interpretation of the poem as an account of a wake. The poem's two halves cut between the kitchen where preparations (including ice-cream) are being made for the funeral wake, and an upstairs bedroom where the corpse of an old woman is laid out on a bed waiting to be properly covered. This is one of those rare readings that unlocks a poem. Once you read it as a poem see-sawing between life and death, the sensuality and vitality of the kitchen and the deathly pallor of the bedroom, it is difficult to read it any other way.

★

The Dean's wife and son head back into the house, and they give us permission to wander around, to take some pictures if we want. We walk to the back of the house, and there's a sports car parked behind it. Neither of us can imagine Wallace Stevens in a sports car. The rear of the house, white-painted and wood-panelled, looks even more grand and stately than the front. One of us stands under the poet's study window for a picture. Then we swap positions, but the other shrugs away: 'I don't want my picture taken here. I've got a bad feeling about it.'

Before we leave, we knock on the door again. Can one of us use the toilet? We have a long drive ahead of us. The house is, as she warned us, stacked high with boxes. The toilet seems to be the only box-free room in the house. 'Would the bathroom be unchanged since Wallace Stevens used it?' Yes, she thought it probably would.

★

The Dean's wife points to a field at the end of the road, where once or twice a year there is a huge gathering of blackbirds, lasting a day or so. She has no idea why this happens, but is convinced that this is where Stevens got the idea for his poem. And likewise his poem 'The Snowman'. She thinks of it every year, because they get such harsh winters in Hartford.

We are impressed with the blackbird trail, we tell her. It's good to see a community taking pride in its poets. Ah well, she says, it's not quite as simple as that. And she explains that the trail was set up by a society in Hartford called 'The Friends and Enemies of Wallace Stevens'. She tells us the locals are proud to have such a famous poet as one of their sons, but he's also remembered in the city as something of a curmudgeon.

We wonder how many of the residents of this road have actually read any of Stevens's poems, beyond 'Thirteen Ways . . .', of course. One of us recalls a comment made by a former student when confronted with the *Collected Poems* – 'Did he publish the answers?' The Dean's son laughs. 'They're in the house,' he says. 'He hid them under the floorboards.'

★

We leave, wishing them well with their move, but with one question still nagging: is the myth true?

Why would the poet, on his deathbed, convert to Roman Catholicism and then want it kept secret? Some have speculated that Stevens feared upsetting his wife or scandalizing his social circle of respectable Connecticut Protestants at a time – pre-JFK – when Roman Catholicism was still infra dig in much of middle America. These are plausible reasons, but for a man as single-minded as Stevens, would he really give a damn for the good opinion of Hartford's establishment?

★

We are talking about blackbirds as we drive out of Wallace Stevens's neighbourhood. Would they flock in vast numbers like that? And if so, why? We are talking, and not taking proper notice of the satnav as it tries to direct us back to the freeway. We cross some traffic lights and suddenly it is as if we are in a different city. This is more like WCW's Paterson than Wallace Stevens's respectable, well-heeled and well-insured Hartford. We keep having to slow down, because there are groups of people in the road and they are not moving so we can pass. In fact, they either ignore us entirely as we steer around them or they stop talking and stare as we roll past. They are mainly men in their teens or twenties. We keep driving, but the satnav has gone silent and we feel like we're getting deeper into somewhere we shouldn't be. We start to wonder if we're heading for a *Bonfire of the Vanities* scenario, but in a Ford Something-or-Other instead of a Mercedes, and a pair of middle-aged English poets instead of a young bond trader and his lover. We start to consider the ironies of being shot whilst researching a book on the deaths of poets, a couple of miles down the road from Wallace Stevens's executive townhouse.

Suddenly a car races up behind us, skids past and cuts us up. We slam on the brakes and the driver swerves violently to the right, then across to the left. We drop back and he drops back with us. We try to pull past him, but he blocks us. Now he leads us slowly through the neighbourhood at the speed of a funeral cortège. We can't pass him and he won't let us fall back. Is he going to pull us over? Are we about to get robbed here? He puts his foot down again and speeds forwards. We keep up the slow pace, following him. He moves aside and seems to be waiting for us to overtake. We're not sure how to play this, so we ease up slowly alongside him. As we draw level with the back of his car, we get a shock.

'There's no one driving.'

'What? How can there be?'

'Look! There's no one in it.'

What are we dealing with here? The car is clearly under *some-one's* control. Perhaps he's trying to freak us out by lying down across the passenger seat? Slowly, we slide up alongside the driver's window. And there's the answer. The driver is a boy of about seven years old. He glances across at us, not with any sense of threat and certainly no sense of fear, just complete indifference.

★

When a letter emerged, apparently written by Father Arthur Hanley to Professor Janet McCann in 1977, the rumour of Wallace Stevens's deathbed conversion took another twist.

Fr Hanley was the Roman Catholic priest assigned to St Francis Hospital in Hartford, when Stevens was admitted with stomach cancer in 1955. According to his letter – in response to questions from Prof. McCann about the alleged conversion – the poet asked to see the priest, and this was followed by '9 or 10' further meetings. They talked about theology and in particular the doctrine of hell, which Stevens struggled with, but according to Hanley 'we later got thru that alright'.

The letter describes Stevens's sense of 'emptiness in his life', and the sense of 'peace and tranquility' he felt when he stepped inside Catholic churches, before declaring that 'he was baptized absolutely'. Since Stevens was a noted and prominent figure, it was felt that this conversion should not be made public, as it might 'cause a scene', but Fr Hanley goes on to stress that 'the sister and the nurses on the floor were all aware of it and were praying for him.' The two men discussed Stevens's poetry, and the letter ends with the poet reportedly assuring the priest that 'if he got well, we would talk a lot more and if not – he would see me in heaven.'

Why should the truth or otherwise of this letter and the story behind it be of such concern? Within a family, the truth about a father or husband's death is of great importance, so their strong feelings are entirely understandable. But what was at stake for the pundits and critics who weighed in to scotch or support it? In short, why does it matter if Wallace Stevens converted to Catholicism or not?

The answer to that lies somewhere close to the heart of this book. The deaths of poets matter because they become a lens through which to look at the poems. If we read Stevens's work as a project built on the absence of God, trying to forge a secular metaphysics for a new age, then what do we do with an alleged deathbed Catholic conversion? How do we read the work then? The answer, of course, should be that we read it as a series of negotiations with uncertainty. For most of his life, Stevens was no atheist, and no card-carrying believer either. Like most poets (and most people) he lived in a space between faith and doubt, and that is where his work lives too.

★

The poet Daisy Fried was our friend and guide on the streets of Greenwich Village, chasing Dylan Thomas's ghost. We are with her in New York again, because we felt that she should travel with us to the other pole, perhaps the least bohemian, least Chattertonian poet we could find. We are standing at the door to Marianne Moore's apartment block on West 9th Street. Daisy loves Marianne Moore, and so do we. Moore's strange, angular Modernist poems, built out of her own measures of syllable counts, manage against all the odds to achieve a shimmering beauty and profundity. A poem like 'What Are Years?' is as devastating in effect as it is complex in structure, with its unforgettable declaration that: 'All are / naked, none is safe.'

This is Marianne Moore's last home in New York. Or rather, this is the apartment block. She lived in Apartment 7b, but it has long since changed hands. The lobby is very plush. This is an exclusive street on the edge of Greenwich Village, lined with ginkgo trees, which produce an incongruous but inescapable reek of vomit. Perhaps this is a deliberate planting, to put off people like us hanging around on the sidewalk. It has been raining for an hour, really tipping it down, which seems to make the trees smell worse. Garbage trucks and taxis keep streaming past and covering us in spray, but we are soaked already. There is a small, discreet plaque on the wall outside. It describes Moore as a 'Pulitzer Prize-winning poet, baseball enthusiast, and lifelong New Yorker'.

This was her last home. Daisy remarks on how much nature and animal imagery is in Moore's work, and yet how utterly urban this place is, in the heart of the city, not a sniff of green except the all too redolent sniff of the ginkgos. The lobby extends on to the sidewalk with a carpet and a long thin awning of the kind favoured by expensive restaurants with uniformed doormen. We look up to get a sense of the place. It's a low-ceilinged, pre-war block. It has clearly been refurbished. Apartment 7b would be nothing like it was in Marianne's day.

★

As we wait under the Manhattan shitberry trees, a very elderly woman is brought in past us, with a great deal of fuss and not much grace. She is complaining bitterly about the way her handlers are lifting her over the kerb and through the narrow doorway. A postman walks past, pushing a trolley, wearing surgical gloves. 'I guess he has to touch a lot of letters other people have touched,' says Daisy.

Of the three phrases in Marianne Moore's memorial plaque, it's 'baseball enthusiast' that sings out to us. 'Pulitzer Prize-winning poet' is no surprise, and 'lifelong New Yorker' figures too for this sophisticated, Francophile woman of letters, famous for her trademark get-up of flowing cape and tricorne hat. But baseball enthusiast she was, as a famous devotee of the Brooklyn Dodgers. In fact, she wrote an ode to them in 1956, which was published in the *New York Herald Tribune* under a suitably declamatory introductory paragraph:

> The Greeks had their Homer, the Romans had their Vergil, and the Dodgers have their Marianne Moore. Miss Moore, prize-winning poetess, might be imagined more at home among trochees and iambs, but, as the ode to her admired ball team appearing below will testify, is just as at home among the epic data of her team's recent bid for fame.

The poem itself is a playful squib, to be recited to the tune of 'Hush Little Baby' to mark the opening game of the 1956 season, against local rivals the New York Yankees. It is full of Moore's wordplay, wit and oddly angular phrasing, so it's hard to imagine it ringing out from the terraces:

> 'Millennium,' yes; 'pandemonium'!
> Roy Campanella leaps high. Dodgerdom
>
> crowned, had Johnny Podres on the mound.
> Buzzie Bavasi and the Press gave ground;

the team slapped, mauled, and asked the Yankees' match,
'How did you feel when Sandy Amoros made the catch?'

Two years later, to the abject horror of its fans, the Dodgers
quit Brooklyn and decamped 2,500 miles to Los Angeles, becoming the LA Dodgers in the process. It was essentially a business
move, to secure the future of the club, with land to build a new
stadium. But it crossed a line that sports fans know all too well.
You can change the kit (as long as you keep the same colour), the
players, even the stadium, but you don't swap cities. Marianne felt
betrayed and horrified. Like many fans, she dropped the Dodgers
and switched her allegiance to the Yankees.

When we try to imagine what this would feel like, we think
of the sorry English example of Wimbledon Football Club –
the so-called Crazy Gang – who won the FA Cup Final in 1988
and relocated to Milton Keynes six years later under the new
brand MK Dons. But the Dodgers' move must have felt like
even more of a betrayal, swapping a great East Coast city for
a great West Coast city with a different spirit, ethos, climate. It
would be (almost) like Liverpool FC moving to Manchester, or
United moving to the banks of the Mersey. It's enough to keep
a fan awake at night.

But Marianne managed to make the switch. Within three years
of the Dodgers leaving New York, she wrote a tribute poem to
her new team, under the title 'Baseball and Writing', and published it in the *New Yorker*. It is a better poem than the Dodgers
squib, full of energy and swagger.

> Assign Yogi Berra to Cape Canaveral;
> he could handle any missile.
>> He is no feather. 'Strike! . . . Strike *two*!'
>>> Fouled back. A blur.
>>> It's gone. You would infer
>>> that the bat had eyes.

The Yankees suited the famous poet. In her final years she became a public figure, feted on television and radio, lauded in newspapers. In 1964 the CBS television network purchased the Yankees, and their network executive Michael Burke became firm friends with Marianne. Burke was, according to Yankees historian and museum curator Brian Richards, 'a World War II hero, CIA agent and circus general manager', on top of his job in TV. Burke was appointed team president in 1966 and began to develop innovative ways of promoting the Yankees. And the best of those ideas involved a famous poet.

★

There cannot be many eminent American poets who have 'baseball enthusiast' on their memorial plaque. But then, there can't be many American poets who have been invited to throw out the first pitch to launch the new season at the Yankee Stadium. Marianne was and did, on 10 April 1968, at the age of eighty.

The ceremonial first pitch is a special moment. First in line to be asked to make the throw are politicians or team alumni. Not poets. Brian Richards believes it was Moore's friendship with the iconoclastic team president Michael Burke that led to her being invited.

But why a poet of all people? That year, 1968, was no ordinary baseball season. Civil unrest in the wake of the assassination of Martin Luther King led to concern about public events that might give rise to riots. The start of the season was put back to allow the public mood to settle. University campuses were in uproar against the Vietnam War.

While the poet Allen Ginsberg on the West Coast was refusing to pay tax and intoning Hare Krishna mantras into microphones at mass rallies, the poet Marianne Moore on the East Coast was tossing a baseball from the crowd at the Yankee Stadium. But perhaps they were working to the same end. Historian Brian Richards suggests that at a moment when many Americans thought the nation was 'tearing itself apart', and political figures were divisive and unpopular, the selection of a poetic grande dame to make the opening pitch could be a gesture towards 'beauty, civility and healing'.

And what of the throw itself? We pore over two press photographs. One looks like it's taken a second before, and one a second after. In the first, the poet stands in a statuesque – of Liberty, indeed – pose, her right arm aloft and her skinny fingers gripping the ball. Two rows behind, a young guy photobombs her, waving at the camera, and a Mister Magoo lookalike one row closer sits open-mouthed in anticipation. Marianne is in her famous tricorne hat, pale twin-set and a lacy white blouse with lavish cuffs. Her facial expression is blank, strangely distant.

The second picture has the ball floating in the top-left corner of the frame. The poet's friend Michael Burke sits a couple of seats away from her, looking on delightedly. Her hand is open, fingers outstretched as if she's pointing out the ball to those around her. Again, her face is impassive, her mouth slightly open, as if to recover her breath after the throw.

The ball was tossed to rookie catcher Frank Fernandez. The *New York Times* report has Frank confessing that the poet looked so nervous and frail that he took two steps towards her to shorten the throw. He caught the ball knee-high. 'They tell me it's best to keep pitches low,' the poet had told a reporter the previous week. Then, caught up in the glory of the moment, the twenty-three-year-old catcher ran to the railing, leaned in and kissed Marianne on the cheek. 'I just did it on the spur of the moment,' he told the paper. And talking to the *Sporting News* he added 'she just looked so lost and confused, that I just couldn't help myself.' As Frank kissed Marianne, he passed the ball back over the railing for her to take home as a memento. She sat down and the game began.

★

Don DeLillo's epic novel *Underworld* begins with the game-winning home run known in baseball as the 'shot heard round the world'. The 'shot' in question was a decisive, league-winning home run hit by the New York Giants' Bobby Thomson in 1951. It so happens that the shot was aimed at Marianne Moore's first baseball love, the Brooklyn Dodgers. That moment becomes pivotal in the lives of many characters in the novel, as does the fate of the ball – caught in the stands, stolen, sold and endlessly pursued by collectors.

After Frank Fernandez ran to the railing to kiss the eminent poet and to hand her the ball she had thrown, the first game of the season began. Frank was nervous, as a relative newcomer, and this was his first time in the opening day line-up. He stood to face another throw, this one from California Angels pitcher George Brunet. 'I knew I hit it good,' Frank told the *Sporting News*. And he did. It soared into the left field seats. It was not just the first home run of the season, but the only one of the game, securing the Yankees' victory.

Fernandez went on to play for the Yankees, then Oakland Athletics, Washington Senators and finally Chicago Cubs. He earned a place in baseball stats books with a very niche record: most home runs (39) for a player with a batting average less than .200. He retired from the game in 1972, and on the back of his baseball card he cited that home run in 1968 as his 'greatest baseball thrill'.

For Marianne Moore that opening season Yankees game was a turning point too. She had suffered a stroke the previous decade, and by April 1968 her health was of sufficient concern that she had live-in help at her New York apartment.

In the weeks following that final public flourish of a throw in front of nearly 16,000 Yankees fans at the stadium, and many thousands watching on TV at home, Marianne suffered a series of strokes. Like her friend and fellow-Modernist William Carlos Williams, her death crept up on her slowly through repeated strokes, finally catching her in February 1972.

As for Michael Burke, the flamboyant Yankees president who befriended the famous poet, he retired to a farm in Ireland and died in 1987. In Marianne Moore's final year, Mr Burke successfully oversaw the rebuilding of the Yankee Stadium, allowing the team to stay in New York, and fending off a threat to move to New Jersey.

★

Marianne Moore was perhaps an unlikely public poet. Shy and eccentric in her dress and manner, uncompromising in the 'difficulty' of most of her poems, she caught the imagination of broadcasters, journalists and the public, becoming something of a celebrity in later life. When she moved to that final apartment in West 9th Street, Manhattan, both the *New York Times* and the *New Yorker* sent reporters to interview her about her move. She was interviewed by the singer Harry Belafonte for *The Tonight Show* and wrote the sleeve notes for Cassius Clay's (later Muhammad Ali) record release *I Am The Greatest!*.

Her eccentric reputation may have been part of the reason why David Wallace, Marketing Director of the Ford Motor Company, approached her in 1955 to come up with a name for their latest family coupé. But Ford took fright at the exoticism of her suggestions, finally naming it themselves – the Edsel. According to *Time* magazine, it qualifies as one of 'The 50 Worst Cars of all Time'. Moore came up with some of the most beautiful car names you could imagine, loads of them:

> *The Ford Silver Sword, Hurricane Hirundo, Turcotinga, Mongoose Civique, Symmecromatic, Bullet Cloisonné, The Intelligent Whale, Turbotorc, Fee Rapide, Dearborn Diamante, Taper Racer, Angelastro, Cresta Lark, Triskelion, Andante con Moto, Utopian Turtletop . . .*

Any of Marianne Moore's beautiful suggestions for the name of the latest Ford would have been better than the Edsel. In fact, had they plumped for Utopian Turtletop, it may well have been in *Time*'s list of the 50 Greatest Cars. A name is not a small thing in the making of a classic car, as British owners of the Ford Capri know well.

It dawns on us that we have no idea what hire car we are driving on our American travels. We just hired it, found the right number plate in the hotel parking lot, got in and drove off. We can see it's a Ford from the badge in the middle of the steering wheel. How much better it would be if the guy who handed us the keys said, 'You can have the cayman blue Triskelion.' Our whole trip would have been different.

★

It sounds like one of the oddest deaths of the poets. The story goes that in her dotage, and with a history of strokes, Marianne Moore threw out the ball to start the Yankees' season, but the strain of such a public spectacle, combined with the physical stress of making the throw itself, brought on a final series of debilitating strokes. The poet never recovered, and died in her sleep at the age of eighty-four. The catcher's account of taking a step towards her because she looked so frail, then going up to kiss her after the throw because she looked so bewildered, makes it all too easy to believe. It is a quirky tale to tell about the quirkiest of poets, and indeed we have told it ourselves in bars where poets gather to talk about their looming sense of mortality.

But the dates don't add up. It was months between Marianne's televised pitch and a series of minor strokes in spring of 1969. A major stroke that summer almost finished her off and left her debilitated, but her death did not catch up with her until February 1972. Despite her lifelong reputation for frailty, Marianne Moore was a survivor. And if the baseball pitch played any role in her death, then that clot or bleed must have been the slowest acting in medical history.

★

We know the fate of the pitcher, the catcher and the president, but what became of the baseball itself?

As was customary, Frank Fernandez signed it, then it was mounted on a plinth and given to the poet as a memento. Marianne found a niche for it among the animal figurines and ornate glassware of her Greenwich Village living room, and that's where it remains. Except that her living room is no longer in her old apartment block. In fact, it isn't in New York at all. In the same year as her season-opening throw, the poet bequeathed all her books and papers to the Rosenbach Museum and Library in Philadelphia. A year later – according to the museum's catalogue – she added a codicil, leaving all her apartment's furnishings too. The Rosenbach honoured the completeness of this bequest by reconstructing the poet's living room on the museum's third floor.

It is on our own completists' list, to visit the Marianne Moore room one quiet weekday afternoon, pretending to take notes on the details of upholstery and ceramics. Then when the curator's back is turned, to pick the crimson-stitched ball from its brass plinth and pitch it back and forth across her duck-egg blue sofa, minding not to trip over the footstool (a gift from T. S. Eliot), until we are escorted off the premises.*

★

Marianne Moore's poems were every bit as idiosyncratic and uncompromising as she was. She built many of them out of syllabic measures, establishing odd patterns of lines to create angular

---

* Self-flagellation in the footnotes. Some time later, one of us *did* in fact make it to Philadelphia, but the visit was a flying one, and in a spectacular dereliction of duty he opted instead to jog up the 'Rocky Steps' at the Museum of Art; the same ascent Sylvester Stallone makes as *Rocky* in training. There is also a bronze statue of the fictional boxer Rocky Balboa at the foot of these steps (queues to have pictures taken with Rocky are supposedly longer than those for the Museum), and maybe there's an unintended correspondence with Moore here: popular sports right on the doorstep of High Art? Yes. That's exactly it.

stanzas, out of which she made her poems. Poet and critic Jeffrey
Wainwright has produced something like a car mechanic's chart
to explain the fantastically complex workings of her poem 'What
Are Years?' The poem looks like this:

> What is our innocence,
> what is our guilt? All are
>   naked, none is safe. And whence
> is courage: the unanswered question,
> the resolute doubt, –
> dumbly calling, deafly listening – that
> in misfortune, even death,
>   encourages others
>   and in its defeat, stirs
>
>   the soul to be strong? He
> sees deep and is glad, who
>   accedes to mortality
> and in his imprisonment rises
> upon himself as
> the sea in a chasm, struggling to be
> free and unable to be,
>   in its surrendering
>   finds its continuing.
>
>   So he who strongly feels,
> behaves. The very bird,
>   grown taller as he sings, steels
> his form straight up. Though he is captive,
> his mighty singing
> says, satisfaction is a lowly
> thing, how pure a thing is joy.
>   This is mortality,
>   this is eternity.

And Wainwright's chart, like the vital statistics of a Utopian Turtletop coupé, reads like this:

#	stanza 1		stanza 2		stanza 3	
	no. sylls.	rhyme	no. sylls.	rhyme	no. sylls.	rhyme
1	6	a	6	a	6	a
2	6	b	6	b	6	b
3	7	a	7	a	7	a
4	9	c	9	c	9	c
5	5	d	5	d	5	d
6	9	d	9	a	9	e
7	7	e	7	a	7	f
8	6	f	6	e	6	e
9	6	f	6	e	6	e

There is a glory to such intricate architecture. Each stanza following the same looping pattern like a menorah, so if you turn each stanza's syllable count through ninety degrees, every line finds an echo on the other side of the stanza – first line with last, second with penultimate, etc.

But why do this? What on earth is the point in making this sudoku poetry? Syllabics is essentially a technique for deciding where a poetic line should end based not on 'beats' or metric feet (the iambic pentameter famously has five) but on counting every syllable. This technique was attractive to Modernist poets, especially American Modernists who wanted to break the hegemony of the English poetic line. If you want to break free from Shakespeare, Keats, Byron et al. and forge a new American poetic line, how do you do it? The disruptive power of syllabics seemed like part of the answer to Marianne Moore.

There is also, as Wainwright argues, an element of puzzle or game in this buried structure. The poet was famous for her bone-dry wit, and it's not hard to see a mischievous satisfaction in laying down treasures for diligent students to unearth.

But perhaps the most compelling reason for such intricate
architecture comes from the poem itself. It is far from an empty
word-game. Essentially, 'What Are Years?' is a meditation on mortality. More than that, it amounts to a confrontation with death
and a challenge as bold as John Donne's 'Death be not proud'. In
the image of the caged bird finding the strength to sing, the poem
is – as Wainwright puts it – 'an effortful, determined acceptance,
and therefore defiance, of death.'

★

In April 1966, Marianne Moore gave an introductory speech
for her friend Langston Hughes at a glitzy season launch for the
Academy of American Poets, held at the Guggenheim Museum.
Both were born in Missouri, both were devoted adoptive New
Yorkers. The following year, at the Plaza Hotel for a Poetry Society
of America dinner, Hughes was able to return the compliment.
As one of the key voices in the Harlem Renaissance, Hughes's
lyrical, jazz-inflected poetry had been part of the great flower-
ing of African-American arts and literature in the Twenties and
Thirties. At the dinner, following Robert Lowell's slightly awk-
ward declaration of Marianne as 'the best woman poet in English',
Hughes pronounced her 'the most famous Negro woman poet
in America'. According to Moore's biographer Linda Leavell,
'Marianne loved the uneasy joke'.

Within weeks of that dinner, Langston Hughes was admitted to
the New York Polyclinic Hospital in great pain, for an emergency
operation on his prostate. The operation went well, but within
three days he developed an infection. A week later he was dead at
the age of sixty-five. A private service was held at Benta's Funeral
Home in Harlem, with more than two hundred guests including
some of New York's finest jazz and blues musicians. The disjunction
between the music (including Duke Ellington's 'Do Nothing Till
You Hear from Me') and the presence of Hughes's body in an open
coffin was too much for some, including the singer Lena Horne

who, according to Hughes's biographer Arnold Rampersad, said on the way out 'I was so confused. There I was, tapping my toes and humming while you all played, and I didn't know whether to cry for Langston or clap my hands and laugh!' Hughes was cremated at the Ferncliff Crematory in Hartsdale, just north of Manhattan.

★

A photograph: Two poets, Amiri Baraka and Maya Angelou, are dancing on a patterned circle in the floor of the New York Public Library's Schomburg Center for Research in Black Culture. Guests in evening dress stand at the edge of the circle, caught mid-clap, mid-laugh, mid-cheer. In a *New York Times* essay to mark his retirement from the newspaper, the photographer Chester Higgins Jr described it as 'one of my favorite photos'. It was taken in 1991 at a ceremony honouring the memory of Langston Hughes. As Higgins describes it:

> At the conclusion of the programme, filled with poetry readings and accolades for Langston Hughes, a jazz combo livened the tempo. As I watched, Amiri Baraka asked Maya Angelou to dance and walked with her to the *I've Known Rivers* cosmogram – the focal point of the celebration, newly set into the floor over the ashes of Langston Hughes. As the two poets danced, the energy of the crowd focused on them. The room came alive as everyone applauded.

We trip back a few lines. Yes, it really did say 'over the ashes of Langston Hughes.' We've heard of poets metaphorically dancing on each other's graves, but not literally. Yet what an honouring, what a tribute. The cosmogram was created as an 'art installation, dance floor and peace memorial' and laid in the atrium of the Schomburg Center just a short walk from the Yankee Stadium where Marianne Moore threw out that famous pitch. Moore's memorial service was meticulously planned, by her, down to the colour ('morning glory blue') of the order of service. It sounds like a beautiful send-off, with its strings and harp, its closing 'Hallelujah Chorus'. But given the choice we'd go for an impulsive dance on our graves any day. Some reports at the time claimed this celebration for Langston was a traditional African ritual, but that was news to Maya Angelou. When she saw the reports, she telephoned Baraka to ask if he had been doing an African dance, because she had been doing the Texas hop. 'No, I was doing the jitterbug', he said.

★

Langston Hughes was a private, diligent man, a prolific writer and a great champion of other writers. Politically engaged and passionate, Hughes's life seems to avoid the self-destructive tendencies of some of his contemporaries. He appears, on the face of it, to be a clear candidate for the poetic survivors' list, up there with Wallace Stevens and his friend Marianne Moore, even if that final illness robbed him of a stretch of his old age. Yet his friend the poet Arna Bontemps reportedly spoke at his funeral about 'the death wish which had haunted this gentle man all his life', then underlined the point by reading Hughes's poem 'Dear Lovely Death':

> Dear lovely Death
> That taketh all things under wing –
> Never to kill –
> Only to change
> Into some other thing
> This suffering flesh,
> To make it either more or less,
> But not again the same –
> Dear lovely Death,
> Change is thy other name.

★

The debate about what makes a poem, and how the poet's life and death impact on it, is only half complete without some discussion of form. When Elizabeth Bishop took at least seventeen drafts to make her poem 'One Art' work in the form of a villanelle, she wasn't trying to solve a cryptic crossword, she was writing about an intensely difficult subject: the estrangement of her lover Alice Methfessel, but also a litany of past losses, including the suicide of her former partner Lota and the death of her mother after eighteen years in an asylum.

So why didn't she just let her anguish pour out on to the page? Why attempt to express such suffering in such a needlessly complex vessel as a villanelle? The reasons are many: because poetry is an act of making rather than simply an expression, because a struggle with form renders impossible subject matter possible, because the unfettered expression of strong feeling on the page almost always results in a dissipation of that feeling, rather than its evocation in the reader.

It is no accident that some of that generation of British and American poets (Keith Douglas, Anthony Hecht, Richard Wilbur) who witnessed the horrors of the battlefields and concentration camps of the Second World War built their bodies of work out of negotiations with form. Of course, the answer doesn't have to be a villanelle. In our experience, the answer is very rarely a villanelle or a sestina. It might not even be a sonnet. It could be a scheme of half-rhymes or syllabics, like Marianne Moore's angular and individualistic exercises in syllable counting. Or it could be so-called free verse, arguably the hardest form of all, which arises out of – and often subverts – speech patterns and demands real rigour to avoid what Thom Gunn diagnosed as 'not quite free verse and not quite metre'.

But there is another side to the importance of poetic form. Sculptors talk about the resistance of the material – the grain of the wood, the toughness of stone – and the way that a sculpture or carving emerges from engagement with that resistance. It works in just the same way with poetry. The resistance of the material in a poem is the language itself, its rhythms and patterns and syllable counts and stresses and networks of associations. It is the resistance of the material that forces you, as you draft and redraft a poem, beyond your first word choice, to your second, third, fourth, because your first choice wouldn't match the metre, or wouldn't make a half-rhyme, or had one syllable too many. This process is one of the key ways in which poets can make new discoveries, can push their work on to the next level. It helps poets to avoid writing the same poem over and over, slipping into habits of self-parody.

Death is the big line break. One crude but basic distinction between poetry and prose is the way the former refuses continually to reach the right margin of the page (prose poets: please don't write in, we know you're there). If poetry has its rootstock in song and dance, one way of accounting for this broken line in the age of the page is its jig between being here and not being here, presence and absence, its duration falling somewhere between the top of the breath and the pit of the stomach, lasting as long as the notional present, from moment to moment. Even those poems that have broken away from long-accumulated shapes that we call 'traditional' are still, line by irregular line, always stepping off an edge. Maybe all poems put us in mind, however subtly, however peripherally, of interruptions, breaks, ends. Or maybe the line break makes a death-defying, perpetual motion.

The great poems, the ones that last the centuries, are often the product of intense feeling and thought, and therefore unarguably rooted in the poet's life. But they are equally rooted in the poet's engagement with form, the way in which that poet negotiated and struggled with the resistance of the poetic material. The fascinations and challenges of form are endlessly addictive; the affliction is lifelong.

★

Lifelong, yes. But does it have to be fatal? Clearly not, or at least, not always prematurely. The likes of Marianne Moore, Wallace Stevens, William Carlos Williams and R. S. Thomas attest to that. There is a survivors' list of major poets who died in their beds at a ripe old age. But the list of victims is a long one too: John Berryman, Hart Crane, Anne Sexton, Frank O'Hara, Sylvia Plath, Dylan Thomas, Lord Byron, and on and on. The deaths of great poets are as various as the deaths of great novelists or playwrights, but the expectation of poets' deaths seems differently inflected. Other writers may well be depressive or drunk or suicidal, but there is no necessary link between those behaviours and the authenticity or power of their work. Since Chatterton died in his garret aged seventeen, we have created a myth that true poetry can – even should – cost you your life. Almost 250 years on, it still feels as potent as ever. The contagion has spread too. Musicians like Kurt Cobain and Amy Winehouse are still viewed through the prism of this myth.

★

Philip Larkin was once asked, in an interview with the critic John Haffenden, what he meant by his declaration that 'poetry is an affair of sanity'. His answer was typically blunt:

> There certainly is a cult of the mad these days: think of all the boys who've been in the bin – I don't understand it. Chaucer, Wordsworth, Hardy – it's the big, sane boys who get the medals. The object of writing is to show life as it is, and if you don't see it like that you're in trouble, not life.

Then he adds, rather winningly, 'Up to you, of course.'

So where do Marianne Moore and Wallace Stevens fit into the pantheon of poetic lives? Were they the kind of myth-busters championed by Larkin, the ones who give the lie to the sacrificial legend? They certainly won their share of medals between them, and both – like Larkin – lived quietly respectable lives. Two more for the survivors' team? Like William Carlos Williams and R. S. Thomas, these two lived to a ripe old age, then died in bed of natural causes. Both were, on the surface at least, politically and socially conservative. Stevens was a soft Republican, and Moore – when interviewed for *Paris Review* on the eve of the 1960 presidential election – only chose not to wear her Nixon button because it 'clashed with her coat and hat'.

Perhaps, as with that other great Modernist innovator T. S. Eliot, a surface respectability and a structured life allowed for more revolutionary energy to be poured into the work. Like many of the Modernists (David Jones, Marianne Moore, John Riley) Eliot held to a broadly orthodox set of religious beliefs. In an essay on William Blake, Eliot argued that what Blake's genius required, and what it was sadly denied, was 'a framework of accepted and traditional ideas which would have prevented him from indulging in a philosophy of his own, and concentrated his energy upon the problems of the poet'.

I Am

On Saturday 4 June 1825 John Clare wrote in his journal: 'Saw three fellows at the end of Royce Wood who I found were laying out the plan for an Iron Rail Way from Manchester to London – it is to cross over Round Oak Spring . . . I little thought that fresh intrusions would interrupt . . . my solitudes after the Inclosure . . .' Royce Wood – now Rice Wood – lies just to the south of Helpston, Clare's native village a few miles west of Peterborough, and this entry would have been written when Clare was already beginning to feel his bloom of fame as 'the Northamptonshire Peasant Poet' wilt, having published two collections of poetry with a London house. The 'Inclosure' he mentions resulted from the Acts of Parliament that changed the distribution and allotment of common land, shifting the emphasis from shared community ownership to wealthier, individual stakeholders. Clare's early life coincided with it, and he witnessed the disintegration of his childhood landscape and places. The entry has a resigned tone – *just when I thought I'd seen everything* . . . It's also surprisingly early for a railway, taking place four years before the Rainhill Trials between Liverpool and Manchester, and the tendering to supply locomotives for the world's first passenger line. But there was a speculative bubble inflating in the new railways, and investors could smell a profit. For Clare, who knew Royce Wood as a place of old oaks, bubbling springs and nightingales, it was one further disastrous incursion (the encounter almost has the feel of – and is contemporary with – the indigenous tribal meetings with European trappers and settlers in the woods of North America). Men with theodolites and sighting rods traipsing into Eden.

We change from a Virgin train at Birmingham International and pick up a London Midland service to Northampton. The 'Iron Rail Way' won. John Clare outlived his own brief 'Peasant Poet' fame, and ended his days largely forgotten in the Northamptonshire General Lunatic Asylum (now St Andrew's Healthcare). We've visited Clare's home patch of Helpston before, and have walked the various boundaries and mosaics of landscape familiar from his poetry, but we know less about his later experiences. And Clare spent a long time in Northampton, over twenty-two years, until his death, aged seventy, probably following a series of strokes, in the spring of 1864. Clare had experienced fame and the attentions of a wide readership before falling into obscurity, but his longevity meant it was a long slow fade. He outlived all of the major Romantic poets, though it was only during his deathtime that he came to be counted among their starry number.

*

Northampton on a monochrome day, a Midlands day. The short walk from the train station into town, the gauging of scale in a new town, the rough comparisons to known towns. There is a subdued market in a broad open square. There is a Boot and Shoe Quarter Conservation Area. This is the centre of English shoemaking, and some of the world's finest footwear is still made here. Soon after publishing his first book of poems, the young John Clare was invited for an audience with the Marquess of Exeter at Burghley House, where the poet's dirty, hobnailed shoes were a source of shame and embarrassment: 'I went upstairs & thro winding passages after the footman as fast as I could hobble almost fit to quarrel with my hard-nailed shoes at the noise they made on the marble & boarded floors & cursing them to myself as I set my feet down in the lightest steps I was able to utter.' Twenty years after this, Clare's shoes make another memorable appearance, letting in gravel and almost losing a sole during his famous flight from Essex, absconding from the first asylum he'd known at High Beech and walking over eighty miles in four days, sleeping rough aligned to the Pole Star for directions and eating grass.

We both take a seat in the two inviting stone recesses under All Saints' Church portico. The clock chimes the hour high above. We feel like a pair of earthbound automata, sitting this one out, tired from trains. There looks to be the possibility of graffiti carved into the pinkish limestone, and we scour it for any sign of Clare's name or initials, but find nothing (though nowhere near as well represented in the common graffiti archive as Byron, there is a good 'John Clare' scratched into the stone under an old bridge arch crossing the River Welland near Helpston).

When we think of 'poor Clare' shut up in the nineteenth-century madhouse, we might imagine a windowless dark, restraints, chains, squalor, loneliness. Except it wasn't quite like that. While he was at the Northampton Aslyum Clare often used to sit here under the high clock tower in the centre of town. He sat here for years. It was only a twenty-minute walk up the road, and the poet became a well-known local figure – the shrunken precinct of his fame – chewing his quid and composing verses for the price of a screw of tobacco. There's a remarkable echo with another poet, who was also incarcerated due to madness a century later. Between 1945 and 1958 Ezra Pound was held at St Elizabeth's Hospital for the Criminally Insane in Washington D.C. Indicted in absentia for treason in 1943, the poet, who was living in Italy, was handed over to the United States Army by Italian partisans, arrested, flown to Washington, found medically unfit to stand trial, and was committed as a psychiatric patient. He was only released following the campaigning of many fellow writers and poets, including William Carlos Williams and T. S. Eliot. While there, Pound once told the critic Hugh Kenner how 'Sometimes the guards ask *me* . . . to write poems . . . for them to give their sweethearts'. Asked if he obliged, 'Why, yes,' said Pound. It's odd to think of poetry having this private currency.

We can easily imagine Clare sitting here. The front of the church is now the All Saints' Bistro, all metal tables and chairs set out Continental style, overlooking a small, pigeon-haunted square. We watch the comings and goings on its benches: canoodling couples, solitary vapers, young mothers with buggies equipped for polar exploration, two elderly women who seem to be engaged in synchronized pastie-eating, a beggar asking for change. Even though the buses that advertise their routes along their sides, the relict High Street clearing banks and the McDonald's all work against it, we get the sense that this view – or perhaps the experience of sitting here – hasn't changed much: the church as a still point, albeit one where you can now sip a double espresso. Just inside the church's porch, the building remembers: Clare's sonnet 'I Am' has been painted on to a wall, alongside his bust, and the assertion that 'John Clare composed this poem on the portico of All Saints' Church BETWEEN . . . 1842 – 1864.' But it's a gloomy room, a penitential narthex next to the toilets beyond the main café, and a deeply melancholic version of 'Moon River' is being piped into it, so we don't linger long.

★

As we have learned on our travels, a hospital death usually means having to turn our attentions elsewhere for traces of a poet's final places. Hospitals, when they're not bulldozed or redeveloped into boutique hotels or luxury apartments, tend to morph. It would be like wandering into one of today's open-plan, hot-desking offices, with their breakout zones and meeting pods, expecting to find the exact place where somebody once sat in the serried ranks of the typing pool. To die in hospital is often to die backstage, behind the scenes, screened off from the tempo of our days. Behind their facades and main entrances, hospitals are an endless scene-shifting. Despite the big exeunt, there's usually nothing to locate.

St Andrew's has been added to and developed, but is still providing mental health care, and a walk around its grounds with Bobbie
Judd, the Archive Manager here, reveals how the old buildings and
original layout are easily navigable. There is a huge lawn opposite
the main entrance wing's grand neoclassical design: pretty swanky
for John Clare. Bobbie points out the Hospital Chapel across on
its other side and tells us it was completed in the year before Clare
died. It was designed by George Gilbert Scott – architect of the
Midland at St Pancras, Reading Gaol and the Albert Memorial –
and Clare would surely have watched it go up during his final
years here. Outside its entrance we find the only memorial to
Clare at the hospital: a wooden planter filled with fresh earth.

St Andrew's is clean-cut, landscaped, an English arcadia of fine
trees and leafy pathways. Even in the middle of the nineteenth
century it must have felt a world away from Clare's childhood:
untidy heath furze and springs that gurgled with a shared history,
significant kinks in a road as ancient meeting places, the workplace and playgrounds of rough pasture, the scorch marks of a
Gypsy fire in the woods, all the teeming variety of its plant and
birdlife. We picture his life in new terms, from all of that to this
tidiness.

The archive itself is held in the Tennent Building. Asking
around before our visit, Bobbie says it has a strong claim to being
the part of the hospital where Clare lived and died, though it's
impossible to be certain. There's a moment of bureaucracy when
we're asked to sign a consent form for access to a deceased patient's
records: we almost flinch, as if Clare is suddenly here and in the
quick, not simply a literary figure. He was being cared for in these
rooms. He was a patient here.

A lot of the original clinical notes have been lost to damp
while in storage, but there are a couple of things here worth
looking at. The casebooks of St Andrew's Hospital still survive,
and we glimpse the grim record of his deterioration. Nevertheless,
the poet seems to have been in reasonable nick approaching

his seventies. One entry (for 6 February 1861) lifts the gloom, because it mentions poetry:

> Is in very good bodily health, but of very feeble intellect, though he has within the last few months written several little sonnets which are very pretty and show but slight traces of his usual incoherence. His memory is bad and he occasionally becomes excited, noisy and abusive using both profane & filthy language.

Sadly, these poems were a rare late blooming in Clare's long asylum years. During his first decade here he'd been productive, and also lucky with the stewards of the hospital, who had encouraged and even collected his work. But by the early 1850s the words trail off. Around this time Clare had also grown too unwell to make the walk into Northampton to resume his post under the portico. We get excited by the idea of a hidden stash of unseen Clare poems turning up, perhaps in a papered-over niche or crawlspace or locked box, somewhere in the fabric of the hospital. Hospitals are always changing, always a work in progress. But Bobbie isn't having any of it: 'No. There's nothing else.'

★

I saw Clare frequently during his residence at the asylum here. At first he was allowed to come into the Town (the Asylum is a mile out of it) unattended, and his favourite resort was beneath the portico of All Saints' Church, where in summer time he would sit for hours together. He was moody and taciturn and rather avoided society. He would talk rationally enough at times, about poetry especially, but on one occasion in the midst of a conversation in which he had betrayed no signs of insanity, he suddenly quoted passages from *Don*

Juan as his own. I suggested, gently, that they were usually attributed to Byron, upon which he said that was true, but he and Byron were one; so with Shakespeare; Shakespeare's plays were his composition when he was Shakespeare; and turning round on me suddenly he said: 'Perhaps you don't know that I am Jan Burns and Tom Spring?' In fact he was any celebrity whom you might mention. 'I'm the same man,' he said, 'but sometimes they called me Shakespeare and sometimes Byron and sometimes Clare.'

Frederick Martin was Clare's first biographer – he'd previously produced an edition of Chatterton's poems, with a memoir – and this account of Clare 'in residence' under the Northampton church portico was related to him by a local journalist the year after the poet's death.

Clare *had* written his own versions of *Don Juan* and *Childe Harold*. Clare started out as a poet in the age of Byron, and the famous poet loomed over his later years. The summer before his encounter with the railway men in Royce Wood, Clare had been in London for eleven weeks. It was his third visit, and one day while making his way into Oxford Street, he found himself caught up in a gathering crowd. He realized at some point that a funeral was shivering through the streets, and no ordinary funeral, going by the looks on peoples' faces. There was low, excited talk. As the cortège drew close, a young girl nearby gave out a sigh, and said: 'Poor Lord Byron!'

Clare must have been stunned. 'I coud almost feel in love with her for the sigh she had uttered for the poet ... It was almost worth all the News paper puffs and Magazine Mournings that ever was paraded after the death of a poet since flattery and hypocrisy was babtizd as the name of truth and sincerity.' Clare was crossing paths with Byron's body on the home leg of a journey that had originated in Missolonghi in Greece three months before. Refused entry into Westminster Abbey, after lying in state in rooms nearby, the hearse was now taking the dead poet north towards Hucknall in Nottinghamshire and the Byron family vault, leading a long procession of carriages.

What struck Clare that day was the way in which London came out for Byron. 'The common people felt his merits & his power & the common people of a country are the best feelings of a prophecy of futurity they are the veins & arteries that feed & quicken the heart of living fame.'

We think of Clare here under the portico in Northampton town centre, having absorbed Byron to the point at which their identities merge, the one poet seemingly continuous with the other. There couldn't be two poets from greater extremes of the social spectrum: the aristocratic lord whose fame had outlived him, and the son of the labourer, feeling himself growing fainter every day, telling anyone who'd listen he wrote *Don Juan*.

★

The iron railway from London to the north was never built through Royce Wood, but the tracks did arrive eventually in a roundabout way, connecting Clare's village to Stamford and Peterborough. Before Dr Beeching did for this offshoot of the Midland Railway a century later, they took John Clare's body home to the landscape of his childhood and buried him in Helpston churchyard, where he lies next to his parents. The poet who got as far away from Helpston as London, who only saw the sea once in his lifetime, travelled – for the first and last time – by train, on the kind of railway he'd seen men planning forty years before, while he was out walking in the woods.

★

Roundhay Park, Leeds. At its southern, Oakwood end, a clock tower is being taken apart. The ornamental owl is removed from its Edwardian perch; a blessing of unicorns is rounded up from its cupola. At the beginning of 2015, time stops: the power to the clock mechanism is switched off, the hands are removed from the dial face and the structure is slowly dismantled. The clock is a local landmark, and the entire process is filmed using time-lapse photography. For a few months the residents of Oakwood are unable to say 'I'll meet you at the Clock,' or if they do they'll mean a patch of opened ground, rubble, and a gaggle of bright plant machinery. The casings and mechanism have been taken away for restoration, and the rust and corrosion and blistered gilding of just over a century of Leeds weather is being cleaned and shotblasted all through the late winter and spring. By March, lucky money is buried under the new foundations, and a copper lightning conductor is earthed at the spot where the restored clock will be re-erected. And up it goes again.

But throughout this spring our eyes are on what remains of the old public toilet block in the background. This is the site where the poet John Riley was murdered on an October night in 1978. A week before we are due to visit in early May, images start arriving of this more prosaic building being demolished, taken by a friend in Leeds. Nobody records any time-lapse footage of this particular phase of the redevelopment project, nobody will be sorry to see the back of these bogs, and it has suddenly become a race against time to view the site, before all trace of it has been wiped from the face of the earth.

★

Obliteration and neglect are part of the John Riley myth, such as it is. We travel to Leeds to find out more about the near-forgotten John Riley, the undervalued John Riley, the neglected John Riley, the unsung John Riley, timing our visit to coincide with an appreciation of Riley's work that's being held at Leeds University's School of English.

Dead poets have afterlives, the things they made finding their way into the collective imagination of subsequent generations of readers, surviving the immediate tastes and circumstances of their making, or fading and growing fainter in time. Some poets are met mostly with silence during their lifetimes, only to do well in this afterlife; others sense themselves – their work – becoming extinct before their actual deaths.

But one factor in all of this, increasingly, is the attention of the academy, and the penumbra of this afterlife is the academic conference. This is a busy funerary complex, with its calls for papers, suggested angles of approach, plenaries, parallel panels, screenings, readings, interviews and themed walks; its name badges, delegate packs, hotel assignations and coffee bitter as gall from regulation, pump-action flasks. Humanist ritual, gathering of the tribe, networking opportunity . . . And at the centre of it all, the dead poet, surely grateful that anybody is still listening?

Though with Riley, we're not entirely sure. This event is sparsely attended, but good humoured and more intimate and engaging than most. Two of the confirmed speakers have cancelled at the last minute, but the organizers roll with the punches and improvise. At one point, during a discussion of Riley's early years as a poet during the Sixties, one speaker remarks on how the poets he had aligned himself with were all more or less ignored at the time. To which an audience member, and veteran of this same scene, replies: 'Yes, but we worked hard to be neglected.'

Riley's first book, *Ancient and Modern*, appeared in 1967, the poet's thirtieth year. He'd become closely associated with the Cambridge School – or should that be 'Cambridge School': the label can seem a handy way of lumping together some fairly dissimilar writers. The Leeds-born Riley was working in and around Cambridge as a schoolteacher at the time *The English Intelligencer* first appeared in 1966, a foundational broadsheet and perhaps the moment a movement gathered shape and collective purpose. These poets – Riley's peer group included J. H. Prynne, Tom Pickard, Andrew Crozier, Peter Riley (no relation) and Barry MacSweeney – were an English underground with its own tributaries and presiding spirits, a countercurrent, a corrective, working against the grain (or twin-sided veneers) of Philip Larkin and Ted Hughes. But maybe pre-eminence wasn't the point. While we might struggle to understand an awkwardness when it comes to readership and reception, there's no doubting the seriousness of the endeavour. Maybe a willed or accepted obscurity is a position of strength, a margin in which to get the work done.

By 1970 Riley had moved back to his home town, and took with him Grosseteste Press, which he had founded with his friend Tim Longville in 1966, in effect establishing a northern arm of Cambridge in the West Riding. Reading Riley, we don't encounter much of a self-ghettoizing tendency. Yes, the poems are quiet and singular, understated and serious, strengthened when read in sequence by a unity of purpose. But they want to be read. Might they have seemed so different from the dominant voices of their day, even in their day? As somebody points out during the appreciation in Leeds, they're sometimes not a million miles from Larkin, still active (just about) a few miles up the M62.

> the sadness
> of good poems
>
> consider an estuary
> and expanse of light

Riley's poems seem to face in two directions: tuned in to an English tradition, while attempting something more bracing, clear, alive to the astronauts orbiting above in their historical moment. *Ancient and Modern.* There are plenty of love lyrics, wind, rain, the trees in the parks and gardens, a witness to seasonal and diurnal forces, the plainsong of quiet praise, night thoughts, and the moon. Lots of moons.

But Riley was attracted to other traditions too, and attempting to work in the realm of the visionary, particularly attuned to the iconographic East. A few years before his death, he had converted to Russian Orthodoxy (originally hoping to join the Polish Orthodox Church in Leeds, an absent cleric meant he was received into the Russian Orthodox Church for convenience's sake), and seemed temperamentally drawn to a form of religious illumination that set him somewhat apart not only from the dominant poets of the overground, but those he'd hitherto been loosely affiliated with.

He turned his native city into a place called Czargrad. Have such ambitions made it difficult for us to see or hear Riley? Does his writing resist easy categorization (and is 'easy categorization' the master key to the kingdom of wide readership)? Perhaps his poems are like Leeds itself, plain and no-nonsense on the face of it, but on closer inspection woven and riven with history, held together with mysterious and contradictory forces.

★

We're boarding a bus in the city centre, down near the Corn Exchange, with the poet Ian Duhig, who has lived in Leeds since 1974. We travel on the top deck of the Number 12 towards Roundhay Park with Ian as our growling tour guide. Tea-time commuters heading home from town are earwigging in on an extraordinary presentation: we're heading towards Chapel Allerton, and Chapeltown (or Chap) is really a corruption of this place name; the Irish have been coming to Leeds since before the Great Famine; they were originally settled in Richmond Hill, but after the slum clearances in the Thirties satellites like Chapeltown were created; this is where the Lithuanian Jews settled, followed by Ukrainians, Hungarians, Latvians and Poles; this is Harehills, big Afro-Caribbean and Asian communities are established here, and the oldest street carnival in Europe. He tells us about Róisín Ban and Róisín Dubh, the white rose of Yorkshire and the black rose of Ireland. He tells us about pubs that lie on subtle fault lines, the Zm Zm Bakery on Harehills Road, the site of the Roots Club, once Leeds's premier Punk venue (though Jimi Hendrix had played there too, in one of its earlier incarnations). In fact, Ian tells us so much, so quickly, we only manage to scribble down half of it. He quotes Wallace Stevens's line about not living in places, but descriptions of places. By the time we reach Roundhay Park, we're alighting at the outskirts of a richer, stranger city.

The park is huge, on a different scale from the other northern park we've visited on the trail of a poet, Pearson Park in Hull, where Larkin once lived. We might be at the wrong end of the year to see it, but Ian mentions the artist John Atkinson Grimshaw, a northern master of Victorian landscapes and city nocturnes, moonlight and gaslight, painter of burnished, autumnal Wapping and Liverpool and Manchester and Leeds, the city of his birth. Grimshaw lived not far from here, and painted Roundhay Park several times. Something of Grimshaw's vision chimes with Riley's: both Loiners seem drawn to English skies of brass and iron, and were acquainted with the night, artists tuned in to the moonlit walk after dark, the view from the streets of lit windows and unknowable interior lives going on. It's detectable in some of Riley's prose pieces, though his world can seem caught in its own time-lapse disintegration:

> The city crumbles, stupified by its own nonentity. It may be well to distinguish, since it is not a matter of poetic pre-cision, between observable fact and observer's prejudice. It is a fact that the streets are filthy; grim, grimy nineteenth century solidity replaced by the glass and cardboard con-structions of architectural rabbits; fields beyond the outskirts sprawling slums; and the centre a bomb-site. Replaced by nothing, the house I was born in is gone, the house from whose perspective the gardened suburb I now live in had no reality, not as fact, not as fantasy. Not until later the prowling round night streets . . .

We think of another Grimshaw, Urban Grimshaw, and a savage kingdom called 'Ashtrayland', in Bernard Hare's book about young Leeds
gangs, a place that's lying in wait on the other side of the Eighties.

★

The trees in Roundhay Park are turning up the green. The new
growth is sizzling a little brighter in the light rain, and we've come
to look at a toilet block, which by now has almost completely
gone. Ian leads us down behind the newly restored clock tower
to a shattered pile of railed-off brickwork and rubble. The only
clues to what once stood here are shiny red ballcocks, rolled from
their broken cisterns, miniature planets among the space junk and
asteroid debris. Ian's been sending us pictures for days taken on his
phone, and we can't say we haven't been warned.

This is the only crime scene we've visited on our travels, and
although the police tape has long vanished, the area emits a grim
force field. A few days ago we pieced together the events of that
night from the smudgy press reports on microfilm. MURDER IN A
LEEDS COPSE. Riley had been playing dominoes at the Nag's Head
in Chapel Allerton, and had drunk his usual five or six pints. His
body, beaten and bloody, had been found behind the toilets in the
morning by an attendant making his rounds; a bunch of keys lay
nearby; his wallet was discovered half a mile away, still containing
£15, though the police believed the motive for the attack was
robbery, a senseless killing for a few quid, but the assailants had
panicked. Riley's widow Carol told police he frequently walked
about late at night to gain inspiration for his writing.

A familiar squeamishness we felt at Thom Gunn's archive, or
while sitting in a car outside Anne Sexton's house, comes back.
We don't want to go any further. Riley's sudden and violent death
is not the most interesting thing about this poet, and why should
it distract or detain us from his poems? In one of the newspaper
cuttings, there is a picture of Riley. The print is old and unstable,
and his beard turned a carbonized jet, but we can recognize the

description we overheard somebody offer of him as resembling something like a Russian diplomat or dignitary: keen and intelligent, austere, learned, perhaps slightly dandyish. It clashes with the banal horror of the reporting. A voice comes to us from one of David Peace's *Red Riding Quartet*, and the old newsdesk maxim: If it bleeds, it leads. Two worlds colliding.

★

Years after Riley's death, 1996, and an IRA bomb exploded in the centre of Manchester. The offices of the publisher Carcanet in the Corn Exchange were severely damaged. Ian tells us how stock of John Riley's *Selected Poems*, published just the previous summer, was mostly lost in the devastation.

★

A writer working in ways that were different enough to set him apart from his wider peer group, never easily disposed to or sitting easily with the more popular currents of his day, killed suddenly in mid-career, the stock of a revival edition of his work mostly destroyed … Why are we still wondering about the neglect of John Riley?

What might have happened if there had been a few more books? The sudden meaningless death certainly seems to have contributed to the arrest of his reputation. There is no need to play counterfactuals: all any writer has to do is consider how an indifferent world will simply and implacably move on without them, the way a quayside seems to recede from an unmoored ship. We know so little about John Riley, and even though that shouldn't matter, a body of work has been cut loose from the self's custodianship, and is lying in wait for its possible audience. Maybe Riley and his readers haven't yet been properly introduced.

★

The night of 27–28 October. That awful, uncertain hyphen seems part of the violence of Riley's death. Beyond the shadows at the edge of the park, and the luminary stare of the Oakwood clock tower, Friday night turned into Saturday morning. At the poly-technic a mile or so across town, a Rock Against Racism gig has ended, and the amps and flight cases are being packed into a van. A band from Manchester called The Fall have just played to a handful of people; the support acts, including a young per-formance poet called John Cooper Clarke, had failed to show. In the city of Tetley Bittermen, the last pints of Sam Smiths and Timothy Taylors and Boddingtons and Stones are being swilled back (only 28p in the student union bars). Towards Headingley, in a polytechnic hall at Beckett Park, a cigarette end left smoulder-ing after the Friday night disco isn't noticed when the building is locked up at two o'clock, and is burning steadily towards dawn, when more than fifty firefighters will be needed to contain the blaze. Towards three o'clock, a waning crescent moon will rise over the West Riding. The body of a forty-one year-old man will be found, and in the local newspaper's offices the ink-stained compositor will set the metal type of the headline, next to a reminder that the following night the clocks will go back and it will be winter.

★

In the short term there seems no doubt that a dubious kind of fame can attach to dead poets if their deaths are deemed bohe-mian, premature, self-inflicted. Even more so if the death is seen to arise out of frustration, neglect, poverty or a despair borne of devotion to the muse. But obscurity can smoulder for years, dec-ades, even centuries. Tragedy isn't a guarantee of staying in print.

With Clare and with Riley, obscurity and the possibility of redis-covery long after death happened (or is still happening) within a certain cultural landscape. Looking beyond its horizons, how many poets have died tragic deaths in recent years, the kind that should – if dying really is the first basic requirement – have attracted wide readerships? In the dense shanties of sub-Saharan Africa, the ports of the Gulf of Guinea, in the humid canyons of Asian megacities or scattered across tiny Micronesian island communities, there must be poets working tonight, but their standing, their relationships to readers, depend on social and cultural complexions beyond the purview of this book (or probably any single book).

How valued are poets anywhere today? We sometimes joke about death being a good career move for the neglected poet, but perhaps that easy formulation only has any real purchase in the anglophone West? The only thing we can say with any certainty is that the designation 'poet' is never really fixed. While writing this book, we came across a blogger's story of Xu Lizhi, a young poet in Guangdong Province in eastern China who killed himself by jumping from the seventeenth floor of a mall in Shenzhen in September 2014. Xu was an economic migrant, working in the factory of a Taiwanese electronics company assembling parts for Western consumer products (when *Time* magazine picked up the story, the article was called 'The Poet Who Died for Your Phone'). What catches our eye is the blogger's description of how 'poet' might once have meant something in China, might once have carried real cachet. But in the reforming, post-1989 country, things began to change; today 'none of the papers would waste space on a poem, even as filler; if a self-advertised "poet" turned up on a dating site there'd be no takers and plenty of eye-rolling: poets must be weird or poor, or both.' Sound familiar? But the *dagong shiren* – or migrant poets – must still be writing between shifts, tonight, capturing the experience of villagers drawn to the big city. And John Clare might have recognized the anonymous migrants in Xu Lizhi's 'Sleepless', trying to work and survive in an indifferent world:

> We ran along the railway,
> arriving in some place called 'the City'
> where we trade in our youth, and our muscle.
> Finally we have nothing to trade, only a cough
> and a skeleton nobody cares about.

On the Circuit

On the evening of Friday, 28 September 1973, England's most famous poet completed a sixteen-minute reading of his poems in the baroque Großer Saal of the Palais Palffy in Vienna. He turned down an offer from his hosts to buy him dinner, asking instead for a 'nice car' to take him back to his hotel. It was an unusual request, since Wystan Hugh Auden, by his own admission, could not 'tell a Jaguar from a Bentley', but doubly so because he was staying at the Altenburger Hof in Walfischgasse, less than a five-minute stroll from the Palais. His reading for the Austrian Society of Literature had been well received, but now he was tired and ready for bed.

We imagine the poet hauling himself out into Walfischgasse, apologizing to the driver for the brevity of the journey, as he offers a five-schilling tip. The evening has likely contained his customary mix of lethal vodka martinis and wines. Perhaps, as he often did, he topped it off with a brandy before leaving the Palais. As the taxi pulls away, he lights a final cigarette and shuffles towards the lobby. The Altenburger Hof is not a smart hotel, rather a plain, gaunt building sandwiched between office blocks and bars. But its location is perfect, just yards from the Opera House in one direction and the Moulin Rouge nightclub in the other. For Auden and his partner Chester Kallman, it has become a second home on visits from their country cottage in Kirchstetten.

Cigarette on lip as ever, a folder of typescripts under his arm, Auden struggles for breath as he climbs the narrow stairs up one flight to Room 6. For the patrons of the Moulin Rouge and the

Opera House, the night is still young. But Auden, in his sixty-sixth year, is a poet of habit. Early to bed, early to rise and to write.

★

We are being driven – unnervingly fast – through the tight back streets of Kirchstetten. We are in the back seat, and our host, the archivist Dr Helmut Neundlinger, is in the passenger seat. Our driver is Paul Horsak, the Mayor of Kirchstetten. Whenever we turn a hairpin and meet an oncoming truck or tractor, the looks of rage and terror melt into smiles as they see their Mayor waving them past. He is clearly a popular man. And he has been generous to us, the visiting British poets. Breaking off from an animated conversation (and a half-drained glass) at the Audenhaus, the Mayor has offered to show us a precious relic of the late, great W. H. Auden.

We flash through a tunnel under the main Linz–Vienna autobahn, past the onion-domed church and into farmland broken up by workshops, barns and garages. Even Kirchstetten has its edgelands, and we glimpse them as we break on to open fields, northwards into the neighbouring village of Totzenbach, where we turn by a low warehouse. The Mayor swings into a courtyard behind it, parks, and waves an arm with pride at a battered VW Beetle in the corner, with a sickly paint job somewhere between custard and mustard. 'This was Auden's car,' he says. We get out and walk around it. We've both seen film footage of the poet driving – faster even than the Mayor, carpet-slippered foot to the floor – on his way to the village shop.

The car looks like Herbie, *The Love Bug* from the hit Seventies movie series (Robert Lowell, in his last letter to Elizabeth Bishop, described how his children and their nanny 'have gone off to a movie about a car without a driver, more or less engaging to three different ages'). It even has a chirpy sticker on the boot lid, saying *'Wer holt mich hier raus?'* meaning 'Who will get me out of here?' One of us suggests renaming the car the *Tell-Me-the-Truth-about-Love-Bug*, but the joke falls flat. The Beetle's tyres, surprisingly, are not flat, though we're not sure this vehicle would make it through an MOT. Rust has taken hold of the bodywork, scabbing every dint. We've heard there are bullet holes somewhere, and scour over each pockmark in the paint like a pair of claims adjusters.

Holt mich hier raus! is now the title of the German version of *I'm a Celebrity . . . Get Me Out of Here!,* the reality TV show in which actors, sports stars and singers are dropped into a jungle and have to survive on a diet of rice and insects. The thought of Auden undergoing a Bushtucker Trial seems ridiculous but, unusually for a poet, he did have a foothold in popular culture. Such was his fame by 1972 that he appeared on the BBC1 prime-time chat show *Parkinson,* telling his host that he is worried about a creeping epidemic of boredom among the young: 'when I was young one was often unhappy, but I don't ever remember in my life being bored.' Recalling the interview years later, Michael Parkinson said, 'I found myself inspecting his face as I was talking to him and I swear there was dust in some of the crevices.'

★

Auden's final reading, arranged by the Austrian Society of Literature, took place in an opulent upstairs room at the Palais Palffy. The Society held most of its readings on its own premises nearby, where there was (and still is) a small performance space, but such was Auden's fame that they decided to hire a special room for it.

The Großer Saal has now been renamed the Beethoven Saal. We buy tickets for a 'Mozart & Strauss Konzerte' so we can see it in action. The function rooms are accessed via an impressive stone staircase. At the foot of the stairs is a large locked door with a sign saying 'Palffy Club'. A piece of paper stuck to the door says it's still closed for the summer. Helmut, the archivist, our Vienna guide, mutters something about the cellar club being a magnet for rich Russians. He's seen them dropped off in their limousines outside.

It must take careful scheduling to keep the Ambient House apart from the Ambient Strauss.

We can't find a lift. And it seems Auden couldn't either, since he was seen on arrival struggling, breathless, up the stairs, then recovering on the landing with a cigarette. In Vienna today it is not hard to locate concert tickets, save for the ever-sold-out Opera House. Faux Mozarts in wigs, brocaded coats and lacy jabots hang out on street corners and palace courtyards, their pockets stuffed with glossy leaflets. Some hunt in packs. To the surprise of the Palais Palffy dandies, we seek them out, while other tourists dive into busy roads to avoid them, risking the horse-drawn carriages that clatter past.

More dandies are waiting upstairs for us, insisting on every coat and bag being checked in to the cloakroom. The elderly man in front of us enters into detailed negotiations as to whether his leather coat is, in fact, a jacket. He finally loses the argument, takes it off and hands it over. We are ushered through the Figaro Saal, where the real Mozart gave a concert at the age of six, and into the Beethoven Saal, where the real Auden gave his last reading at the age of sixty-six. It's easier to imagine the boy wonder than the aged bard in these halls. The whole place is so primped and poodled, walls adorned with gaudy nymphs in glades. We try to picture Auden as he was at the opening of that last reading, sifting through his papers at a desk onstage, while the eminent Austrian actor Achim Benning read German translations of his poems.

The audience is different too. We are not the only ones trying to capture the Beethoven Saal on cameraphones. We are among tourists who have paid through the nose for this Viennese experience and are keen to come away with something to show for it. On that September night in 1973 the audience was made up of Vienna's high art connoisseurs, equally at home in this literary salon or the opera house down the road.

★

At the Österreichische Mediathek across the city we are settling behind desks and donning huge headphones. As radio buffs, we were beguiled by the shelves of vintage sound recorders – reel-to-reels as intricate as the finest watches – now seized by silence. But we have to steel ourselves. We are here because this national sound archive has a digitized recording of W. H. Auden's last ever reading. Indeed, it has some of his last ever words, shortly before he left, alone, for his hotel room. There is a prurient fascination to this, but a trepidation too. We are about to hear the poet's voice, knowing (as he didn't) that this was his last night on earth.

We press play. As Achim Benning concludes his reading, W. H. Auden stands and clears his throat. Pages turn. A heavy lorry outside rumbles across the stereo spectrum. The sound quality is superb. It's 1973.

★

Five minutes from the Palais Palffy, at the magnificent Wiener Staatsoper, a similarly rumpled, ravaged and paunchy old man stands on a stage and sings. Rigoletto is Verdi's fool, a court jester who loses the one thing he truly loves – his only daughter. Although the plot creaks a bit (curses, assassins, implausible seductions) the music is sublime and its themes – the destructive and redemptive power of sex, the mystery of love – also drive Auden's work as a poet. He would rather be here than giving a reading in the Palais Palffy. After all, this opera house is one of the main reasons for his move to Austria in the late Fifties. But although he is missing tonight's performance of *Rigoletto*, his partner Chester Kallman is there. Having heard Wystan read countless times, Chester travelled in from Kirchstetten with him, but opted to attend *Rigoletto* instead. They dropped their bags at the Altenburger Hof and walked from Walfischgasse to their separate venues.

Three decades before, in New York, Chester had introduced Auden to the glories of opera. They were not just partners in love, but in work too, co-writing libretti for Stravinsky and

Hans Werner Henze. For the older Auden, his relationship with Kallman was the marriage he had longed for. But the consummation of that marriage was brief. They met in 1939 and by 1941 their sexual relationship was over. Chester was spending months at a time with a new lover in Athens. But their days together in Kirchstetten were a source of profound joy for Auden. As with many poets, Auden's contradictions fuelled his work. His promiscuity, hard-drinking and drug-use were countered by a rage for normality. He was obsessively punctual, regular and diligent in his writing habits and longed for a settled domesticity. Now, for the first time in his life he felt rooted – in a house of his own, in a village he loved, with the man he felt married to.

★

Auden begins his reading. He says a few lines in German that delight his audience. Then he starts reading an elegy for his former Kirchstetten housekeeper, in his rich mahogany voice, arresting and musical, despite wheeziness from years of chain-smoking. By now, his characteristic late vowel sounds are set, tilted by years spent in New York – 'mester' for 'master'. The poem ('In Memoriam Emma Eiermann, ob. November 4th, 1967') is a fine and honest elegy, a picture of Emma and her brother Josef, Sudetendeutsche refugees who made a home – and a family of cats – in the Vienna woods. He paints her as innately suspicious of visitors, protective of the house and its owners, fiercely loyal:

Liebe Frau Emma,
na, was hast Du denn gemacht?
You who always made
such conscience of our comfort,
oh, how could you go and die,

as if you didn't know
that in a permissive age

so rife with envy,
a housekeeper is harder
to replace than a lover

★

To understand Auden's last years, you have to visit Kirchstetten.
Vienna only shows you the half of it. We arrive at the pickup point –
on the corner of Grillparzerstraße and Rathausplatz – at 2.25 p.m.,
but there is no shuttle bus. Departure time is 2.30 and we were
warned to be on time or we would miss it. We get talking to the
only other person waiting on the corner – a lawyer from Germany.
He is semi-retired and trying to expand his range of interests. He
has heard of W. H. Auden and is keen to find out more. We can't
help but notice that a crowd of people is pouring into a shuttle bus
a hundred yards down the road, but it is not the precise location
described in the paperwork, so the lawyer thinks we should stand
firm. He apologizes for his legal precision. We apologize for backing a hunch, and run for the bus down the road, which is about to
leave. In the windscreen a piece of paper says 'Audenhaus'.

It is a Saturday in September, but a special one. Today is the
reopening of Auden's work-room, the loft study of his Kirchstetten
home, following refurbishment of the archive there. The hope is
that more tourists will make the hour-long trip west of Vienna
if there is a visitor centre to greet them there. We are here at a
volatile moment. The war in Syria has driven thousands of people
across European borders in search of refuge and hope, and Austria
finds itself on route one up through the Balkans and Hungary
towards Germany. As we drive through the Viennese suburbs we
pass signs in shops and graffiti on walls saying 'Migrants Welcome'.

★

At the Palais Palffy reading Auden moves on to his second poem –
'Lines to Dr Walter Birk on his Retiring from General Practice'.

We've forgotten we are in an archive, on headphones, listening to it. This poem in tribute to his doctor is full of the love of his adopted home village – 'The healer I have faith in is / someone I've gossiped // and drunk with before I call him to touch me.'

But the poem then describes the 'dialects' of the body and how easy it is to 'misconster' those dialects and misunderstand our bodies. We hear him read the line 'the organs of old men / suffer in silence', and rewind to listen again. Auden does poet-as-prophet rather well (see the online frenzy about his 'September 1, 1939' being read as a foretelling of 9/11) but this seems particularly ominous – a fear that his body is not telling him how damaged it is, just hours before his heart gave in.

And a doctor might say Auden's body has every right to be damaged – years of chain-smoking, heavy drinking and amphetamines would have seen off many poets years earlier. He was as fastidious about his addictions as he was about his work. His biographer Humphrey Carpenter documents his daily use of alcohol in later life as follows:

> Several strong vodka martinis before dinner
> Much wine with dinner
> More wine after dinner
> Retire to bed early (around 9) with more wine
> Vodka as sleeping draught.

All this accompanied by heavy smoking and – to allow him to work well in the mornings – a Benzedrine (speed) pill on waking. He might then take a second pill to get past the midday slump. According to Carpenter, Auden gave up taking Benzedrine pills in the mid-Sixties 'because he found they were no longer having any effect'. In later life all his teeth had gone. One dinner guest at Kirchstetten remembered him biting into a Greek sesame and honey cake during the dessert course and leaving a full set of dentures embedded in it.

This reading we're listening to is Auden's final one after many such evenings spent before microphone and lectern. How much of his later weariness was induced by the long hours of airports and hotels and engagements? In a poem he wrote in the early Sixties called 'On the Circuit' there's a clear picture of the discombobulated poet in motion, an 'airborne instrument' on a tight schedule across America, unable to garner any sense of place, forgetting 'where I was / The evening before last'. It ends on a note of gratitude, but not before nailing that particular anxiety familiar to those poets and public speakers that like to take a drink in order to survive such events, who don't like going on alone. O for a Shakespeare's Sonnet. Or even a bottle of Buckfast.

> Then, worst of all, the anxious thought,
> Each time my plane begins to sink
> And the No Smoking sign comes on:
> *What will there be to drink?*
>
> *Is this a milieu where I must*
> How grahamgreeneish! How infra dig!
> *Snatch from the bottle in my bag*
> *An analeptic swig?*
>
> Another morning comes: I see,
> Dwindling below me on the plane,
> The roofs of one more audience
> I shall not see again.
>
> God bless the lot of them, although
> I don't remember which was which:
> God bless the U.S.A., so large,
> So friendly, and so rich.

★

The bus journey from central Vienna to Kirchstetten is not short, over an hour, and the landscape changes: we'd imagined a shift from *The Third Man* to *The Sound of Music*, though the village itself sits among plain, rolling fields, 'a tractored sugar-beet country', as Auden himself described it. We are dropped in the centre of the village and follow our party up the hill. We have arranged to meet Dr Helmut Neundlinger – archivist for the Audenhaus – on arrival, and we have seen his pictures online. He shouldn't be hard to spot: a tall, slim, dark-haired, scholarly-looking man in his thirties, in round, wire-framed spectacles. We go over to introduce ourselves. 'I'm not Helmut,' he says, 'I'm his twin brother.' We decide we are being taken for fools. If Helmut wants to play games on foreign visitors, then he can pick on the German lawyer instead. We make our own way up to the Audenhaus, pausing only to photograph the sign for 'Audenstraße'. This honour of a street in his name was bestowed while Auden was still living here, which made him feel grateful but uneasy, since it sounded rather posthumous.

We walk up to the house to find a tidy Tyrolean cottage with a marquee set up next to it. This is the house the fifty-year-old Auden bought using the proceeds from an Italian literary prize in 1957 (who said poetry makes nothing happen?). Local dignitaries are already in place at trestle tables, sampling the beer and wine and canapés. They have been waiting for the shuttle bus of academics from Vienna. Now we are here the speeches can start. It becomes clear that there will be many speeches. A man approaches us, claiming to be the real Helmut. He apologizes for the confusion with his twin earlier. Doubles again. The real Helmut warns us that the speeches will be lengthy and all in German. He advises us to take this opportunity to look inside the house.

The house is now a hybrid. Part-house, part-museum. On the front gate the only nameplates still read 'W. H. Auden' and 'Chester Kallman', despite their absence for the last four decades. It's as if they left for a work trip to the States and are expected back any day. We snoop around, and it looks just like what it is now – a desirable country home with a trampoline in the garden, and the lush Vienna Woods rising from the back of the well-kept lawn. On a warm September afternoon it's not hard to see why Auden found his longing for domestic bliss fulfilled here. He threw himself into village life, attending church and befriending his neighbours in the bar and shop. They took him to their hearts, but then, they knew what it meant to live with a famous poet. Auden was himself doubled, shadowed. He was not the only poet.

★

Auden's third poem at the Palais Palffy is written in honour of Josef Weinheber, the other poet who made Kirchstetten his home. For a small village to lay claim to two famous poets is remarkable. Auden would point out Josef's house when he picked up visitors from the railway station in his yellow Beetle. Weinheber's widow is buried in Kirchstetten churchyard alongside Auden, but the poet himself is not. He has a simple stone memorial on the street outside the church, but was laid to rest in his garden, as Auden explains: 'where (under / the circs they had to) / they buried you like a loved / old family dog'.

The poet's absence from the graveyard is for the saddest of reasons: suicide. Weinheber killed himself in 1945, and his dates give a clue to the greater tragedy beyond his death. One of Austria's most celebrated pre-war poets, Weinheber was seduced by Nazism. Auden's elegy only mentions this in the third stanza, after a passage lamenting the fact that the two poets never had a chance to meet and drink and talk about poetry:

> Yes, yes, it has to be said:
> men of great damage
> and malengine took you up.
> Did they for long, though,
> take you in, who to Goebbels'

offer of culture
countered – *In Ruah lossen?*

By the time Goebbels asked Weinheber what the Nazis could 'do' for Austrian culture, the poet's reply – translated as 'Leave us alone' – suggests he realized what a terrible mistake he had made. In despair, he took his own life. Auden's approach to Weinheber is humane, sympathetic, lamenting the fact that: 'Rag, Tag and Bobtail / prefer a stink, and the young / condemn you unread.' He finishes reading the poem. His voice is clear and light, if a little breathy between lines. He moves on to the next poem.

★

We stand in the poet's attic workroom in the Audenhaus at Kirchstetten. In the marquee outside, local and national dignitaries make speeches in honour of the reopening. Auden's desk is set up under the window where he worked. Poking out of his typewriter is a half-finished poem – 'The Cave of Making' – his elegy for Louis MacNeice, abandoned after the line 'is turned into objects'. It's as if he wasn't sure of the next line and went for a walk in the woods to work it out, only pausing to cover his typewriter with a large protective perspex box. It's a good job the box is there. It would be too tempting, since we have the advantage of seeing the poem published, to help him out by typing 'I wish, Louis, I could have shown it you' . . .

Elsewhere in the attic there are videos on loop – one of a film made for Austrian TV with Auden showing the camera round his house. He speaks fluent German, but even we near-monoglots can tell that his English public-school vowel sounds are ringing through. Another loop shows footage of him being carried in a coffin down from the house to the cemetery, accompanied by the village band. A close-up of Chester at the graveside has him looking broken, eyes tight closed, clenched fist clutched against his chest. The same close-up comes round every couple of minutes.

We move along, pore over notebooks and letters in display cases. Would Auden have been horrified or flattered to see his chattels laid out under glass? A winding tower of the poet's books, a Cinzano bottle, an ashtray and a pair of battered carpet slippers form a display (by now, we've gathered enough material for a small companion volume to this one: *Footwear of the Poets*). Perhaps it's meant to hint at some former dishevelment: a concrete poltergeist. By the door there are more empty bottles – Nikita Vodka, Bols Silver Top Gin – to remind us of the role drink played in his life. It's a strange cross between a museum and a film set.

In one glass case is a die-cast toy of a yellow VW Beetle. It has become an emblem of Auden's eccentricity. There is a note with it referring to Hugerl, Auden's Austrian lover. The poet explains it clearly enough in his poem 'Glad', where he gives thanks for meeting the young car mechanic at a time when 'You were in need of money / And I wanted sex.' The arrangement lasted and deepened into genuine fondness over more than a decade, even surviving Hugerl's use of the yellow Beetle in a series of robberies in and around Kirchstetten, including Auden's own house. This would explain the bullet-hole story.

We mind our step back down the steep wooden staircase, and notice how, underneath the sound of the speeches, we can hear the soft and constant roar of the autobahn passing nearby. 'East, West, on the Autobahn / motorists whoosh', the poet wrote in the spring of 1967 when he turned sixty. The A1 was only completed that year, so perhaps the days were quieter when Auden and Chester first lived here, but it turns out to be quite a road that cuts through this modest agricultural landscape, forming the Austrian section of the E60 Trans-European route. You could climb in to your VW Beetle at Brest on France's Atlantic coast, and drive eastwards without leaving this highway until you reached Erkeshtam in Kyrgyzstan, just short of the People's Republic of China. Not Auden's Beetle. That isn't going anywhere.

★

We sneak into Auden's garden and find a bench where we sit and drink cold Stiegl beer. All those empties in the study have made our mouths dry. And the long road has put us in mind of another poet, often to be found behind the wheel of a car in his work.

Last spring we stood on a back road in Co. Derry, which, so far as we could tell, was Seamus Heaney's walk to school, the Langan's Road. Around us lay the landscape of Heaney's childhood, one he returned to imaginatively throughout his writing life, in poetry and in prose. To get there we'd driven through Toomebridge, where the River Bann leaves Lough Neagh and flows northwards on its way to the Atlantic, but not before pausing to pool and lose itself in Lough Beg. We saw the Lough Neagh Fisherman's Co-operative, the eelworks, and thought of that strange fish that swims a course to its origins. Road signs pointed to half-familiar places: Toome, Magherafelt, Bellaghy. Leaving the car and its satnav somewhere near Mossbawn, the poet's first farmstead home, which as Heaney said has come to resemble something more like a small industrial estate, we tried to get our bearings, a triangulation of map, interviews and poems.

Heaney wrote about the wildness of this rural place 'between the archaic and the modern', its local spirits and birds and animals, individual trees known intimately, its scarier presences, 'mankeepers and mosscheepers', its mysteries. Speaking to the poet Dennis O'Driscoll in *Stepping Stones* (a book that, like *Treasure Island*, is all the more evocative because it sets out with its own prefatory map), Heaney helpfully laid out the cardinal points of his childhood home like a clock face. We walked in a direction between one and two o'clock, along what must have been the Langan's Road. It was still a lonely byway, the land through its scribbly hedges swampy, sumpy, perhaps a little forlorn, when we came across dumped plastic feed bags, tyres, an old television set. And all the time, in the distance, the hum of traffic from the main Belfast road, the road that had brought us. Plans are afoot to build a four-lane dual carriageway right through here, slicing the townland of Anahorish in two.

Heaney had not long died the previous year, and no doubt like many other poets we were still figuring out what to make of the loss. For writers of our generation he had simply always been there, a huge and calibrating presence, one of a very few poets audible and visible on a world stage. Famous Seamus and all that. But the whole day was a kind of wavering, a boundary walk between past and present, poem and place name, local and universal. A mural had appeared on a Dublin wall before Christmas: DON'T BE AFRAID, in stark white letters the height of blockbuster credits, was the work of Maser, a Dublin graffiti artist, clearly inspired by the widely reported story of Heaney's final text to his family, that had ended with the Latin phrase *Noli timere*. The very existence of poetry might feel like cultural lag in some quarters, but we remembered Heaney's Nobel Prize acceptance speech some years before in Sweden, how he'd described the aerial wire in the chestnut tree passing down through the Mossbawn farmstead to the family wireless set, with its names – Leipzig, Oslo, Stuttgart, Warsaw, Stockholm – that fascinated him as a child fifty years before, the voice of the 'absolute speaker' of the BBC. We began to tune in to another animating spirit, that day in the back lanes of Co. Derry, the technological, the little leaps that speed the world up and close down distances and bring *everywhere* to *here*, and vice versa. From the turnip-snedder to digital packet switching. And the internal combustion engine. We remember all those poems in motion, things witnessed through windscreens, the drives around a peninsula or down country roads at night, through checkpoints or along a wind-struck coastline. In Belfast as a young man, finding his feet as a writer among other poets, wasn't Heaney the first among that group with his own set of wheels? On the bench outside the Audenhaus, we dig into our bags to find the Kindle, and scroll though its library to *Stepping Stones*. Yes. A VW Beetle, sometime around 1963.

★

In the Palais Palffy Auden is coming to the end of his reading. He gives the audience a final poem about Austria – 'Stark bewölkt', meaning 'mostly overcast'. It's a warm portrait of his adopted home, in spite of moans about dangerous drivers and 'standards at the Staatsoper' declining each year. Then he closes the reading on a crowd-pleaser with a few of his clerihews gathered under the title *Academic Graffiti*. The applause is loud and long. The famous poet has read for little more than a quarter of an hour, but now he is ready for bed. A car is requested to take him round the corner to the Hotel Altenburger Hof.

On the way to Walfischgasse, his car passes the Staatsoper, where, in spite of declining standards, *Rigoletto* is drawing to a close, with Auden's partner Chester Kallman in the audience. Once the stars have taken their curtain calls, Chester slips out and walks a couple of minutes back to the hotel. As was their custom, they have booked separate rooms. Before he heads to bed himself, Chester knocks on Wystan's door to compare notes on their respective evenings. But he gets no response. Assuming Wystan is already asleep, Chester goes to bed. It will keep until breakfast.

The Altenburger Hof is no longer a hotel, though the building is still there. It's now a block of offices with four company nameplates bolted to the wall by the door. Second from top, between 'Big Bus Vienna' and 'Breiteneder – Attorneys At Law' is a plate to mark the fact that W. H. Auden died here. We take photographs standing by the plaque. A waiter is setting lunch tables outside the café next door. He asks us why we're taking pictures. After all, it's just an office block. He has never heard of Auden, but we tell him the story and he writes it all down. He wants to be ready when the next poetic tourist comes his way.

We look up the performance schedule outside the perpetual aria-machine that is today's Staatsoper. We have one more evening here to piece together Auden's last night on earth, and by sheer chance we find that – of all the operas in the repertoire – *Rigoletto* is playing tonight. We ask at the box office, but we're being naïve. Tickets here sell out weeks in advance. We are told there will be a small number of standing tickets on sale just before the performance. We queue for an hour and get two. The standing areas are rammed and it's a warm evening. At first we only catch the briefest glimpses of the Duke and his titular jester, cricking our necks trying to see the action onstage. We've good views of the lighting rig. A woman in heels starts to sway and is led out. The huddle we're in becomes part of the performance, a drama of sideways looks, daggers when toes are trod on, micro-nods and gestures between couples that mean: *Please, can we go for a drink now?* After a while, the crowd thins out so much that we are no longer staring at the backs of necks beaded in sweat – but we'll never make it to the death of Gilda, and at the interval we flee, stopping by the toilets to splash cold water on our faces and blast our sodden shirts under the hand dryers. We are guessing that Chester Kallman didn't do this.

★

We are sipping coffee at a table in the battered but authentic Café Tirolerhof watching Helmut the archivist open his Auden files. The archive is in St Pölten, regional capital for Lower Austria and home of much paperwork relating to Kirchstetten, including a stack of papers from 1973. He shows us the bills for food and drink at the wake, the cost of the coffin (with details and trimmings itemized) and the printed cards handed to those who attended the funeral.

The death certificate is here, describing Auden as a 'Professor, *anglikanisch*', and setting the time of death at 9.30 a.m., though this is more likely to be the time when his body was discovered. The cause of death is given as 'Arteriosclerosis, fibrosis myocardii, hypertrophia cordis, endocarditis recens.' In other words, his heart gave out.

The most unsettling document Helmut shows us is the bill from Room 6 at the Hotel Altenburger Hof, as presented to – and settled by – Chester Kallman. The bill includes itemized charges for replacing the bed sheets, pillows, pillowcases and a blanket. There is a separate list for cleaning that includes, bizarrely, the curtains. Then we remember the (very) short story by Lydia Davis, 'How W. H. Auden Spends the Night in a Friend's House'. The poet couldn't sleep, it seems, without the help of some reassuring weight:

> Then his stealthy excursion over the floor for a chair to stand on and his unsteady reach for the curtains, which he lays over the other coverings on his bed . . .

It was an old nocturnal habit of his. If there weren't enough blankets to supply the necessary anchoring, the curtains might be pulled from their rail. And if the curtains weren't enough, the carpet might come up. According to Carpenter, Auden was once discovered in the morning 'sleeping beneath (among other things) a large framed picture'. And so we imagine Auden's final night in the Altenburger Hof, one last sweep of the room for mats, rugs, throws, curtains; one last self-burial for the hibernating bear, bedding down for his long winter sleep.

We are shown correspondence between Chester Kallman and the then President of the Austrian Society of Literature negotiating what was to become of the Kirchstetten house, how it might be turned into a library or museum or both, how that might be funded and what would be a fitting price. We are struck by how quickly the remains of this poet were itemized, costed, billed and paid for. We sift through more letters and bills relating to the purchase of the garden, house and car by various authorities. Auden was reputedly a terrible driver. Too fast and reckless in those carpet slippers. Back at the Beetle we had asked the Mayor what plans they had for the car, now that the house is refurbished and open to visitors. He said they were still mulling it over. One idea was to park it permanently outside the house, encased in glass.

★

Of all the twentieth-century poets' deaths, Auden's seems somehow the most fitting. Yes, he was too young, but with the lifelong
caning he gave his heart, lungs and liver, reaching sixty-six is a
testament to his strength. He was a poet of dichotomies – rootless
and wandering (he set up homes in five different countries), yet
longing for domesticity and routine. He was obsessively punctual,
a maker of rules and schedules, yet that schedule included a mix of
drink, drugs and hook-ups. On his final night he entered the belly
of 'Whale Alley' and was found washed up lying on his wrong
side, 'turning icy-blue' the next morning.

That he died on a street between Verdi and vaudeville seems
almost too perfect for him. But more than that, it was exactly the
death he predicted. In an interview with the *Daily Mail* a year
before his death Auden said: 'I smoke a little less than 50 cigarettes
a day . . . All that worries me about the smoking is the expense . . .
My heart is perfectly sound but what I'm frightened of is a lingering illness . . . The nicest way I think would be a heart attack.
It's cheap and it's quick.' Confiding in a friend, he was even more
specific: 'I shall probably die at midnight, in a hotel, to the great
annoyance of the management.'

★

On our last morning in Vienna we are invited to visit the
archive of the Austrian Society of Literature. Their President,
Dr Manfred Müller, shows us folders full of papers and photographs. Here, on foolscap sheets as thin as onion skins, are typed
letters from the poet trying to fix a date for the event, plus photographs almost certainly taken on the afternoon before that
final reading. These are some of the last photographs of him,
hours before his death. We pore over them. They bear all the
hallmarks of Wystan in his final decade – the unmistakeable face,
riven like a walnut, shirt stretched tight over belly, tie at an angle,
almost always caught with mouth gaping, mid-anecdote. There
are one or two pictures without a cigarette between his fingers

or an exhaled cloud above his head. But that's only because the frame is cropped too tight to see it. We are reminded of the photographs at the Bonhams poets' relics sale. They are fine pictures, but utterly lifeless. As we leave Austria, it's the voice recording of his final reading that we can't shake off, the soft, mid-Atlantic growl, the breathlessness, and the closing line of the last poem he ever read aloud, a clerihew about the philosopher Kant being asked to kiss his aunt: 'He obeyed the Categorical Must / But only just.' Now there's a line worth carving on your gravestone.

★

While on a walking tour through Devon in the spring of 1798 the poet Samuel Taylor Coleridge and the critic and essayist William Hazlitt stopped to have breakfast at an inn near Lynton. Coleridge had already written 'Kubla Khan' and 'Frost at Midnight', and later that year would publish *Lyrical Ballads*, his collaboration with William Wordsworth, which would include his 'The Rime of the Ancient Mariner'. But the world knows none of this yet. There, on a window seat in the parlour, the two writers came across a battered and well-thumbed copy of *The Seasons* by James Thomson, and Hazlitt recorded how Coleridge picked it up and declared: 'That is true fame.'

We could claim Auden to be the twentieth-century's most famous English poet – famous, in a more farsighted sense of that word, taking it beyond the clamminess of celebrity – though there'd be other plausible contenders. Auden might even have been one of the century's most famous poets on a world stage. He was certainly something of an international poet, famous for quitting England on the eve of the Second World War and turning himself into a kind of lyrical migrant, summering for many years on Ischia in the Bay of Naples and spending his winters in New York's East Village (a squalid apartment on St Marks Place) before he set up home with Chester in Kirchstetten. But we can think of another poet working in English who became at least as famous as Auden.

★

In 1956 Auden was a guest at a birthday dinner for Robert Frost, sitting alongside other guests, including the poet Richard Wilbur and the literary critic Lionel Trilling. We didn't really understand just how famous Robert Frost actually was until we found some of his birthday menus.

We're in the archive at Boston University. As we've discovered time and again in the course of our amateur research, poets' archives can often throw up a lot more than manuscripts and letters. Opening the storage boxes, we've been surprised by the smells, the clutter, the rummage and texture of the past. It can feel more like beachcombing along a tideline than a solemn page-turning in white gloves. We've been surprised by the sudden, creaturely nearness of our subjects. Here, we've ordered up what looked like materials related to Robert Frost's later years, his death and its aftermath, and the first things to catch our eyes are the finely printed menus from long-ago dinners.

A Robert Frost birthday dinner at Amherst College, 26 March 1954. Frost, who was seated between Thornton Wilder and Archibald MacLeish, ate:

> Clear Green Turtle Soup
> Celery, Olives, Rose Radishes
>
> Broiled Filet Mignon, Mushroom Buttons, Au Gratin
>   Potatoes
> Fresh Asparagus Spears, Hollandaise Sauce
>
> Tossed Green Salad, French Dressing
>
> Assorted Rolls and Butter

Baked Alaska

Mumm's Extra Dry Champagne

Demitasse

It's pure ephemera, but its details transport us to a long forgotten evening. Is that a fleck of Hollandaise? We see that the poet and Librarian of Congress MacLeish was Toastmaster, and that the poet and editor Louis Untermeyer also spoke. We hear the chink of brandy glasses.

By the time of Frost's final birthday party on 26 March 1962, guests included the Ambassador of Nicaragua, the Ambassador of Argentina, Senators from Illinois, New Mexico, Vermont, Minnesota and Oregon, as well as the Under Secretary of the Treasury, the Ambassadors of Great Britain, Germany, Sweden and Gabon, the Attorney General and Mrs Kennedy, and the Chief Justice. Frost was eighty-eight. A gold medal was struck in his honour. We can smell the recently embargoed Cuban cigars.

★

As poetry readings go, this one is about as big as they get. The newsreel shows the eighty-six-year-old Robert Frost take to the podium, slightly stooped, a shock of white hair caught in the January sunlight, and a scarf around his neck. Gouts of breath freeze and cloud the air. The newsreel reports that battalions of snow-fighters have kept Pennsylvania Avenue clear for the ceremony. Just to the poet's right is John F. Kennedy, the newly elected President of the United States, who is being sworn in. This is the first time a poet has ever read at an inauguration (and it will be thirty-two years to the day before another, Maya Angelou, will be invited to do so by Bill Clinton). Even though we know what's coming, we experience the footage from early 1961 with some anxiety each time we view it, because the poet is about to fluff his lines, or not be able to read his lines. Each time we will him on. Vice President-Elect Lyndon B. Johnson even gets up and tries to shield the wintry glare from Frost's page using his top hat. But the poet waves him away. He has a Plan B. Instead of squinting at the poem he has written for Kennedy's inauguration, he reads an older poem, one which he can manage from memory:

> The land was ours before we were the land's.
> She was our land more than a hundred years
> Before we were her people. She was ours
> In Massachusetts, in Virginia . . .

This quick switch from 'For John F. Kennedy His Inauguration' to 'The Gift Outright' is Frosty. It looks like it's one thing – genial old poet, dazzled by the glare on a snow-blinded day, fumbles his way to the practical solution of reading one of his greatest hits off by heart – but think of what would have happened had Frost's random shuffle flicked to 'Design' or 'Provide, Provide'. How random was it? Frost also changes the last line to suit the occasion in such a particular way that you feel he must have planned it. More than this, planned it with the President elect – whose own address, with its famous 'Ask not what your country can do for you; ask what you can do for your country', echoes the rhetorical shapes found in 'The Gift Outright':

> Possessing what we still were unpossessed by,
> Possessed by what we now no more possessed.

Frost had been persuaded by Kennedy to alter the poem's ending from 'Such as she was, such as she would become' to read 'such as she will become', underlining a new start and a change of administration, the country's future about to happen. In the event, watching Frost deliver 'The Gift Outright' at the inauguration, the poet always jazzes the ending up: 'Such as she was, such as she would become, has become – and, for this occasion, let me change that to *will* become.'

★

Of course, we knew Robert Frost was famous, *famous* as in reputed, renowned, spoken of widely. Is there another poet from the last century whose writing has rippled through the wider culture to such an extent? Whose work has embedded itself so securely or reached such a wide audience following the poet's death?

Take cinema and television, which became the dominant cultural forms during Frost's long lifetime. In *The Sopranos*, young A. J. struggles with his homework, a poem called 'Stopping by Woods on a Snowy Evening' (by 'asshole Robert Frost'), while listening to Slipknot. His elder sister Meadow tries to help him (she did Frost in High School, too), explaining that the white snowfield symbolizes death ('I thought *black* was death?' protests A. J.) and that the speaker's sleep is the Big Sleep. In Jim Jarmusch's movie *Down by Law*, Roberto Benigni suddenly recites 'The Road Not Taken' in Italian, and asks his two deadbeat companions if they too 'like Bob Frost'. At the close of the film, this pair come upon a road that forks in a wood, and go their separate ways. Another movie, Don Siegel's spy thriller *Telefon*, has Soviet sleeper agents planted all over the United States, waiting to be activated and turned into instruments of total destruction: all it takes is a phone-caller reciting the closing lines from 'Stopping by Woods on a Snowy Evening'. They have promises to keep. And in *The Shawshank Redemption* Tim Robbins instructs fellow convict Morgan Freeman to look for a field outside Buxton, Maine, 'like something out of a Robert Frost poem', where a secret lies hidden in the base of a drystone wall.

In each of these examples, Frost feels familiar and available – to the different characters involved, or to us, the audience. His maxims continue to be drawn into arguments; his lines are quoted out of context; his words and phrases enter language's mainstream, and whether we know their source or not, they have a different kind of afterlife there. A movie about an ageing actor shooting a whisky commercial in Tokyo, crossing paths with a photographer's girlfriend, takes one of Frost's definitions of poetry for its title. But if we thought we knew the reach of Frost's writing, the archive at Boston University reveals the apparatus behind the scenes, the building blocks of reputation, the small print of huge honour and prestige. We hadn't grasped the scale of how famous Frost had become in his own lifetime.

★

If Auden carried a kind of itinerant bohemianism with him, by middle age he was looking to settle down, to set up home. Frost, on the other hand, appears rooted, firmly planted in New England, and close to the centre of political power in a way unimaginable for Auden. Still, even into his eighties, the poet travelled. On his death, the Frost family received a Western Union telegram from N. Khrushchev, and we are holding it now: 'I am deeply saddened by the news of the passing away of your father, renowned poet and citizen of the United States of America – Robert Frost'. Frost had travelled to the Soviet Union on a goodwill mission (at the request of President Kennedy) and met Khrushchev at his dacha in the Crimea in early September 1962, just a few weeks before the Cuban Missile Crisis. Frost's daughter Lesley Frost Ballantine received a similar message from Vice President Lyndon B. Johnson. We can't find anything from President Kennedy, but then discover how there followed a ground-breaking for the Robert Frost Library later that year, a Convocation to Honour the President of the United States, on 26 October 1963. On that day, JFK spoke at the dedication ceremony for the new building, though he didn't wield the ceremonial shovel because of a back injury sustained while planting a tree in Ottawa. We imagine the

President's motorcade shimmering away, heading towards Dallas and the Book Depository just a few weeks later.

★

We've retreated to the air-conditioned archives of Boston University, because Massachusetts in May is broiling. Once again, the weather in the United States seems to be against us. It's closer to the climate of those poems of Frost's which contain hay gangs and summer showers and blueberries, rather than what we're most familiar with: the strange turn in the seasons and the lid of ice from 'After Apple-Picking', the drear and bleakness of 'The Wood-Pile', or the midwinter dark of 'Stopping by Woods on a Snowy Evening' or 'An Old Man's Winter Night'. Boston in a heatwave is nothing like a Robert Frost poem. We burn our noses and ears walking along the Charles River, taking time out for an unprofessional look at Fenway Park, where the Red Sox play; the traffic fumes seem heavier in the unseasonal heat.

While we're in Boston and Cambridge, we look for Robert Frost places. This isn't easy. Frost died in his sleep, in hospital, in late January 1963. He'd been admitted for cancer surgery several weeks earlier, but succumbed to a pulmonary embolism. He was eighty-eight. The Peter Bent Brigham Hospital in Boston has long since merged with other Harvard-affiliated hospitals (today it's the Brigham and Women's Hospital) and in some ways this was an unremarkable death, even though the life, the position Frost had reached as a poet and public figure, was extraordinary.

There is one definite destination in Cambridge, in the form of a house – it's called the Robert Frost House, on Brewster Street, and is all spick and span, Stick style and bargeboard – where the poet lived for some twenty years leading up to his death. Another poet, and a very different Bostonian, Robert Lowell, recalled walking by this house a few weeks before Frost died:

The lights were out that night; they are out for good now, but I can easily imagine the barish rooms, the miscellaneous gold-lettered old classics, the Georgian poets, the Catullus by his bedside, the iron stove where he sometimes did his cooking, and the stool drawn up to his visitor's chair so that he could ramble and listen.

Years later, Lowell would write a sonnet called 'Robert Frost' that begins: 'Robert Frost at midnight, the audience gone / to vapor, the great act laid on the shelf in mothballs . . .', which all suggests he knew this house, and spoke into the night with Frost not long before his final illness. This is the house we visit.

But we had to choose. It comes as a surprise to us to discover that Frost moved about so much, a kind of internal-flights Auden. Lots of Frost's homes have been consecrated, too many to explore. There's The Frost Place in Franconia, New Hampshire, where the poet lived for five years upon his return to America from England in 1915. Then there's the Robert Frost Farm up in Ripton, Vermont, where Frost summered from the late Thirties until his death. The curatorial calm at Ripton was recently disturbed when youths broke in on a December evening to party. The *New York Times* had a field day:

> Mix 30 or more young people with 150 cans of beer, a few bottles of liquor and some drugs, put them in a museum-like, unheated house in the dead of winter, and the ensuing discussions will not center on the sublime construction of 'Stopping by Woods on a Snowy Evening'. Some played drinking games, some got sick, some did damage, and all followed that snowy path out, bound together by a secret that could not keep.

Actually, there are *two* farms: the Robert Frost Homestead in Derry, New Hampshire, is where the poet farmed for over a decade before his pivotal trip to England. And Vermont is also where you'll find the Robert Frost Stone House, where the poet lived in the Twenties. But wait: Frost lived at a house in Ann Arbor, Michigan, for a time during the middle of that decade. It's now in an open-air museum. And these are only the 'official' residences, places preserved, celebrated and consecrated by societies, counties and states happy to claim Frost as – at least partly – their own. Which of Frost's houses is the more authentic? Does it depend on what was written where?

Some of Frost's real estate lies much closer to home. At Beaconsfield in Buckinghamshire, north of London, Frost settled in a bungalow during his English journey, from 1912 through to early 1914. It's said that he saw a sign for A. C. Frost estate agents when alighting from the train at Beaconsfield for the first time, and took the sign as a *sign*. Renting from his namesake, he addressed himself variously as being resident at The Bung Hole, The Bung or Bung Beak Bucks. But, far from the protective force field of American heritage, Frost's bungalow was demolished years ago. Talk about missing a trick! Robert Frost's Bung Hole: they'd be queuing up around the block. This was where Frost was living when he met Ezra Pound, H. D., Ford Madox Ford, W. B. Yeats and, perhaps most importantly, Edward Thomas. It was here that he put together his first collections, *A Boy's Will* and *North of Boston*. Between here and the Derry farm in New Hampshire, Frost wrote many of the poems that made his name and have entered the language in the century since, lodging in places where they are hard to get rid of.

Frost's the estate agents have also gone from strength to strength, establishing themselves as the leading residential sales and let-tings specialists within the Chilterns, the Thames Valley and West Middlesex. We find them offering a new-build, five-bedroom family home in a cul-de-sac called The Birches, just across the train line from where The Bung Hole once stood. Not long ago, the Theodore Roethke Home museum in Saginaw, Michigan,

sent out a call to all owners of the poet's first collection, *Open
House*. Published in 1941, the print run of a thousand books was
individually numbered, and the museum holds hopes of tracking down as many current owners of this book as possible, to
hear their stories about *Open House* and Roethke's poems. Paul
Celan once said a poem can be 'a message in a bottle'; does that
mean the writer's house can also be a bottle bank, a place where
we can redeem the empties? Or is the house acting like a proud
and curious source, checking up on its many identical progeny,
listening to a thousand ways in which a poem can make its way
in the material world? Indeed, whole regions claim dead poets
as their own. Dylan Thomas is for ever linked with Laugharne
on the Carmarthenshire coast, with its 'heron-priested shore' and
shades of Milk Wood and the poet's writing shed facing out over
the estuary's lamé shimmer, even though he died on the other
side of the Atlantic. But there was a Swansea Thomas, too, before
the Chelsea Hotel and Laugharne and London and the BBC, a
younger suburban poet whom Swansea would like to reclaim. We
imagine Ted Hughes fishing in a crow- and hawk-haunted ripar-
ian Devon landscape, in pre-swinging London with Sylvia Plath,
or perhaps as a child in the windswept gritstone of the Calder
Valley around Heptonstall and Mytholmroyd. But there is also
a Mexborough Hughes, a railway and colliery town boy whose
parents ran a newsagent's in the South Yorkshire town for years.
Mexborough wouldn't mind having him back. Recently, a poet
has even discovered the route of Hughes's paper round. Hughes
once said 'Poets are like pigs – only worth money when they're
dead.' And he was half-right, because today a famous dead poet
can power a local economy like a wind farm.

Anyway: why do we beat these paths to the doors of writers' houses? Why bother making these pilgrimages? Some might
answer: so you don't have to read *The Prelude*. Saying it's replaced
the staff-and-scallop-shelled variety of pilgrimage seems facile
somehow. OK, in some cases the merchandise can be off-putting.

We'd been warned about quills and antique typewriters, though there have been surprisingly few of those where we've been. But it can feel intimate. It can feel like looking for something: if not answers exactly then at least a confirmation.

The house can still be occupied. The journey isn't always purposeful. It can be reluctant. In a recent essay, 'Pilgrimage', Geoff Dyer – himself making a pilgrimage to the former Los Angeles home of philosopher Theodor Adorno – described how the fourteen-year-old Susan Sontag once had to be persuaded to pay a visit to the home of Thomas Mann in Pacific Palisades (her friend had looked him up in the phone book, and cold-called). Years later, Sontag wrote a story about her subsequent audience and tea with the great novelist, called 'Pilgrimage'.

And both of us have experienced the jolt and surprise of coming across a writer's place by complete accident. Our favourite accidental pilgrimage is the sparking-off of Muriel Spark. Stranded in London during the blackout in 1944, she was invited to stay the night at a house in St John's Wood where a maid she had met on the train worked. Fascinated by the books in this house's study, where she'd been billeted while the owners were away, their dedications told her the maid's employer was Louis MacNeice, a poet she admired. Years later, she wrote a story about it called 'The House of the Famous Poet', and an essay too, 'The Poet's House'. Something about it turned her into a writer.

★

A few weeks after the Kennedy inauguration in Washington, a debut by a new French film director was released in American cinemas. *Breathless – À bout de souffle* in Europe – had created a stir when first screened across the ocean, and the bracing wind of the French *nouvelle vague* arrived as an early harbinger of the new decade. It's odd to think of Jean-Luc Godard and Robert Frost occupying the same cultural time frame (just about), in the same way Kennedy's Camelot makes its own strange overlap with the august poet. But there's one famous scene in Godard's film that we think Frost might have enjoyed and recognized (though it's hard to imagine him buying popcorn and settling down on the plush to see what all the fuss was about). At Orly Airport, Jean Seberg is part of a press cadre interviewing a literary celebrity, played by another French director Jean-Pierre Melville (whose name was the nom de guerre he'd used while fighting in the French Resistance, a homage to the great American novelist and poet Herman Melville, which stuck for the rest of his life). The questions and answers are flip: 'Do you like Brahms?' 'Like everybody, no.' 'And Chopin?' 'Makes me want to puke.' Then Seberg asks him: 'What's your greatest ambition?' Melville whips off his shades, fixes her and replies: 'To become immortal, and then die'.

★

A mountain was named after Frost, near Bristol in Vermont, his home state. We don't have time to visit this living monument, and anyway our mountain-climbing days are probably behind us now, though according to peakery.com, it isn't very high, coming in at the 40,612th highest mountain in the United States; even within Vermont it only ranks at the 295th highest. But have you ever had a mountain named after you? No, us neither. We remember how one of Shakespeare's contemporaries, Michael Drayton, once had a memorial bus shelter named after him in his home village of Hartshill, near Nuneaton, long since removed because of vandalism. Even a bus shelter seems unlikely.

★

In 1974 a centennial stamp was issued in the United States: 10¢, Robert Frost, American Poet. The closest Auden has come to postal immortality is a stamp specially issued to celebrate great British films in 2014, and the work of the GPO Film Unit for which Auden wrote 'Night Mail'. Mind you, it was the world's first intelligent stamp. Neither poet has yet appeared on a banknote. We tend not to associate poets with money, despite Wallace Stevens's observation that 'Money is a kind of poetry'. However, beyond the Anglophone world, and those territories where the dollar and the pound circulate, it's surprisingly common. The Scots are an exception proving the rule with Robert Burns (£5 and £10), together with Banjo Paterson in Australia ($10).

★

'To become immortal, and then die.' How did Frost do it? It would be difficult to imagine a fate any further removed from Thomas Chatterton's. This is the poet as visible spokesman, tribal elder at the court of Camelot, elevated, venerable and widely celebrated. Frost's was a long writing life. It encompassed Atlantic crossings on steamships and airliners, and stretched from Ulysses S. Grant to John F. Kennedy. When he was born, there were still Indian Wars and a Frontier; by the time of his death, the Apollo Space Program was underway. At a White House dinner in April 1962, Lionel Trilling's wife Diana wrote of how she spotted Frost talking to Colonel John Glenn, the first American to orbit the Earth, with half a dozen people trying to listen in on what they were saying. Frost started late, or late for a poet, not publishing *A Boy's Will* while in England until he was just shy of forty. But from the very beginning, Frost had a sense of what kind of readership he wanted for his work. Acutely self-aware, he was interested in reaching the widest possible audience, and knew this even before his first collection had appeared:

> There is a kind of success called 'of esteem' and it butters no parsnips. It means a success with the critical few who are supposed to know. But really to arrive where I can stand on my legs as a poet and nothing else I must get outside that circle to the general reader who buys books in their thousands. [. . .] I want to be a poet for all sorts and kinds. I could never make a merit of being caviare [*sic*] to the crowd the

way my quasi-friend Pound does. I want to reach out, and
would if it were a thing I could do by taking thought.

It almost goes without saying that none of this would mean
anything if the poems themselves weren't able to draw so richly
and inventively on living speech and to convince as such (just
as Wordsworth thought a poem ought to), to tap into the language as he knew and spoke it, and return it back into the world
renewed. Often deceptively simple on first encounter, they fuse
the hands-on, hands dirty, everyday rural world with deep, classical resource, and a nihilism that is breathtaking in the way it
reached a mass readership. Frost managed the trick of presenting himself, or his work, on two levels: the genial Yankee codger,
capable of affirming folksy traditional values and a kind of home-
spun wisdom; but also something much darker, bleaker. At a party
thrown for Frost's birthday in New York by his publishers at the
Waldorf Astoria in 1959, Lionel Trilling famously declared Frost
to be 'a terrifying poet':

Call him, if it makes things any easier, a tragic poet, but it
might be useful to come out from under the shelter of that
literary word. The universe that he conceives is a terrifying
universe.

Frost being as famous as he was, these remarks became a cause
célèbre. It's a shame we didn't find any archived menu of this
event, and so don't know what might have been choked on that
evening in surprise and indignation. Writing to apologize for his
remarks later, Trilling received a reply from Frost assuring him
that no distress had been caused: 'You made my birthday party a
surprise party . . . You weren't there to sing "Happy Birthday, dear
Robert", and I don't mind being made controversial. No sweeter
music can come to my ears than the clash of arms over my dead
body when I am down.'

And sometimes the poems themselves can seem intriguingly explicit on what it might take to make the best of whatever one makes, to be custodian and caretaker of the self's gifts. His poem 'Provide, Provide' has an unusual genesis. It seems to have been provoked by news of a charwomen's strike supported by students at one of the Ivy League universities, and in the light of that can be read as a critique of the New Deal. 'Provide, provide', Frost is supposed to have added after a public reading of this poem, 'or somebody else'll provide for you.' But as the poem long outlives the occasions of its making, we can really feel the self-reliant cold:

> The witch that came (the withered hag)
> To wash the steps with pail and rag,
> Was once the beauty Abishag,
>
> The picture pride of Hollywood.
> Too many fall from great and good
> For you to doubt the likelihood.
>
> Die early and avoid the fate.
> Or if predestined to die late,
> Make up your mind to die in state.
>
> Make the whole stock exchange your own!
> If need be occupy a throne,
> Where nobody can call *you* crone.
>
> Some have relied on what they knew,
> Others on being simply true.
> What worked for them might work for you.
>
> No memory of having starred
> Atones for later disregard
> Or keeps the end from being hard.

> Better to go down dignified
> With boughten friendship at your side
> Than none at all. Provide, provide!

★

Boston is our final stop in America, and we fly back to England via Frankfurt with Lufthansa. One of us has a birthday as we cross a certain line of midnight longitude, and we make sure to mention it when we meet our cabin crew. This pathetic ruse gets duly rewarded with champagne, chocolates, and the pity of the attendants. Robert Frost never had to drop any hints. By 1961 he was so famous that on a flight from New York to Tel Aviv on 9 March, a keepsake was distributed to passengers as Frost travelled with El Al Israel Airlines: a copy of the 'Dedication' for JFK, together with 'The Gift Outright'. That is true fame. The port light blinks on the wing, and we feel insignificant above the dark and deep ocean.

Afterword

We rise from the Underground to find Euston Station busy. This great concrete retail-fringed shed is the north-westerner's gateway in and out of the capital, as old as we are now, built in the International Style that had once seemed so shining and new. Many of the faces in the crowd don't only look like they'd rather be somewhere else, they are; our handheld devices are turning us all into phantoms, occupying but barely sharing the same concourse we cross. Maybe technology has just made it easier nowadays to see how we've always moved through the city. Ezra Pound managed to get a signal a century ago on the Paris metro:

> The apparition of these faces in the crowd;
> Petals on a wet, black bough.

Many of our journeys have ended up here, waiting in the seated area of the AMT Coffee Lounge, between Platform 14 and Left Luggage, before saying our farewells and splitting up for our final legs homeward. Our travels are nearly over, but we've decided there's one more place to visit, so close by it's the shortest of detours on foot. We exit the station into daylight, and remember that this is the last day of winter according to the weather forecasters, *and* the February leap day. The city feels a little lighter on its feet in the pale sun, unburdened somehow. Spring seems to be lifting the lid on the world. Although walking out of Euston often produces this effect.

★

Three days before his death in the Holborn garret, Thomas
Chatterton fell into an open grave in St Pancras Churchyard. He'd
been so absorbed in reading the epitaphs that he'd wandered from
the path, missed his footing and stumbled into the earth; the poet
had to be helped out by a friend, who remarked how he was
happy to help in the resurrection of genius.

It's a good story, but might only be so much speculative
Chatterton chat, an ominous anecdote based on a lost letter to the
poet's mother, embellished by his earliest biographers, redeveloped and built upon during the young poet's rise to posthumous
fame. Though if Chatterton had ended up in the ground at St
Pancras, he wouldn't have remained there for long. Another poet
would have seen to that.

We've tended to avoid graves and last resting places on our
journeys to the sites where poets left this world. As we've discovered, the places we associate with writers and artists can be
manifold, and a lot of ground hallowed. There might be a birth
site, one or many 'life sites', a place of death and a grave. We
wanted to visit war graves and record those visits. The scholar
Robert Pogue Harrison reminds us that the Latin *sepulcrum*
comes from *sepelire*, meaning 'to bury', but within which lies
buried an Indo-European root that means 'to render honour'.
The dead recovered from the battlefield are interred in a larger
symbolic structure that links their sacrifice with our identity and
sense of nationhood.

But we've been wary of turning this book into a necropolis,
too much of what David Jones described as a Cook's Tour to the
Devastated Areas, or a Boot Hill of the lyrical dead. We've walked
up the fractious Euston Road, turning left after the British Library,
and found ourselves in the calm of St Pancras Churchyard, not for
a poet's grave but for a tree.

It's a mature ash, whose base has been surrounded by a flinty
wheel of worn gravestones. Dozens of them, as if they have
uprooted themselves and been drawn towards the gravity of the

living tree, gnomons that have deserted their sundials and flocked to its roots and bole, which over time have grown around them, enfolded them, absorbed them, a writhing dance between the mineral and the organic. The tree seems buoyed up by the gravestones, borne aloft on the mound of them, a warden ash from northern folklore. Yggdrasil fed by the buried Fleet River. A poet made this.

★

About a year ago, on a hazy spring morning, we'd stood outside the Palazzo Guiccioli in Ravenna, where Byron lived as *cavalier servente* with his lover Teresa and her elderly husband. The building was covered in tarpaulins. Following extensive restoration, it is hoped that this will become one of Ravenna's great tourist attractions, a multi-media Byron museum and literary centre. But no matter how remarkable the restored Palazzo may be, it can only aspire to be the city's runner-up poetic shrine.

A five-minute walk to the south-east and you find yourself standing at the end of a side road, staring up at a tall, narrow white stone monument with an open door. Above the door are three words: DANTIS POETAE SEPULCRUM. Four or five tourists is enough to fill the small tomb with chatter and camera flashes. You wait for them to leave, then step inside, taken aback by the sudden drop in light and temperature.

A single lamp burns in this place, but it makes a powerful difference. The low flicker of the flame lends it a votive silence, a sense of sacred space. On the wall opposite the doorway, you can just make out a marble carving of the greatest of all poets, fingers on lips, deep in thought, poring over one book open at a lectern, his right hand to his side, marking his place in another. Other books lie scattered across the table in front of him, and a single bottle of ink. Here is the poet at work, it wants us to believe. Here he is putting in the hours that produced the *Divine Comedy*. Below the carving, a marble sarcophagus holds Dante's bones. If any poet has achieved immortality, it is this one. Yet even he had to achieve it through his work, rather than the preferred option – in Woody Allen's words – of achieving it by 'not dying'.

Dante has not always been left to rest in peace. Two centuries after his death, the Pope tried to arrange the transfer of his bones back to his beloved Florence, but Ravenna's monks were having none of it and hid them for another three centuries, until they turned up again in 1865. The bones were placed in this sarcophagus, where they have remained ever since. Well, mostly remained. They were removed again between 1944 and 1945 and buried in the garden next door to protect them from war damage. This temporary haven is now marked with a heap of earth like a termite mound, covered in ivy. A sign beside the temple informs visitors who may be spooked by counting chimes that the bell in the tower will ring thirteen times each dusk, in honour of the 8th Canto of the *Purgatorio*: '. . . to hear, far off, the evening bell / that seems to mourn the dying of the day'.

A footnote bubbles to the surface. Some seventy miles north of Ravenna, Dante's compatriot and near contemporary Petrarch has been similarly unsettled in the long home of the grave. After loving and losing his Laura, after the spring source of the River Sorgue and the limestone hills of Vaucluse, the poet died back in his native Italy in 1374. After being interred at the cathedral at Arquà Padua, Petrarch's remains were moved to a permanent tomb in the town six years later, and for over six hundred years all was dusty silence, though in 1630 a drunken friar broke into the grave, looking for relics to sell, and disturbed the bones. In 2003 a team of forensic scientists were given permission to carry out genetic analysis of Petrarch's remains, and opened the grave in what since 1870 has been called Arquà Petrarca. They examined mitochondrial DNA from a tooth and a rib and discovered that each belonged to different individuals, one male and one female. A sentimental (if also slightly macabre) thought arises: what if Petrarch had somehow been posthumously reunited with his Laura? But no: radiocarbon analysis revealed the skull to be two centuries older than the bone sample. This is more an episode of *CSI: Poetry* than a pilgrimage, and brings to mind Jacques Cousteau's descent into the pool and cavern at Vaucluse. We wondered, as we have done so many times on our travels, what sources in the physical world ever have to tell us about poems that find a home in the heart and on the living tongue.

As you step back into the sunlight at Ravenna, you can't help but wonder where Dante is now. You can be pretty confident where his bones are, but where is *he*? Is he in some circle of his own painstakingly mapped out afterlife, passing eternity with liars or illicit lovers or lost souls? Or has he got a free pass to the Empyrean with his Beatrice, granted safe passage due to the enduring beauty of his work?

★

One year on. Spring is returning to the northern hemisphere. St Pancras Churchyard still feels threadbare, but the bulbs are raising their shoots like green letter-openers; the sun is warm on our backs. This is our final act of pilgrimage, though it breaks step with much of what's gone before. We've not come here seeking the grave or death of a poet, but the work of a poet, perhaps even the place where a poet began.

St Pancras Churchyard lies in the hinterlands of the three great stations – Euston, St Pancras and King's Cross – where the lines into London from the north converge and thicken into broad estuaries of rails. Victorian modernity and expansion sometimes disturbed consecrated ground where generations lay buried, and here, where the Midland Railway Company approached its new terminus, it found the dead of St Pancras Churchyard directly in its path. The architects Sir Arthur William Blomfield and Sons were assigned by the Bishop of London with the task of removing the bones from the earth, and in the late summer and autumn of

1866 Blomfield delegated the work to his assistant, the twenty-six-year-old Thomas Hardy.

Hardy wasn't a published poet or novelist yet, but these early years in London were important, formative ones, and he had begun writing stories and poems, some of which would finally see the light of day thirty years later when his first collection appeared. It's tempting to imagine how the young poet's dismal overseeing, working by the light of flare-lamps as the evenings drew in, must have left many deeply engrained feelings and images. Hardy's oeuvre would contain more graves than most. We think of the confused rabble of 'human jam' from 'The Levelled Churchyard', Drummer Hodge thrown 'uncoffined' into a hole in the African veldt, the green blades and daisies on the mound of 'Rain on a Grave', the separate mounds of 'In Death Divided', the skeletal speakers of 'Channel Firing' disturbed by the racket of the living . . .

And on a mound here in the churchyard today we find the ash tree memorial Hardy made and left to grow, built from the stones of the dismantled graveyard. The poet himself would end up in Westminster Abbey many years later, though his heart – like a king or knight's from the Middle Ages – was removed and buried separately in Wessex earth. There was a rumour that Hardy's heart, kept in a biscuit tin following its removal, was set upon by the cat of the local doctor. We hear the thud of Chatterton falling face down into the opened grave again. Some poets' disappearances and deaths attract stories and fables, just as this tree has drawn an entire graveyard to its bosom.

★

The chances of a poem surviving its maker aren't great. The chances of a poem surviving any greater length of time are bleak. After we've burned in time's wind tunnel and the oxygen that makes complex life possible has used up our cells, a poem's best chance might be to stick and inhere in the collective memory of a culture, the fabric of its language, though over generations this resilience is impossible to predict, and the odds are massively stacked against it happening.

Maybe this is part of the appeal. You're almost certainly doomed to failure, if a longevity measured in centuries rather than decades is your yardstick. What a game to get into. Have we really thought this through? And immortality, like nostalgia, isn't quite what it used to be. Ever since Horace told us he'd finished a monument more lasting than bronze, poets have tried to future-proof their work, to colonize the ages to come, to speak across what Larkin called the 'lengths and breadths of time' to readers unborn, to live for ever. The poet might not live to see it – like Sylvia Plath – or might live to witness the completion of their monument – like Robert Frost – while plenty more – like John Clare – might die having watched the foundations going in, only to see the weeds and roots obscuring and undermining and weakening it. Without proper upkeep, without diligent caretakers, the whole thing might end up cleared away and backfilled.

Much as a poem is a made thing, it isn't simply a structure, and this monument is as much an agreement of the soft tissues – the brains and the tongues – of a people over time, a meeting place, an open secret. But poets themselves have sometimes taken a longer view. 'There's no posterity to write for,' Peter Reading once wrote. 'I'm writing now for mutated arthropods.' Today it's hard to escape the knowledge that, as a species, the chances are we won't be in business for much longer. The planet grows warmer. Yggdrasil suffers dieback. As children of the Cold War, who grew up afraid of the Bomb in their beds at night, we both recognize how we live in an age where the idea of posterity itself has been eroded and discredited. But whether the world ends in fire or in ice, there are even longer prospects. The Northern Irish poet Derek Mahon takes things several degrees further by looking back to the Classical world and Horace, but also Heraclitus, who famously told us nobody steps into the same river twice:

You will tell me that you have executed
A monument more lasting than bronze;
But even bronze is perishable.
Your best poem, you know the one I mean,
The very language in which the poem
Was written, and the idea of language,
All these will pass away in time.

And that will have been poetry, about as long-lived as a bristle-cone pine; those final few inches of dirty snow in a core sample drawn up from the sheet ice. Maybe we should be grateful to find any readers where we live, here and now, closer to home.

★

Spending so much time on the trail of dead poets has had its unpredictable side effects. We've been walking along the rim of a crater called The Past, or through an odd doll's house of linked interiors.

By the time we get back to Euston, we're discussing the actual location of the long-demolished Euston Arch, the Rough Rock, soot-blackened, Doric propylaeum that had stood at the entrance to the old station for over a century, before being knocked down to make way for the new one in the early Sixties. Even John Betjeman couldn't save it, although the neighbouring St Pancras Station might not be standing today if it wasn't for the future Poet Laureate. We reckon the Arch would have stood somewhere *here*, near the centre of what's now the main concourse. An amputee pigeon struggles on the shiny tiles, searching for crumbs a long way from daylight.

★

Euston, for any north-westerner, is a portal. You board in *the north*, and you alight in *the south* five degrees warmer. At the tail-end of the nineteenth century a young Lancastrian made the trip to launch his career as a poet, and was swallowed whole. Francis

Thompson's fall from medical student in Manchester to homeless junkie in London was precipitous. One night he bought a fatal draught of laudanum and withdrew to a rubbish tip at the back of Covent Garden market, determined to end it all. He was barely halfway down the bottle when he felt a restraining hand on his. Looking up, he saw the ghost of Thomas Chatterton, forbidding him to drink the rest. When the marvellous boy tells you to stop, you stop. Within a day Thompson's luck turned, with a letter from the influential Wilfred Meynell praising his poems, and the rest is literary history.

Thompson has been on our radar since childhood, a famous poet born in Preston. Except he was only really famous for 'The Hound of Heaven', and all we could remember of that was how doggedly the hound pursued him. We knew the drama of his story, his geographical and metaphorical descent, but we didn't know then that he was rescued from the brink of suicide by the shade of Thomas Chatterton.

Telling this tale to a friend in 1907, the poet was asked how he knew it was the legendary *wunderkind* who saved him. 'I recognized him from the picture,' Thompson replied. Chatterton is one of those rare figures who, as the historian Richard Holmes puts it, 'seems at times to have taken command of certain areas of the psychic landscape'. Here he was still vivid in the opium visions of Francis Thompson, a relay transmitter pushing the *poète maudit* myth across from the nineteenth to the twentieth century where it was picked up by a green and carefree bard in Swansea.

★

Time is out of joint, because we've been spending too much time in the long view, like our own ghosts. 'There's some reason why you guys are doing this . . .' – Kate Donahue's words come back to us. But somewhere between the tree and the arch, we've decided we want to head home now, back to our lives. In a way, we've only been doing what poets have always done, paying our respects in the final haunts of writers important to us, but among all the epitaphs and grave goods, it's easy to fall into a hole.

This long view opens out backwards and forwards. The future returns no echoes. Our voices barely carry. Poetry doesn't have a definite destination; we can't even be sure of the next calling points on the journey. Any poet today might hope to have some small part to play in the direction it will take, but for all we know the poems that readers in the twenty-third and twenty-fourth centuries will value and admire (assuming there are any) are being written in those blind spots in our midst that are not regarded as poetry places. Some mute inglorious programmer using Python script.

So, what of our central question: is it true that great poems come at a heavy – perhaps ultimately fatal – price? Looking back, we can see how poetry likes squaring up to the big safe themes – which turn out not to be very safe, because, in the absence of love or death or raw nature, the poet might go looking for a heightened state, taking risks that imperil them emotionally or physically in order to spark a poem. The poetic exceptionalist will point to patterns of depressive introspection. Even those poets who keep up appearances and give the impression of leading routine and orthodox lives seem to harbour unrulier, disruptive energies, a poltergeist behind closed doors and beyond public view.

But isn't this part of a wider artistic affliction? There are plenty of painters, composers, playwrights and musicians who have taken such risks. The non-exceptionalist view looks at things the other way, the big cultural narrative that began with Chatterton, was reified by Keats and exported in scores of ways into the faraway century that followed. Looked at this way, there is nothing particularly 'doomed' about poets; if anything, those poets who lived on a screeching edge that we picked up in our youth were assuming a role, doing what the world expected of them.

If we're honest, this is where our own 'we' starts to split. At the end of this odyssey, one of us would say the myth of the doomed poet is simply that – a myth we need to debunk – while the other thinks there's an unquiet spirit in many poets that means the myth still holds.

Our trains are announced. One thing is absolutely certain. When we get home, we are both going to have a little bonfire in our back gardens.

★

Places like this are where poems tend to begin or stir: while in transit, in motion. We both have workplaces a few hours to the north, but while there is no lectern or ink to be found, those places can feel as inert as Dante's tomb-study. It suddenly seems laughable to call either – a shed in the garden and a box room – *studies*. Both are more like shrines to vanity, or at best places where we can hide and stall, get things finished or at least make them presentable. But if this is true for us, what of all the places we've visited over the last few years? If poems begin in the wind, while driving along or staring vacantly through the window of a train, what kind of sources do the living look for in the haunts of dead poets?

Time to return to the poems, which have their own lives to lead and will make their own ways in the world to come. That we are all going to die, that a poem can happen anywhere, the most unlikely spot, and inscribe its shape despite our awful foreknowledge, means it's also time to admit it will definitely happen to us – though hopefully not before we hand this in – and to leave behind the plural pronoun, the shelter of the average rate we've been travelling at, to run for our separate trains after saying our goodbyes as Michael and as Paul.

walks around New York City, then reprised the role and indulged
one of our own enthusiasms for *Rocky* in Philadelphia; to the
poet George Green (and the poet Billy Collins for putting us
on to him), knowledgeable leader of the most definitive literary tour of lower Manhattan; to the staff of the Library Hotel,
New York; to Richard Thomas, organizer of the Dylan Weekend
at Laugharne, Wales; and, over the water, to the organizers of the
Dún Laoghaire Festival in Ireland; in Minneapolis, to the poets
Steve Healey, Dobby Gibson and Peter Campion for showing
us the Twin Cities; back in Bristol, to Andrew Kelly, who runs
the Festival of Ideas, and gave us a chance to search for Savage
and Chatterton and the Ancient Mariner in that city; to Michael
Doble for his knowledge of Chatterton's Bristol and to the staff
of Bristol Central Library; to the poet Jo Shapcott for helping
us look again at Sylvia Plath in Primrose Hill and Stevie Smith
in Palmers Green; in Athens, to the staff of the British Embassy,
especially Katerina Korompli and Ambassador John Kittmer, for
allowing a viewing of their Byron portrait at such short notice; in
Messolonghi, to Rosa Flourou and all at the Messolonghi Byron
Society; to the poet August Kleinzahler for useful tips on Thom
Gunn and San Francisco; in Hull, to the poet Sean O'Brien,
who led us through the landscape of Larkin and his own childhood; to Professor Stephen Regan for his keenness for all things
Larkin, and the story of meeting the Librarian; to Miriam Porter,
who allowed us into Larkin's house, and her home, in a show of
great generosity; to Richard Heseltine, University Librarian, and
his staff at the Brynmor Jones Library, the University of Hull; to
Simon Wilson at the Hull History Centre; in Boston, we're grateful to the poet and critic Stephen Burt for late breakfast/early
lunch and talk near Harvard; at the Lewis Wharf Quayside apartments, to Michael the Building Manager, and his tip for Legal
Seafood; in Devon, to Mair Bosworth who did the driving and a
boundary walk around Stevie Smith's places under Dartmoor; in
Palmers Green, to Lisa and Kevin, who very kindly allowed a look

around their flat, once Stevie's house; to Siobhan Maguire at BBC Bristol, for helping us track down elusive MacNeician sound files; in Normandy, we were taken on a tour of Keith Douglas's last days with Stéphane Jacquet, Curator of the Museum of the Battle of Tilly-sur-Seulles, and we wouldn't have got far without his knowledge on the ground; at BBC Salford, to Geoff Bird for an eventful few days spent with one of us in New York, looking for Frank O' Hara's *Lunch Poems;* on Long Island, to the staff of Sip n'Twirl at Fire Island Pines, who made us both very welcome; back in London, to Vivian Wright and Jonathan Barker, our wonderful hosts during a walking tour of David Jones's Harrow; to Julian May at the BBC, for travelling to the Somme for the first time with one of us, in the footsteps of Wilfred Owen, and to the late Dominic Hibberd; in Paterson, New Jersey, to Professor Steve Hahn from William Paterson University; to Della Rowland and Rod Leith, for their enthusiasm and insights into William Carlos Williams; and to Daphne Williams Fox for her great hospitality and for making so much of our work on her grandfather possible; we're grateful to the poet and critic Jeremy Hooker for being with one of us at the longhouse of R. S. Thomas, and to Dr Jeremy Noel-Tod; to all the staff at the Emily Dickinson Homestead at Amherst, Massachusetts; in Bournemouth, to the publisher Neil Astley for opening our eyes to Rosemary Tonks: he has given us a great deal towards this book; we're also grateful to Nigel Still and Lisa Stillman at Stephen Noble Estate Agents, and Duncan Ross, who let us look around Rosemary's house; to the poet Anne Stevenson, who talked to us about Sylvia Plath and Anne Sexton; in Hartford, Connecticut, to the wife of the Dean of Christ Church Episcopal Cathedral and her son, gracious after we came cold-calling; to Brian Richards of the New York Yankees Museum in New York, who taught us baseball; we thank St Andrew's Healthcare in Northampton, and in particular the Archive Manager Bobbie Judd, who shared her knowledge of John Clare; the poet Ian Duhig was a brilliant guide in Leeds, and also a mover and shaker in 'Riley's Light: an appreciation of the poetry of John Riley' at the University of Leeds, where we're also grateful to Helen Mort, Andrew McMillan and Professor John Whale; to Antony Ramm at the Local and Family History Archive, Leeds Library; in Austria on the trail of W. H. Auden, we were lucky to meet Dr Helmut Neundlinger: he, his colleague Katharina Strasser at the Centre for Museums Collection Management, Danube University Krems, and the Documentation Centre for Literature in Lower Austria couldn't have been more helpful; to the staff of the Österreichische Mediathek who allowed us to travel back in time to 1973, and to Dr Manfred Müller and Ursula Ebel at the Austrian Society for Literature; we're also grateful to the staff of the Beethoven Saal at the Palais Palffy; in Kirchstetten, to Maria Rollenitz, who arranged us access to the Audenhaus; we had the good fortune to meet the German-language poet E. A. Richter, who told us his story and brought Auden and Chester's world at Kirchstetten to life; to the Mayor of Kirchstetten, Paul Horsak, who took us in his car to see Auden's car, and gave us the heartiest of welcomes; we'd also like to offer our thanks to the author and historian Michael O'Sullivan: Michael was due to travel from Budapest to give us a tour of Auden in Austria, but was prevented from doing so when international train services between Budapest and Vienna were suspended due to the migrant crisis; but his goodwill and suggestions made much of our Auden journey plausible.

We wanted to say a particular thank you to Kate Donahue in Minneapolis, for inviting us into her home and agreeing to talk about her husband John Berryman with a couple of English poets. The example of her generosity at an early stage in this project was galvanizing.

Making all these meetings and journeys happen took some serious logistics. Carole Romaya booked many flights and hotels, and generally made sure we got to the gig. We owe a huge debt of gratitude to Caroline Hawkridge. Caroline took our barely formed plans and lists of names and transformed them into itineraries. She told us who had what and where. She got us though the doors. She checked what we were writing.

Our agents David Godwin, Anna Webber and Peter Straus have made the whole two-author-shuffle thing easy once again. At Jonathan Cape our editor Robin Robertson, together with Clare Bullock and Ceri Maxwell Hughes, gave us everything we needed, and then some. Also, thanks to Ian Pindar for his copy-editing of the manuscript. Any errors or faults escaped into the text are down to the other guy.

This book received support from the Society of Authors thanks to an Authors' Foundation Award in 2012, for which we're both enormously grateful.

In particular, Paul Farley would like to thank: the Society of Authors (again) for the award of a Travelling Scholarship in 2009, the American Academy of Arts and Letters for the E. M. Forster Award the same year, and the Faculty of Arts and Social Sciences Research Fund at Lancaster University. An early version of the half-chapter on Wilfred Owen was published in the *Independent* (10 November 2006), as 'Journey to the Trenches'. Along with those BBC producers already mentioned, I want to thank Tim Dee and Emma Harding for their company and forbearance while on the road. I'm deeply grateful for the hospitality and encouragement of many people, including Adam Sutherland and Karen Guthrie at Grizedale Arts/Lawson Park, my students Matt Haw and Karen Lockney, the poet Julian Turner; and I also wanted to remember two friends, Michael Donaghy and Robert Woof. Finally, warm and constant thanks to Carole.

Michael Symmons Roberts would like to thank: the Humanities Research Centre at Manchester Metropolitan University, the commissioners of BBC Radio 2, 3 and 4, and BBC2 and BBC4 television, for sowing the seeds of some of these chapters; and in particular Sebastian Barfield, Faith Lawrence, Susan Roberts, Sharon Sephton and Matt Thomas for their company and forbearance on various travels. Also the editors, including those of the *Guardian*, *Telegraph* and *Tablet*, where some of these ideas were first explored. At MMU I'm indebted to Jess Edwards and Berthold Schoene for their interest in, and support for, the making of this book. I'm grateful for the conversation and insights of many friends and colleagues, but especially the poet Jean Sprackland and producer Geoff Bird. As ever, my last words of gratitude must go to Ruth, Joe, Paddy and Griff, for all the talk of poets – dead and living – they have had to live with over many years.

Notes and Further Reading

We would like to thank the following archives, and everyone who answered our queries and allowed us to visit their collections and granted us permission to quote materials:

The Elmer L. Andersen Library, Archives & Special Collections Department, University of Minnesota, Minneapolis, USA (John Berryman Papers); Audenhaus Memorial, Kirchstetten, Austria (W. H. Auden); the Bancroft Library, University of California, Berkeley, USA (Thom Gunn Papers); the BBC Archive (Keith Douglas, David Jones, Louis MacNeice, Dylan Thomas, R. S. Thomas); the Biblioteca Classense, Ravenna, Italy (Lord Byron); the Henry W. and Albert A. Berg Collection of English and American Literature, the New York Public Library, Astor, Lenox and Tilden Foundations, New York, USA (Robert Lowell Collection of Papers 1943–1977); the Dokumentationsstelle für Literatur in Niederösterreich [Documentation Centre for Literature in Lower Austria], St Pölten, Austria (W. H. Auden); the Howard Gotlieb Archival Research Center, Boston University, USA (Robert Frost (1874–1963) Collection); the Houghton Library, Harvard College Library, Harvard University, USA (Elizabeth Bishop and Robert Lowell Papers); the Hull University Archives, the Hull History Centre (Papers of Philip Arthur Larkin and Stevie Smith Collections); Local and Family History Archive Leeds (John Riley); the Museum of Modern Art Archives, New York, USA (Frank O'Hara Papers); the Österreichische Gesellschaft für Literatur [Austrian Society for Literature], Vienna, Austria

(W. H. Auden); the Österreichische Mediathek, Vienna, Austria (W. H. Auden); the Rare Book & Manuscript Library, Columbia University Library, New York, USA (Weldon Kees Papers); the Rosenbach Museum & Library, Philadelphia, USA (Marianne Moore Collection); the St Andrews Healthcare Archive, Northampton (John Clare); the Estate of Rosemary Tonks (Rosemary Tonks); Daphne Williams Fox's family archive, Rutherford, New Jersey, USA (William Carlos Williams).

★

★

INTRODUCTION

John Betjeman sits . . . : Christopher Barker, *Portraits of Poets* (Carcanet Press, 1986).

in the words of Bonhams' cataloguer . . . : Bonhams Catalogue, *The Roy Davids Collection, Part III – Poetry: Poetical Manuscripts & Portraits of Poets Volume I: A–K.* (Bonhams, 2013).

according to Alan Bennett . . . : Alan Bennett, *London Review of Books*, Vol. 31, No. 21 (5 November 2009).

All photographs are memento mori . . . : Susan Sontag, *On Photography* (Farrar, Straus and Giroux, 1977).

posthumous message to the living . . . : *Dead Poets Society* (1989), directed by Peter Weir.

One of the survivors . . . : 'Poetic justice: UK auction house planning to sell celebrated Canadian poet's early manuscripts, journals agrees to give them back', *National Post*, Canada (15 April 2013).

lot Number 17 . . . : Bonhams Catalogue, *The Roy Davids Collection, Part III, Volume I.*

It was famously read . . . : *Four Weddings and a Funeral* (1994), directed by Mike Newell.

As the numbers settle . . . : Bonhams Auction Records: Lot 17, Auden, Wystan Hugh (1907–73), autograph revised manuscript of his celebrated poem 'Stop all the Clocks' [?1937].

John Berryman, in an interview . . . : John Berryman, 'The Art of Poetry No. 16', interview in *Paris Review*, No. 53 (Winter 1972).

Our British contemporary . . . : Don Paterson interview by J. P. O'Malley, *The Bottle Imp*, issue 12.

W. B. Yeats sets out . . . : W. B. Yeats, 'The Choice' in *Collected Poems* (Macmillan Collector's Library, 2016).

Robert Graves blamed . . . : Robert Graves, 'The Art of Poetry No. 11', interview in *Paris Review*, No. 47 (Summer 1969).

Lot 480 at the . . . : Bonhams Catalogue, *The Roy Davids Collection, Part III – Poetry: Poetical Manuscripts & Portraits of Poets Volume* II: L–Y. (Bonhams, 2013).

standing in shafts of moonlight . . . : James Kirkup, in 'I would much rather torment dinosaurs than play golf' Michael Deacon, *Daily Telegraph* (7 December 2010).

to invoke Johnson . . . : Samuel Johnson, *The Lives of the Poets*, ed. John H. Middendorf, *The Yale Edition of the Works of Samuel Johnson* XXI–XXIII (Yale University Press, 2010).

The road of excess . . . : William Blake, 'Proverbs of Hell', *The Complete Poems*, ed. Alicia Ostriker (Penguin Classics, 2004).

He lodged as much by . . . : Samuel Johnson, *The Lives of the Poets*.

to have discovered the manuscripts . . . : James Boswell, *The Life of Samuel Johnson*, ed. David Womersley (Penguin Classics, 2009).

warned by a friend not to depend on it . . . : Thomas Percy letter to William Shenstone in *The Percy Letters*, ed. Cleanth Brooks (Yale University Press, 1977).

THE MINUTE THEY BECOME DEAD . . . : Mary Ruefle, *Madness, Rack, and Honey* (Wave Books, 2012).

A PORTABLE SHRINE

Standing in front of . . . : Henry Wallis, *Chatterton* (1856), Tate Britain, Millbank, London.

What Ruskin called . . . : Frances Fowle, Tate notes on Wallis's *Chatterton* (2000).

Harry Wildfire, Decimus and Flirtilla . . . : Linda Kelly, *The Marvellous Boy: The Life and Myth of Thomas Chatterton* (Weidenfeld & Nicolson, 1971).

Grant me, like thee . . . : Samuel Taylor Coleridge, 'Monody on the Death of Chatterton', *Poetical Works* (Oxford, 1912).

claiming Chatterton as one of his heroes . . . : *NME* on the Libertines (May 2011).

Exhibitions like the colossal . . . : BBC History features, 'The Greatest Art Show Ever?' (2007/8).

Manchester Arena sold . . . : Source: PollstarPro.com Top 200 Arena Venues 2014.

I always somehow associate Chatterton . . . : John Keats, *Selected Letters* (Oxford World's Classics, Oxford University Press, 2009).

I know the colour . . . : John Keats to Charles Brown (*Life of John Keats*), cited in Andrew Motion, *Keats* (Faber and Faber, 1997).

liked to recite its best-known stanza . . . : According to Keats's friend Benjamin Bailey, in Daniel Cook, *Thomas Chatterton and Neglected Genius 1760–1830* (Palgrave Macmillan, 2013).

Comme, wythe acorne . . . : Thomas Chatterton, *Selected Poems*, ed. with introduction by Grevel Lindop (Carcanet Press, 1972).

part of the lyric of a Serge Gainsbourg song . . . : Serge Gainsbourg, 'Chatterton' (1967).

pleasingly amateurish of art thefts . . . : Edward Dolnick, *The Rescue Artist* (Harper Collins, 2010).

In what he called his 'last Will and Testament' . . . : Thomas Chatterton, *Selected Poems*.

to dull the pain of his medicines . . . : This thesis is discussed in Linda Kelly, *The Marvellous Boy*. See also Richard Holmes, *Sidetracks* (Harper Perennial, 2005).

A lyric poet is one who is . . . : Donald Davie on Dylan Thomas in the *New York Times* Book Review (9 November 1975).

eighteen straight whiskies . . . : Andrew Lycett, *Dylan Thomas, a New Life* (Orion, 2004).

the title of the drama, A Poet in New York . . . : Writer Andrew Davies, BBC Television (2014).

Twenty years ago . . . : 'Heritage as Formal Education', Prentice, Light, in *Heritage, Tourism and Society* (Mansell, 1995).

In a 1977 interview . . . : Kane on Friday, *Leftover Wife: Caitlin Thomas* (1997), produced by Brian Turvey, BBC Television.

In an early letter . . . : Dylan Thomas (9 May 1934), letter to Pamela Hansford Johnson, in *Collected Letters* (Weidenfeld & Nicolson, 2014).

And there's an early poem, too . . . : Dylan Thomas, *Collected Poems*, ed. John Goodby, Centenary Edition (Weidenfeld & Nicolson, 2014).

with evidence suggesting . . . : 'The death of Dylan Thomas: a conspiracy theory', *British Medical Journal*, 341: c4595 (16 September 2010). See also David N. Thomas, *Fatal Neglect: Who Killed Dylan Thomas?* (Seren, 2008).

He wouldn't have lived, anyway . . . : John Berryman, 'The Art of Poetry No. 16', *Paris Review*.

subsumed into Dylan the legend . . . : Donald Davie in the *New York Times Book Review*.

only six poems . . . : Andrew Lycett, *Dylan Thomas: A New Life*.

THE NAMES OF THE BRIDGES

Searching through Robert Lowell's . . . : Robert Lowell Papers (MS Am 1905), Houghton Library, Harvard University. References to Dylan Thomas's death in letters to Lowell from John Berryman (14 November 1953).

The Minneapolis Star . . . : Cited in John Haffenden, *The Life of John Berryman* (Ark Paperbacks, 1982). But also from authors' private archive.

Poetry exacts a price . . . : Kate Donahue, interview with authors, 2013.

having suffered an irreversible loss . . . : John Berryman, prefatory note to *The Dream Songs* (Faber and Faber, 1964).

W. B. Yeats believed . . . : W. B. Yeats, letter to Olivia Shakespear (1927).

Michael Hofmann has described . . . : Michael Hofmann, introduction to *John Berryman: Selected Poems* (Faber and Faber, 2004).

Next stop on the tour is Zipps Liquors . . . : Steve Marsh, 'Homage to Mister Berryman', Mpls St Paul Magazine (September 2008).

At the post mortem there was no trace . . . : John Haffenden, *The Life of John Berryman*.

more recently his autobiography . . . : Bob Dylan, *Chronicles* (Simon & Schuster, 2004).

Completely familiar now . . . : Adam Kirsch, 'Reckless Endangerment', *The New Yorker* (5 July 2004).

The extent of the archive . . . : Details of collection from Literary Manuscripts Collections, Manuscripts Division, 213 Elmer L. Andersen Library, University of Minnesota.

We start to work backwards from . . . : John Berryman Papers (Mss 43), Literary Manuscripts Collections, Manuscripts Division, University of Minnesota Libraries.

his thought made pockets . . . : John Berryman, '*Dream Song* 5', *The Dream Songs*.

and we begin to talk . . . : Kate Donahue, interview, ibid.

can be found in that infamous interview . . . : John Berryman, interview, ibid.

Donald Davie, writing in . . . : Donald Davie, 'John Berryman's Freedom of the Poet', in *New York Times* Book Review (25 April 1976).

in a US edition . . . : Published by Farrar, Straus and Giroux, 1969.

Those days before I knew . . . : Joan Didion, 'Goodbye to all that', *Slouching Towards Bethlehem* (Farrar, Straus and Giroux, 1968).

The one could not exist . . . : Al Alvarez, *Beyond All This Fiddle: Essays 1955–1967* (Allen Lane, The Penguin Press, 1968).

The woman who launched . . . : Christina Patterson, 'In search of the poet', *Independent* (6 February 2004).

deathtime . . . : Julian Barnes, 'Selfie with "Sunflowers"', *London Review of Books*, Vol. 37, No. 15 (30 July 2015).

A letter home . . . : Sylvia Plath, letter (7 November 1962), Sylvia Plath and Aurelia Schober Plath, *Sylvia Plath. Letters Home 1950–63: Correspondence* (Faber and Faber, 1999).

Tomorrow morning some poet . . . : Randall Jarrell, *Poetry and the Age* (Faber and Faber, 1996).

She wrote to her mother . . . : Sylvia Plath, letter (16 January 1963), *Letters Home*.

Sylvia . . . : Hugo Williams, 'Freelance', *The Times Literary Supplement* (29 November 2002).

Ocean 1212-W . . . : Sylvia Plath, *Johnny Panic and the Bible of Dreams: Short Stories, Prose and Diary Excerpts* (Harper Collins, 2008).

according to Hughes . . . : Ted Hughes, 'Sylvia Plath', *Poetry Book Society Bulletin*, No. 44 (February 1965).

In a paper from 2003 . . . : J. C. Kaufman, 'The Cost of the Muse: Poets Die Young', *Death Studies 27*.

The New York Times picked up on the research . . . : Felicia R. Lee, 'Going Early Into That Good Night', *New York Times* (24 April 2004).

Mark Lythgoe et al., 'Obsessive, prolific artistic output following subarachnoid haemorrhage', *Neurology* 64 (2) 2005.

A serious person . . . : Christopher Hitchens, 'Introduction', *Arguably: Selected Prose* (Atlantic Books, 2011).

My Mother died there . . . : Frieda Hughes, quoted by Adam Sonin, *Hampstead Highgate Express* (2 February 2013).

The pram in the hall . . . Cyril Connolly, 'The Charlock's Shade', *Enemies of Promise* (Andre Deutsch, 1996).

Hughes's poem . . . : Ted Hughes, 'Last Letter', *New Statesman* (7 October 2010).

drifting, rootless rage . . . : Elizabeth Hardwick, 'On Sylvia Plath', *The New York Review of Books* (12 August 1971).

Plath wrote an account . . . : Sylvia Plath, *The Journals of Sylvia Plath: 1950– 1962*, ed. Karen V. Kukil (Faber and Faber, 2000).

THE DUST OF ENGLAND

shawl-girt head and. . . : Lord Byron, *Childe Harold's Pilgrimage*, LVIII, Canto II

O thou, Parnassus! . . . : Lord Byron, *Childe Harold's Pilgrimage*, LXII, Canto I.

It was a world of . . . : Patrick Leigh Fermor, *Roumeli: Travels in Northern Greece* (John Murray, 2004).

And thou, the Muses'. . . : Lord Byron, *Childe Harold's Pilgrimage*, LXII Canto I.

Tony Harrison, 'Polygons', *London Review of Books*, Vol. 37, No. 4 (19 February 2015).

one known extant line . . . : Tony Harrison, 'Remains', *Collected Poems* (Viking, 2007).

Where'er we tread . . . : Lord Byron, *Childe Harold's Pilgrimage*, LXXXVIII, Canto II.

But who, of all the . . . : Lord Byron, *Childe Harold's Pilgrimage*, XI, Canto II.

'*spaciousness*' *and* '*claustrophobia*' : Stefania Michelucci, *The Poetry of Thom Gunn: A Critical Study* (McFarland & Co., 2009).

Dennis O'Driscoll, *Stepping Stones: Interviews with Seamus Heaney* (Faber and Faber, 2008).

It is a part solution . . . : Thom Gunn, 'On the Move', *Collected Poems* (Faber and Faber, 1994).

My methedrine . . . : Thom Gunn, 'Street Song', *Moly* (Faber and Faber, 1971).

It's like a house . . . : Thom Gunn, 'The Art of Poetry No. 72', interview by Clive Wilmer in *Paris Review*, No. 135 (Summer 1995).

There are different floors . . . : Tom Sleigh, 'Sex, Drugs and Thom Gunn: The life and work of a true servant of Eros', *Poetry* (10 June 2009).

We have the archival boxes . . . : Letters, postcards and diaries, Carton 2, folders 33–34 and 41, Thom Gunn Papers, BANC MSS 2006/235, The Bancroft Library, University of California, Berkeley.

acute polysubstance abuse . . . : Tom Sleigh, 'Sex, Drugs and Thom Gunn'.

He kept his freak . . . : Billy Lux, quoted by Edward Guthmann in 'A Poet's Life: Part Two', *San Francisco Chronicle* (26 April 2005).

gerontophile . . . : Mike Kitay, quoted by Edward Guthmann, 'A Poet's Life', ibid.

as though raft-bourne . . . : Patrick Leigh Fermor, *Roumeli*.

I love Greece . . . : Thomas Medwin, *Conversations of Lord Byron Noted During a Residency With His Lordship at Pisa* (Henry Colburn, 1824).

I should prefer . . . : Letter to Lord Blessington (23 April 1823), Marguerite Countess of Blessington, *Conversations of Lord Byron with the Countess of Blessington* (Henry Colburn, 1834).

And I will war . . . : Lord Byron, *Don Juan*, XXIV, Canto IX.

Among the arranged trees . . . : Louis MacNeice, 'Ten Burnt Offerings, III, Cock o' the North', *Collected Poems*, ed. Peter McDonald (Faber and Faber, 2007).

light, slender, faded . . . : Patrick Leigh Fermor, *Roumeli*.

Take these: peach-stones in a Petri dish . . . : Biblioteca Classense, Ravenna, Italy.

But, no. It's his skin . . . : Biblioteca Classense.

many more die . . . : Pietro Gamba, *A Narrative of Lord Byron's Last Journey to Greece* (John Murray, 1825).

and some doctors today . . . : Theodore Dalrymple, 'Safety in Death', *British Medical Journal*, Vol. 342 (21 May 2011).

The next day . . . : Pietro Gamba, *A Narrative of Lord Byron's Last Journey to Greece.*

story of a monk . . . : Zoe Wilkinson, 'Byron's Greek Self', *Athens News* (13 June 2008).

GOING TO THE INEVITABLE

like free bloody birds . . . : 'High Windows'; *Swerving East* . . . : 'Here'; *awful pie* . . . : 'Dockery and Son'; *shoeless corridors* . . . : 'Friday Night at the Royal Station Hotel'; all Philip Larkin, *Collected Poems*, ed. Anthony Thwaite (Faber and Faber, 1990).

the tall heat that slept . . . : Philip Larkin, 'The Whitsun Weddings', ibid.

Coined there among . . . : Philip Larkin, 'Solar', ibid.

new Larkin poem . . . : Philip Larkin, 'Aubade', *Times Literary Supplement* (23 December 1977).

egg sculpted in lard . . . : Philip Larkin to Fay Godwin (16 September 1984), from Andrew Motion, *Philip Larkin: A Writer's Life* (Faber and Faber, 1994).

A wild white face . . . : 'Ambulances'; *The white hours* . . . : 'Cut Grass'; *unseen congregations* . . . : 'The Building': *Though white is not* . . . : 'Sympathy in White Major'; *lambs that learn* . . . : 'First Sight'; *white as clay* . . . : 'Aubade'; all Philip Larkin, *Collected Poems.*

Death is what gets . . . : Billy Collins at the Rubloff Auditorium of the Chicago Historical Society, reported by Patrick T. Reardon, '83 per cent of poetry is not worth reading', *Chicago Tribune* (14 November 2001).

Larkin never included . . . : Stephen Regan, in correspondence with the authors, 10 July 2015.

An April Sunday . . . : Philip Larkin, 'An April Sunday brings the snow', *Collected Poems.*

late getting away . . . : Philip Larkin, 'The Whitsun Weddings', ibid.

blurred playground noises . . . : Philip Larkin, 'Toads Revisited', ibid.

BBC Monitor interview . . . : Philip Larkin interview with John Betjeman, BBC Monitor: *Down Cemetery Road*, Episode 140 (12 December 1964), directed by Patrick Garland.

the classy part . . . : ibid. (at 12' 46").

I am in love with . . . : Sean O'Brien, 'Walking', *Collected Poems* (Picador, 2012).

The trees are coming . . . : 'The Trees'; *the leaves are falling* . . . : 'Afternoons'; all Philip Larkin, *Collected Poems*.

the ugliest one-roomed . . . : The Larkin Trail www.thelarkintrail.co.uk

The Mower . . . : Philip Larkin, 'The Mower', *Collected Poems*.

sixteen stone six . . . : Philip Larkin to Kingsley Amis (3 January 1982), *Selected Letters of Philip Larkin*, ed. Anthony Thwaite (Faber and Faber, 1992).

When Potter was dying . . . : Dennis Potter, interview by Melvyn Bragg, Channel 4 (15 March 1994).

Paul Muldoon's New York Times review . . . : Paul Muldoon, *New York Times* Book Review (19 April 2012).

I'm writing to ask . . . : Correspondence between Philip Larkin and Michael Kustow (Associate Director of the National Theatre), mainly discussing Larkinland (3 September 1976 to 31 October 1977 (Ref U DPL2/3/42/1), Papers of Philip Arthur Larkin, Hull University Archives, Hull History Centre.

LARKINLAND sounds a . . . : ibid.

Larkinland . . . : BBC Radio 4 (28 July 1977).

It is all rather like a mixture . . . : Correspondence between Charles Monteith (Faber and Faber) and Philip Larkin, reporting on the success of Larkinland (26–30 May 1977) (Ref U DPL2/3/24/41), Papers of Philip Arthur Larkin, Hull University Archives, Hull History Centre.

All that remains of Larkin's diaries . . . : Diary remnants and holiday journals (Ref U DPL4/1) Papers of Philip Arthur Larkin, Hull University Archives, Hull History Centre.

Monitor documentary . . . : *Down Cemetery Road*.

University Librarian takes an archive box . . . : Personal items belonging to Philip Larkin that were part of his office and inherited by his successors, but which remain in the University Librarian's office at Brynmor Jones Library, University of Hull, and were made available for viewing courtesy of the current University Librarian, Richard Heseltine.

Shetland pony . . . : Philip Larkin, *Times Educational Supplement* (19 May 1972).

I came away rather . . . : Philip Larkin's response to Larkinland (31 May 1977) (Ref U DPL2/1/55/8), Papers of Philip Arthur Larkin, Hull University Archives, Hull History Centre.

Deprivation is . . . : Philip Larkin, *Required Writing* (Faber and Faber, 1983). See earlier (p 90) *Depression is* . . . : in *Viewpoints: Poets in Conversation with John Haffenden* (Faber and Faber, 1981).

Writing in the New York Times . . . : Paul Muldoon review.

Larkin wrote, perhaps more in hope . . . : Philip Larkin, interview with John Haffenden, published in *Further Requirements: Interviews, Broadcasts, Statements and Reviews, 1952–85*, ed. Anthony Thwaite (Faber and Faber, 2013).

art just isn't worth that much . . . : Elizabeth Bishop, ed. Robert Giroux, *One Art: Letters, Elizabeth Bishop* (Farrar, Straus and Giroux, 1994).

ruptured cerebral aneurysm . . . : Obituary by Tony Schwartz, *New York Times* (8 October 1979).

by Elizabeth Spires . . . : Elizabeth Bishop, 'The Art of Poetry No. 27', interview in *Paris Review*, No. 80 (Summer 1981).

a book of her 'uncollected poems, drafts and fragments' . . . : Elizabeth Bishop, *Edgar Allan Poe and the Juke-Box, Uncollected Poems, Drafts and Fragments*, ed. and annotated by Alice Quinn (Farrar, Straus and Giroux, 2006).

wrote in the New Republic . . . : Helen Vendler, *New Republic* (3 April 2006).

This is one of Elizabeth Bishop's notebooks . . . : MS Am 2115. Houghton Library, Harvard University.

famous poem 'The Fish' . . . : Elizabeth Bishop, 'The Fish', *Poems, Centenary Edition* (Chatto & Windus, 2011).

awful but cheerful . . . : Elizabeth Bishop, 'The Bight', ibid.

POET INTERRUPTED

Oh no, no, no, it was . . . : Stevie Smith, *Collected Poems and Drawings of Stevie Smith*, ed. Will May (Faber and Faber, 2015).

I am an addict . . . : Linda Anderson, 'Gender, feminism, poetry: Stevie Smith, Sylvia Plath, Jo Shapcott' in *The Cambridge Companion to Twentieth-century English Poetry*, ed. Neil Corcoran (Cambridge, 2007).

I had a very peculiar . . . : Handwritten letter from Stevie Smith to Anthony Thwaite (17 January 1971) (Ref U DP214/3/14), Letters from Philip Larkin and Stevie Smith to Anthony and Anne Thwaite, with related material (1955–1983), Hull University Archives, Hull History Centre.

While in hospital . . . : Letter to John Guest, in *Me Again: Uncollected Writings of Stevie Smith*, ed. Jack Barbera and William McBrien (Virago, 1981).

when reading 'Come Death' to visitors at her bedside . . . : Frances Spalding, *Stevie Smith: A Critical Biography* (Faber, 1988).

I feel ill . . . : Stevie Smith, 'Come, Death', *Collected Poems and Drawings*.

this awful medical case. . . : Letter (lost) to John Guest, cited in Jack Barbera and William McBrien, *Stevie: a Biography of Stevie Smith* (Heinemann, 1985).

Her [Molly's] capacity for boredom . . . : Frances Spalding, *Stevie Smith*, ibid.

that day in 1971 . . . : Sanford Sternlicht, *Stevie Smith* (Twayne Publishers, 1990).

How sweet the birds . . . : Stevie Smith, 'Avondale', *Collected Poems and Drawings*.

It is a house . . . : 'A House of Mercy', ibid.

self-described 'Anglican Agnostic' . . . : Kay Dick, *Ivy & Stevie* (Duckworth, 1971).

under the culvert . . . : Frances Spalding, *Stevie Smith*.

when the wind blows . . . : *Me Again*.

a feature film . . . : *Stevie* (1978), directed by Robert Enders.

Persons from Porlock . . . : Louis MacNeice, *Persons from Porlock* (30 August 1963), BBC Third Programme.

MERVYN: *Sit down . . .* : Louis MacNeice, *Persons from Porlock and Other Plays for Radio* (BBC Books, 1969).

letter to his daughter . . . : Louis MacNeice, letter (8 August 1963), *Letters of Louis MacNeice*, ed. Jonathan Allison (Faber and Faber, 2010).

August 1963 was . . . : Met Office Monthly Weather Report: www.metoffice.gov.uk

HANK: *I find it . . .* : Louis MacNeice, *Persons from Porlock*.

HANK: *What I like . . .* : ibid.

letter to his daughter . . . : Louis MacNeice, letter (8 August 1963), *Letters of Louis MacNeice*.

composed in a sort of . . . : S. T. Coleridge, 1797, *Crewe Manuscript*: www.bl.uk

Samuel Taylor Coleridge, *Poems*, ed. John Beer (J. M. Dent & Sons, 1974).

On awakening he . . . : S. T. Coleridge, 'Preface to *Kubla Khan*' (1816), *Poems*, ibid.

between Porlock & Linton . . . : S. T. Coleridge, 1797, *Crewe Manuscript*.

Coleridge received . . . : Stevie Smith, 'Thoughts about the Person from Porlock', *Stevie Smith: A Selection*, ed. Hermione Lee (Faber and Faber, 1983).

St Leonard's Hospital still . . . : Hannah Parham, 'St Leonard's Hospital. Kingsland Road, Built 1863–66', *The Story of Healthcare in Hackney*, The Hackney Society: www.health.hackneysociety.org

a brangle of talk . . . : Louis MacNeice, 'Carrick Revisited', *Collected Poems*, ed. Peter McDonald (Faber and Faber 2007).

a black labyrinth . . . : Louis MacNeice, *The Strings are False: An Unfinished Autobiography* (Faber and Faber 1996).

Where the bottle-neck . . . : Louis MacNeice, 'Carrickfergus', *Collected Poems*.

a sense in which . . . : Tom Paulin, 'The Man from No Part: Louis MacNeice', *Writing to the Moment: Selected Critical Essays 1980–1996* (Faber and Faber 1996).

Transported across . . . : Louis MacNeice, *The Strings are False*.

THRILLING BROADCAST . . . : Belfry Bulletin 552 (Summer 2005): www.bec-cave.org.uk

Silbury Hill . . . : Louis MacNeice, letter to Georgina Beatrice MacNeice (6 May 1932), *Letters of Louis MacNeice*.

Pause: sudden increase . . . : Louis MacNeice, *Persons from Porlock*.

which in turn . . . : Louis MacNeice, *The Strings are False*.

Our worst experience . . . : Jacques Cousteau, *The Silent World: A Story of Undersea Discovery and Adventure* (Hamish Hamilton, 1953).

Once, when by . . . : Frederic Mistral, *Mirèio*, trans. Harriet W. Preston (Robert Bros, 1885).

Louis MacNeice, *The Burning Perch* (Faber and Faber, 1963).

A month from . . . : Robert Lowell, 'Louis MacNeice 1907–1963', *Collected Poems*, ed. Frank Bidart and David Gewanter (Faber and Faber, 2003).

will not stir . . . : Derek Mahon, 'At Carrowdore Churchyard', *Collected Poems* (Gallery Press, 1999).

picked up frequencies . . . : Michael Longley, 'Introduction', Louis MacNeice, *Selected Poems*, ed. Michael Longley (Faber and Faber, 1988).

his 'unwritten book' . . . : Louis MacNeice, 'Landscapes of Childhood and Youth' in *The Strings Are False*.

Coda . . . : Louis MacNeice, 'Coda', *Collected Poems*.

TWO FERRIES

On the headland east . . . : Arromanches 360, Chemin du Calvaire, 14117 Arromanches les Bains.

One of Keith Douglas's most famous lines . . . : 'Simplify me when I'm dead', Keith Douglas, *The Complete Poems* (Oxford University Press, 1978).

The literary scholar . . . : Jean Moorcroft Wilson, *Edward Thomas: From Adlestrop to Arras: A Biography* (Bloomsbury, 2015).

The army padre, Skinner . . . : Stuart Hills, *By Tank into Normandy* (Cassell, 2002).

at the end of his poem 'How to Kill' . . . : Keith Douglas, 'How to Kill', *The Complete Poems*.

In 'Vergissmeinnicht' . . . : Keith Douglas, '*Vergissmeinnicht*', ibid.

if you want to move your reader . . . : Anton Chekhov, letter to Lidya Alexyevna (19 March 1892), Project Gutenberg.

If at times my eyes are lenses . . . : Keith Douglas, 'The Bête Noire Fragments', *The Complete Poems*.

It is tremendously illogical . . . : Keith Douglas, *Alamein to Zem Zem* (Faber and Faber, 1966).

a man with no head . . . : Keith Douglas, 'Cairo Jag', *The Complete Poems*.

were given the nickname 'Ronsons' . . . : Stuart Hills, *By Tank into Normandy*.

Keith Douglas landed at Gold Beach . . . : On Jig sector, Gold Beach. See Desmond Graham, *Keith Douglas: A Biography* (Oxford University Press, 2012).

In a feature for BBC Radio . . . : Sean Street, *Keith Douglas: Landscape with Figure*, Radio 3 documentary.

The padre recorded . . . : Stuart Hills, *By Tank into Normandy*.

According to Hills . . . : Sean Street, *Keith Douglas*.

opposite a Commonwealth War Cemetery . . . : Tilly War Cemetery, D13, 14250 Tilly-sur-Seulles, Calvados, France.

One might ask . . . : W. H. Auden, 'The Art of Poetry No. 17', interview in *Paris Review*, No. 57 (Spring 1974).

like a young man man, full of longing . . . : Keith Douglas, 'The Prisoner', *The Complete Poems*.

a policy of land remembrement . . . : Hedgelink report 2010: www. hedgelink.org.uk.

The bare facts . . . : Brad Gooch, 'Death', *City Poet: The Life and Times of Frank O'Hara* (Harper Perennial, 1994).

On the street . . . : Charles Simic, 'Terra Incognita', *Dime-Store Alchemy: The Art of Joseph Cornell* (New York Review Books, 2006).

I liked the . . . : Edmund Leites, 'Frank's Charm', *Homage to Frank O'Hara*, ed. Bill Berkson and Joe LeSueur (Bolinas, 1978).

I remember . . . : Joe Brainard, *I Remember* (Granary Books, 2006).

I can't even . . . : Frank O'Hara, 'Meditations in an Emergency', *The Collected Poems of Frank O'Hara*, ed. Donald Allen (University of California Press, 1995).

exhibition catalogue . . . : Frank O'Hara, *Nakian* (MoMA, 1966).

in the memos and minutes . . . : Frank O'Hara Papers [folder 11], Museum of Modern Art Archives, New York.

hum colored . . . : Frank O'Hara, 'A Step Away From Them', *Lunch Poems* (City Lights Books, 1964).

where Billie Holiday . . . : *Village Voice* (16 February 1976).

this desert of . . . : Albert Camus, journal entry (April/May 1946), in *American Journals*, trans. Hugh Levick (Hamilton, 1989).

private boat . . . : Brad Gooch, *City Poet*.

I remember . . . : Joe Brainard, *I Remember*.

When you see . . . : Frank O'Hara, 'Lament and Chastisement, 4', *Frank O'Hara: Early Writing*, ed. Donald Allen (Grey Fox Press, 1977).

Lana Turner . . . : Frank O'Hara, 'Poem', *Lunch Poems*.

there is no . . . : Marie Heaney, *The Bloodaxe Book of Poetry Quotations*, ed. Dennis O'Driscoll (Bloodaxe, 2006).

I was sorry . . . : Elizabeth Bishop, letter to Robert Lowell (25 September 1966), in *Words in Air: The Complete Correspondence Between Elizabeth Bishop and Robert Lowell*, ed. Thomas Travisano and Saskia Hamilton (Farrar, Straus and Giroux, 2008).

lost more than . . . : R. Darren Price, 'Half of Fire Island's Beaches, Dunes Washed Away by Sandy': www.nbcnewyork.com

a romantic death . . . : Larry Rivers, quoted in Brad Gooch, 'Prologue', *City Poet*.

In City Poet . . . : Brad Gooch, 'Death', ibid.

Nevertheless I am . . . : Frank O'Hara, 'Autobiographical Fragments', *Standing Still and Walking in New York*, ed. Donald Allen (Grey Fox Press, 1983).

Don't be bored . . . Frank O'Hara, in the television film *David Smith: Sculpting Master of Bolton Landing*, WNDT-TV, New York (18 November 1964). Reprinted in *Frank O'Hara, What's With Modern Art?* ed. Bill Berkson (Mike & Dale's Press, 1999).

THE DUGOUT

Douglas ended up in a rain-soaked . . . : Desmond Graham, *Keith Douglas.*

that the job of a poet was . . . : David Jones, Preface to *The Anathemata* (Faber and Faber, 1952).

you find yourself alone . . . : David Jones, *In Parenthesis* (Faber and Faber, 1937).

a certain cure for lust of blood . . . : Robert Graves, 'A Dead Boche', *The Complete Poems* (Penguin, 2015).

he declared himself 'deeply moved' . . . : T. S. Eliot, Introduction to *In Parenthesis* (Faber and Faber, 1961 reissue).

Fifties dramatization of the poem . . . : *In Parenthesis*, adapted by David Jones and Douglas Cleverdon (1903–87), produced by Douglas Cleverdon, BBC Third Programme (30 January 1955).

The poet Kathleen Raine visited . . . : Essay published in Merlin James's exhibition catalogue *A Map of the Artist's Mind* (Lund Humphries Publishing Ltd, 1995).

Another friend, Nest Cleverdon . . . : Essay published in *A Map of the Artist's Mind*, ibid.

For us amateur soldiers . . . : David Jones, Introduction to *In Parenthesis* (Faber and Faber, 1937).

The memory of it is like a disease . . . : Thomas Dilworth, *David Jones and the Great War* (Enitharmon Press, 2012).

I have to try and paint now . . . : Letter to Harman Grisewood (24 August 1947), reproduced in *Dai Greatcoat: A Self-Portrait of David Jones in His Letters* (Faber and Faber, 1980).

On the making of Vexilla Regis . . . : Letter to Mrs Ede (28 August 1949), ibid.

The poet Robert Graves . . . : Robert Graves, *Goodbye to All That* (Penguin, 2000).

Leave it for a Cook's tourist . . . : David Jones, *In Parenthesis*, Faber and Faber, 1937.

Those fifty hours…: Wilfred Owen, letter to Susan Owen (16 January 1917), *Collected Letters* (OUP, 1967).

Miners…: Wilfred Owen, *The Collected Poems* (Chatto & Windus, 1977).

I get mixed up with…: Wilfred Owen, 'Notes', *The Poems of Wilfred Owen* (Chatto & Windus, 1933).

for half an hour's…: Wilfred Owen, letter to Susan Owen (8 February 1918), *Collected Letters*.

Purest, it is…: Wilfred Owen, 'Purple', *Collected Poems*.

cobbled with skulls…: Wilfred Owen, letter to Mary Owen (25 March 1918), *Collected Letters*.

For I so repassed…: Wilfred Owen, *The Complete Poems and Fragments* ed. Jon Stallworthy (Chatto & Windus, 1983).

fine biography…: Dominic Hibberd, *Wilfred Owen* (Weidenfeld & Nicolson, 2002).

Full ninety autumns…: Wilfred Owen, 'Written in a Wood, September 1910', Appendix, *Collected Poems*.

perceptibly provincial…: Siegfried Sassoon, *Siegfried's Journey 1916–1920* (Viking, 1946).

If you could hear…: Wilfred Owen, 'Dulce et Decorum Est', *Collected Poems*.

Head to limp head . . . : Wilfred Owen, 'Smile, Smile, Smile', ibid.

Down the close . . . : Wilfred Owen, 'The Send-Off', ibid.

his Military Cross . . . : Duncan Campbell, 'War poet's medal turns up in attic', *Guardian* (10 May 2007).

HOUSE CALLS

this is perhaps why . . . : Martin Amis, 'Career Move', *Heavy Water* (Vintage, 1999).

This was underlined for many in a discovery . . . : Story reported in article by Madeleine Davies in *Church Times* (10 January 2014).

'This Is Just to Say' . . . : William Carlos Williams, 'This Is Just to Say', *Selected Poems*, ed. Charles Tomlinson (New Directions, 1985).

So much depends upon . . . : William Carlos Williams, 'The Red Wheelbarrow', ibid.

Some biographers . . . : Herbert Leibowitz, *Something Urgent I Have to Say to You: the Life and Work of William Carlos Williams* (Farrar, Straus and Giroux, 2011).

According to WCW's biographer . . . : Paul Mariani, *William Carlos Williams: A New World Naked* (McGraw-Hill, 1981).

In a late interview . . . : 'On Women' in *Interviews with William Carlos Williams: Speaking Straight Ahead*, ed. Linda Welshimer Wagner (New Directions, 1976).

No ideas but in things . . . : William Carlos Williams, in *Paterson*, revised edition prepared by Christopher McGowan (New Directions, 1992).

not 'distinguished or varied enough' . . . : 'A Statement by William Carlos Williams about the Poem *Paterson*' (31 May 1951), ibid.

In his short, vivid memoir . . . : Robert Coles and Thomas Roma, *House Calls with William Carlos Williams, MD* (Powerhouse Books, 2008). Plus Robert Coles's interview for the BBC Radio 3 programme *Paterson* (2015).

a twelve-year-old girl was shot dead . . . : report by Rebecca D. O'Brien and Joe Malinconico, *Record and Paterson Press* (6 July 2014).

One of the letters WCW includes . . . : William Carlos Williams, *Paterson*.

That God damned . . . : James Laughlin, *Remembering William Carlos Williams* (New Directions Publishing, 1996).

biographer Paul Mariani . . . : Paul Mariani, *William Carlos Williams*.

According to Mariani. . . : ibid.

Rainfalls and surfeits . . . : William Carlos Williams, *Paterson*.

The refrain, he told Pound . . . : Notes to William Carlos Williams, *Paterson*.

Robert Coles reveals . . . : *House Calls with William Carlos Williams, MD*, and Robert Coles BBC Radio 3 interview.

24 shirts at .82 ½ cents . . . : William Carlos Williams, *Paterson*.

His final letter to Laughlin . . . : James Laughlin, *The Way It Wasn't* (New Directions, 2006).

We are making a radio programme . . . : *Daring the Depths* (15 November 1991), presented by Jeremy Hooker, BBC Radio 3.

In one of R. S. Thomas's most celebrated . . . : R. S. Thomas, 'The Empty Church', *Collected Poems 1945–1990* (Dent, 1993).

In an interview . . . : Contemporary Authors Autobiography Series, Vol. 4 (Gale, 1986), as quoted in Poetry Foundation Biography of R. S. Thomas.

You must wear your eyes out . . . : R. S. Thomas, 'Sea-Watching', *Collected Poems*.

What troubles me . . . : *Daring the Depths*.

Dr Robert Coles . . . : Robert Coles BBC Radio 3 interview.

THE BURNING OF SOME IDOLS

In April 2014 . . . : Neil Astley, Rosemary Tonks obituary, *Guardian* (2 May 2014).

like the 2009 Radio 4 . . . : *Lost Voices* (March 2009), presented by Brian Patten, BBC Radio 4.

'Story of a Hotel Room' . . . : *Bedouin of the London Evening: Collected Poems* (Bloodaxe Books, 2015).

Philip Larkin, in an essay . . . : Collected in *Required Writing: Miscellaneous Pieces 1955–1982* (Faber and Faber, 1983).

Most of the Collected . . . : Emily Dickinson, *Complete Poems* (Faber and Faber, 1976).

This, in a letter Emily Dickinson . . . : Emily Dickinson, letter to Mrs J. G. Holland (early May 1866), in *The Letters of Emily Dickinson* (Harvard University Press, 1997).

In her poem 'Wild Nights' . . . : Emily Dickinson, 'Wild Nights', *Complete Poems*.

Mabel's affair with . . . : Lyndall Gordon, *Lives Like Loaded Guns: Emily Dickinson and Her Family's Feuds* (Virago, 2010).

Standing in Emily's room . . . : Emily Dickinson Museum, The Homestead and The Evergreens, 280 Main Street, Amherst MA 01002, USA.

Because I could not stop . . . : Emily Dickinson, 'Because I could not stop for Death', *Complete Poems*.

an abandoned 1954 . . . : Anthony Lane, 'The Disappearing Poet: What ever happened to Weldon Kees?', *New Yorker* (4 July 2005).

Ann & I were divorced . . . : Weldon Kees, letter to Bob and Lorraine Wilbur (November 1954); Weldon Kees papers; Box 1, Folder 2; Rare Book and Manuscript Library, Columbia University Library.

Dear Herbert, my book . . . : Weldon Kees, card to Herbert Cahoon (December 1954); Weldon Kees papers; Box 1, Folder 1, ibid.

Poems about Kees. . . : Dana Gioia, 'Introduction', *The Bibliography of Weldon Kees* (Parrish House, 1997).

I'd heard it said . . . : Simon Armitage, 'Looking for Weldon Kees', *Around Robinson* (Slow Dancer, 1991) and the BBC2 programme *Looking for Robinson* (1993).

Appearing in just . . . : Weldon Kees, *Collected Poems of Weldon Kees* (Faber and Faber, 1993).

The strangest item . . . : Envelope containing frames of 35mm film; Weldon Kees papers; Box 1, Folder 3, ibid.

Her notebooks . . . : Courtesy of the estate of Rosemary Tonks.

Her search for a spiritual home . . . : See Neil Astley's Introduction to *Bedouin of the London Evening*.

29 December 2013 . . . : Rosemary Lightband, notebook 136, December 2013–February 2014, courtesy of the estate of Rosemary Tonks.

be living in poverty . . . : Neil Astley, 'Rosemary Tonks, the lost poet', *Guardian* (31 May 2014).

In his introduction . . . : Neil Astley, Introduction to *Bedouin of the London Evening*.

Addiction to an Old Mattress . . . : *Iliad of Broken Sentences* is out of print, but the poems are republished in *Bedouin of the London Evening*, ibid.

CONFESSIONAL

a natural death . . . : Robert Lowell, 'Death of a Critic', *Day by Day* (Farrar, Straus and Giroux, 1978).

Life Studies . . . : Robert Lowell, *Life Studies* (Faber and Faber, 1988).

My own poems . . . : Robert Lowell, cited in 'On Robert Lowell's "Skunk Hour"', a symposium, in *The Contemporary Poet as Artist and Critic*, ed. Anthony Ostroff, (Little, Brown, 1964).

what influenced me . . . : Robert Lowell, *Collected Prose*, ed. Robert Giroux (Farrar, Straus and Giroux, 1987).

from the anxiety . . . : Seamus Heaney, 'Lowell's Command', *Finders Keepers: Selected Prose 1978–2001* (Faber and Faber, 2002).

My namesake, Little Boots . . . : Robert Lowell, 'Caligula', *For the Union Dead* (Faber and Faber, 1985).

They all also have . . . : Elizabeth Bishop, letter to Robert Lowell (14 December 1957), *Words in Air*.

the details are always . . . : Elizabeth Hardwick, letter to Elizabeth Bishop (20 January 1958), ibid.

he wrote back . . . : Robert Lowell, letter to Elizabeth Bishop (15 March 1958), ibid.

I am tired . . . : Robert Lowell, 'Eye and Tooth', *For the Union Dead*.

Hospitalization became art . . . : Robert Lowell, 'Waking in the Blue', *Life Studies*.

I was so out of . . . : Robert Lowell, 'Memories of West Street and Lepke', ibid.

the first typed draft . . . : 'Memories of West Street and Lepke', typescript of poem with the author's ms. corrections. Robert Lowell Collection of Papers 1943–1977, The Henry W. and Albert A. Berg Collection of English and American Literature, The New York Public Library.

There's a good deal . . . : Robert Lowell, 'The Art of Poetry No. 3', interview in *Paris Review*, No. 25 (Winter–Spring 1961).

might seem as open . . . : Robert Lowell, interviewed by Ian Hamilton, 'A Conversation with Robert Lowell', *Robert Lowell: Interviews and Memoirs, ed.* Jeffrey Meyers (University of Michigan Press, 1988).

Those blessèd structures . . . : Robert Lowell, 'Epilogue', *Day by Day*.

The tendency is . . . : Elizabeth Bishop, quoted in 'The Poets: Second Chance', *Time* (2 June 1967).

They had collected . . . : Robert Lowell, letter to Elizabeth Bishop (14 June 1967), *Words in Air*.

the dead poet's arms . . . : Interview with Elizabeth Hardwick, quoted by Richard Tillinghast, 'Robert Lowell's *Day by Day*: "Until the wristwatch is taken from the wrist"', *New England Review*, Vol. 16, No. 3 (1994), which gives the source of quote as *Town and Country*, September 1993.

Berryman rejected the term . . . : See, for example, his interview in *Paris Review*.

portraits from The Dolphin . . . : Robert Lowell, *Collected Poems*, ed. Frank Bidart and David Gewanter (Farrar, Straus and Giroux, 2003).

Her letters and notebooks are . . . : See *Anne Sexton: A Self-Portrait in Letters*, ed. Linda Gray Sexton and Lois Ames (Mariner Books, 2004).

Sexton poured out her feelings . . . : Anne Sexton, 'Sylvia's Death', *The Complete Poems* (Houghton Mifflin, 1981).

Beth Hinchliffe's account . . . : Beth Hinchliffe, 'Wellesley and Weston's Hometown Poets', *Wellesley Weston Magazine* (21 May 2008).

The Awful Rowing Toward God . . . : Published in 1975. See in Anne Sexton, *The Complete Poems*.

Anne Sexton went home and locked herself inside . . . : Diane Wood Middlebrook, *Anne Sexton: A Biography* (A Peter Davison Book/ Houghton Mifflin, 1991).

Denise Levertov made a plea . . . : Denise Levertov, *Light up the Cave* (New Directions, 1982), written as an obituary for Anne Sexton in the *Boston Globe*.

Adrienne Rich put it even more starkly . . . : Diane Wood Middlebrook, *Anne Sexton, A Biography*.

wrote about her near contemporary . . . : Anne Stevenson, *Bitter Fame: A Life of Sylvia Plath* (Penguin, 1990).

a satire on the Confessional aesthetic . . . : 'Letter to Fuller', James Fenton, *The Memory of War and Children in Exile: Poems 1968–1983* (Penguin, 1983).

Don't look now, God . . . : Anne Sexton, *The Complete Poems*.

In a letter reflecting . . . : T. S. Eliot, *The Letters of T. S. Eliot, Volume 1: 1898–1922*, ed. Valerie Eliot and Hugh Haughton (Faber and Faber, 2009).

THE INTELLIGENT WHALE

I am not an atheist . . . : Wallace Stevens, letter to Sister M. Bernetta Quinn, Hartford (21 December 1951) in *Letters of Wallace Stevens*, ed. Holly Stevens (University of California Press, 1996), Letter 808.

the story goes that he . . . : Letter from Father Arthur Hanley to Professor Janet McCann (24 July 1977), reproduced in *The Wallace Stevens Journal*, 18.1 (Spring 1994): 3, under the title 'A Letter from Father

Hanley on Stevens' Conversion to Catholicism'. See also Peter Brazeau, *Wallace Stevens Remembered: An Oral Biography* (Random House, 1983) and William J. Hartigan, 'Wallace Stevens at the Hartford', in the *Wallace Stevens Journal*, Vol.1, No.2 (Summer 1977).

'Thirteen Ways of Looking at a Blackbird' . . . : Wallace Stevens, 'Thirteen Ways of Looking at a Blackbird', *Collected Poems* (Faber and Faber, 1955).

'The Emperor of Ice-Cream' . . . : Wallace Stevens, 'The Emperor of Ice-Cream', ibid.

The critic Helen Vendler . . . : Quoted in Austin Allen's 'Guide to "The Emperor of Ice-Cream"', www.poetryfoundation.org.

The Friends and Enemies . . . : The society's website (www.stevenspoetry.org) explains in full why the 'enemies' are included.

When a letter emerged . . . : 'A letter from Father Hanley on Stevens' conversion to Catholicism'.

A poem like 'What are Years?' . . . : Marianne Moore, *The Complete Poems of Marianne Moore* (Macmillan/Viking, 1956).

she wrote an ode to them . . . : *New York Herald Tribune* (3 October 1956).

'Millennium,' yes: 'pandemonium' . . . : Marianne Moore, 'Hometown Piece for Messrs. Alston and Reese', *The Complete Poems*.

Assign Yogi Berra . . . : Marianne Moore, 'Baseball and Writing', ibid.

Yankees historian and museum curator . . . : In correspondence with the authors.

public mood to settle . . . : Leonard Koppett, 'Season Opens Today With All 20 Clubs Listed for Action; Yankees, Angels Play at Stadium', *New York Times* (10 April 1968).

Historian Brian Richards . . . : In correspondence with the authors.

We pore over two press photographs . . . : 'Poet Marianne Moore tosses first ball', news photo: Bettmann Pictures, 1968, Getty Images, and Bob Olen, 1968. Marianne Moore Collection, The Rosenbach Museum & Library, Philadelphia.

The New York Times report . . . : *New York Times* (11 April 1968).

talking to the Sporting News . . . : *Sporting News* (27 April 1968).

Don DeLillo's epic novel . . . : Don DeLillo, *Underworld* (Picador, 1998).

Frank confessing . . . : *Sporting News* (27 April 1968).

She had suffered a stroke . . . : Linda Leavell, *Holding On Upside Down: The Life and Word of Marianne Moore* (Farrar, Straus and Giroux, 2013).

As for Michael Burke . . . : *New York Times* obituary (7 February 1987).

She was interviewed by . . . : Linda Leavell, *Holding On Upside Down*.

According to Time Magazine . . . : *Time* online: Dan Neil, 'The 50 Worst Cars of All Time'.

some of the most beautiful car names . . . : Names sourced from letters from and to the Ford Motor Company, Marianne Moore and David Wallace, Pierpont Morgan Library, 1958. Also *Letters of Note* (www.lettersofnote.com) and Linda Leavell, *Holding On Upside Down*.

It was months between . . . : Linda Leavell, *Holding On Upside Down*, ibid.

to the Rosenbach Museum . . . : Marianne Moore Collection, The Rosenbach Museum & Library, Philadelphia.

the museum's catalogue . . . : The Marianne Moore Collection, General Introduction, The Rosenbach, Philadelphia.

pick the crimson-stitched ball . . . : Autographed baseball signed 'To Miss Marianne Moore' by Frank Fernandez. The Rosenbach, Philadelphia, 2006.3034.

'What Are Years?' . . . : Marianne Moore, 'What Are Years?', *The Complete Poems*.

Wainwright's chart . . . : Jeffrey Wainwright, *Poetry: The Basics* (Routledge, 2004).

according to Moore's biographer . . . : Linda Leavell, *Holding On Upside Down*.

Within weeks of that dinner . . . : Full details of these final weeks can be found in Arnold Rampersad, *The Life of Langston Hughes: Volume II: 1941–1967* (Oxford University Press, 2002).

according to Hughes' biographer . . . : ibid.

In a New York Times essay . . . : Chester Higgins, Jr, 'A Dance of Rivers', *New York Times* (18 December 2014).

The cosmogram was created . . . : *Africana Heritage*, Volume 2, No. 2 (2002), published by the New York Public Library.

as an 'art installation . . .' : Cosmogram created by Houston Conwill, Estella Conwill Majozo and Joseph DePace, in honour of Langston Hughes and Arturo A. Schomburg, according to *Africana Heritage*, ibid.

morning glory blue . . . : Linda Leavell, *Holding On Upside Down*.

news to Maya Angelou . . . : In Maya Angelou's response to the death of Amiri Baraka on her Facebook page, reported by Buzzfeed books on 13 January 2014.

Arna Bontemps reportedly spoke . . . : Reported in the *New York Post* (26 May 1967), according to Arnold Rampersad, *The Life of Langston Hughes*.

'Dear Lovely Death' . . . : Langston Hughes, 'Dear Lovely Death', *Collected Poems of Langston Hughes* (Vintage Classics, 1995).

Thom Gunn diagnosed as . . . : Thom Gunn, 'The Art of Poetry No. 72'.

A cult of the mad . . . : Philip Larkin, interview with John Haffenden, published in *Further Requirements*.

Moore – when interviewed . . . : Marianne Moore, interview, 'The Art of Poetry No. 4', *Paris Review*, No. 26 (Summer–Fall 1961).

Eliot argued that . . . : T. S. Eliot, *The Sacred Wood: Essays on Poetry and Criticism* (Faber and Faber, 1997).

I AM

Saw three fellows . . . : John Clare, journal entry (4 June 1825), cited in *John Clare by Himself*, ed. Eric Robinson and David Powell (Carcanet, 1996).

I went upstairs . . . : John Clare, 'The Nature of Society: The Thousands and the Few', in Johanne Clare, *John Clare and the Bounds of Circumstance* (McGill-Queens University Press, 1987).

Sometimes the guards . . . : Hugh Kenner, *The Pound Era* (Faber and Faber, 1972).

Is in very good . . . : The Case Books of St Andrew's Hospital, at St Andrew's Archive, St Andrew's Healthcare, Billing Road, Northampton.

I saw Clare frequently . . . : Frederick Martin, *The Life of John Clare* (MacMillan and Co, 1865).

I could almost feel . . . : John Clare, 'Byron's Funeral' (composed 1825), in *Selected Poetry and Prose*, ed. Merryn and Raymond Williams (Methuen, 1986).

The common people felt . . . : ibid.

John Riley, *Ancient and Modern* (Grosseteste Press, 1967).

As somebody points out . . . : David Wheatley, '"Name Your Realities": Thoughts on John Riley', presented at *Riley's Light: An Appreciation of the Poetry of John Riley (1937–1978)* on 24 April 2015 at the School of English, the University of Leeds.

the sadness . . . : John Riley, 'Chronographia Continuata', *The Collected Works* (Grosseteste Press, 1980).

the city crumbles . . . : John Riley, 'Between Strangers', ibid.

We think of another . . . : Bernard Hare, *Urban Grimshaw and the Shed Crew* (Sceptre, 2006).

MURDER IN A LEEDS . . . : *Yorkshire Evening Post* (28 October 1978).

picture of the poet . . . : 'Two help police over killing of writer', *Yorkshire Evening Post* (30 October 1978).

a blogger's story . . . : Sheng Yun, *Accidental Death of a Poet*, London Review of Books blog (11 November 2014): www.lrb.co.uk.

We ran along the railway . . . : Xu Lizhi, 'Sleepless', quoted in Sheng Yun, *Accidental Death of a Poet*, ibid.

ON THE CIRCUIT

sixteen-minute reading of his poems . . . : W. H. Auden und Achim Benning 'Gedichte/Poems', 1978.09.28. Österreichische Mediathek (www.mediathek.at).

a nice car . . . : Humphrey Carpenter, *W H. Auden: A Biography* (Faber and Faber, 2011).

tell a Jaguar from a Bentley . . . : In 'Three Posthumous Poems', W. H. Auden, *Collected Poems*, ed. Edward Mendelson (Faber and Faber, revised 1991).

Moulin Rouge nightclub in the other . . . : See Alan Levy, *W. H. Auden: In the Autumn of the Age of Anxiety* (The Permanent Press, 1983).

have gone off to a movie . . . : Robert Lowell, letter to Elizabeth Bishop (4 September 1976), in *Words in Air*.

on the BBC1 prime-time chat-show Parkinson . . . : Clip shown in *The Addictions of Sin: W. H. Auden in his Own Words*, BBC4 (17 May 2009).

Recalling the interview . . . : Michael Parkinson, *Parky: My Autobiography* (Hodder & Stoughton, 2008).

landing with a cigarette . . . : Alan Levy, *W. H. Auden*.

At the Österreichische Mediathek . . . : Österreichische Mediathek, Gumpendorfer Straße 95, 1060 Wien.

Liebe Frau Emma . . . : W. H. Auden, 'Eleven Occasional Poems', *Collected Poems*, ibid.

The healer I have faith . . . W. H. Auden, 'Lines to Dr Walter Bick on his Retiring from General Practice', ibid.

Humphrey Carpenter documents his daily use . . . : Humphrey Carpenter, *W. H. Auden*.

a full set of dentures embedded in it . . . : Jane Rule, *A Hot-Eyed Moderate* (Naiad Press, 1985).

called 'On the Circuit' . . . : W. H. Auden, 'On the Circuit', *Collected Poems*.

a tractored sugar-beet country . . . : W. H. Auden, 'For Friends Only', part of 'Thanksgiving for a Habitat', ibid.

an Italian literary prize in 1957 . . . : The Antonio Feltrinelli Foundation Prize is worth more than $33,000, according to Richard Davenport-Hines in his *Auden* (Heinemann, 1995).

in honour of Josef Weinheber . . . : W. H. Auden, 'Eleven Occasional Poems', *Collected Poems*.

I wish, Louis . . . : W. H. Auden, 'The Cave of Making', part of 'Thanksgiving for a Habitat', ibid.

Hugerl, Auden's Austrian lover . . . : W. H. Auden, 'Glad', part of 'Three Posthumous Poems', ibid.

East, West, on the Autobahn . . . : W. H. Auden, 'Prologue at Sixty', ibid.

between the archaic . . . : Seamus Heaney, *Crediting Poetry: The Nobel Lecture 1995* (Gallery Books, 1996).

mankeepers and mosscheepers . . . : Seamus Heaney, 'Mossbawn', in *Finders Keepers: Selected Prose 1978–2001* (Faber and Faber, 2002).

Speaking to the poet Dennis O'Driscoll . . . : Dennis O'Driscoll, *Stepping Stones*.

Heaney's Nobel Prize acceptance speech . . . : See www.nobelprize.org

absolute speaker . . . : Seamus Heaney, 'A Sofa in the Forties', *The Spirit Level* (Faber and Faber, 1996).

Chester slips out and walks . . . : Accounts of these events can be found in Humphrey Carpenter, *W. H. Auden*, and Richard Davenport-Hines, *Auden*.

His archive is in St Pölten . . . : Dokumentationsstelle für Literatur in Niederösterreich, Landhausplatz 1, Haus1, 3109 St Pölten, Austria.

short story by Lydia Davis . . . : Lydia Davis, *The Collected Stories of Lydia Davis* (Farrar, Straus and Giroux, 2009).

According to Carpenter . . . : Humphrey Carpenter, *W. H. Auden*.

In an interview with the Daily Mail . . . : ibid.

to the great annoyance of the management . . . : Letter to Ursula Niebuhr (1947), ibid.

Their President, Dr Manfred Müller . . . : Österreichische Gesellschaft für Literatur (Austrian Society for Literature), Palais Wilczek, Herrengasse 5, 1010 Wien, Austria.

Here, on foolscap sheets . . . : Letters, Subject: Auden's lection in the Austrian Society for Literature on 28 September 1973, Ring binder: A-Z XV. Vom 1.5. 1973 bis zum 1.1.1974, Archive of the Austrian Society for Literature, www.ogl.at/archiv.

plus photographs almost certainly taken on the afternoon . . . : Photographs of W. H. Auden, Archive of the Austrian Society for Literature, www. ogl.at/archiv.

That is true fame . . . : S. T. Coleridge, quoted by William Hazlitt, 'My First Acquaintance with Poets', in *Hazlitt: Selected Essays*, ed. George Sampson (Cambridge University Press, 2015).

we're in the archive at Boston . . . : Menus for Robert Frost's birthday dinners and guest lists in Frost, Robert (1874–1963) Collection, Howard Gotlieb Archival Research Center at Boston University.

The land was ours . . . : Robert Frost, 'The Gift Outright', *Robert Frost: Selected Poems*, ed. Ian Hamilton (Penguin, 1973).

In The Sopranos . . . : 'Proshai, Livushka', *The Sopranos*, directed by Tim Van Patten, Series 3, Episode 2 (US Broadcast: 4 March 2001).

Down by Law (1986), directed by Jim Jarmusch.

Teflon (1977), directed by Don Siegel.

The Shawshank Redemption (1994), directed by Frank Darabont.

Western Union telegram . . . : From the Frost, Robert (1874–1963) Collection, Howard Gotleib Archival Research Center at Boston University.

The lights were out . . . : Robert Lowell, 'Robert Frost: 1875–1963', *New York Review of Books* (1 February 1963).

Robert Frost at midnight . . . : Robert Lowell, 'Robert Frost', *Collected Poems*.

Mix 30 or more . . . : Dan Barry, 'A Violation of Both the Law and the Spirit', *New York Times* (28 January 2008).

A. C. Frost estate . . . : Mark Richardson, *Robert Frost in Context* (Cambridge University Press, 2014).

The Bung Hole . . . : *The Letters of Robert Frost: Volume I 1886–1920*, ed. Donald Sheehy, Mark Richardson and Robert Faggen (Harvard University Press, 2014).

sent out a call . . . : Nate Pedersen, 'Roethke Museum Seeks Owners of "Open House"', *Fine Books and Collections* (30 December 2015).

Poets are like . . . : Ted Hughes, *The Bloodaxe Book of Poetry Quotations*.

In a recent essay . . . : Geoff Dyer, 'Pilgrimage', *White Sands: Experiences from the Outside World* (Canongate, 2016).

Sontag wrote a story . . . : Susan Sontag, 'Pilgrimage', *The New Yorker* (21 December 1987).

Our favourite accidental . . . : Muriel Spark, 'The House of the Famous Poet', *The New Yorker* (2 April 1966).

a memorial bus shelter named . . . : Erected in 1972 and listed by the Public Monuments & Sculpture Association (www.pmsa.org.uk); since replaced with a plaque. See 'Village honours its poet son', *Coventry Telegraph* (14 June 2006).

At a White House dinner . . . : Joshua Rothman, 'Robert Frost: Darkness or Light?' *New Yorker* (29 January 2013).

There is a kind of . . . : Letter to John Bartlett, early November 1913, *The Letters of Robert Frost*.

a terrifying poet . . . : Lionel Trilling, 'A Speech on Robert Frost: A Cultural Episode', *Partisan Review*, Vol. 26, No. 3 (Summer 1959).

Call him, if it makes . . . : ibid.

You made my birthday . . . : Letter from Robert Frost to Lionel Trilling (18 June 1959), quoted by Christopher Benfey, 'The Storm over Robert Frost', *New York Review of Books* (4 December 2008).

It seems to have been provoked . . . 'Provide, Provide', *The Cambridge Companion to Robert Frost*, ed. Robert Faggen (Cambridge University Press, 2001).

The witch that came . . . : Robert Frost, 'Provide, Provide', *Complete Poems of Robert Frost* (Holt, Rinehart & Winston, 1964).

a copy of the 'Dedication' . . . : From the Frost, Robert (1874–1963) Collection, Howard Gotlieb Archival Research Center at Boston University.

AFTERWORD

The apparition of . . . : Ezra Pound, 'In a Station of the Metro', *Selected Poems and Translations*, ed. Richard Sieburth (Faber and Faber, 2010).

the Latin sepulcrum . . . : Robert Pogue Harrison, 'Hic Jacet', *The Dominion of the Dead* (University of Chicago Press, 2003).

a Cook's Tour . . . : David Jones, *In Parenthesis* (Faber and Faber, 1937).

turned up again in 1865 . . . : 'Discovery of Dante's Remains', *New York Times* (2 July 1865).

In 2003 a team . . . : 'Genetic Analysis of the Skeletal Remains Attributed to Francesco Petrarca', *Forensic Science International* 173 (2007).

lengths and breadths . . . : Philip Larkin, 'An Arundel Tomb', *Collected Poems*, ibid.

There's no posterity . . . : Peter Reading, *The Bloodaxe Book of Poetry Quotations.*

You will tell me . . . : Derek Mahon, 'Heraclitus on Rivers', *Collected Poems.*

as the historian Richard Holmes puts it . . . : Richard Holmes, *Sidetracks.*

★

Above and beyond the cited texts, this book takes its bearings from a galaxy of biographical work, broadcasts and conversations about these poets over many years. We are standing on the shoulders of numerous writers, critics and other poets, and wish to acknowledge our debt to as many as possible, including the following:

W. H. Auden, *Selected Poems*, ed. Edward Mendelson (Faber and Faber, 1979)

————, *Collected Poems*, ed. Edward Mendelson (Faber and Faber, 1991)

Jonathan Bate, *John Clare: A Biography* (Picador, 2003)

Robert Beaton, *Byron's War: Romantic Rebellion, Greek Revolution* (Cambridge University Press, 2013)

John Berryman, *Recovery* (Farrar, Straus and Giroux, 1973)

————, *The Dream Songs* (Faber and Faber, 1990)

————, *Selected Poems*, ed. Michael Hofmann (Faber and Faber, 2004)

Elizabeth Bishop, *One Art: Letters*, ed. Robert Giroux (Farrar, Straus and Giroux, 1994)

————, *Edgar Allan Poe & The Juke-Box*, ed. Alice Quinn (Farrar, Straus and Giroux, 2006)

————, *Poems, Prose and Letters* (The Library of America, 2008)

Elizabeth Bishop and Robert Lowell, *Words in Air: The Complete Correspondence Between Elizabeth Bishop and Robert Lowell*, ed. Thomas Travisano and Saskia Hamilton (Farrar, Straus and Giroux, 2008).

Bonhams Catalogue *The Roy Davids Collection, Part III – Poetry: Poetical Manuscripts & Portraits of Poets*, Volume I: A–K, Volume II: L–Y.

James Booth, *Philip Larkin: Life, Art & Love* (Bloomsbury, 2015)

Humphrey Carpenter, *W. H. Auden: A Biography* (Faber and Faber, 2011)

Thomas Chatterton, *Selected Poems*, ed. with an Introduction by Grevel Lindop (Carcanet Press, 1972)

John Clare, *Selected Poems*, ed. Geoffrey Summerfield (Penguin, 1990)

Robert Coles and Thomas Roma, *House Calls with William Carlos Williams MD* (Powerhouse Books, 2008)

Barbara Coulton, *Louis MacNeice in the BBC* (Faber and Faber, 1980)

Theodore Dalrymple, *The Death of Dylan Thomas: A Conspiracy Theory* (BMJ, 2010)

Richard Davenport-Hines, *Auden* (Heinemann, 1995)

Kay Dick, *Ivy & Stevie* (Duckworth, 1971)

Emily Dickinson, *Complete Poems* (Faber and Faber, 1976)

————, *The Letters of Emily Dickinson* (Harvard University Press, 1997)

Thomas Dilworth, *David Jones in the Great War* (Enitharmon Press, 2012)

Keith Douglas, *Alamein to Zem Zem* (Faber and Faber, 1966)

————, *The Complete Poems* (Oxford Paperbacks, 1978)

T. S. Eliot, *The Letters of T. S. Eliot, Volume 1: 1898-1922*, ed. Hugh Haughton, Valerie Eliot (Faber and Faber, 2009)

Robert Frost, *Complete Poems* (Holt, Rinehart and Winston, 1964)

————, *Frost: Collected Poems, Prose, and Plays*, ed. Mark Richardson and Richard Poirier (Library of America, 1995)

John Fuller, *W. H. Auden: A Commentary* (Faber and Faber, 1998)

Brad Gooch, *City Poet: The Life and Times of Frank O'Hara* (Knopf, 1993)

Lyndall Gordon, *Lives Like Loaded Guns: Emily Dickinson and Her Family's Feuds* (Virago, 2010)

Desmond Graham, *Keith Douglas: A Biography* (O.U.P, 2012)

Thom Gunn, *Collected Poems* (Faber and Faber, 1994)

John Haffenden, *Poets in Conversation* (Faber and Faber, 1981)

———, *The Life of John Berryman* (Ark Paperbacks, 1983)

Ian Hamilton, *Robert Lowell: A Biography* (Random House, 1984)

———, *Against Oblivion: Some Lives of the Twentieth-Century Poets* (Viking, 2002)

Victoria Harrison, *Elizabeth Bishop's Poetics of Intimacy* (Cambridge University Press, 1993)

Seamus Heaney, *Finders Keepers: Selected Prose 1971 –2001* (Faber and Faber, 2003)

Alistair Heys, ed. *From Gothic to Romantic: Thomas Chatterton's Bristol* (Redcliffe Press Ltd, 2005)

Dominic Hibberd, *Wilfred Owen: A New Biography* (Weidenfeld & Nicolson, 2002)

Stuart Hills, *By Tank into Normandy* (Cassell, 2002)

Richard Holmes, *Dr Johnson and Mr Savage* (Harper Perennial, 2005)

———, *Sidetracks* (Harper Perennial, 2005)

Langston Hughes, *Collected Poems* (Vintage Classics, 1995)

Merlin James, *David Jones: A Map of the Artist's Mind* (Lund Humphries Publishing Ltd, 1995)

Samuel Johnson, *The Lives of the Poets*, ed. John Middendorf, *The Yale Edition of the Works of Samuel Johnson*, XXI–XXIII (Yale University Press, 2010)

David Jones, *In Parenthesis* (Faber and Faber, 1937)

———, *The Anathemata* (Faber and Faber, 1952)

Linda Kelly, *The Marvellous Boy: The Life and Myth of Thomas Chatterton* (Weidenfeld & Nicolson, 1971)

Philip Larkin, *Required Writing: Miscellaneous Pieces 1955-1982* (Faber and Faber, 1983)

———, *Collected Poems*, ed. Anthony Thwaite (Faber and Faber, 2003)

———, *Further Requirements: Interviews, Broadcasts, Statements and Reviews 1952–1985*, ed. Anthony Thwaite (Faber and Faber, 2013)

James Laughlin, *Remembering William Carlos Williams* (New Directions, 1996)

———, *The Way It Wasn't* (New Directions, 2006)

Linda Leavell, *Holding On Upside Down: The Life and Work of Marianne Moore* (Farrar, Straus and Giroux, 2013)

Alan Levy, *W. H. Auden: In the Autumn of the Age of Anxiety* (The Permanent Press, 1983)

Robert Lowell, *Collected Poems*, ed. Frank Bidart and David Gewanter (Farrar, Straus and Giroux, 2003)

Andrew Lycett, *Dylan Thomas: A New Life* (Orion, 2004)

Louis MacNeice, *The Strings Are False: An Unfinished Autobiography* (Faber and Faber, 1965)

———, *Collected Poems*, ed. Peter McDonald (Faber and Faber, 2007)

Janet Malcolm, *The Silent Woman: Sylvia Plath & Ted Hughes* (Knopf, 1994)

Paul Mariani, *William Carlos Williams: A New World Naked* (McGraw Hill, 1981)

———, *Dream Song: The Life of John Berryman* (Trinity University Press, 2016)

Brett C. Millier, *Elizabeth Bishop: Life and the Memory of It* (University of California Press, 2015)

Marianne Moore, *The Poems of Marianne Moore*, ed. Grace Schulman (Faber and Faber, 2003)

Andrew Motion, *Philip Larkin: A Writer's Life* (Faber and Faber, 1994)

———, *Keats* (Faber and Faber, 2003)

Stella Musulin, 'Auden in Kirchstetten', *In Solitude, For Company*, ed. Catherine Bucknell and Nicholas Jenkins (Oxford University Press, 1996)

Dennis O'Driscoll, *Stepping Stones: Interviews with Seamus Heaney* (Faber and Faber, 2008)

Frank O'Hara, *Lunch Poems*, Pocket Poets 19 (City Lights Books, 1964)

———, *Selected Poems*, ed. Mark Ford (Random House, 2009)

Charles Osborne, *W. H. Auden: The Life of a Poet* (Eyre Methuen, 1979)

Paris Review interviews, collected in various books, but also online at http://www.theparisreview.org/interviews, is an unparalleled collection of insights into writers and writing.

Denis Pellerin and Brian May, *The Poor Man's Picture Gallery: Stereoscopy versus Paintings in the Victorian Era* (The London Stereoscopic Company, 2014)

Sylvia Plath, *Collected Poems*, ed. Ted Hughes (Faber and Faber, 2002)

Arnold Rampersad, *The Life of Langston Hughes: Volume II: 1941–1967* (Oxford University Press, 2002)

Kay Redfield Jamison, *Touched With Fire* (Free Press Paperback, 1994)

Anne Sexton, *The Complete Poems* (Houghton Mifflin, 1981)

———, *A Self-Portrait in Letters*, eds Linda Gray Sexton and Lois Ames (Mariner Books reprint edition, 2004)

Stevie Smith, *Me Again: Uncollected Writings of Stevie Smith*, ed. Jack Barbera and William McBrien (Vintage Books, 1983)

———, *Collected Poems and Drawings of Stevie Smith*, ed. Will May (Faber and Faber, 2015)

Frances Spalding, *Stevie Smith: A Critical Biography* (Faber, 1988)

Jon Stallworthy, *Louis MacNeice* (Faber and Faber, 1995)

Sanford Sternlicht (ed.), *In Search of Stevie Smith* (Syracuse University Press, 1991)

Wallace Stevens, *Collected Poems* (Faber and Faber, 1955)

———, *Letters of Wallace Stevens*, ed. Holly Stevens (University of California Press, 1996)

Anne Stevenson, *Bitter Fame: A Life of Sylvia Plath* (Mariner: Houghton Mifflin, 1998)

John Strausbaugh, *The Village: 400 Years of Beats and Bohemians, Radicals and Rogues – A History of Greenwich Village* (Ecco Press, 2013)

David N. Thomas and Simon Barnes, *Dylan Remembered 1935–1953* (Seren, 2004).

Dylan Thomas, *Collected Letters* (Weidenfeld & Nicolson, 2014).

———, *Collected Poems*, Centenary Edition, ed. John Goodby (Weidenfeld & Nicolson, 2014)

R. S. Thomas, *Collected Poems 1945–1990* (Dent, 1993)

Claire Tomalin, *Thomas Hardy: The Time-Torn Man* (Penguin, 2006)

Rosemary Tonks, *Bedouin of the London Evening: Collected Poems* (Bloodaxe Books, 2015)

William Carlos Williams, *The Autobiography of William Carlos Williams* (New Directions, 1948)

———, *Interviews: Speaking Straight Ahead*, ed. Linda Welshimer Wagner (New Directions, 1976)

———, *Selected Poems*, ed. Charles Tomlinson (New Directions, 1985)

———, *Paterson*, revised edition, prepared by Christopher McGowan (New Directions, 1992)

Diane Wood Middlebrook, *Anne Sexton: A Biography* (Virago, 1992)

Index